CANADIAN LITERATURE
the beginnings to the 20th century

edited by Catherine M. McLay

McClelland and Stewart Limited

0-7710-5813-6

The Canadian Publishers
McClelland and Stewart Limited
25 Hollinger Road, Toronto

Printed and bound in Canada

Contents

III PRE-CONFEDERATION: THE CANADAS

Preface

While this anthology is intended primarily for the use of university students studying Canadian literature, it should also meet the needs of the general reader interested in the backgrounds of our literature and in our early writers in prose and poetry from the beginnings in the 1760's to the early twentieth century. The introduction is designed to give a general overview of literary activity in this period with some comment on central themes and preoccupations of these writers; the introduction to each author provides biographical information, and attempts to suggest the relationship of each writer to his period and his contemporaries.

The anthology is devised in the hopes of fulfilling a need that the editor has observed teaching a survey course in Canadian literature. Until recently, this early material has been available only in A. J. M. Smith's *Book of Canadian Poetry*, Klinck and Watters' *Canadian Anthology*, and a number of individual volumes, mostly fiction, reprinted in the McClelland and Stewart New Canadian Library Series. Much of the early poetry in particular has been out of print and is available only in rare book collections in the library. Thus many of the works, and indeed authors, referred to in books such as *The Literary History of Canada*, Desmond Pacey's *Creative Writing* or Northrop Frye's *The Bush Garden* are inaccessible or accessible only in anthologies which must needs devote much of their space to the important developments in our literature since the 1920's. As a result, students miss much of the breadth of the period, and also an opportunity to observe the prevalence in the modern Canadian imagination of themes and patterns which draw from a common background of ideas extending back into two centuries of Canadian life. The new Holt, Rinehart and Winston four volume collection, *The Evolution of Canadian Literature in English*, which was designed at the same time as this work, makes some attempt to meet this demand, at least for the specialist, but there still remains a need for a work in one volume to relate different times and genres in our early history for a more general audience.

The selections in this anthology are drawn from the areas of poetry, fiction, drama, autobiography and the essay, and include thirty-five authors who appear commonly in critical estimates of the period. Where possible, individual selections have been chosen which have not been frequently reprinted, but where familiar selections are germane to an understanding of the author or are the best-known works of major writers, they are included. Occasionally, selections are chosen from a novel or long dramatic work where that is the author's most significant piece and where no alternate selection is equally suitable. Of necessity, a few selections have been abridged because of space limitations; an effort has been made to convey the scope of the work and the overall argument and tone while omitting secondary material, digressions or detailed comment on specific works.

In most literatures, there is a significant gap between the end of the nineteenth century and the new writers coming into vogue in the years after World War I. Most of the writers in this anthology remain within the confines of the eighteenth and nineteenth centuries. A number, however, were just beginning literary careers towards the last decade of the nineteenth century and were writing into the 1920's and 30's. Where possible, selections have been chosen from works published before 1900 as in the case of E. W. Thomson or Gilbert Parker. With Charles G. D. Roberts, Bliss Carman and D. C. Scott, the emphasis here is upon early works but later pieces have also been chosen to illustrate the continuance of themes or techniques into this century. These authors clearly belong to a period before the age of Yeats and Eliot, and it is against this world that they must be measured rather than that of succeeding generations with new values and new techniques. This is true also of Robert Service whose first publication does not appear until 1907 but who is, in a physical sense only, a contemporary of Leacock. A number of transitional writers such as Marjorie Pickthall might have been represented, but it was felt that this was merging into modern territory.

The authors are arranged in approximate chronological order with some attention to grouping such as the Confederation Poets, the secondary Confederation Poets and the Confederation novelists and short-story writers. The individual works, however, are arranged thematically to bring together poems on a common subject such as nature, art, patriotism, love or death from different periods of the writer's career. The texts from which the selections have been taken are indicated at the end of the introduction to each author, along with suggestions of helpful books or articles; a short bibliography of suggested reading is included at the end. Biographical information has been drawn from these sources and from the following works in general:

The Literary History of Canada. Toronto: University of Toronto Press, 1965

Norah Storey. *A Companion to Canadian Literature and History.* Toronto: Oxford University Press, 1966.

Desmond Pacey. *Creative Writing in Canada.* Toronto: Ryerson, 1962.

E. M. Morgan. *Canadian Men and Women.*

Macmillan's *Dictionary of Canadian Biography.*

R. E. Watters. *A Bibliography of Canadian Literature.* Toronto: University of Toronto Press, 1972.

I would like to thank many people who have assisted with this anthology: the library staff in many universities and archives across Canada, the students of my Canadian literature classes over the past several years, and the secretaries of the English department of the University of Calgary, especially Miss Merrigold Archibald. I would also like to express my appreciation to my colleagues and friends in the department who have been helpful in their advice, in particular Dr. Hallvard Dahlie, Dr. Grant McGregor, and Dr. Charles Steele, and to my mother and family for their support and encouragement.

Introduction

"Part of you is where you have been," remarks Margaret Atwood in *Survival*, her recent commentary on Canadian literature, and she continues:

> Literature is not only a mirror; it is also a map, a geography of the mind. Our literature is one such map, if we can learn to read it as *our* literature, as the product of who and where we have been .... For the members of a country or a culture, shared knowledge of their place, their here, is not a luxury but a necessity. Without that knowledge, we will not survive.[1]

To-day in Canada, when an interest in our own native culture is at a peak, it seems an appropriate time to look backwards, to re-consider our literary ancestors of the eighteenth and nineteenth centuries and replace them in the lineage of modern Canadian literature. In his conclusion to *The Literary History of Canada*, Northrop Frye questions the value of tracing a lineage for writers back to "earlier writers whom they may not have read or greatly admired," yet he continues: "There does seem to be such a thing as a literary continuum ... writers are conditioned in their attitudes by their predecessors, or by the cultural climate of their predecessors, whether there is conscious influence or not."[2]

The process of re-evaluating these early writers has begun rather recently. In the thirties and forties, the emerging poets and novelists were engaged in casting off the bonds of the past in order to explore fully the new themes and techniques of the twentieth century. F. R. Scott's "The Canadian Authors Meet" has become a classic statement of their attitudes to these predecessors and their descendents:

> O Canada, O Canada, Oh can
> A day go by without new authors springing
> To paint the native maple, and to plan
> More ways to set the selfsame welkin ringing?[3]

Yet it was his colleague, A. J. M. Smith, also a critic of this generation of poets, who was the first in 1943 to publish a comprehensive modern anthology of Canadian literature which makes accessible to modern students the representative and the best literature of the previous century.[4] In the past few years, a number of publications have appeared which make more available these early works. In addition to McClelland and Stewart's New Canadian Library which since 1959 has published many of the early novels and a few selections of the poetry, there are the Coles

Canadiana Series, the new University of Toronto reprints which include Dewart's anthology *Selections from Canadian Poets,* Joseph Howe's *Poems and Essays*, Sangster's *The St. Lawrence and the Saguenay*, and Isabella Valancy Crawford's *Collected Poems*. As well, a new anthology in four volumes has recently appeared, two of these devoted to the period before World War I. It seems that a reconsideration of our early literature is well underway.

For nearly a century, debate raged as to whether Canada had a distinctive literature of her own and even if such a literature is necessary, when we have in Britain and America "the best that has been said and thought" in the English language. The recent publication of such books as *Read Canadian* or *Survival* points to the preoccupation even to-day with our cultural identity and its preservation from foreign contamination which stirred E. H. Dewart in his introduction to *Selections from Canadian Poets*. Dewart states: "A national literature is an essential element in the formation of national character. It is not merely the record of a country's mental progress; it is the expression of its intellectual life, the bond of national unity."[5] Eighty-four years later, E. K. Brown in his *On Canadian Poetry* asserts again a need for literature where the artist and the audience may share "a peculiar and passionate interest in the kind of life that exists in the country where they live," but continues, "There is a Canadian literature, often rising to effects of great beauty, but it has stirred little interest outside Canada" and indeed "even within the national borders the impact of Canadian books and Canadian literature has been relatively superficial."[6]

When we look then at the literature which Canada has produced in its period as a colony and in the three and a half decades following Confederation, it is important to retain a perspective. These writers are not literary giants; we will look in vain for an undiscovered Keats or Arnold or Tennyson, an Austen or George Eliot. In the nineteenth century, America produced Emerson, Melville, Hawthorne, Whitman, Emily Dickinson, Mark Twain, and Henry James. In Canada before 1900, there are no such major literary figures. We did indeed achieve recognition beyond our own borders in the writings of Henry Alline, Thomas Haliburton, Susannah Moodie, and Catharine Parr Traill, John Richardson, Charles Heavysege, Charles G. D. Roberts, Bliss Carman, Robert Service, W. H. Drummond, Pauline Johnson, William Kirby, Gilbert Parker, and Ernest Thomson Seton. But the literature of this period is important, not so much for its eminent artists, as for its expression of the voice of a people, the record of our society and the world from the unique centre of vision which is Canada. These writers are earnest and sincere, and they have much to convey to us, not only of the life and perspective of their times, but also of universal human nature and society, universal joys and sorrows.

The literature of the eighteenth and nineteenth centuries is of interest in reflecting the cultural patterns of the new colony and later, the new Dominion. Many of these early writers came to this country as pioneers. Most came at an early age and remained, contributing to the intellectual and cultural life of their adopted land. A few returned to their homelands within a few years and, like Frances Brooke and Joseph Stansbury, left little mark upon the literature of Canada. Yet their records are relevant here, for they suggest the first cultural imprint of a new country upon a receptive mind, and they indicate for us what many felt who came to stay but left no record. Of the thirty-five authors represented over one third here were British, from England, Scotland or Ireland: Frances Brooke, Thomas McCulloch, Catharine Parr Traill, Susannah Moodie, Alexander McLachlan, Charles Heavysege, Thomas D'Arcy McGee, Isabella Valancy Crawford, William Henry Drummond, Robert Service, William Kirby and Gilbert Parker. A few such as Henry Alline and Jonathan Odell were American, and Stansbury, McGee, and Kirby came to Canada by way of the States. But a surprising number were born in Canada. Oliver Goldsmith, Joseph Howe, Thomas Haliburton, and John Richardson made their mark on the literature of the country before 1850 and were followed in the next two decades by Charles Sangster, Charles Mair and James de Mille. The "Confederation Group" of poets and novelists were born in Canada in the 1860's and came to maturity after Confederation; they include Charles G. D. Roberts, his cousin Bliss Carman, Archibald Lampman, Duncan Campbell Scott, William Wilfred Campbell, George Frederick Cameron, F. G. Scott, Pauline Johnson, Sara Jeannette Duncan, and Gilbert Parker.

The majority of these writers, whether immigrant or Canadian, were staunchly middle-class, and their literature reflects the middle class virtues of nineteenth century Canada. A few were from the labouring classes such as Kirby whose father was a tanner and who at one time was apprenticed to him, Heavysege, a cabinet-maker and self-educated after the age of nine, and McLachlan, a farmer and a tailor. Of these, only McLachlan wrote poems which expressed working class views in opposition to those of the gentry such as Susannah Moodie; McLachlan's "Jack's As Good as his Master," "Acres of Your Own," "The Man Who Rose from Nothing," "The Emigrant," and a few others were very popular in their day but do not form a large proportion of his total output. Service was a bank clerk, a white collar worker, but he wrote of miners, and W. H. Drummond, D. C. Scott and E. W. Thomson were in medicine and the Civil Service, although they wrote of habitants, lumbermen, and the simple people of the little French Canadian villages. Not surprisingly, the writers represent the upper levels of the middle class, the professionals, merchants and civil servants (although as late as 1901 only 4.6 per cent of the employed population were in the professions and 1.0 per cent in the Civil Service[7]). Chief among the classes represented is the clergy, and, indeed, six of the thirty-five writers were ministers (Henry Alline, Thomas McCulloch, Jonathan Odell, E. H. Dewart, F. G. Scott, and William Wilfred Campbell) and five were the children of clergymen: Campbell again, Frances Brooke, Charles G. D. Roberts, Archibald Lampman, and D. C. Scott. The army is represented by Goldsmith and Richardson, by the husbands of Susannah Moodie and Catharine Traill, and the father of Gilbert Parker, law by Haliburton, McGee, Lighthall, Cameron, and Carman Senior, and medicine by W. H. Drummond and the fathers of Richardson, Crawford, and F. G. Scott. Only three, Thomas McCulloch, Charles G. D. Roberts, and James de Mille, were teachers for any length of time, although Carman, Lampman, Kirby, Duncan and, Parker taught for brief periods. Business and merchandising is represented by eight: Stansbury and the fathers of Mrs. Traill and Mrs. Moodie, of Sangster, Mair, Seton, de Mille, and Duncan, while Sangster, Mair, Lampman, D. C. Scott, and Campbell were civil servants. A large number of these writers were also engaged in journalism as reporters or editors for at least a part of their career: Joseph Howe, Sangster, McGee, Heavysege, Roberts, Carman, Duncan, Kirby, Parker, and Thompson.

The majority of these writers also lived in Ontario, particularly in the late years of the century. There is, however, an early flowering in the Maritimes in the 1770's with Henry Alline, and in the 1820's and 30's with Oliver Goldsmith, Joseph Howe, Thomas McCulloch and Thomas Haliburton, and a second flowering in the 1870's and 80's with James de Mille, Roberts, and Carman. An English tradition also flourished in Quebec from 1760 on, and D. C. Scott, Charles Mair, Gilbert Parker and Robert Service mark the beginnings of a movement into the North and West.

The literature provides us with a panorama of the times. In the century that passed between 1800 and 1900, Canada emerged from the bush and entered the twentieth century. Thus in the lifetime of one author such as Catharine Parr Traill who was born in 1802 and died in 1899, Canada developed from a primitive frontier to a modern nation, a process which, in England, took place over some ten centuries. At the signing of the Treaty of Paris in 1763, Canada became a colony, an entity stretching from Gaspé to Cornwall in length and two hundred miles in width along the St. Lawrence River. The eastern portion of this area had been settled for over a century by the French, but there were only a handful of English colonists when Frances Brooke arrived in 1763 with her clergyman husband to record in the first North American novel the flavour of the new Canadian society.

In 1791 the Constitutional Act divided the country into two sections, Lower Canada with a population of about 130,000 and Upper Canada with only 50,000. The western section remained almost unsettled until 1783 when the end of the Revolutionary War led to the inrush of over 25,000 Loyalists into British North America, drawn by the generous land grants of the British government; about 10,000 of these settled in Upper Canada and formed a nucleus for incoming immigrants. In 1796 the population of York, newly created capital of Upper Canada, was estimated at under twenty families. Quebec City in 1795 had 7,700 English inhabitants and Montreal, 1,300. By 1825 Toronto had reached 1,600, Kingston, 2,800 and Montreal and Quebec each slightly over 22,000. Ottawa began in 1827 with the incorporation of Bytown and did not achieve national significance until the 1850's when it was renamed Ottawa and chosen by Queen Victoria as the new national capital.[8]

Long before the settlement of Upper Canada, the British colonies in the Maritimes had been established with the first permanent English settlement in Halifax in 1749 and the surge of frontiersmen from New England into Nova Scotia and New Brunswick to claim lands available after the Expulsion of the Acadians in 1855. The inrush of some 10,000 Loyalists into the Maritimes at the end of the Revolutionary War was the impetus which led to the establishment of this area, and Halifax in particular, as the first real cultural centre in British North America. The West and North, as a part of the colony, did not really exist. Until 1870, the huge area including all of present day Manitoba, Saskatchewan, Alberta, British Columbia, and the North-West Territories, was under the ownership of the privately-operated Hudson's Bay Company chartered in 1670 by Charles II.

In one hundred years, the face of the country had changed completely. In 1867 the Dominion of Canada united four provinces, Ontario, Quebec, New Brunswick and Nova Scotia, joined in 1870 by Manitoba, in 1871 by British Columbia, and in 1873 by Prince Edward Island. Two decades later, Saskatchewan and Alberta were carved out of the existing territories, and Manitoba reconstituted to include a larger northern section. Victoria, established in 1843, became a city in 1862 and Vancouver, beginning in 1865 as a sawmill at Granville, was by 1890 a thriving urban area.

In 1800 the series of little villages in the British colonies were linked by a network of waterways and by mud and corduroy roads across marsh and bush which were passable comfortably only in mid-winter by sleigh and in mid-summer by light wagon. By 1900 paved highways linked the major cities and towns across the length and breadth of the continent. The hammering of the symbolic "Last Spike" at Craigellachie on November 7, 1885 signalled the success of that heroic affirmation of faith in the new Dominion, the Canadian Pacific Transcontinental Railway, which linked Quebec on the St. Lawrence with Vancouver on the Pacific Ocean and so realized the vision of a "Dominion from sea to sea." Ten years later, in 1895, the first Canadian canal at Sault Ste. Marie made possible an all-Canadian shipping route from the head of the Lakes to the Atlantic Ocean some two thousand miles away. In 1800 the only real industry was agriculture and the pioneer industries which developed to serve the needs of the small farming communities. By 1901,

Eastern Canada was still predominantly rural and agricultural with 73.8 per cent of the population, and 40 per cent of the labour force. But commerce and manufacturing represented another 23 per cent of the employed and there were fifty-nine "urban" centres with a population of over 5,000 people and twenty-two with over 10,000. The total population of Canada was 5,371,000 and Toronto alone had over 208,000 people, Montreal 267,000 and Ottawa 59,900.[9] It was not until after World War I that the literature of Canada reflected successfully this immense surge of population and this recent expansion in the economy, and in commerce, industry, transportation, and urban growth; nevertheless the changes between 1800 and 1900 paved the way for the emergence in the twentieth century of a literature which is mature, rich, and distinctive.

By 1900, Canadian culture too had reached maturity. As early as 1824, the Quebec Literary and Historical Society was founded by the Earl of Dalhousie and encouraged a flurry of literary activity. In 1859, the Nova Scotia Literary and Scientific Society was established "for the reading and discussion of original communications . . . in Literature, Science, Political Economy, Commerce, Statistics, and the Arts . . . to foster a spirit of enquiry and enterprise and generally promote the advancement of science, learning and the useful arts."[10] In 1882, at the suggestion of the Governor General, the Marquis of Lorne, the Royal Society of Canada was inaugurated. Among its charter members were William Kirby, Charles Sangster, John Reade, literary editor of the Montreal *Gazette*, and James LeMoine who wrote *Maple Leaves* from which both Kirby and Parker derived information for their historical romances of early Quebec. Later members included Charles G. D. Roberts, Bliss Carman, Archibald Lampman, D. C. Scott, Charles Mair, W. D. Lighthall, F. G. Scott, and William Wilfred Campbell.

By 1900 there also existed in Canada seventeen universities and nineteen colleges, agricultural schools, and ladies' colleges, among them King's College, Windsor (1790), The University of New Brunswick (1859 but chartered as King's College, Fredericton in 1826), McGill (1821), Dalhousie (1821), Victoria College (1836), Acadia College (1838), Queen's (1841), Bishop's, Lennoxville (1843), The University of Ottawa (1848), The University of Toronto (originally King's College, 1827, and now University College), Trinity College, Toronto (1852), St. Michael's College, Toronto (1852), Laval (1852), Mount Allison (1862), University of Manitoba (1877), and McMaster (1887).[11] These universities prepared the ground academically and culturally for the literary harvest.

Also by 1900, the foundations have been laid for Canada's publishing industry. The first printing-press was introduced into British North America in 1751 and from this point on, small presses began to flourish. Indeed there are estimated to have been over 1200 documents published in Canada between 1751 and 1800.[12] In the early years of the 1800's, the first bookstores appeared in the Maritimes, a number of these combining bookselling with publishing. Out of these and the newspaper offices and government printing departments, the publishing houses of Canada emerged and gradually gravitated to Toronto. One of the earliest full-fledged houses was Hunter-Rose which in 1848 was taken over by Irwin's. The Methodist Book and Publishing House emerged from the printing presses on which Egerton Ryerson published *The Christian Guardian* in 1829; it was bought out by William Briggs in 1879 and became Ryerson Press in 1918. John Lovell, co-editor of the *Literary Garland*, began printing in Montreal in 1835 and brought out a number of minor literary works as well as Sangster's *Hesperus and Other Poems*, Heavysege's *Saul*, McGee's *Canadian Ballads and Occasional Verses*, Joseph Howe's *Poems and Essays*, and the first edition of William Kirby's *The Golden Dog*. The largest firm in Toronto in the 1860's and 70's was James Campbell and Son who published mostly religious biographies, sermons, and travel books and was the supplier of texts for Canadian schools. Copp Clark was established in 1869 from the firm of Thomas MacLear who edited the *Anglo-American Magazine* (1852-5) and W. J. Gage was also established by the turn of the century. The most significant of these publishers in stimulating native literature was William Briggs. In the years preceding July of 1883, Briggs published 211,714 bound books as well as 34,000 pamphlets and sermons.[13] Briggs also brought out editions by William Kirby, Charles G. D. Roberts, F. G. Scott, Charles Mair, Catharine Parr Traill, Isabella Valancy Crawford, William Wilfred Campbell, Robert Service, and E. W. Thomson.

As well as a multitude of local newspapers in towns and cities across the country, the century also produced a host of cultural and literary journals, most of them rather short-lived. In the Maritimes appeared *The Nova Scotia Magazine* (1789-92), the *New Brunswick Religious and Literary Journal* (1829-30), *The Halifax Monthly Magazine* (1830-1), *The Bee* (1835-8), *The Colonial Pearl* (1837-40), *The Maple-Leaf* or *Canadian Annual* (1847-9), *Stewart's Quarterly* (1867-72), the *Maritime Monthly* (1873-5) and the *New Brunswick Magazine* (1898-1905), as well as Joseph Howe's famous weekly *The Novascotian* in the 1820's. Periodicals were more numerous in the Canadas: *the Quebec Magazine* (1792-4), *the Christian Examiner* (1819-20), *The Literary Miscellany* (1822-3), *The Canadian Magazine and Literary Repository* (1823-5), *The Canadian Review and Literary and Historical Journal* (1824-6) which became *The Canadian Review and Magazine*, *The Canadian Literary Magazine* (1833), the *Canadian Magazine* (1833), *The Literary Garland* (1838-51), the *Victoria Magazine* (1847-8), *The Canadian Journal* (1852), the *Anglo-American Magazine* (1852-5), the *British American Magazine* (1863-4), *The Canadian Monthly and National Review* (1872-8) becoming *Rose-Belford's Canadian Monthly* (1878-82), *The Nation* 1874-6, *The Week* (1883-96), and *The Canadian Magazine* (1893-1939). Around 1900 Winnipeg appeared on the literary scene with two periodicals, *The Canadian West Magazine* and *The Manitoban*.

Most of these magazines were publishing some Canadiana although a staple was American poetry and fiction and British literature which often arrived via America. The pronouncement in 1823 of David Chisholme, the young editor of the *Canadian Magazine and Literary Repository* represents the policy of the most national of this group:

> It shall form one of the most prominent parts of our labours to select and transfer into our pages . . . such articles as we deem of importance, in promoting the diffusion of useful knowledge throughout this country. . . . Besides selected articles from other publications, we intend that this work shall also contain *original* matter of such a local and general character as shall render it at once useful and entertaining to all classes of society. . . . A due proportion of our pages shall be allotted for the selection of published and unpublished verse.[15]

The Literary Garland, edited by John Lovell and his brother-in-law John Gibson from 1838-52, is one of the best-known of these periodicals and published in its pages works by Major John Richardson, Anna Jameson, Susannah Moodie, Catharine Parr Traill, John Dunbar Moodie, Charles Sangster, Rosanna Leprohon, and two daughters of a popular American lady novelist, Mrs. Elizabeth Cushing and Mrs. Harriet V. Cheney. Susannah and John Moodie's *Victoria Magazine,* published in Belleville, was short-lived and lasted only from 1847 to 1848. Goldwyn Smith, one of the prime movers of the Canada First Group, was also one of the most influential promoters of literature in his magazines *The Canadian Monthly and National Review, The Nation,* and *The Bystander. The Week,* which he established in 1883, was edited for a period of several months in 1883 and 1884 by Charles G. D. Roberts and published selections by Roberts, Carman, Lampman, D. C. Scott, and Sarah Jeanette Duncan among others. Two newspapers, the Montreal *Gazette* and the *Toronto Star,* were also significant in stimulating native literature, in particular short fiction.

Despite this predominance of Canadian literary and cultural magazines, however, the role of the Canadian writer was a hard one, as William Kirby complained to the Royal Society in his address on publishing in 1883. There were no Canadian copyright laws to protect local authors from American pirates. Indeed Kirby's own *Golden Dog* appeared in several editions before the authorized one and he received from this novel only $100 during his lifetime in addition to a small sum from the French Canadian translation. Both publishing houses and magazines reprinted extensively from British and American works and a flood of American books and pirated editions of British authors crossed the border. As a result of public apathy and the marginal finances of native publishers, Canadian authors usually found it more profitable to publish in Britain and the United States, and in the 1890's and the early years of this century many writers left Canada to seek an audience else-where, among them Roberts, Carman, Gilbert Parker, Seton, Duncan, and E. W. Thomson.

Writers throughout the period reflect their awareness of their country and of its potentialities in their choice of theme, subject, and form. The earliest literary response to Canada apart from the travelogue was expressed primarily in the form of poetry, in lyrics, songs and sonnets, even narratives. By 1880, after a century of development and thirteen years of nationhood, Canadian poetry entered a phase of maturity, as suggested by Thomas Marquis in his essay of 1912 "Canadian Litera-ture." Fiction, Marquis states, was slower to ripen and matured about 1890.[16] By the end of the century, literary criticism was still young, and Canadian drama in its infancy.

The central themes of Canadian poetry are those of any country and any age, a concern with the physical environment and nature, with patri-otism, religion or the artistic process, and with personal relationships and experiences, in particular with love and death. Of these, an absorp-tion with physical nature, with the land itself, is the dominant theme in Canadian poetry and remains central in both poetry and fiction even to-day as Margaret Atwood indicates in *Survival*. Indeed it must have seemed to Canadian writers of the nineteenth century, in competition with many centuries of English literature and one hundred years of American writing that our only distinctive characteristic was the land and our relationship to it. In his essay "Wanted: Canadian Criticism," A. J. M. Smith indicates how close the association was between his predecessors and their choice of nature as theme:

> If you write, apparently, of the far north and the wild west and the picturesque east, seasoning well with allusions to the Canada goose, fir trees, maple leaves, snow shoes, northern lights, etc., the public grasp the fact that you are a Canadian poet whose works are to be bought from the same patriotic motive that prompts the purchaser of Eddy's matches or a Massey-Harris farm implement.[17]

Both Lighthall and Dewart comment at some length on the native scene in their introductions. Dewart asserts that the wildflowers and songbirds of Canada, her "magnificent lakes, forests, and rivers" are "as worthy of being enshrined in lyric numbers" as those of older countries and more distant ages,[18] while Lighthall celebrates Canada's "four-thousand-mile panorama of noble rivers, wild forests, ocean-like prairies; her towering snow-capped Rockies, waking to the tints of sunrise in the West; in the east her hoary Laurentians."[19] In Lighthall's anthology, for example, three sections can be loosely described as concerned with landscape: eighteen poems of "Sports and Free Life," twenty-eight poems of "Places," and all thirty-seven poems of "Seasons," or one half of the selections in the volume. In these poems we find a land of seasons, a brief spring, a rapid summer, a brilliant fall, and again winter, and the poetry of Sangster, McLachlan, Mair, Roberts, Carman, Lampman, Campbell, and Pauline Johnson captures the changing face of the year. With A. J. M. Smith, these poets write of a "lonely land," its "strength broken by strength/And still strong." Their trees and rocks and cliffs, their wild geese and ducks symbolize man's struggle against the very physical universe for survival.

Nor are these poets alone. Frances Brooke is the first to record for us the appeal of the landscape to those from the Old World, its sublimity and romance, its combination of grandeur and starkness, terror and awe. These elements appear also in the prose of Susannah Moodie and Catharine Parr Traill, and the latter records for us in detail the life of the forest, the trees and flowers and animals. John Richardson and Rosanna Leprohon employ natural description as background for their historic romances while Roberts and Seton depict the struggle for survival of the forest creatures. Nor is this theme less prevalent to-day. Man is pitted against the land for survival, both mental and physical, in poems by E. J. Pratt, Earl Birney, George Bowering, and Al Purdy among others, and in novels by Frederick Philip Grove, Sinclair Ross, W. O. Mitchell, Hugh MacLennan, Gabrielle Roy, Ernest Buckler, Fred Bodsworth, and Margaret Atwood to name only a few.

A corollary to the theme of physical nature is the relationship of man to an urban environment. While poems on this theme form a small proportion of verse in the century, they are significant in underlining the theme of nature. The nineteenth century view that "God made the country, Man the town" is prevalent. Cities are seen not as positive creations of man, as vertical and progressive elements of civilization established on the horizontal and static landscape, but as sterile and anti-life. McLachlan's "Sighs of the City" is in this tradition as well as his "Wilson's Grave" but its chief exponent is Lampman, whose sonnet "Reality" presents as unpleasant a view of urban Ottawa as Wordsworth's or Blake's descriptions of London. And his view here is borne out by other poems as "The City," "A Night of Storm," and his nightmare vision "The City of the End of Things," his prophecy of doom for a mechanical and industrial civilization. Other writers escape to the land. While Sangster worked in Kingston and later in Ottawa where D. C. Scott and William Wilfred Campbell were also employed, they write of open fields and lakes, the north or west rather than the city. William Henry Drummond and F. G. Scott spent most of their lives in Montreal, Service was in the Yukon for less than ten years, and Isabella Valancy Crawford lived in Lakefield, Peterborough, and Toronto; while they, like Roberts and Carman, lived predominantly in urban areas, they wrote largely of the land or personal experience. This trend away from the city is still evident today and George Bowering can still write in his poetry of Mexico "My face is lost in the city" or of Calgary as a "box social of a city" with its "steel haystacks" and its "box people/pushed into cubes."[20]

A second major theme in Canadian poetry is patriotism, a popularity attested to by the predominance of nationalistic poetry in any early collection of Canadian verse. For example, in Lighthall's *Songs of the Great Dominion*, at least three of nine sections could be categorized as patriotic: "The Imperial Spirit," "The New Nationality," and "The Spirit of Canadian History," or thirty-two poems in a book of about one hundred and thirty selections. Indeed the whole book is clearly a product of patriotic fervour, as indicated by the sub-title: "Voices from the Forests and Waters, the Settlements and Cities of Canada." The best of these pieces are illustrated by such works as Sangster's "Brock" and "Ode for the Canadian Confederacy" or Roberts' "Canada." Perhaps more typical is the verse of John Reade, literary editor of the Montreal *Gazette* which begins "Canada, Canada, land of the maple,/ Queen of the forest and lake" and concludes "A new reign of beauty on earth has begun." Northrop Frye suggests that the patriotic poet is divided by two urges, "one scribbling ready-made poetic doggerel and the other attempting to communicate the real feelings his country inspires him with."[21] Too often the former predominates and the result is cliché, abstraction, and bombast. Few of these poems remain of interest to-day and they have virtually no successors among the major poems of the twentieth century.

The same is true of the religious verse of the period which is prolific but minor. As noted already, eleven of these writers were clergymen or the children of clergymen and religion was a major preoccupation of the period, although Lighthall includes few interesting examples. Thirty ministers published works of fiction alone from 1880 to 1920, and the chief of these, Ralph Connor, published nearly thirty novels and books of short stories which E. W. McCourt estimates to have sold over five million copies.[22] As well, the publishers of poetry and fiction were often religiously oriented, as in the case of The Methodist Book and Publishing House which became William Briggs, while Hunter-Rose, and many periodicals such as Ryerson's *Christian Endeavour* were organs of the church. And the first Canadian anthologist of note was the Reverend W. H. Dewart, editor of the *Christian Guardian* of the Methodist Church from 1869-94 and author of several religious pamphlets and three books on church doctrine. His choices for his collection were, however, not primarily religious. Of the writers represented in this present volume, only Henry Alline wrote centrally and almost exclusively of religious questions, in an introspective and personal style reminiscent of Donne. Jonathan Odell has few extant apolitical poems, none of these primarily religious, while William Wilfred Campbell is concerned with landscape, nationalism and imperialism more extensively than with religion. A few of F. G. Scott's poems such as "The Wayside Cross" and "The Crucifixion" are effective in conveying a religious sense of life, and elsewhere there are occasional pieces such as Carman's "Vestigia" and Pauline Johnson's "Christmas Tide" which are successful in handling a religious theme.

Personal poetry is also popular in Canadian literature of the nineteenth century, in particular poetry of personal emotions such as those associated with love and death. It has long been a critical commonplace of Canada that we are bad lovers and have written love poetry of little consequence. Yet surprisingly, Irving Layton remarks in his anthology, *Love Where the Nights are Long*: "Canadian poets have written some of the best love poetry in the world." And he collects selections from twenty-eight Canadian poets to prove his point, including pieces by Charles G. D. Roberts, D. C. Scott, and three by Bliss Carman. He explains in his introduction:

> In this vast, empty space, in this white blankness, love defines us, gives us a habitation and a name. More than others, our poets have known this to be true, and therefore their lyrics have a concreteness and particularity, an authenticity, unmatched by those of any other country.[23]

On the whole, love poetry was not a major strength of British or American poets of the nineteenth century apart from Browning. Although most of the writers have tried their hand at the subject, they rarely succeed in capturing the subtle cadences of love in language free from cliche or sentimentality. The love poems which do succeed however are often surprisingly fresh, thoughtful or perceptive, as Howe's witty "To Mary," McLachlan's "Lovely Alice" and "My Love is Like the Lily Flower," Sangster's "The Impatient Lover" and "Love While You May," Carman's classic "Low Tide on Grand Pré" and his Sappho Poems, Crawford's "Love's Forget-Me-Not," and "Where, Love, Art Hid?" and several of F. G. Scott's poems. On the whole, these writers are more successful in handling death, perhaps because the intense and personal nature of grief is more likely to break through the bonds of convention and ritual to achieve poignancy and depth, perhaps also because the poems may express a later phase of life while love poems often belong to youth. An intensification of life in contact with the sudden realities of death has long been a staple of short-story writers and is predominant in such recent novels as Laurence's *The Stone Angel,* Mitchell's *Who Has Seen the Wind* and *The Kite,* MacLennan's *The Watch That Ends the Night,* Gabrielle Roy's *The Cashier*, and Margaret Atwood's *Surfacing*. Again most of these poets have at some time written elegies. In a day when early death was a common feature of life and where many families lost mothers and babies or young children, the theme of death was of pressing concern. Perhaps the closest of these to death are Archibald Lampman and George Cameron, both of whom died before the age of forty. As well as personal poems such as "To Death," "White Pansies," and "We Too Shall Sleep," Lampman indicates his awareness of death in his poems on fall and winter, as in "In November" where the season induces in him a "spectral happiness" and "a nameless and unnatural cheer,/A Pleasure secret and austere." Other works which treat this theme are McLachlan's "Wilson's Grave," Roberts' "The Place of His

Rest" and "Severance," Carman's "The Ghost-Yard of the Golden-Rod" and "Threnody for a Poet," D. C. Scott's "Memory," "At Delos," "The Leaf," "The Closed Door," and several of the "Thirteen Songs," F. G. Scott's "Death and the Child" and "By the Sea," Campbell's "Return No More," and Johnson's "Through Time and Bitter Distance" and "Good-bye" as well as most selections of George Frederick Cameron.

Another favourite theme of Romantic and Victorian poets is a concern with the role of the poet and with the artistic process, a concern which was iterated first in Romantic poetry and in the 1880's and '90's became an element of fiction as in the works of Henry James or Thomas Hardy's *Jude the Obscure*. In modern poetry, this theme appears in A. M. Klein's "Portrait of the Poet as Landscape" and elsewhere in his works, in A. J. M. Smith, Irving Layton, Leonard Cohen, and many recent writers. In the novel, it is treated in MacLennan's *Two Solitudes*, Ross' *As For Me and My House*, Davies' *A Mixture of Frailties*, Roy's *The Hidden Mountain*, Richler's *The Acrobats* and Buckler's *the Mountain and the Valley*. In view of the marginal situation of the artist in Canada before 1915, however, it is not surprising that artists are more concerned with public and popular subjects rather than with their own personal dilemma of communication. In *Life in the Clearings*, Susannah Moodie indicates the common view of the artist when her son recalls the taunt of a comrade that "his ma said Mrs. M.—invented lies, and got paid for them." Yet another woman, after looking Mrs. Moodie up and down and inquiring after her age and the condition of her teeth, remarks disappointedly: "Well, I've he'rd a great deal about you, and I wanted to see you bad for a long time; but you are only a humly person like myself after all."[24] The prevailing view of the artist is Romantic, both from inside and outside. Society views him with curiosity, apprehension, and moral concern while the poet feels himself torn by contrary impulses. Lampman, the poet most concerned with this process, expresses this view explicitly; the poet is a child of Pan, "half God, half brute, within the selfsame shell," and "halfway twixt hell and heaven," yet he is fitted to be an interpreter of the life of man for:

> Life with its hope and error, toil and bliss,
> Earth-born, earth-reared, ye know it like it is.

And in "Why Do Ye Call the Poet Lonely" he replies "He is not desolate, but only/Sees where ye cannot, hidden faces." George Frederick Cameron too is centrally concerned with this theme and, like Keats, also aware of the nearness of death, hopes to record his vision of the world before he is silenced. While a number of other poets deal occasionally with the role of the poet, particularly in tributes to their predecessors and contemporaries such as Shakespeare, Milton, Keats, Shelley or Tennyson, the most remarkable treatment of art is D. C. Scott's "The Piper of Arll," the long narrative which is reminiscent of Coleridge's "Ancient Mariner" in its choice of the ballad form and stanza and its oblique narration without authorial commentary. But while Coleridge's artist-mariner is doomed to wander the world in search of an audience, Scott's piper passes swifly from innocence to experience and dies at the moment of achieving the fullest expression of his art. The final vision of the static poet at the bottom of the sea has been interpreted as a comment on the predicament of the artist in Canada.

While the majority of poems written in the century were short lyrics, sonnets or odes or more sustained verse, the narrative tradition was remarkably strong, as Northrop Frye indicates in his essay on narrative poetry in *The Bush Garden*.[25] The narrative poem was established as a genre almost as early as the lyric and is represented by such works as Goldsmith's "The Rising Village" and Howe's "Acadia" which like McLachlan's later "The Emigrant" deal not so much with the story of an individual as that of a people. Other poems such as Sangster's "The St. Lawrence and the Saguenay" employ a narrative framework for a description of the Canadian landscape and a philosophical comment on human life. While Crawford's "Malcolm's Katie" relates a story of individuals, the characters become, like those of Howe, Goldsmith, and McLachlan, representative of a process of development within Canada itself. Many other narrative poems are more concerned with individuals than with symbols. Howe's light satire "Once More I Put My Bonnet On," McLachlan's "Auld Hawkie's Dream," and Crawford's "The Deacon and his Daughter" are carefully controlled narratives which satirize human pretensions and vanities. The ballad tradition is strong in Canadian poetry with a large number of works by Service and Drummond such as "The Shooting of Dan McGrew," "The Cremation of Sam McGee," and "The Wreck of the Julie Plante" and in D. C. Scott's "The Piper of Arll," "At the Cedars," and "On the Way to the Mission"; in these poems the often-tragic tone, the interrelation of love and death, and the predominance of action and the absence of authorial comment mark the resemblance to the ballad. Scott's Indian ballads too are at the height of a tradition which includes such earlier works as Howe's "Song of the Micmacs" and "The Micmacs," McGee's "The Arctic Indian's Faith," Sangster's "Taapookaa: A Huron Legend" and "The Lament of Shingwakonce," and Richardson's early poem "Tecumseh" as well as the work of his contemporaries Pauline Johnson in her Indian narratives such as "Ojistoh" and F. G. Scott in "Wahonomin." In theme and form these narratives resemble the short story. They involve conflict, frequently a conflict with the physical universe but often a conflict between old and new, the native and the imported, the primitive and the "civilized." This tradition culminates in the poetry of E. J. Pratt. In "The Cachalot," "The Titanic," and "Towards The Last Spike," man struggles against the alien forces of sea and ice and rock, against an indifferent universe, and in "Brébeuf and his Brethren," this struggle becomes a conflict between civilization and primitivism for the soul of man.

As T. G. Marquis has suggested, the year 1890 marks the real emergence of the novel in Canada on the literary scene. Before 1880, 250 works of fiction appeared in Canada, written by 150 authors; two-thirds of these were written in the '60's and '70's and 100 of them by only five authors: Thomas Haliburton, Susannah Moodie, Agnes Fleming, James de Mille, and Mary Anne Sadlier. From 1880 to 1920, four hundred Canadians produced fourteen hundred volumes of fiction, among them Charles G. D. Roberts, his brother Theodore, Gilbert Parker, Sarah Jeanette Duncan, Ralph Connor, E. W. Thomson, and Ernest Thompson Seton.[26]

Frances Brooke was the first writer to import to Canada the novel which, in the past twenty-five years, had emerged in England as a new and popular genre. She selected her themes and techniques, not from Defoe, Fielding or Smollett, but from the more refined Richardson, a friend and acquaintance whose *Pamela* had appeared in 1740. Like him, Mrs. Brooke chose the technique of letters to develop the romance of her characters. The Canadian setting is in many ways incidental to the action but it does function, in Shakespearian terms, as a "green world" where the characters, away from the pressures of society, come to a knowledge of themselves and their true identity. The work has no real counterpart in Canadian fiction until a century later. The first native-born novelist, was Julia Beckwith Hart who published her *St. Ursula's Convent or The Nuns of Canada* in 1824 and *Tonnewonte or The Adopted Son of America* in 1831, works which are primarily of historic interest. John Richardson lays claim to recognition as the earliest native novelist of consequence with his *Wacousta*, published in 1832. He was the first important novelist to make use of Canada's historic past and he later lamented that he was unrecognized as "the only Author this country has produced or who has attempted to infuse in it a spirit of literature."[27] He followed this work with a sequel, *The Canadian Brothers; or The Prophecy Fulfilled* (1840). In the Maritimes during the same period, Thomas Haliburton was producing his famous Clockmaker Series with its successors the Sam Slick series which ran through six volumes; like Thomas McCulloch's *Stepsure Letters, The Clockmaker* employs fiction to examine the problems of Nova Scotian society and to satirize its attitudes and beliefs with the hope of reform. McCulloch also published two novels *William* and *Melville*, but these are essentially didactic tracts and are of little interest today.

Catharine Parr Traill's *The Backwoods of Canada* and her sister Susannah Moodie's *Roughing It in the Bush* are also contemporary with the works of Richardson and Haliburton but belong in part to the category of travel literature, a staple of early Canadian writing and appearing in such Canadian classics as George Heriot's *Travels Through the Canada's* (1807), John Lambert's *Travels Through Lower Canada and the United States of North America* (1810), Anne Langton's *A Gentlewoman in Upper Canada* (1837), Anna Jameson's *Winter Studies and*

Summer Rambles in the Canadas (1838), Paul Kane's *Wanderings of an Artist,* and later accounts at the end of the century of Kipling, Rupert Brooke, and Lady Dufferin. In the decade that Mrs. Traill's *The Female Emigrant's Guide* appeared, there were published over one hundred books of the same type, few of which are of more than passing interest to-day. But the Moodie and Traill accounts differ from those of most of their contemporaries in the immediacy and vividness of the naration and description. *Roughing It in the Bush* in particular is close to autobiography and fiction in its narrative techniques and its character depiction. Both Susannah and Catharine also published novels which are less interesting, more conventional, and inclined to be didactic. Catharine wrote many books for children, among these a number of animal stories, including *Afar in the Forest* (1850) and *Cot and Cradle Stories* (1895), as well as two adventure stories, *The Young Emigrants* (1826) and *Canadian Crusoes* (1852).

In the 1860's and 70's several important figures emerged on the fictional scene. The most financially successful novelist in this period was Mary Agnes Fleming of Saint John (1840-80) who wrote forty-two novels in a lifetime of forty years and who received as much as $10,000 in one year from her New York publishers; she is thus the first successful professional novelist in Canada.[28] Her contemporary, James de Mille, also published prolifically in a short lifetime, thirty books in twenty years, among them boy's stories, historical romances, and popular fiction with exotic settings. His *A Strange Manuscript Found in a Copper Cylinder*, published posthumously in 1888, is unique in Canadian literature and traces its history to Swift's *Gulliver's Travels* and such anti-Utopian works as Butler's *Erewhon*. Like Swift's work it is a satiric examination of contemporary mores and codes of ethics disguised as an autobiographical account of a journey to a remote country, here Antarctica. William Kirby's classic novel *The Golden Dog,* his one major work of fiction, also appeared in this period, in 1877 after eleven years of intensive research. An historical romance in the vein of Walter Scott, it draws like Richardson's *Wacousta* on the indigenous past for both setting and plot structure. Set in French Canada in the period of the *ancien régime* just before the victory of Wolfe, it effectively evokes the atmosphere of decadence which pervaded the upper levels of society and the French administration and recreates in fiction the power of that influential figure Francis Bigot. The novel marks a rising interest in Canada both in the genre of historical romance and in the French Canadian setting which was to inspire a large volume of novels in the next decades.

In the late 1880's, the output of fiction in Canada increased rapidly in volume. From 1888 to 1914, nearly every year saw the appearance of a new Canadian fiction-writer, and some years of two or three.[29] The most popular vogue was the historical romance which reached a peak of interest between 1886 and 1904. Gilbert Parker's *The Seats of the Mighty* is in this tradition, and deals with the same period as *The Golden Dog,*

Quebec before the French defeat in 1759. Charles G. D. Roberts also wrote several novels of the Acadian past, as *The Raid of Beausejour* (1894), *The Forge in the Forest* (1896), *A Sister to Evangeline* (1898), and *The Prisoner of Mademoiselle* (1904). The regional novel was also in vogue, in particular, the novel set in French Canada which between 1890 and 1914 inspired seventy-five volumes of historical romances, local colour stories, tales, and legends.[30] As well as Parker's *Seats of the Mighty*, his *The Trail of the Sword* (1894), *When Valmond Came to the Pontiac* (1895), *The Pomp of the Lavilettes* (1894), and *The Right of Way* (1901), Lighthall's *The Young Seigneur* (1888) and Grey's *The Curé of St. Philippe* (1899), also draw on this tradition. D. C. Scott's volume of short stories *In the Village of Viger* (1895), E. W. Savarin's *Old Man Savarin*, and the narrative poems of W. H. Drummond are also in this vein. Elsewhere too regionalism is in the ascendent, with the novels of Ralph Connor in Scots Ontario and the prairies and foothills of the West, of Lucy Maud Montgomery in the Maritimes, and of Gilbert Parker in the lands of the Hudson's Bay Company, later Saskatchewan, and of many minor authors in each of these areas.

Another variety of fiction which emerged after 1890 is the animal story, a peculiarly Canadian phenomenon which was developed by Charles G. D. Roberts and Ernest Thompson Seton.[31] Earlier writers produced animal tales for children, such as Mrs. Traill and Susannah Moodie with her *Little Black Pony and Other Stories* (1850), and Marshall Saunder's *Beautiful Joe* (1894) is a successor to this tradition. But Roberts and Seton wrote for adults. Drawing from allegory and classical legend, they adapted the form to depict the Darwinian struggle for survival in the animal and human worlds, the sacrifice of the individual to the species and the balance between prey and predator. Although Seton published first his animal biography "The Life of a Prairie Chicken" in the *Canadian Journal* of 1883, it was not until "Lobo: King of the Currumpaw" (Scribner's, 1894) that he really moved into the area of fiction. Meanwhile, Roberts had published "Do Seek Their Meat from God" in *Harper's* (December 1892) and fifteen similar stories appeared in *Earth's Enigmas* of 1895, three years before Seton's first book *Wild Animals I Have Known* made the genre popular. Together after 1898, Roberts and Seton published over thirty books of this type. Among their descendents are Jack London, James Oliver Curwood, Grey Owl, and Fred Bodsworth.

In Canadian literature, the novel of manners or society was also popular. It was often related to the small town as depicted successfully by Leacock in his *Sunshine Sketches* (1912). The most successful of these early works and anticipating both the wit of Leacock and his irony is Sara Jeannette Duncan's *The Imperialist* (1904) which evokes the life of the bustling little town of Elgin, Ontario, with its sense of selfimportance, its provincialism and preoccupation with local concerns, its religion and commerce and local politics. Although the romances of the hero and his sister are in the traditional manner, more novel is the choice, particularly by a woman, of a political subject, the campaign of the hero to represent Elgin in the Liberal government in Ottawa. Here and elsewhere, in *An American Girl in London, A Voyage of Consolation, A Daughter of To-Day*, and *Cousin Cinderella: A Canadian Girl in London*, Duncan handles successfully another popular theme, the relationships between Europe and America in the manner of Henry James and Mark Twain's *Innocents Abroad*. Her first work *A Social Departure*, her record of a trip with a friend around the world, is of interest in particular for its description of an epic rail journey across Canada little over one year after the completion of the Canadian Pacific Railway to Vancouver.

Thus by 1910, the Canadian novel was well established in the popular imagination. In the forefront were historical romances but other popular patterns include regional fiction, adventure stories, the animal story, sentimental domestic fiction, novels of social manners, travel fiction, a number of works of mystery and crime fiction and even a few artist novels.

Drama was very late in appearing on the Canadian scene and may be said to have emerged as a major literary force as late as the 1950's and '60's. In fact, there were theatres in Canada at a very early date. In the Maritimes well before 1880 professional companies which toured New York and Boston also performed in Halifax, St. John and sometimes Chatham, and amateur theatre was established very early. In his *Travels through Lower Canada and the United States of North America in the years 1806, 1807 and 1808*, the Englishman John Lambert commented on the fledgling drama:

> There is, indeed, a building at Quebec called a theatre, and also one at Montreal; but the persons who perform there, are as bad as the worst of our strolling actors; yet they have the conscience to charge the same price nearly as the London theatres. Sometimes the officers of the army lend their assistance to the company; but I have seen none, except Colonel Pye, and Captain Clark of the 49th, who did not murder the best scenes of our dramatic poets.[32]

In 1822, the Halifax Garrison organized a theatrical company and in the same year presented Oliver Goldsmith's *She Stoops to Conquer*, with the part of Tony Lumpkin played by the author's grand-nephew, the Canadian Oliver. But such companies as these almost always chose works by established authors to ensure popular and financial support rather than plays of unknown native artists, a practice still common and satirized in Robertson Davies' witty novel on amateur Canadian theatre *Tempest Tost* (1951). By the end of the nineteenth century, every city and little town across the country sported a theatre or "Opera-House" where local entertainment was presented, even the Dawson of the

Gold-rush. Dramatic readings were also given in many centres by travelling writers from Britain and the United States, as Charles Dickens and Mark Twain, and by Pauline Johnson, accompanied after 1897 by Walter McRaye who recited the verses of Drummond. Later readings in this tradition were given by Bliss Carman and by Stephen Leacock.

Native Canadian drama, however, barely existed until late in the century. Frances Brooke who wrote the first North American novel also published several plays: *Virginia* (1756), *Sinope* which ran for ten days at Covent Garden in 1779, and a light opera *Rosina,* also produced for ten days at Covent Garden in 1782. Barnabas Bidwell who emigrated to Upper Canada in 1810 published a poetic tragedy while at Yale in 1784 and later contributed to Canadian literature in the form of eleven sketches included in Robert Gourlay's *Statistical Account of Upper Canada* (1822). But these are hardly native dramatists. In the Maritimes, *The Poetical Remains of Peter John Allan,* published after the author's death in 1853, include a romantic play, while Frederick Augustus Dixon published three plays and John Hunter-Duvar two poetic dramas, *The Enamerado* (1879) and *De Roberval* (1888). In Ontario, Kirby's *Joseph in Egypt* was performed in the Niagara Court House in 1876, and his *Queen Esther* in 1880; Kirby also wrote *The Queen's Own,* a poetic farce, and his novel *The Golden Dog* was dramatized and produced as *Beaumanoir.* William Wilfred Campbell also published four plays: *Mordred* and *Hildebrand* (1895) and *Daulac* and *Morning* (1908) and wrote a number of others: "Brokenfield," "Robespierre," "Sanio," and "The Admiral's Daughter." In 1889 George Frederick Cameron's opera *Leo, A Royal Cadet* was performed in Kingston and later in Ottawa, Utica, Guelph, Stratford, Woodstock and Toronto, and Gilbert Parker at the beginning of his career had three plays produced in Australia by the actor George Rignold: an adaptation of Faust, *No Defence* and *Heart of Gold.* Sarah Jeanette Duncan published *Julyann and other Plays* and her novel *His Royal Happiness* was dramatized and put on at the Royal Alexandra in Toronto. Bliss Carman collaborated with Mary Perry King on the masques *Daughters of the Dawn,* (1913) and *Earth's Deities* (1914), while D. C. Scott's one-act play *Pierre* was produced by the Ottawa Little Theatre in 1923. Thus towards the end of the century, a number of writers who were more successful in poetry and fiction did experiment with the drama and did often succeed in getting their plays staged, although these have little literary interest. Two other writers, however, did succeed, if not in creating notable drama, at least in conceiving dramatic pieces of literary and historic interest. Heavysege published his *Saul* first in 1857 and *Count Filippo* in 1860 while Mair's *Tecumseh* was a popular success when it appeared in 1888. These works are closet-dramas and unsuited to the stage; too unwieldy for performance they are perhaps closer to the traditions of the narrative poem. Yet they do employ effectively a sense of conflict, the dramatic character of their heroes, at times a vivid action and again at times effective dialogue.

While Heavysege employs foreign subject-matter, the Bible or Renaissance Europe in accord with his Shakespearean form, Charles Mair brings to the drama a theme already employed by Richardson in fiction and becoming increasingly popular in the next few years, the Canadian historical past. His is thus the forerunner of such modern dramas as John Coulter's *Riel*.

The essay and, in particular, literary criticism was also late in evolving. Reviews of current literary works, British, American and native, were common in the pages of the numerous daily and weekly newspapers published in the cities and towns across the country and, in particular, in the Toronto *Globe*, or *Saturday Night*, the Montreal *Star* or the Ottawa *Gazette*. But a large part of these are interesting more as a commentary on the opinions of the writers themselves and the taste of the period than as enduring literary evaluations. Many of them were adulatory, and indeed this is one of the dangers of provincialism where authors may be over-rated for patriotic reasons as well as minimized by comparison to the best international standards, as Dewart warns in his first anthology of Canadian literature. Here Dewart expresses ideas to appear later in 1944 in the classic statement of E. K. Brown's *On Canadian Poetry*: the difficulties encountered in both publishing and distribution, the indifference of Canadians themselves to their own literature, an over-dependence upon Britain and America both for techniques and for the literature itself, and the problems of the double standard applied to foreign and to native authors.[33] Dewart also examines issues more contemporary to his own century such as the interpretation of the word "poetry." Bliss Carman in his aesthetic essays also comments on the meaning of poetry, on the role of the artist in society, and on the nature of art in general and its quality of "realism," which he defines as a reflection of both life as it is and life as it ought to be. Dewart's successor Lighthall, in his introduction to *Songs of the Great Dominion*, concentrates on emphasizing the appeal of his authors to their society and suggests that native scenes, flora and fauna are as capable of inspiring poetry as the scenes, flowers and birds sung by British authors. His essay is thus less interesting to-day than Dewart's as cultural comment.

The state of Canadian culture and literature in the period is examined by several critics. Joseph Howe's "Local Patriotism" is a plea to Nova Scotians to create "a high mental and moral cultivation, infusing into every branch of industry such a degree of intellectual vigour as shall insure success, multiply population, and endow them with productive power," in order to produce a society of distinction. Howe encourages local initiative not only in agriculture and commerce, but in science, literature and the other arts.[34] McGee too demands a distinctive intellectual and cultural life for Canada. In "The Mental Outfit of the New Dominion," he surveys the present cultural life and calls for a mental self-reliance to match the physical beauty of the new capital and its new architecture. He urges native authors to express Canadian needs and ideals rather than depending on British and American sources and prophesies that, in the next generation, at least forty men should emerge capable of the mental discipline and power necessary to the creation of a great civilization. Archibald Lampman considers the present state of Canadian culture, in particular its literature, in his speech delivered in Ottawa in 1891. Canada, he remarked, is "still in the house-building land-breaking stage" where capable minds are "engaged in making fortunes and founding families. Their descendants ... will be the writers or the readers of the age when a Canadian literature comes to be."[35] Lampman also contributed with D. C. Scott and William Wilfred Campbell to a weekly column which ran from 1892 to 1893 in the Toronto *Globe.* Under the title "At the Mermaid Inn," this column discussed affairs of cultural interest, both national and international. A number of these articles represent the best of literary criticism in their period. The most extensive comments on Canada's literature before 1900 are the books of the historian John George Bourinot: *The Intellectual Development of the Canadian People: an Historical Review* which appeared in 1881 and *Intellectual Strength and Weakness,* a speech delivered before the Royal Society of Canada and printed in 1893 as a book of nearly one hundred pages. Subtitled "A Short Review of Literature, Education and Art in Canada," it includes thirty pages of notes on important historical events, authors, and works of the period.

These, then, are the literary reflections of the nineteenth century. During this period from 1790 to 1910, Canada emerged onto the world literary scene in poetry and in fiction. Canadian authors experimented with a variety of themes and subjects, a variety of techniques and forms and, while not achieving complete success in all areas, they have left as a legacy to the modern generation much of their inspiration and enthusiasm, their belief in the future of Canadian literature and their vision of Canada as a nation of the world. No anthology can sample all the most interesting works of these writers or of their many contemporaries in the fields of poetry, fiction and literary criticism. We can merely note Northrop Frye's suggestion in his review of A. J. M. Smith's *Canadian Poetry* that all anthologies conclude with several blank pages for the readers to add their own "neglected favorites."[36]

Notes

[1] Margaret Atwood, *Survival,* Toronto: Anansi, 1972, pp. 112, 18-19.

[2] Northrop Frye, *The Literary History of Canada,* ed. Carl F. Klinck, Toronto: University of Toronto Press, 1965, pp. 848-49. Also in *The Bush Garden,* Toronto: Anansi, 1971, p. 250.

[3] F. R. Scott, "The Canadian Authors Meet," first published in *McGill Fortnightly Review,* April 27, 1927.

[4] See A. J. M. Smith *The Book of Canadian Poetry,* Toronto: W. J. Gage, 1943 (1948, 1957) and *The Book of Canadian Prose,* Toronto: W. J. Gage, 1965.

[5] E. H. Dewart, Introduction to *Selections from Canadian Poets,* Montreal: Lovell, 1864. See text p. 217.

[6] E. K. Brown, *On Canadian Poetry*, Toronto: Ryerson, 1943, pp. 3, 5.

[8] *Statistical Year-Book of Canada* for 1901, p. 600.

[8] *Statistical Year-Book*, 1901 and Robert Legget, *Rideau Waterway*, University of Toronto Press, 1955, p. 23.

[9] *Statistical Year-Book*, 1901, pp. 80, 85-86.

[10] Quoted in *The Literary History of Canada*, p. 447.

[11] *Statistical Year-Book*, 1901, p. 587.

[12] *Literary History of Canada*, p. 175. For information and background on this area see the section "Literary Publishing" by H. Pearson Gundy, pp. 174-88.

[13] *Literary History of Canada*, p. 187.

[14] *Ibid.*, pp. 176-86.

[15] Quoted in the *Literary History of Canada*, p. 176.

[16] Thomas G. Marquis, *English-Canadian Literature*, ed. Clara Thomas, Toronto: University of Toronto Press, 1973, p. 548.

[17] A. J. M. Smith, "Wanted: Canadian Criticism," in *The Making of Modern Poetry in Canada*, ed. Dudek and Gnarowski, Toronto: Ryerson, 1967, p. 32.

[18] Dewart, *Selections from Canadian Poets*. See text p. 221.

[19] W. D. Lighthall, *Songs of the Great Dominion*, London: Walter Scott, 1889. See text. p. 227.

[20] George Bowering, "Mexico City Face," in *Touch*, Toronto: McClelland and Stewart, 1971 and "Calgary," in *Rocky Mountain Foot*, McClelland and Stewart, 1968.

[21] *The Bush Garden*, p. 133.

[22] E. W. McCourt, *The West in Canadian Fiction*, Toronto: Ryerson, 1970, p. 25.

[23] Irving Layton, *Love Where the Nights Are Long*, Toronto: McClelland and Stewart, 1962, pp. 13, 14.

[24] Susannah Moodie, *Life in the Clearings Versus the Bush*, ed. R. L. McDougall, Toronto: Macmillan, 1959, pp. 42-43.

[25] Northrop Frye, "The Narrative Tradition in English-Canadian Literature," *The Bush Garden*, pp. 145-55.

[26] *Literary History of Canada*, p. 111. For information on this area see Fred Cogswell, "Literary Activities in the Maritime Provinces" (1815-1880), pp. 102-24, Carl F. Klinck, "Literary Activities in the Canadas" (1812-41) and (1841-80), pp. 125-62, and Gordon Roper, "New Forces: New Fiction" (1880-1920), and "The Kinds of Fiction" (1880-1920), pp. 260-312.

[27] Quoted in Desmond Pacey, "A Colonial Romantic," in *Essays in Canadian Criticism*, Toronto: Ryerson, 1969, pp. 163-64.

[28] *Literary History of Canada*, pp. 261, 284.

[29] *Ibid.*, p. 262.

[30] *Ibid.*, p. 286.

[31] See Alec Lucas, "Nature Writers and the Animal Story" in *The Literary History of Canada*, pp. 364-88.

[32] Quoted in *The Literary History of Canada*, p. 89.

[33] See Dewart pp. 183 ff.

[34] Joseph Howe, "Local Patriotism" from *The Heart of Howe*, ed. D. C. Harvey, Toronto: Oxford University Press, 1939, p. 53.

[35] Lampman, "Two Canadian Poets," *University Of Toronto Quarterly*, XIII, July 1944. See text, p. 269.

[36] *The Bush Garden*, p. 130.

CANADIAN LITERATURE
the beginnings to the 20th century

I LITERARY BEGINNINGS

Nova Scotia: A New Ballad (Anonymous)

The Gentleman's Magazine of London published a number of items on life in Nova Scotia in February 1750, following the settling of Halifax the previous May by 2500 British men and women led by Lord Cornwallis. Included were a letter from the flourishing new settlement, an essay on the North American porcupine found in Nova Scotia, a statement of settlers' limits as defined by the Treaty of Utrecht, and several illustrations: a page of drawings of plant life in Nova Scotia with notes, a plan of the harbour of Chebucto and town of Halifax, and the arms of Halifax and its baronets. Also included was the following ballad, to be sung to the tune of "King John and the Abbot of Canterbury." The ballad expresses one pole of Canadian experience, the Canadian dream of a new Eden unmarked by war, political dissension, economic strife, class divisions or any form of inequality. The opposite pole, that of the cultural wilderness, is expressed in Joseph Stansbury's poem "To Cordelia," written some thirty years later.

TEXT:

The Gentleman's Magazine, February, 1750.

Nova Scotia: A New Ballad

Let's away to *New Scotland*, where Plenty sits queen
O'er as happy a country as ever was seen;
And blesses her subjects, both little and great,
With each a good house, and a pretty estate.
    Derry down, [down, down, derry down].

There's wood, and there's water, there's wild fowl and tame;
In the forest good ven'son, good fish in the stream,
Good grass for our cattle, good land for our plough
Good wheat to be reap'd, and good barley to mow.
    Derry down, etc.

No landlords are there the poor tenants to teaze,
No lawyers to bully, nor stewards to seize:
But each honest fellow's a landlord; and dares
To spend on himself the whole fruit of his cares.
   Derry down, etc.

They've no duties on candles, no taxes on malt,
Nor do they, as we do, pay sauce for their salt:
But all is as free as in those times of old,
When poets assure us the age was of gold.
   Derry down, etc.

Frances Brooke (1724-1789)

The first novelist in Canada and perhaps the first in North America, Frances Brooke was an Englishwoman who lived in Quebec for several years in the decade immediately following the British victory of 1759. Although she was not Canadian, she did employ a distinctively Canadian setting and conveyed a firsthand view of a period to become popular a century later in the historical romances of Rosanna Leprohon and her successors. She also presented a realistic account of everyday life and society in a manner not equalled again in Canada until Sara Jeannette Duncan.

Born in Lincolnshire, England in 1724, the daughter of a Church of England clergyman, she married Reverend John Brooke in 1756, and in October of 1763, she followed him to Quebec where he was the first clergyman of the Church of England in Quebec and chaplain of the British garrison. Except for a visit to England in late 1764, Mrs. Brooke probably remained in Canada until 1768 when her husband returned to England; the couple lived there permanently until their deaths in 1789, three days apart.

Mrs. Brooke was a very versatile writer, attempting, before she was forty, journalism, essays, poetry, drama, translation and fiction. In 1760 she was already part of a select London circle which included Samuel Richardson, David Garrick, Fanny Burney, Oliver Goldsmith, Dr. Samuel Johnson and James Boswell. Before her arrival in Quebec, she edited *The Old Maid*, a weekly periodical in which she was the main contributor, and published a volume of poems including a tragedy, *Virginia*, which David Garrick refused to produce (1756), a translation of a French romance by Madame Riccobini (1760), and her first novel, *The History of Lady Julia Mandeville*, which like *The History of Emily Montague*, is in the form of letters (1763). After her return to England, *Emily Montague* (1769), *The Memoirs of the Marquis de St. Forlaix* (1770), and a translation of Abbé Milot's *Histoire de l'Angleterre* appeared in rapid succession, followed in 1777 by a fourth novel *The Excursion*. A play *Sinope* ran in Covent Gardens for ten nights in 1779; a light opera *Rosina*, for which William Shields composed the music, was also performed in Covent Garden in 1782, and there are contemporary references to another opera and another novel.

It is uncertain whether *Emily Montague* was written during Mrs. Brooke's stay in Quebec or after her return to England. The novel employs the form of letters made popular by Richardson's *Pamela*. Two hundred and twenty-eight letters are exchanged by the correspondents, some crossing the Atlantic and some from Sillery to Quebec or Montreal; slightly over one third are written by Ed. Rivers, the hero, and another third by Arabella Fermor, a close friend of Emily. These letters and those of Arabella's father provide the fullest information on Canadian landscape and society of the period.

TEXT:

The History of Emily Montague. London: Dodsley, 1769, collated with the New Canadian Library edition by Carl F. Klinck, Toronto: McClelland and Stewart, 1961. Spelling and printing have been modernized in accord with the second text.

See also:

Introduction to *The History of Emily Montague*. ed. Lawrence J. Burpee, with an appendix by F. P. Grove. Ottawa: Graphic, 1931.
Introduction to *The History of Emily Montague*. ed. Carl F. Klinck. Toronto: New Canadian Library, 1961.

From *The History of Emily Montague*

LETTER 6

[ED. RIVERS]
TO MISS RIVERS, CLARGES STREET

MONTREAL, JULY 9.

I am arriv'd, my dear, and have brought my heart safe thro' such a continued fire as never poor knight errant was exposed to; waited on at every stage by blooming country girls, full of spirit and coquetry, without any of the village bashfulness of England, and dressed like the shepherdesses of romance. A man of adventure might make a pleasant journey to Montreal.

The peasants are ignorant, lazy, dirty, and stupid beyong all belief; but hospitable, courteous, civil; and, what is particularly agreeable, they leave their wives and daughters to do the honours of the house: in which obliging office they acquit themselves with an attention, which, amidst every inconvenience apparent (tho' I am told not real) poverty can cause, must please every guest who has a soul inclin'd to be pleas'd: for my part, I was charm'd with them, and eat my homely fare with as much pleasure as if I had been feasting on ortolans in a palace. Their conversation is lively and amusing; all the little knowledge of Canada is confined to the sex; very few, even of the seigneurs, being able to write their own names.

The road from Quebec to Montreal is almost a continued street, the villages being numerous, and so extended along the banks of the river St Lawrence as to leave scarce a space without houses in view; except where here or there a river, a wood, or mountain intervenes, as if to give a more pleasing variety to the scene. I don't remember ever having had a more agreeable journey; the fine prospects of the day so enliven'd by the gay chat of the evening, that I was really sorry when I approach'd Montreal.

The island of Montreal, on which the town stands, is a very lovely spot; highly cultivated, and tho' less wild and magnificent, more smiling than the country round Quebec: the ladies, who seem to make pleasure their only business, and most of whom I have seen this morning driving about the town in calashes, and making what they call, the *tour de la ville,* attended by English officers, seem generally handsome, and have an air of sprightliness with which I am charm'd; I must be acquainted with them all, for tho' my stay is to be short, I see no reason why it should be dull. I am told they are fond of little rural balls in the country, and intend to give one as soon as I have paid my respects in form.

Six in the evening

I am just come from dining with the_____regiment, and find I have a visit to pay I was not aware of, to two English ladies who are a few miles out of town: one of them is wife to the major of the regiment, and the other just going to be married to a captain in it, Sir George Clayton, a young handsome baronet, just come to his title and a very fine estate, by the death of a distant relation: he is at present at New York, and I am told they are to be married as soon as he comes back.

Eight o'clock

I have been making some flying visits to the French ladies; tho' I have not seen many beauties, yet in general the women are handsome; their manner is easy and obliging, they make the most of their charms by their vivacity, and I certainly cannot be displeas'd with their extreme partiality for the English officers; their own men, who indeed are not very attractive, have not the least chance for any share in their good graces.

Thursday morning

I am just setting out with a friend for Major Melmoth's, to pay my compliments to the two ladies: I have no relish for this visit; I hate misses that are going to be married; they are always so full of the dear man, that they have not common civility to other people. I am told however both the ladies are agreeable.

14th. Eight in the evening

Agreeable, Lucy! she is an angel: 'tis happy for me she is engag'd; nothing else could secure my heart, of which you know I am very tenacious: only think of finding beauty, delicacy, sensibility, all that can charm in woman, hid in a wood in Canada!

You say I am given to be enthusiastic in my approbations, but she is really charming. I am resolv'd not only to have a friendship for her myself, but that *you* shall, and have told her so; she comes to England as soon as she is married; you are form'd to love each other.

But I must tell you; Major Melmoth kept us a week at his house in the country, in one continued round of rural amusements; by which I do not mean hunting and shooting, but such pleasures as the ladies could share; little rustic balls and parties round the neighbouring country, in which parties we were joined by all the fine women at Montreal. Mrs. Melmoth is a very pleasing, genteel brunette, but Emily Montague – you will say I am in love with her if I describe her, and yet I declare to you I am not. . . .

I am to give a ball to-morrow; Mrs. Melmoth is to have the honours of it, but as she is with child, she does not dance. This circumstance has produc'd a dispute not a little flattering to my vanity: the ladies are making interest to dance with me; what a happy exchange have I made! what man of common sense would stay to be overlook'd in England, who can have rival beauties contend for him in Canada? This important point is not yet settled; the *etiquette* here is rather difficult to adjust; as to me, I have nothing to do in the consultation; my hand is destin'd to the longest pedigree; we stand prodigiously on our noblesse at Montreal.

Four o'clock

After a dispute in which two French ladies were near drawing their husbands into a duel, the point of honour is yielded by both to Miss Montague; each insisting only that I should not dance with the other: for my part, I submit with a good grace, as you will suppose.

Saturday morning

I never passed a more agreeable evening; we have our amusements here, I assure you: a set of fine young fellows, and handsome women, all well dress'd, and in humour with themselves, and with each other: my lovely Emily like Venus amongst the Graces, only multiplied to about sixteen. Nothing is, in my opinion, so favourable to the display of beauty as a ball. A state of rest is ungraceful; all nature is most beautiful in motion; trees agitated by the wind, a ship under sail, a horse in the course, a fine woman dancing: never any human being had such an aversion to still life as I have.

I am going back to Melmoth's for a month; don't be alarm'd, Lucy! I see all her perfections, but I see them with the cold eye of admiration only: a woman engaged loses all her attractions as a woman; there is no love without a ray of hope: my only ambition is to be her friend;

I want to be the confidant of her passion. With what spirit such a mind as hers must love!

Adieu! my dear!
Yours,

ED. RIVERS

LETTER 10

[ARABELLA FERMER TO MISS RIVERS]

SILLERI, AUGUST 24

I have been a month arrived, my dear, without having seen your brother, who is at Montreal, but I am told is expected to-day. I have spent my time however very agreeably. I know not what the winter may be, but I am enchanted with the beauty of this country in summer; bold, picturesque, romantic, nature reigns here in all her wanton luxuriance, adorned by a thousand wild graces which mock the cultivated beauties of Europe. The scenery about the town is infinitely lovely; the prospect extensive, and diversified by a variety of hills, woods, rivers, cascades, intermingled with smiling farms and cottages, and bounded by distant mountains which seem to scale the very Heavens.

The days are much hotter here than in England, but the heat is more supportable from the breezes which always spring up about noon; and the evenings are charming beyond expression. We have much thunder and lightening, but very few instances of their being fatal: the thunder is more magnificent and aweful than in Europe, and the lightening brighter and more beautiful; I have even seen it of a clear pale purple, resembling the gay tints of the morning.

The verdure is equal to that of England, and in the evening acquires an unspeakable beauty from the lucid splendour of the fire-flies sparkling like a thousand little stars on the trees and on the grass.

There are two very noble falls of water near Quebec, la Chaudière and Montmorenci: the former is a prodigious sheet of water, rushing over the wildest rocks, and forming a scene grotesque, irregular, astonishing: the latter, less wild, less irregular, but more pleasing and more majestic, falls from an immense height, down the side of a romantic mountain, into the river St Lawrence, opposite the most smiling part of the island of Orleans, to the cultivated charms of which it forms the most striking and agreeable contrast.

The river of the same name, which supplies the cascade of Montmorenci, is the most lovely of all inanimate objects: but why do I call it inanimate? It almost breathes; I no longer wonder at the enthusiasm of Greece and Rome; 'twas from objects resembling this their mythology took its rise; it seems the residence of a thousand deities.

Paint to yourself a stupendous rock burst as it were in sunder by the hands of nature, to give passage to a small, but very deep and beautiful river; and forming on each side a regular and magnificent wall, crowned with the noblest woods that can be imagined; the sides of these romantic walls adorned with a variety of the gayest flowers, and in many places little streams of the purest water gushing through, and losing themselves in the river below: a thousand natural grottoes in the rock make you suppose yourself in the abode of the Nereids; as a little island, covered with flowering shrubs, about a mile above the falls, where the river enlarges itself as if to give it room, seems intended for the throne of the river goddess. Beyond this, the rapids, formed by the irregular projections of the rock, which in some places seem almost to meet, rival in beauty, as they excel in variety, the cascade itself, and close this little world of enchantment.

In short, the loveliness of this fairy scene alone more than pays the fatigues of my voyage; and, if I ever murmur at having crossed the Atlantic, remind me that I have seen the river Montmorenci.

I can give you a very imperfect account of the people here; I have only examined the landscape about Quebec, and have given very little attention to the figures; the French ladies are handsome, but as to the beaux, they appear to me not at all dangerous, and one might safely walk in a wood by moonlight with the most agreeable Frenchman here. I am surprized the Canadian ladies take such pains to seduce our men from us; but I think it a little hard we have no temptation to make reprisals.

I am at present at an extreme pretty farm on the banks of the river St Lawrence; the house stands at the foot of a steep mountain covered with a variety of trees, forming a verdant sloping wall, which rises in a kind of regular confusion,

"Shade above shade, a woody theatre,"

and has in front this noble river, on which the ships continually passing present to the delighted eye the most charming moving picture imaginable; I never saw a place so formed to inspire that pleasing lassitude, that divine inclination to saunter, which may not improperly be called, the luxurious indolence of the country. I intend to build a temple here to the charming goddess of laziness.

A gentleman is just coming down the winding path on the side of the hill, whom by his air I take to be your brother. Adieu! I must receive him: my father is at Quebec.

Yours,

ARABELLA FERMOR

Your brother has given me a very pleasing piece of intelligence: my friend Emily Montague is at Montreal, and is going to be married to great advantage; I must write to her immediately, and insist on her making me a visit before she marries. She came to America two years ago, with her uncle Colonel Montague, who died here, and I imagined was gone back to England; she is however at Montreal with Mrs. Melmoth, a distant relation of her mother's. Adieu! *ma très chère!*

LETTER 16

[ARABELLA FERMOR]

TO MISS RIVERS, CLARGES STREET

SILLERI, SEPTEMBER 18

Your brother, my dear, is gone to Montreal with Sir George Clayton, of whom I suppose you have heard, and who is going to marry a friend of mine, to pay a visit to *Monsieur le General*, who is arrived there. The men in Canada, the English I mean, are eternally changing place, even when they have not so pleasing a call: travelling is cheap and amusing, the prospects lovely, the weather inviting; and there are no very lively pleasures at present to attach them either to Quebec or Montreal, so that they divide themselves between both.

This fancy of the men, which is extremely the mode, makes an agreeable circulation of inamoratoes, which serves to vary the amusement of the ladies; so that upon the whole 'tis a pretty fashion, and deserves encouragement.

You expect too much of your brother, my dear; the summer is charming here, but with no such very striking difference from that of England, as to give room to say a vast deal on the subject; though I believe, if you will please to compare our letters, you will find, putting us together, we cut a pretty figure in the descriptive way; at least if your brother tells me truth.

You may expect a very well-painted frost-piece from me in the winter; as to the present season, it is just like any fine autumn in England: I may add, that the beauty of the nights is much beyond my power of description: a constant *Aurora borealis*, without a cloud in the heavens; and a moon so resplendent that you may see to read the smallest print by its light; one has nothing to wish but that it was full moon every night. Our evening walks are delicious, especially at Silleri, where 'tis the pleasantest thing in the world to listen to soft nonsense.

"Whilst the moon dances through the trembling leaves"

(A line I stole from Philander and Sylvia): But to return:

The French ladies never walk but at night, which shews their good taste; and then only within the walls of Quebec, which does not: they saunter slowly, after supper, on a particular battery, which is a kind of little Mall: they have no idea of walking in the country, nor the least feeling of the lovely scene around them; there are many of them who never saw the falls of Montmorenci, though little more than an hour's drive from the town. They seem born without the smallest portion of curiosity, or any idea of the pleasures of the imagination, or indeed any pleasure but that of being admired; love, or rather coquetry, dress, and devotion, seem to share all their hours: yet, as they are lively, and in general handsome, the men are very ready to excuse their want of knowledge.

There are two ladies in the province, I am told, who read; but both of them are above fifty, and they are regarded as prodigies of erudition.

Eight in the evening

Absolutely, Lucy, I will marry a savage, and turn squaw (a pretty soft name for an Indian princess!): never was any thing delightful as their lives; they talk of French husbands, but commend me to an Indian one, who lets his wife ramble five hundred miles, without asking where she is going.

I was sitting after dinner with a book, in a thicket of hawthorn near the beach, when a loud laugh called my attention to the river, where I saw a canoe of savages making to the shore; there were six women, and two or three children, without one man amongst them: they landed, tied the canoe to the root of a tree, and finding out the most agreeable shady spot amongst the bushes with which the beach was covered, which happened to be very near me, made a fire, on which they laid some fish to broil, and, fetching water from the river, sat down on the grass to their frugal repast.

I stole softly to the house, and ordering a servant to bring some wine and cold provisions, returned to my squaws: I asked them in French if they were of Lorette; they shook their heads: I repeated the question in English, when the oldest of the women told me, they were not; that their country was on the borders of New England; that, their husbands being on a hunting party in the woods, curiosity, and the desire of seeing their brethren the English who had conquered Quebec, had brought them up the great river, down which they should return as soon as they had seen Montreal. She courteously asked me to sit down, and eat with them, which I complied with, and produced my part of the feast. We soon became good company, and *brighten'd the chain of friendship* with two bottles of wine, which put them into such spirits, that they danced, sung, shook me by the hand, and grew so very fond of me, that I began to be afraid I should not easily get rid of them. They were very unwilling to part with me; but, after two or three very ridiculous hours, I with some difficulty prevailed on the ladies to pursue their voyage, having first replenished their canoe with provisions and a few bottles of wine, and given them a letter of recommendation to your brother, that they might be in no distress at Montreal.

Adieu! my father is just come in, and has brought some company with him from Quebec to supper.

Yours ever,

A. FERMOR

Don't you think, my dear, my good sisters the squaws seem to live something the kind of life of our gypsies? The idea struck me as they were dancing. I assure you, there is a good deal of resemblance in their persons: I have seen a fine old seasoned female gypsey, of as dark a complexion as a savage: they are all equally marked as children of the sun.

LETTER 22

[ARABELLA FERMOR]
TO MISS RIVERS, CLARGES STREET
SILLERI, SEPTEMBER 25

I have been rambling about amongst the peasants, and asking them a thousand questions, in order to satisfy your inquisitive friend. As to my father, though, properly speaking, your questions are addressed to him, yet, being upon duty, he begs that, for this time, you will accept of an answer from me.

The Canadians live a good deal like the ancient patriarchs; the lands were originally settled by the troops, every officer became a seigneur, or lord of the manor, every soldier took lands under his commander; but, as avarice is natural to mankind, the soldiers took a great deal more than they could cultivate, by way of providing for a family: which is the reason so much land is now waste in the finest part of the province: those who had children, and in general they have a great number, portioned out their lands amongst them as they married, and lived in the midst of a little world of their descendents.

There are whole villages, and there is even a large island, that of Coudre, where the inhabitants are all the descendents of one pair, if we only suppose that their sons went to the next village for wives, for I find no tradition of their having had a dispensation to marry their sisters.

The corn here is very good, though not equal to ours; the harvest not half so gay as in England, and for this reason, that the lazy creatures leave the greatest part of their land uncultivated, only sowing as much corn of different sorts as will serve themselves; and being too proud and too idle to work for hire, every family gets in its own harvest, which prevents all that jovial spirit which we find when the reapers work together in large parties.

Idleness is the reigning passion here, from the peasant to his lord; the gentlemen never either ride on horseback or walk, but are driven about like women, for they never drive themselves, lolling at their ease in a calash: the peasants, I mean the masters of families, are pretty near as useless as their lords.

You will scarce believe me, when I tell you, that I have seen, at the farm next us, two children, a very beautiful boy and girl, of about eleven years old, assisted by their grandmother, reaping a field of oats, whilst the lazy father, a strong fellow of thirty-two, lay on the grass, smoking his pipe, about twenty yards from them: the old people and children work here; those in the age of strength and health only take their pleasure.

A propos to smoking, 'tis common to see here boys of three years old, sitting at their doors, smoking their pipes, as grave and composed as little old Chinese men on a chimney.

You ask me after our fruits: we have, as I am told, an immensity of cranberries all the year; when the snow melts away in spring, they are said to be found under it as fresh and as good as in autumn: strawberries and raspberries grow wild in profusion; you cannot walk a step in the fields without treading on the former: great plenty of currants, plumbs, apples, and pears; a few cherries and grapes, but not in much perfection: excellent musk melons, and water melons in abundance, but not so good in proportion as the musk. Not a peach, nor any thing of the kind; this I am however convinced is less the fault of the climate than of the people, who are too indolent to take pains for any thing more than is absolutely necessary to their existence. They might have any fruit here but gooseberries, for which the summer is too hot; there are bushes in the woods, and some have been brought from England, but the fruit falls off before it is ripe. The wild fruits here, especially those of the bramble kind, are in much greater variety and perfection than in England.

When I speak of the natural productions of the country, I should not forget that hemp and hops grow every where in the woods; I should imagine the former might be cultivated here with great success, if the people could be persuaded to cultivate any thing.

A little corn of every kind, a little hay, a little tobacco, half a dozen apple trees, a few onions and cabbages, make the whole of a Canadian plantation. There is scarce a flower, except those in the woods, where there is a variety of the most beautiful shrubs I ever saw; the wild cherry, of which the woods are full, is equally charming in flower and in fruit; and, in my opinion, at least equals the arbutus.

They sow their wheat in spring, never manure the ground, and plough it in the slightest manner; can it then be wondered at that it is inferior to ours? They fancy the frost would destroy it if sown in autumn; but this is all prejudice, as experience has shewn. I myself saw a field of wheat this year at the governor's farm, which was manured and sown in autumn, as fine as I ever saw in England.

I should tell you, they are so indolent as never to manure their lands, or even their gardens; and that, till the English came, all the manure of Quebec was thrown into the river.

You will judge how naturally rich the soil must be, to produce good crops without manure, and without ever lying fallow, and almost without ploughing; yet our political writers in England never speak of Canada without the epithet of *barren*. They tell me this extreme fertility is owing to the snow, which lies five or six months on the ground. Provisions are dear, which is owing to the prodigious number of horses kept here; every family having a carriage, even the poorest peasant; and every son of that peasant keeping a horse for his little excursions of pleasure, besides those necessary for the business of the farm. The war also destroyed the breed of cattle, which I am told however begins to increase; they have even so far improved in corn, as to export some this year to Italy and Spain.

Don't you think I am become an excellent farmeress? 'Tis intuition; some people are born learned: are you not all astonishment at my knowledge? I never was so vain of a letter in my life.

Shall I own the truth? I had most of my intelligence from old John, who lived long with my grandfather in the country; and who, having little else to do here, has taken some pains to pick up a competent knowledge of the state of agriculture five miles round Quebec.

Adieu! I am tired of the subject.

Your faithful,

A. FERMOR

LETTER 41

[ARABELLA FERMOR]

TO MISS RIVERS, CLARGES STREET

NOVEMBER 10

The savages assure us, my dear, on the information of the beavers, that we shall have a very mild winter; it seems, these creatures have laid in a less winter stock than usual. I take it very ill, Lucy, that the beavers have better intelligence than we have.

We are got into a pretty composed easy way; Sir George writes very agreeable, sensible, sentimental, gossiping letters, once a fort-night, which Emily answers in due course, with all the regularity of a counting-house correspondence; he talks of coming down after Christmas: we expect him without impatience; and in the mean time amuse ourselves as well as we can, and soften the pain of absence by the attention of a man that I fancy we like quite as well.

With submission to the beavers, the weather is very cold, and we have had a great deal of snow already; but they tell me 'tis nothing to what we shall have: they are taking precautions which make me shudder beforehand, pasting up the windows, and not leaving an avenue where cold can enter.

I like the winter carriages immensely; the open carriole is a kind of one-horse chaise, the covered one a chariot, set on a sledge to run on the ice; we have not yet had snow enough to use them, but I like their appearance prodigiously; the covered carrioles seem the prettiest things in nature to make love in, as there are curtains to draw before the windows: we shall have three in effect, my father's, River's, and Fitzgerald's; the two latter are to be elegance itself, and entirely for the service of the ladies: your brother and Fitzgerald are trying who shall be ruined first for the honour of their country. I will bet three to one upon Ireland. They are every day contriving parties of pleasure, and making the most gallant little presents imaginable to the ladies.

Adieu! my dear.

Yours,

A. FERMOR

LETTER 45

[ARABELLA FERMOR]

TO MISS RIVERS, CLARGES STREET

SILLERI, NOVEMBER 23

I have been seeing the last ship go out of the port, Lucy; you have no notion what a melancholy sight it is: we are now left to ourselves, and shut up from all the world for the winter: somehow we seem so forsaken, so cut off from the rest of human kind, I cannot bear the idea: I sent a thousand sighs and a thousand tender wishes to dear England, which I never loved so much as at this moment.

Do you know, my dear, I could cry if I was not ashamed? I shall not absolutely be in spirits again this week.

'Tis the first time I have felt any thing like bad spirits in Canada: I followed the ship with my eyes till it turned Point Levi, and, when I lost sight of it, felt as if I had lost every thing dear to me on earth. I am not particular: I see a gloom on every countenance; I have been at church, and think I never saw so many dejected faces in my life.

Adieu! for the present: it will be a fortnight before I can send this letter; another agreeable circumstance that: would to Heaven I were in England, though I changed the bright sun of Canada for a fog!

DECEMBER 1

We have had a week's snow without intermission: happily for us, your brother and the Fitz have been weather-bound all the time at Silleri, and cannot possibly get away.

We have amused ourselves within doors, for there is no stirring abroad, with playing at cards, playing at shuttlecock, playing the fool, making love, and making moral reflexions: upon the whole, the week has not been very disagreeable.

The snow is when we wake constantly up to our chamber windows; we are literally dug out of it every morning.

As to Quebec, I give up all hopes of ever seeing it again: but my comfort is, that the people there cannot possibly get to their neighbours; and I flatter myself very few of them have been half so well entertained at home.

We shall be abused, I know, for (what is really the fault of the weather) keeping these two creatures here this week; the ladies hate us for engrossing two such fine fellows as your brother and Fitzgerald, as well as for having vastly more than our share of all the men: we generally go out attended by at least a dozen, without any other woman but a lively old French lady, who is a flirt of my father's, and will certainly be my mamma.

We sweep into the general's assembly on Thursdays with such a train of beaux as draws every eye upon us; the rest of the fellows crowd round us; the misses draw up, blush, and flutter their fans; and your little Bell sits down with such a fancy impertinent consciousness in her countenance as is really provoking: Emily on the contrary looks mild and humble, and seems by her civil decent air to apologize to them for being so much more agreeable than themselves, which is a fault I for my part am not in the least inclined to be ashamed of.

Your idea of Quebec, my dear, is perfectly just; it is like a third or fourth rate country town in England; much hospitality, little society; cards, scandal, dancing, and good chear; all excellent things to pass away a winter evening, and peculiarly adapted to what I am told, and what I begin to feel, of the severity of this climate.

I am told they abuse me, which I can easily believe, because my impertinence to them deserves it: but what care I, you know, Lucy, so long as I please myself, and am at Silleri out of the sound?

They are squabbling at Quebec, I hear, about I cannot tell what, therefore shall not attempt to explain: some dregs of old disputes, it seems, which have had not time to settle: however, we new comers have certainly nothing to do with these matters: you can't think how comfortable we feel at Silleri, out of the way.

My father says, the politics of Canada are as complex and as difficult to be understood as those of the Germanic system.

For my part, I think no politics worth attending to but those of the little commonwealth of woman: if I can maintain my empire over hearts, I leave the men to quarrel for every thing else.

I observe a strict neutrality, that I may have a chance for admirers amongst both parties. Adieu! the post is just going out.

Your faithful

A. FERMOR

LETTER 48

[ARABELLA FERMOR]

TO MISS RIVERS, CLARGES STREET

SILLERI, DECEMBER 27.

After a fortnight's snow, we have had near as much clear blue sky and sunshine: the snow is six feet deep, so that we may be said to walk on our own heads; that is, speaking *en philosophe*, we occupy the space we should have done in summer if we had done so; or, to explain it more clearly, our heels are now where our heads should be.

The scene is a little changed for the worse: the lovely landscape is now one undistinguished waste of snow, only a little diversified by the great variety of evergreens in the woods: the romantic winding path down the side of the hill to our farm, on which we used to amuse ourselves with seeing the beaux serpentize, is now a confused, frightful, rugged precipice, which one trembles at the idea of ascending.

There is something exceedingly agreeable in the whirl of the carrioles, which fly along at the rate of twenty miles an hour; and really hurry one out of one's senses.

Our little coterie is the object of great envy; we live just as we like, without thinking of other people, which I am not sure *here* is prudent, but it is pleasant, which is a better thing.

Emily, who is the civilest creature breathing, is for giving up her own pleasure to avoid offending others, and wants me, every time we make a carrioling-party, to invite all the misses of Quebec to go with us, because they seem angry at our being happy without them: but for that very reason I persist in my own way, and consider wisely, that, though civility is due to other people, yet there is also some civility due to one's self.

I agree to visit every body, but think it mighty absurd I must not take a ride without asking a hundred people I scarce know to go with me: yet this is the style here; they will neither be happy themselves, nor let any body else. Adieu!

DECEMBER 29

I will never take a beaver's word again as long as I live: there is no supporting this cold; the Canadians say it is seventeen years since there has been so severe a season. I thought beavers had been people of more honour.

Adieu! I can no more: the ink freezes as I take it from the standish to the paper, though close to a large stove. Don't expect me to write again till May; one's faculties are absolutely congealed this weather.

Yours,

A. FERMOR

Henry Alline (1748-1784)

Henry Alline is Canada's first poet of any note; a recent biographer, J. M. Bumstead, remarks: "[he was] British Canada's most important and prolific intellectual voice in the eighteenth century," and again "within the confines of his own horizons and his own time, Alline was an intellectual and literary giant." He did not, however, influence the direction or techniques of developing national poets, and indeed as a literary figure he is almost unknown today.

Henry Alline was born in Newport, Rhode Island on January 14, 1748 to an old New England family which traced its ancestry back to the *Mayflower*. He was educated here until the age of eleven when his family took up a land grant in Nova Scotia at Falmouth, King's County in the area of the Minas Basin. The Allines were among the first New Englanders to settle here after the Expulsion of the Acadi-ans. As there were neither schools nor churches, Henry received all his education at home, reading in the King James' edition of the Bible, Milton, Pope, Bunyan and Martin Luther, among others. His father operated a grain mill, and after his brother took up land of his own, Henry was left to supervise the family farm. But his inclinations were towards the ministry. Although a social leader among the young people of the community, he underwent a personal conversion in five stages as recorded in his diary: Christian knowledge and conviction, a state of grace, a combat with doubt and despair, and ultimate personal assurance of salvation; this last stage he reached on March 26, 1775. In 1776 he attempted to go to Boston for further studies but was prevented by family illness and war between the American colonies and Britain. On April 19, 1776, he became an itinerant preacher, establishing churches over the next three years in Falmouth, Newport, Cornwallis and Norton. After his ordination as an evangelist on April 6, 1779, he widened his circuit to include the Cumberland area, the St. John Valley, the island of St. John (Prince Edward Island) and western Nova Scotia, and finally in 1783, New England. He died in North Hampton, New Hampshire at the home of a Calvinist Puritan with whom he had been fighting for years, and was given a funeral and burial by the Puritans. After his death, most of his churches either collapsed or became Baptist, and his future influence was to lie largely in the United States where his ideas formed the basis of the Freewill Baptist movement.

Alline published five works in his lifetime: *Two Mites on Some Important Points of Divinity* (Halifax 1781, reprinted in 1804 as *Two Mites Cast into the Offering of God), A Court for the Trial of*

Anti-Traditionist (1783, reprinted *A Gospel Call to Sinners,* 1895) and three sermons. His *Hymns and Spiritual Songs* appeared after his death, in 1786; *The Life and Journal of Rev. Mr. Henry Alline* was found among his personal papers and printed in 1806.

Most of Alline's hymns, like those of his predecessors Isaac Watts and Charles Wesley, were written for his own services; he would travel continuously, stopping only for a few days in each place to preach and to pray in houses or barns, beside roads or rivers. Like his Journal, the poems are deeply introspective, and emphasize the personal experience of Divine Love and a "new birth" rather than set ritual or the vengeance of a Calvinist God. *The Hymns and Spiritual Songs* were immediately popular and went through four editions between 1786 and 1802.

TEXT:

Hymns and Spiritual Songs. Stonington-Port, Connecticut: S. Turnbull, 1802.

See also:

J. M. Bumstead. *Henry Alline 1748-1784.* Toronto: University of Toronto Press, 1971, especially pages 77 and 78.

Book I Hymn XIII – *On Death*

Death reign'd with vigour since the Fall,
    And rides with fury still;
Nor rich nor poor, nor great nor small,
    Can e'er resist his will.
He ravages both night and day,
    Through all our mortal stage;
And ev'ry creature falls a prey,
    To his resistless rage.
Nations and empires he has slain,
    And laid whole cities waste,
And doth his cruel seige maintain
    To sweep the world in haste.
Ride forth, O mighty Prince of Peace,
    And take away his sting,
Then shall his cruel kingdom cease,
    And saints his triumph sing.

(1786)

Book I Hymn XLIII – *The Fame*

O Lord, how dang'rous is the place
  Where my poor soul doth stand,
With all my sins, without thy grace,
  And death on either hand!
Time, like a torrent, swift doth hurl,
  And steals my breath away,
And drives me to the nether world,
  Without the least delay.
Soon will these mortal cords be broke,
  And I shall lose my breath;
Soon must I feel the fatal stroke
  Of an all-conqu'ring death.
Then would it tear my bleeding heart,
  And fill me with despair,
If Christ should bid my soul depart,
  Where hope is known no more.
Extend, extend, O Lamb of God,
  Thy blessed arm of pow'r,
Speak to my soul one saving word,
  In this distressing hour.
O let me now redemption know,
  And taste immortal love;
And let me with thy people go,
  To the bright realms above.

(1786)

Book II Hymn XXXVII – *Christ Inviting Sinners to His Grace*

Amazing sight, the Saviour stands,
  And knocks at every door;
Ten thousand blessings in his hands,
  For to supply the poor.
"Behold, saith he, I bleed and die,
  To bring poor souls to rest;

Hear, sinners, while I'm passing by,
   And be forever blest.
Will you despise such bleeding love,
   And choose the way to hell;
Or in the glorious realms above,
   With me forever dwell?
Not to condemn your sinking race,
   Have I in Judgement come.
But to display unbounded grace,
   And bring lost sinners home.
May I not save your wretched soul,
   From sin, from death, and hell;
Wounded or sick, I'll make you whole,
   And you with me shall dwell.
Say, will you hear my gracious voice,
   And have your sins forgiv'n?
Or will you make a wretched choice,
   And bar yourselves from heav'n?
Will you go down to endless night,
   And bear eternal pain?
Or dwell in everlasting light,
   Where I in glory reign?
Come answer now before I go,
   While I am passing by;
Say, will you marry me or no?
   Say, will you live or die?"

(1786)

Book II Hymn LXXI – *The Christian Surpriz'd at Christ's Love*

And didst thou die for me,
   O thou blest Lamb of God?
And hast thou brought me home to thee,
   By thine own precious blood?
How couldst thou stoop so low?
   O what amazing grace!
He saves me from eternal wo,
   And gives me heav'nly peace.

My soul, how can it be,
That Jesus freely bore
The pangs of death and hell for me,
And yet I love no more!
O let me now arise,
And soar to realms above,
And shouting gaze, with sweet surprise,
On such amazing love!

(1786)

Jonathan Odell (1737-1818)

A representative of the United Empire Loyalists, an important element of Canadian society who had left home and friends to support their King and the British cause, Jonathan Odell was among those who were to make their mark upon their adopted land, influencing education, society, culture, and ultimately, the development of a native Canadian literature. Odell's own literary works are not his chief achievement in Canada and indeed, like his compatriot Joseph Stansbury, he wrote most of his extant poems in the United States for the Loyalist cause. A few poems written in Canada remain among his manuscripts.

Jonathan Odell was born on September 25, 1737 at Newark, New Jersey, a descendant of one of the founders of the colony of Massachusetts. In 1754 he graduated from the College of New Jersey; he studied medicine and became a surgeon with the British Army in the West Indies, but abandoning this profession for the ministry in the Church of England, he studied theology in England and in January of 1767 became rector of St. Mary's Church in Burlington, New Jersey. For eight years he refused to participate in politics although he hoped for a reassessment of colonial rights to be achieved by constitutional means. On June 4, 1776, three days before the Declaration of Independence was presented to Congress, Odell wrote an ode for the birthday of King George which he delivered in Burlington before a group of British officers. Accused of being inimical to American liberty, he was paroled to his own area of Burlington on July 20, but fled in December. Hiding in local homes to escape his pursuers, he made his way to New York and attached himself to the British Garrison as chaplain. He believed in peace, and remarked that he resorted to satire only when Reason and Order no longer prevailed; his satires express clearly his horror at America's crime of treason.

After Britain's recognition of America as a sovereign state, Odell left its shores; he went first to England with Sir Guy Carleton and then to New Brunswick where he was joined by his wife and family. Here he became provincial secretary, the Registrar of Records and clerk of the Council, positions he held until 1812 when he was succeeded by his son William Franklin. He was also one of the founders of the University of New Brunswick. He died in Fredericton on November 25, 1818.

Like Frances Brooke, Joseph Stansbury, and Henry Alline, Jonathan Odell represents the first generation of Canadian writers whose roots and concerns were outside Canada and who never became indigenous literary figures. Odell's work, like Stansbury's, is largely political and his best work was done in the period before he came to Canada. Moses Coit Taylor describes him as "the most powerful and unrelenting of the Tory satirists" and remarks: "as a satirist, none of his fellow Loyalists approaches Odell, either in passionate energy of thought or in pungency and polish of style". The few extant personal poems such as "On our Thirty-Ninth Wedding Day" and "To Molly Odell," a poem to his daughter on the occasion of her fifth Birthday, are tinged with politics as well. Few of the poems concern religious experience as do virtually all of Alline's.

TEXT:

The Loyal Verses of Joseph Stansbury and Dr. Jonathan Odell. ed. Winthrop Sargent. Albany: Munsell, 1860.

See also:

Vernon L. Parrington. *Main Currents in American Thought.* New York: Harcourt Brace, 1927.
Moses Coit Taylor. *The Literary History of the American Revolution.* New York: Ungar Publishing Company, 1957, 98-129.

Inscription

[on a chamber-stove invented by Franklin in
   which the flame descends rather than rising.]

Like a Newton sublimely he soar'd
   To a Summit before unattained;
New regions of Science explor'd,
   And the Palm of Philosophy gain'd.

With a Spark, that he caught from the Skies,
   He display'd an unparallel'd wonder:
And we saw, with delight and surprise,
   That his Rod could protect us from Thunder.

O had he been wise to pursue
   The track for his talents design'd,
What a tribute of praise had been due
   To the teacher and friend of Mankind!

But to covet *political* fame
   Was, in him, a degrading ambition;
A Spark, that from *Lucifer* came,
   And kindled the blaze of *Sedition*.

Let Candor, then, write on his Urn –
   Here lies the renowned Inventor,
Whose flames to the Skies ought to burn,
   But, inverted, descends to the Center!

(1776-1860)

A Birthday Song

[composed at New York, in honor of the anniversary of the King's birthday, June 4, 1777]

Time was when America hallow'd the morn
On which the lov'd monarch of Britain was born,
Hallow'd the day, and joyfully chanted
   God save the King!
Then flourish'd the blessings of freedom and peace,
And plenty flow'd in with a yearly increase.
Proud of our lot we chanted merrily
   Glory and joy crown the King!

With envy beheld by the nations around,
We rapidly grew, nor was anything found
Able to check our growth while we chanted
   God save the King!
O blest beyond measure, had honour and truth
Still nurs'd in our hearts what they planted in youth!
Loyalty still had chanted merrily
   Glory and joy crown the King!

But see! how rebellion has lifted her head!
How honour and truth are with loyalty fled!
Few are there now who join us in chanting
   God save the King!
And see! how deluded the multitude fly
To arm in a cause that is built on a lye!
Yet are we proud to chant thus merrily
   Glory and joy crown the King!

Though faction by falsehood awhile may prevail,
And loyalty suffers a captive in jail,
Britain is rouz'd, rebellion is falling:
   God save the King!
The captive shall soon be releas'd from his chain;
And conquest restore us to Britain again,
Ever to join in chanting merrily
   Glory and joy crown the King!

(1777-1860)

On Our Thirty-Ninth Wedding-Day (6th of May, 1810)

Twice nineteen years, dear Nancy, on this day
Complete their circle, since the smiling May
Beheld us at the altar kneel and join
In holy rites and vows, which made thee mine.
Then, like the reddening East without a cloud,
Bright was my dawn of joy. To Heaven I bowed
In thankful exultation, well assured
That all my heart could covet was secured.

But ah, how soon this dawn of Joy so bright
Was followed by a dark and stormy night!
The howling tempest, in a fatal hour,
Drove me, an exile from our nuptial bower,
To seek for refuge in the tented field,
Till democratic Tyranny should yield.
Thus torn asunder we, from year to year,
Endured the alternate strife of Hope and Fear;
Till, from Suspense deliver'd by Defeat,
I hither came and found a safe retreat.

Here, join'd by thee and thy young playful train,
I was o'erpaid for years of toil and pain.
We had renounced our native *hostile* shore;
And met, I trust, *till death to part no more!*
But fast approaching now the verge of life,
With what emotions do I see a Wife
And Children, smiling with affection dear,
And think – how sure that parting, and how near!
The solemn thought I wish not to restrain:
Tho' painful, 'tis a salutary pain.
Then let this verse in your remembrance live,
That, when from life released, I still may give
A token of my love; may whisper still
Some fault to shun, some duty to fulfill;
May prompt your Sympathy, some pain to share;
Or warn you of some pleasures to beware;
Remind you that the Arrow's silent flight,
Unseen alike at noon or dead of night,
Should cause no perturbation or dismay,
But teach you to enjoy the passing day
With dutiful tranquillity of mind;
Active and vigilant, but still resign'd.
For our Redeemer liveth, and we know,
How or whenever parted here below,
His faithful servants, in the Realm above,
Shall meet again as heirs of his eternal love.

(1810-1860)

Joseph Stansbury (1740-1809)

An Englishman who emigrated to the United States and became a leader in the literary war of the Revolution, Joseph Stansbury, like Frances Brooke, spent only a few years in Canada and then returned to America permanently. His major poetry is not set in Canada and, like Brooke and his compatriot Jonathan Odell, he has had little influence on Canadian literature. Yet his "To Cordelia" is an important record of one pole of the Canadian experience, the antithesis of the optimism of "Nova Scotia: A New Ballad."

Joseph Stansbury was born in London in 1740 and studied at St. Paul's School. In 1767 he came to America and set up in business in Philadelphia. He was at first in sympathy with the colonists' cause, but he sought to achieve freedom within the bonds of empire by constitutional means and in 1776, with the declaration of war against Britain, he began to voice his protests. He sympathized with the British Army in occupation of Philadelphia and left the city with them in the spring of 1778, retiring behind British lines at New York; here he satirized both the revolutionists and the spiritlessness and procrastination of the British leaders. After the defeat of Britain, Stansbury joined those who remained loyal to the United States and burned all his personal papers which referred to his British sympathies. In 1783 he moved with his wife and family to a small village in New Jersey; a week later he was imprisoned and forced to leave the state within nine days. Taking leave of his family, he crossed the border into Nova Scotia in August 1783; here he received a grant of land and remained for about two years. He then returned to Philadelphia, but for the next seven or eight years he was forced to move his family from place to place to avoid local persecution. In 1793 he was allowed to settle in New York and there he remained for the rest of his life. He died in 1809.

Like Odell, Stansbury is noted chiefly for his political verse in the Loyalist cause. Moses Coit Taylor describes him as among the most eminent of the Loyalist writers and "without rival among his brethren as a writer of festive political songs, and of satire in verse characterized by a playful humour". "To Cordelia", the only extant Canadian piece, is the first expression of the negative response to Canadian life noted by many later writers such as Susannah Moodie, and Alexander McLachlan.

TEXT:

The Loyal Verses of Joseph Stansbury and Dr. Jonathan Odell. ed. Winthrop Sergent. Albany: J. Munsell, 1860.

See also:

Vernon L. Parrington. *Main Currents in American Thought.* New York: Harcourt Brace, 1927.

Moses Coit Taylor. *The Literary History of the American Revolution.* New York: Ungar Publishing Company, 1957.

God Save the King

Time was, in defence of his King and the Right,
We applauded brave Washington foremost in fight:
On the banks of Ohio he shouted lustily
   God save the King!
Disappointed ambition his feet has misled;
Corrupted his heart and perverted his head:
Loyal no longer, no more he cries faithfully
   Glory and Joy crown the King!

With Envy inflam'd 'tis in Britain the same;
Where leaders, despairing of virtuous fame,
Have push'd from their seats those whose watchword was constantly
   God save the King!
The helm of the State they have clutched in their grasp
When American Treason is at its last gasp:
When Firmness and Loyalty soon should sing valiantly
   Glory and Joy crown the King!

But Britain, with Glory and Conquest in view,
When nothing was wanted, but just to pursue –
To yield – while her Heroes chanted triumphantly
   God save the King!
With curses consign to the Furies his Name,
Whose Counsels thus cover'd his Country with shame!
Loyalists still will chant, tho' heavily,
   Glory and Joy crown the King!

Tho' ruin'd so deeply no Angel can save:
The Empire dismember'd: our King made a Slave:
Still loving, revering, we shout forth honestly
   God save the King!
Tho' fated to Banishment, Poverty, Death,
Our Hearts are unalter'd, and with our last breath
Loyal to George, we'll pray most fervently
   Glory and Joy crown the King!

(1783 – 1860)

To Cordelia

Believe me, Love, this vagrant life
   O'er Nova Scotia's wilds to roam,
While far from children, friends or wife,
   Or place that I can call a home
Delights not me; – another way
My treasures, pleasures, wishes lay.

In piercing, wet, and wintry skies,
   Where man would seem in vain to toil,
I see, where'er I turn my eyes,
   Luxuriant pasture, trees, and soil.
Uncharm'd I see: – another way
My fondest hopes and wishes lay.

Oh could I through the future see
   Enough to form a settled plan,
To feed my infant train and thee
   And fill the rank and style of man:
I'd cheerful be the livelong day;
Since all my wishes point that way.

But when I see a sordid shed
  Of birchen bark, procured with care,
Design'd to shield the aged head
  Which British mercy placed there –
'Tis too, too much: I cannot stay,
But turn with streaming eyes away.

Oh! how your heart would bleed to view
  Six pretty prattlers like your own,
Expos'd to every wind that blew;
  Condemn'd in such a hut to moan.
Could this be borne, Cordelia, say?
Contented in your cottage stay.

'Tis true, that in this climate rude,
  The mind resolv'd may happy be;
And may, with toil and solitude,
  Live independent and be free.
So the lone hermit yields to slow decay:
Unfriended lives – unheeded glides away.

If so far humbled that no pride remains,
  But moot indifference which way flows the stream;
Resign'd to penury, its cares and pains;
  And hope has left you like a painted dream;
Then here, Cordelia, bend your pensive way,
And close the evening of Life's wretched day.

(1784-1860)

II PRE-CONFEDERATION: THE MARITIMES

Oliver Goldsmith (1794-1861)

The first native-born Canadian poet to receive critical attention, Oliver Goldsmith was a grand-nephew of the famous Anglo-Irish poet Oliver Goldsmith, and had ambitions for a time to become his literary successor in British North America. His "Rising Village", like Joseph Howe's "Acadia", is ambitious in theme and scope; these poems are important today however as illustrations of the problems of young writers faced with a new country and a new experience which they tried to express in ideas and language derived from an older settled civilization and a past literary tradition.

Oliver Goldsmith was born July 6, 1794 in St. Andrews, New Brunswick, son of a British army officer who had fought in the Revolutionary War and who emigrated to Canada with his American wife. The family settled first in St. Andrews, then in 1796 in Annapolis Royal where Goldsmith Senior was Assistant Engineer and in 1800, in Halifax where he was Assistant Commissioner in the Army. Young Oliver was employed successively in a naval hospital, an ironmonger's shop, a bookseller's shop, a lawyer's office, and a wholesale firm; in 1810, after a short session at Halifax Grammar School, he entered the Commissariat Branch of the Army, a career he was to follow for forty-five years, serving in Halifax until 1833, in Saint John, New Brunswick for the following eleven years, in Hong Kong from 1844-5, in St. John's, Newfoundland from 1848 to 1853 and in Corfu from 1854 to 1855. He retired to England where he lived with a sister in Liverpool and died there on June 23, 1861.

While in Halifax, Goldsmith became acquainted with Joseph Howe and his literary circle. His first literary endeavour was an address for the opening of the Halifax Garrison Theatrical Company in 1822 and in the same year he played the role of Tony Lumpkin in his great uncle's *She Stoops to Conquer*. His chief work, *The Rising Village*, was published in London in 1825; a second edition, *The Rising Village and Other Poems*, was brought out in Saint John in 1834 in slightly revised form. Disappointed with the reception of his work, Goldsmith abandoned his literary activities; his *Autobiography*, written in England after his retirement, did not appear until 1943.

"The Rising Village" is an ambitious work deliberately modelled in style and structure on the older Goldsmith's famous poem, "The Deserted Village". The young Oliver hoped to parallel the theme of the decay of village life in the Old World with the rise and prosperity of towns in the New. The poem falls into three sections: a comment on the general growth of the colony since its first days, an intrusive story of two young lovers, Flora and Albert, and a climax praising the peace and prosperity of contemporary Nova Scotia. The second edition included eighteen occasional poems which are little known to-day.

TEXT:

The Rising Village and Other Poems. Saint John: Macmillan, 1834.

See also:
The Autobiography of Oliver Goldsmith. ed. Wilfrid E. Myatt. Toronto: Ryerson, 1943.

From "The Rising Village"

How chaste and splendid are the scenes that lie
Beneath the circle of Britannia's sky!
What charming prospects there arrest the view,
How bright, how varied, and how boundless too!
Cities and plains extending far and wide,
The merchant's glory, and the farmer's pride.
Majestic palaces in pomp display
The wealth and splendour of the regal sway;
While the low hamlet and the shepherd's cot,
In peace and freedom mark the peasant's lot.
There nature's vernal bloom adorns the field,
And Autumn's fruits their rich luxuriance yield.
There men, in busy crowds, with men combine,
That arts may flourish, and fair science shine;
And thence, to distant climes their labours send,
As o'er the world their widening views extend.
Compar'd with scenes like these, how lone and drear
Did once Acadia's woods and wilds appear;
Where wandering savages, and beasts of prey,
Displayed, by turns, the fury of their sway.
What noble courage must their hearts have fired,
How great the ardour which their souls inspired,
Who leaving far behind their native plain,
Have sought a home beyond the Western main;
And braved the perils of the stormy seas,
In search of wealth, of freedom, and of ease!
Oh! none can tell but they who sadly share

The bosom's anguish, and its wild despair,
What dire distress awaits the hardy bands,
That venture first on bleak and desert lands.
How great the pain, the danger, and the toil,
Which mark the first rude culture of the soil.
When, looking round, the lonely settler sees
His home amid a wilderness of trees:
How sinks his heart in those deep solitudes,
Where not a voice upon his ear intrudes;
Where solemn silence all the waste pervades,
Heightening the horror of its gloomy shades;
Save where the sturdy woodman's strokes resound,
That strew the fallen forest on the ground.
See! from their heights the lofty pines descend,
And crackling, down their pond'rous lengths extend.
Soon from their boughs the curling flames arise,
Mount into air, and redden all the skies;
And where the forest once its foliage spread,
The golden corn triumphant waves its head.

* * *

The arts of culture now extend their sway,
And many a charm of rural life display.
Where once the pine upreared its lofty head,
The settlers' humble cottages are spread;
Where the broad firs once sheltered from the storm,
By slow degrees a neighbourhood they form;
And, as it bounds, each circling year, increase
In social life, prosperity, and peace,
New prospects rise, new objects too appear,
To add more comfort to its lowly sphere.
Where some rude sign or post the spot betrays,
The tavern first its useful front displays.
Here, oft the weary traveller at the close
Of evening, finds a snug and safe repose.
The passing stranger here, a welcome guest,
From all his toil enjoys a peaceful rest;
Unless the host, solicitous to please,
With care officious mar his hope of ease,
With flippant questions to no end confined,
Exhaust his patience, and perplex his mind.
Yet, let no one condemn with thoughtless haste,
The hardy settler of the dreary waste,
Who, far removed from every busy throng,
And social pleasures that to life belong,
Whene'er a stranger comes within his reach,
Will sigh to learn whatever he can teach.

To this, must be ascribed in great degree,
That ceaseless, idle curiosity,
Which over all the Western world prevails,
And every breast, or more or less, assails;
Till, by indulgence, so o'erpowering grown,
It seeks to know all business but its own.
Here, oft when winter's dreary terrors reign,
And cold, and snow, and storm, pervade the plain,
Around the birch-wood blaze the settlers draw,
"To tell of all they felt, and all they saw."
When, thus in peace are met a happy few,
Sweet are the social pleasures that ensue.
What lively joy each honest bosom feels,
As o'er the past events his memory steals,
And to the listeners paints the dire distress,
That marked his progress in the wilderness;
The danger, trouble, hardship, toil, and strife,
Which chased each effort of his struggling life.
    While time thus rolls his rapid years away,
The Village rises gently into day.
How sweet it is, at first approach of morn,
Before the silvery dew has left the lawn,
When warring winds are sleeping yet on high,
Or breathe as softly as the bosom's sigh,
To gain some easy hill's ascending height,
Where all the landscape brightens with delight,
And boundless prospects stretched on every side,
Proclaim the country's industry and pride.
Here the broad marsh extends its open plain,
Until its limits touch the distant main;
There verdant meads along the uplands spring,
And grateful odours to the breezes fling;
Here crops of grain in rich luxuriance rise,
And wave their golden riches to the skies;
There smiling orchards interrupt the scene,
Or gardens bounded by some fence of green;
The farmer's cottage, bosomed 'mong the trees,
Whose spreading branches shelter from the
    breeze;
The winding stream that turns the busy mill,
Whose clacking echos o'er the distant hill;
The neat white church, beside whose walls are
    spread
The grass-clod hillocks of the sacred dead,
Where rude cut stones or painted tablets tell,
In laboured verse, how youth and beauty fell;
How worth and hope were hurried to the grave,
And torn from those who had no power to save.

Or, when the Summer's dry and sultry sun
Adown the West his, fiery course has run;
When o'er the vale his parting rays of light
Just linger, ere they vanish into night,
How sweet to wander round the wood-bound lake,
Whose glassy stillness scarce the zephyrs wake;
How sweet to hear the murmuring of the rill,
As down it gurgles from the distant hill;
The note of Whip-poor-Will how sweet to hear,
When sadly slow it breaks upon the ear,
And tells each night, to all the silent vale,
The hopeless sorrows of its mournful tale.
Dear lovely spot! Oh may such charms as these,
Sweet tranquil charms, that cannot fail to please,
Forever reign around thee, and impart
Joy, peace, and comfort to each native heart.
  Happy Acadia! though around thy shore
Is heard the stormy wind's terrific roar;
Though round thee Winter binds his icy chain,
And his rude tempests sweep along thy plain,
Still Summer comes, and decorates thy land
With fruits and flowers from her luxuriant hand;
Still Autumn's gifts repay the labourer's toil
With richest products from thy fertile soil;
With bounteous store his varied wants supply,
And scarce the plants of other suns deny,
How pleasing, and how glowing with delight
Are now thy budding hopes! How sweetly bright
They rise to view! How full of joy appear
The expectations of each future year!
Not fifty Summers yet have blessed thy clime,
How short a period in the page of time!
Since savage tribes, with terror in their train,
Rushed o'er thy fields, and ravaged all thy plain,
But some few years have rolled in haste away
Since, through thy vales, the fearless beast of prey,
With dismal yell and loud appalling cry,
Proclaimed his midnight reign of terror nigh.
And now how changed the scene! the first, afar,
Have fled to wilds beneath the northern star;
The last has learned to shun man's dreaded eye,
And, in his turn, to distant regions fly.
While the poor peasant, whose laborious care
Scarce from the soil could wring his scanty fare;
Now in the peaceful arts of culture skilled,
Sees his wide barn with ample treasures filled;
Now finds his dwelling, as the year goes round,
Beyond his hopes, with joy and plenty crowned.

Nor culture's arts, a nation's noblest friend,
Alone o'er Scotia's fields their power extend;
From all her shores, with every gentle gale,
Commerce expands her free and swelling sail;
And all the land, luxuriant, rich, and gay,
Exulting owns the splendour of their sway.
These are thy blessings, Scotia, and for these,
For wealth, for freedom, happiness, and ease,
Thy grateful thanks to Britain's care are due,
Her power protects, her smiles past hopes renew,
Her valour guards thee, and her councils guide,
Then may thy parent ever be thy pride!

* * *

Then blest Acadia! ever may thy name,
Like hers, be graven on the rolls of fame;
May all thy sons, like hers, be brave and free,
Possessors of her laws and liberty;
Heirs of her splendour, science, power, and skill,
And through succeeding years her children still.
And as the sun, with gentle dawning ray,
From night's dull bosom wakes, and leads the day,
His course majestic keeps, till in the height
He glows one blaze of pare exhaustless light;
So may thy years increase, thy glories rise,
To be the wonder of the Western skies;
And bliss and peace encircle all thy shore,
Till empires rise and sink, on earth, no more.

(1825)

Serenade.

Wake Leila, wake, the stilly night
  Invites thee from repose,
The zephyrs in the moon-beam's light,
  Now sleep on every rose.
Leila, awake, and come to me.

Wake, Leila, wake, in yonder bower,
   Beneath the Acacia tree,
Thy lover waits at this soft hour,
   To breathe his vows to thee.
Leila, awake, and come to me.

Wake, Leila, wake, to thy fond youth
   In beauty's charms appear,
His tale of love, and hope, and truth,
   Thou'lt never blush to hear.
Leila, awake, and come to me.

(1834)

Joseph Howe (1804-1873)

A highly colourful figure in colonial Nova Scotia, an eminent federal politician, a Premier of Nova Scotia and ultimately its Lieutenant-Governor, Joseph Howe was also an important literary figure, and represented the new generation of Canadian-born, descended from Loyalist stock, who brought the colony to an early maturity. As editor of *The Novascotian* Howe influenced a number of Maritime writers including Oliver Goldsmith and Thomas Haliburton, and was instigator of "The Club," a literary coterie of Halifax writers who met to discuss literary problems and their own prose and poetry.

Born in 1804, Joseph Howe was the son of John Howe who had established the *Halifax Gazette* with a printing-press brought with him from Boston when the American Revolution began. In 1817, at thirteen years of age, young Joseph was apprenticed to his father to learn the printing-trade. In 1827, Howe became joint editor and publisher of the *Acadian Recorder* and in 1828, at twenty-four, he purchased *The Novascotian* and became an avowed political reformer. In 1835, accused of publishing a paper which attacked the magistrates of Halifax and the executive and legislative council, he won his own defence in a six-hour speech. Elected to the House of Assembly in 1836 as a Reformer, he began agitation for responsible government; he joined the executive council in 1840 but resigned in 1843 over a difference with the Lieutenant-Governor. From 1848 to 1857 he was provincial secretary in the new responsible government, and chairman-in-chief of the railway board from 1854-7, and again from 1860-1. He was Premier of Nova Scotia from August 1861 to 1863, when he was appointed by the British Government as Fishery Commissioner until 1866. Surprisingly, he opposed Confederation and proposed an imperial federation in which the colonies would be represented in the British parliament, but was eventually convinced by Sir John A. Macdonald and Charles Tupper to join Macdonald's first Federal Cabinet as president of the council and later Secretary of State. In 1873 he was appointed Lieutenant-Governor of Nova Scotia, but his health had been poor and he died three weeks after he took office.

Howe was also involved in several literary activities. In *The Nova-Scotian* he encouraged a number of local writers including Oliver Goldsmith. He published Haliburton's *Sam Slick* in *The Novascotian*; Haliburton's *An Historical and Statistical Account of Nova Scotia* (1829) and the first edition of *The Clockmaker* (1836), which R. Bentley of London pirated the next year. Howe published a volume of poetry, *May-Flowers of Nova Scotia* (1840), and also "Sable Island" which was bound with his *Sable Island, its Past History, Present Appearance, Natural History etc.* (1858), but no collection of his work appeared until *Poems and Essays*, published after his death in 1874. He also wrote a political lampoon on the lieutenant-governor of the province, *The Lord of the Bed-Chamber.* Two collections of his speeches, *The Speeches and Public Letters of the Hon. Joseph Howe,* edited by William Annand (2 volumes, 1909) and *The Heart of Howe*, edited by D. C. Harvey (1939), gather together a number of addresses such as "Address Delivered Before the Halifax Mechanics' Institute" (1834), and "Confederation Considered in Relation to the Interests of the Empire" (1866).

Despite his strenuous political involvement, Howe is quoted as having remarked: "Poetry was my first love but politics was the hag I married". His most ambitious work is also his best-known, "Acadia", an account never completed of the development and present state of Nova Scotia similar to Goldsmith's "The Rising Village". Yet the poetry of *Poems and Essays* is surprisingly varied in theme and style and anticipates the work of many later writers. The essay "Local Patriotism" illustrates the personal force and magnetism which made Howe a leading orator in his time and a noted politician in Canada's history.

TEXT:

Poems and Essays. Montreal: Lovell, 1874.
The Heart of Howe. ed. D. C. Harvey. Toronto: Oxford University Press, 1939.

See also:

Roy Palmer Baker. *A History of English and Canadian Literatures of The Confederation.* Cambridge: Harvard University Press, 1920.
J. W. Longley. *Joseph Howe.* Toronto: Morang, 1904.
J. A. Roy. *A Study in Achievement and Frustration.* Toronto: Macmillan, 1935.

Song for the 8th June

Hail to the day when the Briton came o'er
  And planted his flag where the Mayflower blows,
And gathered the blossoms, unheeded before,
  To entwine with the Shamrock, the Thistle, and Rose.

Let us never forget, while our revels we keep
  'Neath the shade of the green woods that hang over-
    head,
The labors of those in our churchyards who sleep,
  But fill up a bumper to honor the Dead.

Oh! dear to our hearts is the land they bequeathed,
  And the standard they reared proudly waves o'er us
    yet;
While we gather and cherish the flowers they wreathed,
  Let us never the graves of our fathers forget.

They vanquished the forest to make us a home,
  Though the knife of the savage defended each grove;
And, while ocean's proud waves round our headlands
    shall foam,
  This day must be honored where'ever we rove.

The valleys their garments of emerald wear,
  The flocks on the mountains unherried repose,
And the songs of our maidens rise mirthful and clear
  By the side of each stream in the starlight that flows.

The Cities are growing with wealth in their train,
  The Hamlet securely expands in the glen;
And our white sails are glancing far over the main,
  To the islands that nourish'd those stout hearted men.

Then fill up a bumper, uncovered, we'll name,
  And drink to THE DEAD, and the day they've en-
    deared;
May the spirit they left, like a circle of flame,
  Guard forever the homes and the standard they
    rear'd.

(1874)

To the Linnet

Oh! fear me not, sweet little Bird,
   Nor quit the bough for me,
But let your evening song be heard
   Of artless minstrelsy.

Think not I wish to do you harm
   Or drive you from the spray,
In hopes your song my thoughts may charm
   I'm listening to your lay.

Oh! sing the saddest, wildest strain
   You've e'er been taught by grief,
And chaunt it o'er and o'er again
   'Twill give my soul relief.

If you have watched a Parent dear
   Whose life was on the wane,
The mournful song pray let me hear,
   You sang to soothe his pain.

If you have seen his eyelids close
   Without the power to save,
Warble the lay, 'twill bring repose,
   You sang beside his grave.

How oft by yonder aged tree,
   My Father at my side,
I've listen'd many an hour to thee
   At silent eventide.

For then, the merriest roundelay
   You sang on summer eve
Was welcome, to a heart so gay
   It knew no cause to grieve.

E'en yet your simple strain I love
   Altho' by care oppress'd,
To hear thee warbling as I rove
   Relieves my aching breast.

Then fear me not, sweet little Bird
   Nor quit the bough for me,
But let your evening song be heard
   Of artless minstrelsy.

(1874)

The Wild Cherry Tree

Child of the wilderness – gladly I see
Thy blossoms unfolding on hill-side and lea;
By streamlet and river thy white veil is spread,
Where the Witch Elm looks lovingly down on thy head;
In the depth of the forest the Moose turns aside
To gaze on thy branches with pleasure and pride;
And the Salmon leaps higher, if lit by the beam
Of noontide, you gracefully droop o'er the stream.
Oh! dear to all nature, but dearer to me
Is the pride of the Spring time – the Wild Cherry Tree.

Storm-tested, the Oak on the mountain top grows,
And the date of its seedling no living man knows;
The Maple, in Autumn, is lovely to view,
And the tremulous Aspen, that shakes off the dew;
Like a Temple the Pine Grove invites us to prayer,
And we worship 'midst beauty and solitude there;
By the Beech in the pastures, 'tis pleasant to lean,
And the Fir, through the snow wreath, looks cheery and
   green.
Though highly I prize them, yet dearer to me
Is the pride of the Spring time, the Wild Cherry Tree.

The Laurel's pink blossoms look gay on the moor,
The Larch's red berries droop round the church door;
The Alder Clumps, dress'd in their tassels, are fine,
And the Rockets, the Windfalls with beauty enshrine;
The wings of each zephyr the Bay-leaf perfumes,
And, rich in its odors, the modest Fern blooms.
Oh! countless the blossoms the woodlands display,
And varied the scents on the night air that stray –
From childhood I loved them – but dearer to me
Is the delicate flower of the Wild Cherry Tree.

(1874)

The Micmac

Though o'er Acadia's hills and plains
    The wand'ring Micmac listless strays,
While scarce a single trace remains
    Of what he was in other days.

And though he now an outcast seems
    Upon the lands his Fathers trod,
And his dark eye no longer beams
    With pride which bent but to his God, –

Though the fire-water's deadly wave
    Which even pride could not control,
Has drown'd each feeling high that gave
    Such innate grandeur to his soul; –

There was a time when Nature's child
    With nobler port and manner bore him,
And ranged with joy his native wild,
    Or slept with Heaven's blue curtain o'er him.

Long ere the white man's axe was heard
    Resounding in the forest shade,
Long ere the rifle's voice had stirr'd
    The stillness of the Sylvan glade, –

Ere Science, with her plastic hand,
   And Labor, with his patient toil,
Had changed the features of the land,
   And dispossess'd him of the soil.

Then let fair Fancy change the scene,
   While gazing on the Micmac's brow,
And showing what he once has been,
   Make us forget what he is now.

(1874)

To Mary

Oh! blame me not, Mary, for gazing at you,
   Nor suppose that my thoughts from the Preacher
     were straying.
Tho' I stole a few glances – believe me 'tis true –
   They were sweet illustrations of what he was saying.

For, when he observed that Perfection was not
   To be found upon Earth – for a moment I bent
A look upon you – and could swear on the spot,
   That perfection in Beauty was not what he meant.

And when, with emotion, the worthy Divine
   On the doctrine of loving our neighbors insisted,
I felt if their forms were as faultless as thine,
   I could love every soul of them while I existed.

And Mary, I'm sure 'twas the fault of those eyes –
   'Twas the lustre of them to the error gave birth –
That, while he spoke of Angels that dwelt in the Skies,
   I was gazing with rapture at one upon Earth.

(1874)

The Blue Nose
AIR. – *Bumper of Burgundy*.

Let the Student of Nature in rapture descant
   On the Heavens' cerulean hue;
Let the Lover indulge in poetical rant,
   When the eyes of his Mistress are blue.

But fill high your glasses – fill, fill to the brim,
   I've a different toast to propose:
While such eyes, and such skies, still are beaming for him,
   Here's a health to the jolly Blue Nose.

Let the Frenchman delight in his vine-covered vales,
   Let the Greek toast his old classic ground;
Here's the land where the bracing Northwester prevails,
   And where jolly Blue Noses abound.

Long – long may it flourish, to all of us dear,
   Loved and honored by hearts that are true;
But, should ever a foe chance his nose to show here
   He shall find all our Noses true Blue.

(1874)

Once More I Put My Bonnet On

Once more I put my bonnet on,
   And tie the ribbons blue,
My showy poplin dress I don,
   That's just as good as new,
And smooth and stately as a swan
   Go sailing to my pew.

Once more, Ah! me, how oft, how oft,
   Shall I the scene repeat?
With graceful ease and manner soft
   I sink into my seat,
And round the congregation waft
   The sense of odors sweet.

A finer form, a fairer face
   Ne'er bent before the stole,
With more restraint, no spotless lace
   Did firmer orbs control,
I shine, the Beauty of the place,
   And yet I look all soul.

When to the sinful people round
   My pitying glances rove
The dewy tints of Heaven's profound
   Seem in my eyes to move,
Too sorrowful their hearts to wound,
   And hardly asking love.

And thus for four long years I've sat,
   My gloves without a crease,
For two of them I wore a hat,
   For one a blue pelisse,
When will the wicked know what's what,
   The weary heart have peace?

My head gear twenty times I've changed,
   Worn Paris flowers in Spring,
Wheat ears in Autumn, re-arranged,
   Tried birds of every wing,
Bade that from Paradise estranged
   Its lustre o'er me fling.

But yet, as "nether millstones" hard
   The hearts of men appear,
Smooth shaved, "or bearded like the pard"
   They're worse from year to year.
My "virtue is its own reward,"
   I'm sitting single here.

The Rector's eyes, a brilliant pair,
   Lit up with love divine,
Beaming with inspiration rare,
   And phrenzy very fine,
Like nestling birds from upper air,
   Would gently droop to mine.

What could I think, as day by day
   His gaze more earnest grew,
Till half the girls began to say
   He neither cared nor knew,
Though all the Church should go astray
   If he could save my pew.

I read divinity by reams,
   The Bible got by heart,
I studied all the Church's "Schemes,"
   Prepared to play my part
Of Rector's wife, as well beseems
   A lady of high Art.

But, let the truth at once be told,
   Religion's cause was nought,
For Twenty Thousand Pounds in gold
   The Rector's heart was bought,
And I was most completely sold,
   The Blackbird was not caught.

The Curate's hair was crisp and brown,
   His color very high;
His ample chest came sloping down,
   Antinous-like his thigh,
Sin shrank before his gathered frown,
   Peace whispered in his sigh.

So young! I hoped his steps to guide
   From error's devious way;
By bad example sorely tried,
   I feared the youth might stray;
To life's allurements opening wide
   Become an easy prey.

I did my best, I watched and prayed,
   His ardent soul to save,
But by the sinful flesh betrayed,
   What could I do but rave?
Ten stone of blonde, in lace arrayed
   Walked with him down the nave.

If Gospel truth must now be told
   I've selfish grown of late,
The Banker next though somewhat old,
   And limping in his gait,
And quite as yellow as his gold,
   I thought to animate.

I'm sure my Note he would have "done"
  With "two good names" upon it;
I do not think he ever run
  His eye glass o'er my sonnet,
Or counted, in the morning sun
  The feathers in my bonnet.

The widowed Judge I next essayed,
  His orphans kindly viewing,
Read Blackstone nearly through 'tis said,
  All gaudy dress eschewing;
But, am I doomed to die a maid?
  Not yet he comes a wooing.

Once more I'll put my bonnet on
  And tie the ribbons blue;
My showy poplin dress I'll don,
  That's just as good as new,
And smooth and stately as a swan
  Go sailing to my pew.

Merchants and Lawyers, half a score,
  Bow on their hats to pray,
Tho' scattered round, I'm very sure
  They always look my way.
I'll re-appear, encore! encore!
  Who shall I catch to-day?

(1874)

From "Local Patriotism"

The abstract or cosmopolitan idea of knowledge is, that it is of no
country; the world of science and of letters comprises the learned and
the ingenious of every clime, whose intellects, reflecting back the light
which each in turn bestows, serve to illuminate and cheer the dark
places of the earth, and roll off the mists which ignorance and prejudice have gathered around the human mind. To benefit his whole race
and to earn universal applause, are the first great stimulants of the
student and philosopher; but the all-wise Being, who divided the earth

into continents, peninsulas and islands – who separated tribes from each other by mountain ranges and unfathomable seas; who gave a different feature and a different tongue – evidently intended that there should be a local knowledge and a local love, binding His creatures to particular spots of earth, and interesting them peculiarly for the prosperity, improvement and happiness of those places. The love of country, therefore, though distinguished from this universal love, boasts of an origin as divine, and serves purposes scarcely less admirable. It begets a generous rivalry among the nations of the earth, by which the intellectual and physical resources of each are developed and strengthened by constant exercise; and although sometimes abused by ignorance or criminal ambition, has a constant direction favourable to the growth of knowledge, and the amelioration and improvement of human affairs.

Is that feeling alive in your breasts? Is it abroad in this country? Has Nova Scotia received the power to attach her children to her bosom and make them prouder and fonder of her bleak hills and sylvan valleys, than even of the fairer and more cultivated lands from which their parents came?

I must confess that, at a first glance, the youthful native of Nova Scotia would seem to require more than an ordinary share of *amor patriae,* to justify much pride at the present condition of his country or to inspire any ardent hope of her future prosperity and renown. He sees her almost the least in population and extent in the whole range of a mighty continent, and without reference to the glorious nations of the old world, but a child in resources and improvement, as compared with the States and Provinces by which she is more immediately surrounded, and upon which the signs of a manhood, vigorous and advanced, are already deeply impressed. He may love her, but can he hope to render her conspicuous among such competitors? – to raise her up to the level which they may, without any very extraordinary efforts, attain? To the South and West a more generous sun warms a more fertile soil into a higher measure of fruitfulness and beauty than nature bestows on him; and to the North, he finds countries which, from their geographical extent and earlier settlement, have a greater command of resources – are already vastly in advance – and seem destined to leave Nova Scotia far behind in the race of improvement; and to merge, in their own mental effulgence, the feeble light of science which even ardent patriotism may kindle upon her soil. . . .

These splendid individual instances have often been pressed upon your attention; and I only allude to them here, that I may inquire, whether men in masses may not achieve for their common country a moral and intellectual reputation, and a measure of collective prosperity and influence, equally disproportioned to her apparent means; equally honourable to their joint exertions; and equally worthy of that untiring diligence and indefatigable hope, without which nothing valuable can ever be attained? I think they can. I would have you think so;

and, sanctioned by your judgment, I wish the sentiment to go abroad over the Province, and to become strongly impressed upon the minds of my youthful countrymen, until it ripens into a cheerful and fixed determination to raise up their native land to a point of distinction in agriculture, commerce, and the arts, in literature and science, in knowledge and virtue, which shall win for her the admiration and esteem of other lands, and teach them to estimate Nova Scotia rather by her mental riches and resources, than by her age, population, or geographical extent. With nations as with individuals, though much depends on natural endowments, much also depends on first impressions and early culture; and with them, as with us, though in some cases accidents may make or mar, it rarely happens that their ruling passions and fixed determinations do not control their destiny. . . .

Providence has given us a separate country and the elements of a distinct character. We cannot change what the hand of nature has performed. But can we not follow out the benevolent designs of Providence and fill up with pleasing tints and graceful animation the outline which nature has but sketched? Can we endanger our friendly relations with Britain or excite the jealousy of our neighbours, by becoming wise and virtuous, by establishing a high standard of moral excellence and making to Nova Scotians the great truths of religion, philosophy and science familiar as household words, by exciting among our population a desire for distinction, and a taste for literature and art as general as is the taste for music in modern Italy, or as was the love of country which distinguished ancient Rome?

But, it may be said, what can a little society such as this accomplish? Need I remind you that a few intelligent and determined men can do almost anything to which reason and sound policy are not opposed? Have not smaller combinations ere now broken down the superstitions, dispelled the ignorance, and elevated the moral and social character of distant millions who seemed sunken in the lowest depth of barbaric degradation? . . .

You will readily perceive that I wish to show you how national happiness, influence, and glory are comparatively independent of those circumstances which are vulgarly believed to create them, and that a people, though ever so few in numbers and deficient in physical resources, may, by a due appreciation of this truth – by a due estimate of early combination and perseverance, form their own destiny – control their own fortune, and earn for themselves a measure of improvement, influence, and renown, out of all proportion to the gifts of nature and the apparent means at their command.

*   *   *

. . . Beginning with Agriculture, I will suppose that you demand of me how our soil is to be brought up to an equality with that of more favoured lands? and I answer – by higher cultivation; by intense study of its composition and capabilities; by enlightened and assiduous management; and by the application of all those chemical and mechanical improvements which promote fertility and amelioration, and have been treasured by the experience of the past. How are we to raise manufactures? By importing nothing which our own industry can supply at as low a rate, and by multiplying those bulky and cheap productions, which enjoy some protection from the cost of transportation. Though the facility with which we are deluged by European manufactures on the one side and those of the United States, forced into existence by wars and high duties on the other, at present prevents, and may for many years retard, the formation of some establishments that are eminently to be desired; still, as the natural capabilities of our country for the prosecution of this branch of national industry are great, I do not despair. Indeed there can be little doubt that, if the proper encouragement is given, as the cost of subsistence and of labour falls, domestic manufactures will take firm root in the soil, and if once reared they may be carried to any extent.

As respects commerce, there is no reason why Nova Scotia should not be eminently commercial; because, although our power of agricultural production may be restrained by our narrow limits and by the character of our soil and climate; and although the growth of manufactures may be retarded by the trifling domestic demands of a thin population, and the direct competition of older and more wealthy states, there are no such formidable obstacles to the rapid growth of a commercial marine and to the almost indefinite extension of domestic and foreign trade. I know that this opinion will be regarded by many as absurd, but it is the result of some thought and of a firm conviction. It is not essentially necessary that a country should produce largely, in order to secure the advantages of commerce – provided her people have more industry, economy, enterprise and intelligence, than their neighbours, and are contented with smaller profits. The whole world is open to a people possessing these qualities; and, if brought to bear, for any length of time, upon the most sterile and unpromising spot that skirts the ocean, they will infallibly make it wealthy, populous, and powerful.

The Phoenicians produced neither the gold of Ophir, nor the corn of Egypt; the Genoese had no natural claim to the rich harvest of the Crimea, or the sturgeon of the Black Sea; and yet they made more by the interchange of these commodities than the people by whom they were prepared. What gave the Dutch almost a monopoly of the wheat of Poland and the spices of the Indian isles? The qualities to which I have referred. Who will say that it has not been by establishing commercial relations with all parts of the earth, and becoming the factors of all other nations, rather than by the force of domestic production, that Great Britain has attained the unexampled rank and opulence she enjoys?

What natural connection is there between Glasgow and the North American forests? and yet one house in that city, composed of a few enterprising, intelligent, and frugal men, have established stores and mills in every part of Canada and New Brunswick, buy and sell nearly half of all the timber cut, and out of the profits of their trade have created a fleet of ships, the finest ornaments of the Clyde, and which would almost furnish a navy for a third-rate European power. Was it skill, economy, and enterprise, that enriched Salem by the India trade, and Nantucket and New Bedford by the whale fishery? or was there any exclusive privilege, any singular advantage, which enabled their inhabitants thus to outstrip the other seaports of the United States? I might multiply these illustrations without end; but enough has been said to show you the grounds of my belief, that if the requisite qualities are cultivated and maintained, we may attain a degree of commercial greatness and prosperity, to which in the present depressed state of our trade, it would appear like madness to aspire.

Let me not be misunderstood. I am neither seeing visions nor dreaming dreams, but reasoning upon facts sanctioned by the experience of ages. I wish to build up agriculture, commerce, and manufactures, upon the surest of all foundations – the mental and moral cultivation of the people. If knowledge is power, let us get knowledge. If our position presents difficulties, let us study to overcome them; and if we can only surpass others, by a higher measure of patriotism, sagacity, and endurance than they possess, let us never cease to hope and labour until that standard is attained. A German economist, in treating of the elements of national wealth, beautifully characterizes that general intelligence to which I refer, as the "capital of mind" – that capital without which a country, richly blessed by nature, may be poor indeed; but which is capable of raising up even a little Province like this, until its population is swelled to millions, until its canvas whitens every sea, and even its rocky hills are covered with fruitfulness, and its wildest glens are made to blossom as the rose.

But, setting aside all views of political advantage, all hopes of individual or national opulence, is it not worth our while to get knowledge for its own sake? to love and cultivate literature, science, and the arts, for the delight they afford and the honour and distinction they confer? . . .

But, it may be said, how can we earn distinction in literature, science, and art, when we are far removed from those great marts where excellence in these things meets the highest rewards; and where the materials out of which they are created are almost exclusively treasured? . . .

Though there are many walks of literature, where others have earned distinction, from which we are shut out by our position and comparatively infant state, there are others, in which much may be done, even by the ambitious youth of Nova Scotia, by a right application of their powers and a judicious employment of their time. The sonnets of Petrarch, the sublime poems of Milton, the sacred melodies of Byron and Moore, and many of the finest dramas of England and France, might, by the same combination of genius and self-devotion, have been produced in this or in any other country. The history, poetry, and general literature of the world are now open to us, as they were to them; and, except where peculiar associations and minute local knowledge are required, the daring and imaginative spirits of Nova Scotia may learn to imitate, and possibly rival, the great masters by whom they are taught. . . .

As regards the sciences, though we may lack many of the facilities for study and experiment that abound in older countries, still, the materials of all science surround us on every side, and hold out rich rewards to those who shall use them with skill and perseverance. In chemistry, geology, pneumatics, electro-magnetism, optics, natural history, astronomy, and medicine, how many brilliant discoveries are to be made and how splendid a reputation may not the assiduous pursuit of either or all of those sciences, even in this little colony, confer? . . .

. . . In conclusion, I would again remind you that both honour and interest distinctly mark the paths which we should tread. We are few in numbers; our country is but a narrow tract, surrounded by populous States; and we have no prospect of distinction – I had almost said of future safety – but from high mental and moral cultivation, infusing into every branch of industry such a degree of intellectual vigour as shall insure success, multiply population, and endow them with productive power.

As we grow in knowledge, the contrast between Nova Scotia and her neighbours will be less striking; the evidences of their superiority less disheartening and distinct. But this is not all. As the standard of mental and moral character is elevated; as we become distinguished by an ardent pursuit of truth, by the noble flights of genius, the graceful creations of fancy – those things which are independent of mere politics and economy – Nova Scotia may acquire a reputation, which, in peace, will be a universal passport for her sons, and in times of peril must secure for her sympathy and support.

Thomas McCulloch (1776-1843)

A noted Presbyterian minister, an outstanding educator, founder of
Pictou Academy, and the first president of Dalhousie College,
Thomas McCulloch was the author of several religious and political
works, two novels, and the first important satirical work in Canada,
pre-dating Thomas Chandler Haliburton by nearly fifteen years. Of
him Northrop Frye remarks: "McCulloch is the founder of genuine
Canadian humour: that is, of humour which is based on a vision of
society and is not merely a series of wisecracks on a single theme. The
tone of his humour, quiet, observant, deeply conservative in a human
sense, has been the prevailing tone of Canadian humour ever since."

Thomas McCulloch was born in 1776 in Renfrewshire, Scotland in
the parish of Neilston. He attended the University of Glasgow where
he studied Arts and Medicine and taught a private tutorial class in
Hebrew. He subsequently attended the Secession Divinity Hall at
Whitburn and was licensed as a preacher in 1799 by the Presbytery of
Kilmarnock. Ordained in the Secession Church at Stewarton, he held
the position of minister here until 1803, when he decided to become a
missionary in the colonies. Arriving first in Nova Scotia, he took a
temporary appointment at Pictou, and remained until 1838 when he
became active in public education. At this time there was little provi-
sion for elementary education for the general public, and the two
institutions for higher education, Halifax Grammar School, and
King's College and Academy at Windsor which Haliburton attended,
were controlled by the Anglican Church. McCulloch in reaction
founded the Pictou Academy in 1816, a development rising out of his
first log schoolhouse located behind his home and its successor, a
small school across the street. But the Academy was not given the
right to grant degrees, and McCulloch spent many years in a bitter
struggle for educational recognition. At Pictou he taught logic, moral
philosophy, science, Hebrew and theology, and attempted to build up
a library containing works of Hobbes, Descartes, Berkeley, Adam
Smith, Malebranche and Burke among others; he also developed an
up-to-date laboratory and a museum. His contributions to education
were recognized by the University of Glasgow which granted him an
M.A. McCulloch also trained young candidates for the Presbyterian
ministry; this section of the Academy was later expanded into a
Theological Seminary at West River which in 1858 was moved to
Truro. In 1860 it was one of the colleges to unite in The Presby-
aterian College in Halifax, and in 1925 it became Pine Hill Divinity
Hall under the United Church of Canada. In recognition of his
outstanding contribution to education in Nova Scotia, McCulloch was

appointed in 1838 as the first principal of Dalhousie College and established the university as a place of greatness and educational excellence. Here he taught philosophy and political economy and again sought to develop an outstanding library, a well-equipped laboratory and a museum. He died in Halifax in 1843.

McCulloch's writings were largely in the fields of education, religion and politics. His address for the opening of Pictou Academy in 1818, "The Nature and Uses of a Liberal Education Illustrated", was published in Halifax in 1819. The essay defines a liberal education as "the improvement of man in intelligence and moral principle, as the basis of his subsequent duty and happiness", and advocates it not only for the learned professions but for every individual in the community. He also published three religious books *Popery Condemned* (1808), *Popery Again Condemned* (1810) and *Calvinism* (1849) as well as a number of sermons in pamphlet form. In a series of articles for the *Pictou Herald* and the *Acadian Recorder* he advocated the principles of responsible government which were later to influence Joseph Howe. The novels *William* and *Melville* (1824 and 1826), treat in fictional form the economic and social conditions of this period.

The Stepsure Letters was originally a group of letters appearing in the *Acadian Recorder* from December of 1821 to May of 1822. They were prepared and circulated for book publication but were not printed until after the death of McCulloch, by Hugh W. Blackadar in 1862. The series aroused considerable controversy and McCulloch replied in another six letters appearing in the *Recorder* from January to March of 1823. Like Haliburton in *The Clockmaker*, McCulloch employs satire to examine the causes of economic crisis in the Maritimes in the period following the Napoleonic Wars. Like *The Clockmaker*, the structure is basically anecdotal, connected by a central character. Mephibosheth Stepsure, named after a lame son of King Saul, rises to prosperity as an advocate of good taste, simplicity, industry and economy and thus becomes the satiric norm of the work along with his wife, her mother the Widow Scant, Parson Drone and Sancrotesh.

TEXT:

The Stepsure Letters. Halifax: Hugh W. Blackadar, 1862.

See also:

William McCulloch. D. D. *Life of Thomas McCulloch, D. D.* Pictou: 1920.

The Stepsure Letters. New Canadian Library edition with an introduction by Northrop Frye, biographical notes by John A. Irving and bibliographic information by Douglas G. Lochhead. Toronto: McClelland and Stewart, 1960.

From *The Stepsure Letters*

LETTER III

GENTLEMEN, – I formerly observed that it has been, in our town, a time of general distress. This, however, is by no means the effect of carelessness or inactivity; for our townsfolk are in general eager to be rich, and as active as eager. I will venture to affirm that there is not another township in the province, where there are so many bargains every day made. Indeed, the greater part of us spend the half of their time, running about expressly for the purpose of getting rich; yet, by some strange fatality, misfortune has fallen heaviest upon those who were most active. I remember, when Parson Drone came amongst us, he tried to persuade us that the property of the town, at that time, could not make us all wealthy; and, therefore, that, if we would all be rich, we must by labour add as much to its value, as would enrich us all. But it appeared very plain to the most of us, that, if every one made so many bargains and gained by each of them, he would be so much the richer, and no man who can become wealthy by hard work, will ever submit to the drudgery of farming. I am inclined to think that our parson told us the truth; but the Reverend Mr. Shadrach Howl, who, last year, being tired of chopping down trees, converted himself into a preacher of the gospel, affirms that our calamities are a judgment upon the town for rejecting his doctrines. However this may be, certain it is that our most active and enterprising townsmen are either living with the sheriff, or, from a principle of delicacy, keeping themselves out of the way of his invitations.

After the account which I have given of Jack Scorem, I find that I have little else to do than to send you the names of the sheriff's other lodgers. Though the life of each of them has been marked by a diversity of incidents; the original situation of most of them, their views, and the conclusion of their course have been exactly similar. Respecting them, therefore, I shall only send you a few brief notices.

Whoever looks at the soil of our township, would say that nature designed us to be a farming people; and, that every man who gives the ground fair play, will be able to live very snugly. Accordingly, my cousin Harrow, Saunders Scantocreesh, and a few others, who mind only their farms, have everything thriving about them; and whoever goes into their houses, is sure to find plenty and cheerfulness. Yet, though our soil is excellent, and farms very easily got, the most of our townsfolk would rather ride two days round the country to make a bargain, than give the ground one day's labour. Whether this proceeds from the waywardness of human nature, or because, being British subjects, we are born traders, I cannot tell. Our parson is somewhat inclined to think that our parishioners are a part of the ten tribes; and says that the only objections to his opinion are, that, though our folks are great traders in watches, horses, and other things, and as eager to be rich as any of the seed of Abraham; not one of them deals in old clothes, or is as rich as a Jew. But Saunders Scantocreesh, who reads his Bible a good deal, declares, that, from their disposition to meddle with quiet honest men, they must be the Philistines, or else the children of Ishmael; because when the court comes round, they are all at loggerheads among themselves.

Along with my neighbour Gosling, I found Mr. Gypsum, the plaster merchant, who once possessed as fair prospects as any in the town. Like most of our young folks he began the world early. Much about the same time, he married and bought a farm with a good deal of marsh; for which he agreed to pay by easy instalments. The young people were both very active and eager to be out of debt. Now labour in our town is usually succeeded by bountiful returns; so that, in a few years, the farm sent more cattle and hogs to market than any of their neighbours; and Mrs. Gypsum's turkeys always brought the highest price. By these means and using a good deal of thrift, they both owned an excellent farm, and were out of every man's debt. By pursuing this course, Mr. Gypsum had also acquired a habit of labouring, which, in every line of life, is a valuable acquisition. But he had now got his farm in fine order; and, not being disposed to clear up any more wood-land, he had a good deal of spare time upon his hands. Still he was not disposed to be idle; and it occurred to him, that as he had excellent plaster upon his lot, it would be easy for him, when he had nothing else to do, to build a vessel which would carry it to the Lines. Accordingly, the vessel was built, rigged by the help of good credit, and sent off with a cargo. At that time it happened that plaster was giving a great price, so that the rigging was soon paid: and Mr. Gypsum now owned a good farm and a vessel, and had money in his pocket besides. As the best returns were now made by trading, trading chiefly occupied his thoughts. But money in a man's pocket doing nothing, is mere lumber. It occurred to him, therefore, that, as he was now in the way of business he might as well make the homeward voyage productive, by bringing flour and corn, which, in our town, are always in demand. Mr. Gypsum was now in very prosperous circumstances. Beside owning a farm and a vessel, almost the whole town owed him.

It has been rarely found that a state of hardship and poverty has excited envy. But Mr. Gypsum began to be eyed with considerable dislike. There was no reason why he should be growing rich so fast, when everybody else was poor. A great many vessels, therefore, were put upon the stocks; and next year plaster at the Lines was a mere drug.

When a person enters into trade, he cannot always tell exactly when or how he may get out of it. The vessels were now built; to sell them at a fair price was out of the question; and to lay them up, dead loss. Still the Lines afforded a little relief, which my townsmen readily embraced. In the plaster market there are always more goods than money, and it frequently happened that merchants, who would not give cash, would be very willing to exchange goods at a fair profit. The greater part of goods, it is true, could not be got home without smuggling; but this was easily got over. There is not one of my neighbours who would not kick mightily at the name of rogue; and among us, were any person to take a penny from the pocket of another, the whole town would cry out against such a sinful and shameful operation: but cheating the whole community at once, was so far from being considered as either sin or shame, that Deacon Scruple, who allowed nothing to be sung in his vessel but hymns, was the greatest smuggler of the whole.

Beside flour and corn, there were now brought into the town, gin, tea, and a great variety of other articles which persons are very apt to think necessary comforts. But as plaster was now a drug at the Lines, on account of the multitude of carriers; so, in our town, there were more goods than good customers. When goods, however, are on hand, they must be sold. Where the profit, too, is considerable, it is a temptation to traders to make large allowances for the responsibility of buyers. All my neighbours who had been purchasing flour and corn, were equally willing to add the other articles to their comfort; and, as Mr. Ledger, who imported for himself, not only paid the duties, but began to be a little scrupulous about crediting, they carried their custom to the new traders. The young folks, also, who worked at the plaster, were always very ready to buy. In the meantime, the new traders, by appearing to own vessels and do a great deal of business, received credit from everybody who had anything to sell. But, by and by, everybody wanted his own; and when the merchants began to call in their accounts, the young folks had nothing; and the old people who had found it hard to raise grain, found it harder to raise money; and the new merchants in general, finding that, after smuggling in goods for the benefit of the town, they had been dealing with rogues, became dissatisfied, and, at the persuasion of the sheriff, retired from business.

As Mr. Gypsum had been a little forehanded, he stood it longer than any of them. But no man who is always going back, can always keep his feet. The neighbours, in striving to be rich, had ruined his trade. His smuggled goods, also, like theirs, were sold upon trust. Now, however, the other traders had retired, and there was the prospect of doing something; when unfortunately a great storm in the Bay wrecked his vessel with a large cargo of goods, and, at the same time broke through a weak portion of his marsh dyke, which, in the hurry of business, he had neglected to mend. In this state, my cousin Harrow, who had for a long time supplied him with beef and other articles, recollecting how much custom Mr. Gypsum had given him, begged hard with the sheriff to accommodate him in his house, till he could collect his debts.

For the state of Mr. Gypsum's domestic affairs, I must refer to my account of Jack Scorem's family: only Mrs. Gypsum, being a trader's wife, conducted matters in a more genteel way. Her husband was a merchant, and kept company with gentlemen; and everything about his house ought to correspond with his station. One thing I recollect, that go into Mr. Gypsum's house at any hour of the day, you would find the gin bottle standing upon the table. Smuggled gin was cheap; it also helped on trade among the customers; and Mr. Gypsum himself never failed to set them a good example. Not that he was by any means a professed drunkard. But people who are from home, from the want of domestic comforts, are apt to become listless; and hence, when he and the sailors were lolling about the deck without anything to do, they would frequently take a glass to help away the time. I never heard that he was in the practice of anything to do him harm; for, with the exception of a troublesome disease in his nose, he is a sound, healthy man. This, he says, is the effect of beating up the Bay, one night late in the fall, against a violent north-wester: And here, from Mr. Gypsum's sad experience, I would warn all your readers that there is nothing like taking a disease of this kind at its very commencement; for, when it gets far on, the cure is worse than the disease. Through neglect Mr. Gypsum's nose became worse and worse, till it burned like fire. At last he got alarmed, and applied to an old lady in our town, noted for curing cancers. But, after using for a long time, to no purpose, a poultice of cow-dung soaked in cold water, he found out by mere accident, that holding the afflicted member over a glass of spirits, gave him instant relief; and now, as one glass has not the same effect twice, he will never get over the expense of keeping it easy.

Another of the sheriff's lodgers is Mr. Soakem, the tavern-keeper. Like the rest of us, he began the world by settling upon a farm. At first, he was a hard-working man, and soon made himself comfortable. But he was very eager to be rich, and he would frequently compare his hard labour with his little gains, as he called them. At last, one day, passing Mr. Tipple's, and observing the great number of horses which were fastened to the fence, it occurred to him that a large proportion of the township passed by his house, and he might as well keep tavern as not. He would mind the business of the farm, and Mrs. Soakem would attend to the travellers. Accordingly, he applied for license in the usual way.

When our parson, who was then young and spry, heard of it, he used every argument in his power to dissuade him. He begged him to consider what religion could be in a family, open at all hours, to all kinds of company. He entreated him to reflect upon the influence which the profligate conduct of vagabonds must have upon his children. He told him that a person entering upon any line of life should view those who are in it, and asked him, how he would like to see himself and his family like Tipple. He conjured him to prefer his religious character and prospects to a little wealth with such fearful hazards. And lastly, he denounced that, where one man's sin is another man's gain, the judgment of God is the amount of the profit. Still, Mr. Soakem was not convinced. Houses of entertainement were necessary, and might be very decently kept by religious people; and he hoped that the parson knew him better than to compare him to Tipple. When Mr. Drone found his arguments fruitless, he applied to the magistrates. He told them that taverns are at best but necessary nuisances, and ought not to be multiplied. He bid them look round the township, and see how many had been ruined by living in their neighbourhood. And as he got on, becoming gradually more earnest, he said they had received His Majesty's commission for better purposes, than to grant a license to every fool who chose to ruin himself and his family; that they were the guardians of good order; and, that, if they placed temptations in the way of the unwary, they were the partakers of other men's sins; and might assure themselves that the gall and wormwood would be shared between them.

Our magistrates have always been in the practice of giving licenses to all who request them. The town, they say, needs the license money; and, if the taverns increase too much, those who keep them, will get tired of the business. They were, therefore, not well-pleased that Parson Drone should interfere, and pretend to instruct them in their official duties. They never meddled with his preaching, and he had no right to interfere with them. Hence, partly at the solicitation of Mr. Soakem, and partly from opposition to the parson, the license was granted.

When Mr. Soakem opened his house of entertainment, he was eager to get rich. At the same time, he was really an industrious honest man; and he commenced with a firm determination to show Parson Drone and the whole town, that he was a different man from Tipple, and kept another sort of a house. Accordingly, as his character was known, everything at first went admirably on. The young folks went where they could get card-playing and fun; and nobody lodged at Mr. Soakem's tavern, except those sober travellers who wished to take their glass moderately and quietly after the fatigues of the day. As his custom was thus small, and [the] whole attention of the family directed to have everything clean and comfortable, travellers never failed to be pleased; and, frequently, to show their satisfaction, as Mr. Soakem was a very conversable man, they would invite him to chat an hour with them and take a glass of grog.

When there happens to be a good tavern upon the road, everybody soon knows of it. Mr. Soakem's trade began to enlarge very fast. This produced a corresponding exertion to please; and everybody was pleased. About this time I observed, that, from the attention which the tavern required, my neighbour's farm did not look so well as it used to do. From the hurry of travellers, also, family prayers and graces would be sometimes hurried over, and sometimes omitted; but, at first, this only happened in unavoidable cases.

Mr. Soakem was now in prosperous circumstances, and making money very fast. Whether it was on account of his good conduct, or because he was getting rich, I cannot exactly say; but he began to be very much respected, and his friends thought him well-qualified to be one of the justices for the town. He was no longer plain Boniface, but Mr. Soakem; and I have even seen some of his letters from your town merchants, with, Esq[uire] to his name. Mr. Soakem, having thus acquired much respectability, now studied to conduct himself with the decent dignity which became him. Instead of bustling about, as formerly, when a traveller arrived, to get everything comfortable, as his children were now growing up and should learn to do something, the horses were left to the boys, and the girls had the cooking and other indoor affairs. Mrs. Soakem, too, began to assume a lady-like deportment; and though the very best of you Halifax gentry had stopped at the door, she would not have budged from her seat.

With this new arrangement travellers were not always satisfied, and like the discontented in all ages, they looked back with regret to good old times. They complained that, in the house, there were far more attendants than service; and whether it was that the boys had given the horses too much to eat, they could never get them to start from the door without a good deal of whipping and spurring. With these things, it must be confessed, Mr. Soakem was altogether unacquainted, for on account of the enlargement of his business and other causes, he was often from home.

I do not know how it is in Halifax; but, in the country, it is really a great hardship to be a respectable gentleman. Such a person, for the sake of character, must do a great many things which he would otherwise avoid. Accordingly, when Mr. Soakem was abroad, in order to maintain his reputation, he would stop at every tavern on the road, and show how a gentleman ought to behave. In the meantime, the young people were left to manage both the farm and the house of entertainment. This was more than they could well do; and, besides, not very consistent with sober and industrious habits. They had learned, also, whose children they were. Now, this kind of knowledge never fails to influence strongly the conduct of youth. They did not see why Mr. Soakem's children should be always drudging upon a farm like beasts, or be the servant of every fellow who chose to come along the road. Of course, when their father was from home, and he was from home very often, they would visit their companions, and their companions would visit them; and travellers, understanding how things stood, passed on to the New Inn about half a mile distant. In short, Mr. Soakem's gradually became like the habitation of the wicked. He was rarely in it himself; his children were always strolling about; and no traveller came near it; when, at last, one day the sheriff calling and finding him at home, remarked, that he must now be very lonely, and insisted upon introducing him to the company in which I found him.

I remember, when Mr. Soakem began to keep tavern, it happened to be the subject of conversation between Parson Drone and myself.

"I'll tell you," says he, "Mr. Stepsure, how it will turn out." (Among the neighbours I am plain Mephibosheth, but he called me Mr. Stepsure.) "I'll tell you, Mr. Stepsure, how it will turn out. Our neighbour Soakem is a well-meaning, decent man; but eager to be rich, and totally ignorant of the influence of external circumstances upon human character and conduct. He is determined to keep tavern. A tavern must be open at all hours, and to all kinds of company. Irregularity in eating and sleeping requires the comfort of drinking. In a family, too, the want of good order destroys all personal and family religion; and, when our neighbour's children are deprived of his present good example, they will learn to imitate his guests. In short, Mr. Soakem, between tasting at home and drinking abroad, will become a mere sot. His fine family of children will be the prey of ill example and idleness: and Mrs. Soakem, poor woman, who dreams of being rich, will come upon the town. It is well for you, Mr. Mephibosheth Stepsure, that you are lame of both feet, and cannot run about like the rest of the town. They are a bustling, bargaining, running-about sort of folks. But depend upon it, it is, as the wise man says, a sore travail and an evil disease. I have generally seen, that he who, instead of minding his farm, is always running about, needs a long rest at last; but, instead of running home to get it, he stops at the sheriff's."

Accordingly, Mr. Soakem's boys are mere lazy, drunken vagabonds. His daughters, too, who are really finelooking girls, have become pert, idle hussies, without industry and economy. Mrs. Soakem, through the misfortunes of the family, has lost all heart to well-doing; for, what can a woman in such circumstances do? And, when I arrived at the sheriff's, I found Mr. Soakem with eyes like collops, poring upon the cards, and the grog before him.

MEPHIBOSHETH STEPSURE

Thomas Chandler Haliburton (1796-1865)

Called by Artemus Ward "The Father of American Humour", Thomas Haliburton influenced the humour of Ward himself, perhaps of Mark Twain, who parallels certain of his characters and incidents, and possibly of Charles Dickens whose Pickwick Papers appeared in 1835 after a number of reprints of *The Clockmaker*. For a decade at least, Haliburton rivalled Dickens in popularity. He was perhaps the first native-born Canadian to achieve an international reputation in Britain and America and was the first colonial to receive a degree from Oxford University.

Haliburton was born in Windsor, Nova Scotia on December 17, 1796, a third generation Canadian whose paternal grandfather moved from Boston to Nova Scotia after the expulsion of the Acadians in 1755. Educated locally he attended King's College, Windsor, founded in 1789 as an arts college and an Anglican theological centre. Graduating in 1815, he studied law and began practising at Annapolis Royal in 1820. Appointed to the House of Assembly in Halifax in 1826, Haliburton advocated a number of new measures such as the Catholic Emancipation Bill allowing Catholics to hold office, and the permanent endowment of Pictou Academy, a Presbyterian College. While the latter passed the House, it was rejected by Council and Haliburton resigned in 1829. In the same year he was appointed as Chief Justice for the Court of Common Pleas in the Middle Division of Nova Scotia, replacing his father who had died that year. In 1841 he became Judge of the Supreme Court of Nova Scotia and held this position to 1856 when he moved to Great Britain. Here he was elected to the British Parliament in 1859 as member from Launceston but had little influence in the House of Commons from this time until his death, for the members were unable to comprehend his ideal of a world-wide Empire of British peoples, an ideal before its time. In 1858 he received a Doctor of Civil Law from Oxford. He died in England in 1865.

Haliburton first became involved in literary circles when he moved to Halifax in 1826 and became a member of Joseph Howes's "Club" whose members devoted their time to writing witty satires on politics, literature and society. As editor of *The Novascotian*, Howe published in 1829 Haliburton's *Historical and Statistical Account of Nova Scotia*, a revision of an anonymous pamphlet "A General Description of Nova Scotia" appearing in 1823 and reprinted in 1825. In two volumes, the *Account* is a romanticized history which may have influenced the treatment of later historians such as Parkman as well as Longfellow in his "Evangeline". In 1836 Howe also published *The*

Clockmaker; or, The Sayings and Doings of Sam Slick, of Slickville, a work pirated in 1837 by R. Bentley of London. Haliburton capitalized immediately on its popularity with a second series in 1838 and a third series in 1840, followed by *The Attaché; or, Sam Slick in England* (4 volumes, 1843-4), *Sam Slick's Wise Saws and Modern Instances* (1853) and *Nature and Human Nature* (1855). In addition he published *The Letter-Bag of the Great Western; or Life in a Steamer* (1840), *The Old Judge; or Life in a Colony* (1849), *The Season Ticket* (1860) and two anthologies of humour *Traits of American Humour* (1852) and *The Americans at Home; or Byeways, Backwoods and Prairies* (1855). His political works include *The Bubbles of Canada* (1839), "A Reply to the Report of the Earl of Durham" (1839), "Rule and Mis-Rule of the English in America" (1851), and two addresses in Great Britain, "On the Conditions, Resources and Prospects of North America" (1860) and "On the Repeal of Duties on Foreign and Colonial Wood" (1860).

The Clockmaker won Haliburton his reputation. Published first as a series of twenty-one sketches in Joseph Howe's paper *The Novascotian*, the work was an immediate success and appeared subsequently in seventy editions, being translated as well into French and German. Intended to popularize Haliburton's social comments and economic recommendations for the province which, in *The Historical and Statistical Account of Nova Scotia* had fallen on deaf ears, *The Clockmaker* owed its popularity to the inimitable Sam Slick. Inspired by Seba Smith's Jack Downing of Maine, Sam quickly became an international character and was even celebrated in a popular London street ballad of the time.

TEXT:

The Clockmaker. Halifax : Joseph Howe, 1836.

See also:

Ray Palmer Baker. *A History of English Canadian Literature to the Confederation.* Cambridge: Harvard University Press, 1920.

V. O. Chittick. *Thomas Chandler Haliburton.* New York: 1924.

John D. Logan. *Thomas Chandler Haliburton.* Toronto: Ryerson, 1925.

No. II. The Clockmaker.

I had heard of Yankee clock pedlars, tin pedlars, and bible pedlars, especially of him who sold Polyglot Bibles *(all in English)* to the amount of sixteen thousand pounds. The house of every substantial farmer had three substantial ornaments, a wooden clock, a tin reflector, and a Polyglot Bible. How is it that an American can sell his wares, at whatever price he pleases, where a blue-nose would fail to make a sale at all? I will enquire of the Clockmaker the secret of his success. What a pity it is, Mr. *Slick*, (for such was his name,) what a pity it is, said I, that you, who are so successful in teaching these people the value of *clocks*, could not also teach them the value of *time*. I guess, said he, they have got that ring to grow on their horns yet, which every four year old has in our country. We reckon hours and minutes to be dollars and cents. They do nothing in these parts, but eat, drink, smoke, sleep, ride about, lounge at taverns, make speeches at temperance meetings, and talk about *"House of Assembly."* If a man don't hoe his corn, and he don't get a crop, he says it is all owing to the Bank; and if he runs into debt and is sued, why [he] says the lawyers are a curse to the country. They are a most idle set of folks, I tell you. But how is it, said I, that you manage to sell such an immense number of clocks, (which certainly cannot be called necessary articles,) among a people with whom there seems to be so great a scarcity of money.

Mr. Slick paused, as if considering the propriety of answering the question, and looking me in the face, said, in a confidential tone, Why, I don't care if I do tell you, for the market is glutted, and I shall quit this circuit. It is done by a knowledge of *soft sawder* and *human natur*. But here is Deacon Flint's, said he, I have but one clock left, and I guess I will sell it to him. At the gate of a most comfortable looking farm house stood Deacon Flint, a respectable old man, who had understood the value of time better than most of his neighbours, if one might judge from the appearance of every thing about him. After the usual salutation, an invitation to "alight" was accepted by Mr. Slick, who said, he wished to take leave of Mrs. Flint before he left Colchester. We had hardly entered the house, before the Clockmaker pointed to the view from the window, and, addressing himself to me, said, if I was to tell them in Connecticut, there was such a farm as this away down east here in Nova Scotia, they would'nt believe me – why there aint such a location in all New England. The deacon has a hundred acres of dyke – seventy, said the deacon, only seventy. Well, seventy; but then there is your fine deep bottom, why I could run a ramrod into it – Interval, we call it, said the Deacon, who, though evidently pleased at this eulogium, seemed to wish the experiment of the ramrod to be tried in the right place – well interval if you please, (though Professor Eleazer Cumstick, in his work on Ohio, calls them bottoms,) is just as good as dyke. Then there is that water privilege, worth 3 or $4,000, twice as good as what Governor Cass paid $15,000 for. I wonder, Deacon, you don't put up a carding mill on it: the same works would carry a turning lathe, a shingle machine, a circular saw, grind bark, and _____. Too old, said the Deacon, too old for all those speculations – old, repeated the clock-maker, not you; why you are worth half a dozen of the young men we see, now-a-days, you are young enough to have – here he said something in a lower tone of voice, which I did not distinctly hear; but whatever it was, the Deacon was pleased, he smiled and said he did not think of such things now. But your beasts, dear me, your beasts must be put in and have a feed; saying which, he went out to order them to be taken to the stable. As the old gentleman closed the door after him, Mr. Slick drew near to me, and said in an under tone, that is what I call *"soft sawder."* An Englishman would pass that man as a sheep passes a hog in a pasture, without looking at him; or, said he, looking rather archly, if he was mounted on a pretty smart horse, I guess he'd trot away, *if he could.* Now I find – here his lecture on *"soft sawder"* was cut short by the entrance of Mrs. Flint. Jist come to say good bye, Mrs. Flint. What, have you sold all your clocks? yes, and very low, too, for money is scarce, and I wished to close the concarn; no, I am wrong in saying all, for I have just one left. Neighbor Steel's wife asked to have the refusal of it, but I guess I won't sell it; I had but two of them, this one and the feller of it, that I sold Governor Lincoln. General Green, the Secretary of State for Maine, said he'd give me 50 dollars for this here one – it has composition wheels and patent axles, it is a beautiful article – a real first chop – no mistake, genuine superfine, but I guess I'll take it back; and beside, Squire Hawk might think kinder harder, that I did not give him the offer. Dear me, said Mrs. Flint, I should like to see it, where is it? It is in a chest of mine over the way, at Tom Tape's store, I guess he can ship it on to Eastport. That's a good man, said Mrs. Flint, jist let's look at it. Mr. Slick, willing to oblige, yielded to these entreaties, and soon produced the clock – a gawdy, highly varnished, trumpery looking affair. He placed it on the chimney-piece, where its beauties were pointed out and duly appreciated by Mrs. Flint, whose admiration was about ending in a proposal, when Mr. Flint returned from giving his directions about the care of the horses. The Deacon praised the clock, he too thought it a handsome one; but the Deacon was a prudent man, he had a watch, he was sorry, but he had no occasion for a clock. I guess you're in the wrong furrow this time, Deacon, it ant for sale, said Mr. Slick; and if it was, I reckon neighbor Steel's wife would have it, for she gives me no peace about it. Mrs. Flint said, that Mr. Steele had enough to do, poor man, to pay his interest, without buying clocks for his wife. It's no concarn of mine, said Mr. Slick, as long as he pays me, what he has to do, but I guess I don't want to sell it, and beside it comes too high; that clock can't be made at Rhode Island under 40 dollars. Why it ant possible, said the Clockmaker, in apparent surprise, looking at his watch, why as I'm alive it is 4 o'clock, and if I hav'nt been two hours here – how on airth shall I reach River Philip to-night? I'll tell you what, Mrs. Flint, I'll leave the clock in your care till I return on my way to the States – I'll set it a going and put it to the right time. As soon as this operation was performed, he delivered the key to the deacon with a sort of serio-comic injunction to wind up the clock every Saturday night, which Mrs. Flint said she would take care should be done, and promised to remind her husband of it, in case he should chance to forget it.

That, said the Clockmaker as soon as we were mounted, that I call *'human natur!'* Now that clock is sold for 40 dollars – it cost me just 6 dollars and 50 cents. Mrs. Flint will never let Mrs. Steel have the refusal – nor will the deacon learn until I call for the clock, that having once indulged in the use of a superfluity, how difficult it is to give it up. We can do without any article of luxury we have never had, but when once obtained, it is not *in 'human natur'* to surrender it voluntarily. Of fifteen thousand sold by myself and partners in this Province, twelve thousand were left in this manner, and only ten clocks were ever returned – when we called for them they invariably bought them. We trust to *'soft sawder'* to get them into the house, and to *'human natur'* that they never come out of it.

No. III. The Silent Girls.

Do you see them are swallows, said the Clockmaker, how low they fly? Well I presume we shall have rain right away, and them noisy critters, them gulls how close they keep to the water, down there in the Shubenacadie; well that's a sure sign. If we study natur, we don't want no thermometer. But I guess we shall be in time to get under cover in a shinglemaker's shed about three miles ahead on us. We had just reached the deserted hovel when the rain fell in torrents.

I reckon, said the Clockmaker, as he sat himself down on a bundle of shingles, I reckon they are bad off for inns in this country. When a feller is too lazy to work here, he paints his name over his door, and calls it a tavern, and as like as not he makes the whole neighbourhood as lazy as himself – it is about as easy to find a good inn in Halifax, as it is to find wool on a goat's back. An inn, to be a good concarn, must be built a purpose, you can no more make a good tavern out of a common dwelling house, I expect, than a good coat out of an old pair of trowsers. They are etarnal lazy, you may depend – now there might be a grand spec made there, in building a good Inn and a good Church. What a sacrilegious and unnatural union, said I, with most unaffected surprise. Not at all, said Mr. Slick, we build both on speculation in the States, and make a good deal of profit out of 'em too, I tell you. We look out a good sightly place, in a town like Halifax, that is pretty considerably well peopled, with folks that are good marks; and if there is no real right down good preacher among them, we build a handsome Church, touched off like a New-York liner, a real taking looking thing – and then we look out for a preacher, a crack man, a regular ten horse power chap – well, we hire him, and we have to give pretty high wages too, say twelve hundred or sixteen hundred dollars a year. We take him at first on trial for a Sabbath or two, to try his paces, and if he takes with the folks, if he goes down well, we clinch the bargain, and let and sell the pews; and, I tell you it pays well and makes a real good investment. There were few better specs among us than Inns and Churches, until the Railroads came on the carpet – as soon as the novelty of the new preacher wears off, we hire another, and that keeps up the steam. I trust it will be long, very long, my friend, said I, ere the rage for speculation introduces "the money changers into the temple," with us. Mr. Slick looked at me with a most ineffable expression of pity and surprise. Depend on it, Sir, said he, with a most philosophical air, this Province is much behind the intelligence of the age. But if it is behind us in that respect, is is a long chalk ahead on us in others.

I never seed or heard tell of a country that had so many natural privileges as this. Why there are twice as many harbors and water powers here, as we have all the way from Eastport to New Or*leens*. They have all they can ax, and more than they desarve. They have iron, coal, slate, grindstone, lime, firestone, gypsum, freestone, and a list as long as an auctioneer's catalogue. But they are either asleep, or stone blind to them. Their shores are crowded with fish, and their lands covered with wood. A government that lays as light on 'em as a down counterpin, and no taxes. Then look at their dykes. The Lord seems to have made 'em on purpose for such lazy folks. If you were to tell the citizens of our country, that these dykes had been cropped for a hundred years without manure, they'd say, they guessed you had seen Col. Crockett, the greatest hand at a flam in our nation. You have heerd tell of a man who could'nt see London for the houses, I tell you, if we had this country, you could'nt see the harbors for the shipping. There'd be a rush of folks to it, as there is in one of our inns, to the dinner table, when they sometimes get jammed together in the door-way, and a man has to take a running leap over their heads, afore he can get in. A little nigger boy in New York found a diamond worth 2,000 dollars; well, he sold it to a watchmaker for 50 cents – the little critter didn't know no better. *Your people are just like the nigger boy, they don't know the value of their diamond.*

Do you know the reason monkeys are no good? because they chatter all day long – so do the niggers – and so do the blue noses of Nova Scotia – its all talk and no work; now, with us its all work and no talk – in our ship yards, our factories, our mills, and even in our vessels, there's no talk – a man can't work and talk too. I guess if you were at the factories at Lowell we'd show you a wonder – *five hundred galls at work together all in silence.* I don't think our great country has such a real natural curiosity as that – I expect the world don't contain the beat of that; for a woman's tongue goes so slick of itself, without water power or steam, and moves so easy on its hinges, that its no easy matter to put a spring stop on it, I tell you – it comes as natural as drinkin mint julip.

I don't pretend to say the galls don't nullify the rule, sometimes at intermission and arter hours, but when they do, if they don't let go, then its a pity. You have heerd a school come out, of little boys, Lord its no touch to it; or a flock of geese at it, they are no more a match for em than a pony is for a coach-horse. But when they are at work, all's as still as sleep and no snoring. I guess we have a right to brag o' that invention – we trained the dear critters, so they don't think of striking the minutes and seconds no longer.

Now the folks of Halifax take it all out in talking – they talk of steamboats, whalers and rail roads – but they all end where they begin – in talk. I don't think I'd be out in my latitude, if I was to say they beat the women kind at that. One feller says, I talk of going to England – another says, I talk of going to the Country – while a third says, I talk of going to sleep. If we happen to speak of such things, we say: 'I'm right off down East; or I'm away off South,' and away we go, jist like a streak of lightning.

When we want folks to talk, we pay 'em for it, such as ministers, lawyers, and members of congress: but then we expect the use of their tongues, and not their hands; and when we pay folks to work, we expect the use of their hands, and not their tongues. I guess work don't come kind o' natural to the people of this Province, no more than it does to a full bred horse. I expect they think they have a little *too much blood* in 'em for work, for they are near about as proud as they are lazy.

Now the bees know how to sarve out such chaps, for they have their drones too. Well they reckon its no fun, a making honey all summer, for these idle critters to eat all winter – so they give 'em Lynch Law. They have a regular built mob of citizens, and string up the drones like the Vixburg gamblers. Their maxim is, and not a bad one neither I guess, 'no work, no honey.'

No. VII. Go Ahead.

WHEN we resumed our conversation, the Clockmaker said, "I guess we are the greatest nation on the face of the airth, and the most enlightened too." This was rather too arrogant to pass unnoticed, and I was about replying, that whatever doubts there might be on that subject, there could be none whatever that they were the most *modest*; when he continued "we go ahead," the Novascotians go "astarn." Our ships go ahead of the ships of other folks, our steam boats beat the British in speed, and so do our stage coaches; and I reckon a real right down New York trotter might stump the univarse for going "ahead." But since we introduced the Rail Roads if we dont go "ahead" its a pity. We never fairly knew what going the whole hog was till then; we actilly went ahead of ourselves, and that's no easy matter I tell you. If they only had edication here, they might learn to do so too, but they dont know nothin. You undervalue them, said I, they have their College and Academies, their grammar schools and primary institutions, and I believe there are few among them who cannot read and write.

I guess all that's nothin, said he. As for Latin and Greek, we dont valy it a cent; we teach it, and so we do painting and music, because the English do, and we like to go ahead on em, even in them [th]are things. As for reading, its well enough for them that has nothing to do, and writing is plaguy apt to bring a man to States-prison, particularly if he writes his name so like another man as to have it mistaken for his'n. Cyphering is the thing – if a man knows how to cypher, he is sure to grow rich. We are a 'calculating' people, we all cypher.

A horse that wont go ahead, is apt to run back, and the more you whip him the faster he goes astarn. That's jist the way with the Nova Scotians; they have been running back so fast lately, that they have tumbled over a *Bank* or two, and nearly broke their necks; and now they've got up and shook themselves, they swear their dirty clothes and bloody noses are all owing to the *Banks*. I guess if they wont look ahead for the future, they'll larn to look behind, and see if there's a bank near hand em.

A Bear always goes down a tree *starn foremost*. He is a cunning critter, he knows tante safe to carry a heavy load over his head, and his rump is so heavy, he dont like to trust it over hisn, for fear it might take a lurch, and carry him heels over head, to the ground; so he lets his starn down first, and his head arter. I wish the blue-noses would find as good an excuse in their rumps for running backwards as he has. But the bear *'cyphers;'* he knows how many pounds his hams weigh, and he *'calculates'* if he carried them up in the air, they might be top heavy for him.

If we had this Province we'd go to work and 'cypher' right off.

Halifax is nothing without a river or back country; add nothing to nothing, and I guess you have nothing still – add a Rail Road to the Bay of Fundy, and how much do you git? That requires cyphering – it will cost $300,000, or £75,000 your money – add for notions omitted in the addition column, one third, and it makes even money – £100,000. Interest at 5 per cent £5,000 a year. Now turn over the slate and count up freight – I make it upwards of £25,000 a year. If I had you at the desk, I'd shew you a bill of items.

Now comes *"subtraction;"* deduct cost of engines, wear and tear, and expenses, and what not, and reduce it for shortness down to £5000 a year, the amount of interest. What figures have you got now? you have an investment that pays interest, I guess, and if it don't pay more then I dont know chalk from cheese. But suppose it dont, and that it only yields 2½ per cent, (and it requires good cyphering, I tell you, to say how it would act with folks that like going astarn better than going ahead,) what would them are wise ones say then? Why the critters would say it wont pay; but I say the sum ant half stated. Can you count in your head? Not to any extent, said I. Well, that's an etarnal pity, said the Clockmaker, for I should like to show you *Yankee Cyphering.* What is the entire real estate of Halifax worth, at a valeation? I really cannot say. Ah, said he, I see you dont cypher, and Latin and Greek wont do; them [th]are people had no rail-roads. Well, find out, and then only add ten per cent to it, for increased value, and if it don't give the cost of a rail-road, then my name is not Sam Slick. Well, the land between Halifax and Ardoise is worth_____nothing, add 5 per cent to that, and send the sum to the College, and ax the students how much it comes to. But when you get into Hants County, I guess you have land worth coming all the way from Boston to see. His Royal Highness the King, I guess, hasn't got the like in his dominions. Well, add 15 per cent to all them [th]are lands that border on Windsor Basin, and 5 per cent to what butts on Basin of Mines, and then, what do you get? A pretty considerable sum I tell you – but its no use to give you the *chalks*, if you can't keep the *tallies*. Now we will lay down the schoolmaster's assistant, and take up another book every bit and grain as good as that, although these folks affect to sneer at it – I mean human natur. Ah! said I, a knowledge of that was of great service to you, certainly, in the sale of your clock to the old Deacon; let us see how it will assist you now. What does a clock want that's run down? said he. Undoubtedly to be wound up, I replied; I guess you've hit it this time. The folks of Halifax have run down, and they'll never go to all etarnity, till they are wound up into motion; the works are all good, and it is plaguy well cased and set – it only wants a *key*. Put this rail-road into operation, and the activity it will inspire into business, the new life it will give the place, will surprise you. Its like lifting a child off its crawling, and putting him on his legs to run – see how the little critter goes ahead arter that. A kurnel, (I don't mean a Kurnel of militia, for we don't valy that breed o' cattle nothing – they do nothing but strut about and screech all day, like peacocks,) but a kurnel of grain, when sowed, will stool into several shoots, and each shoot bear many kurnels, and will multiply itself thus – 4 times 1 is 4, and 4 times 25 is a hundred, (you see all natur cyphers, except the blue noses.) Jist so, this here rail-road will not perhaps beget other rail-roads, but it will beget a spirit of enterprise, that will beget other useful improvements. It will enlarge the sphere and the means of trade, open new sources of traffic and supply – develop resources – and what is of more value perhaps than all – beget motion. It will teach the folks that go astarn or stand stock still, like the statehouse in Boston, (though they do say the foundation of that has moved a little this summer) not only to go "*ahead,*"*but to nullify time and space.*

Here his horse (who, feeling the animation of his master, had been restive of late) set off at a most prodigious rate of trotting. It was some time before he was reined up. When I overtook him, the Clockmaker said, "this old Yankee horse, you see, understands our word 'go ahead' better nor these blue noses."

What is it, he continued, what is it that 'fetters' the heels of a young country, and hangs like 'a poke' around its neck? what retards the cultivation of its soil, and the improvement of its fisheries? – the high price of labor, I guess. Well, what's a rail-road? The substitution of mechanical for human and animal labor, on a scale as grand as our great country. Labor is dear in America, and cheap in Europe. A rail-road, therefore, is comparatively no manner of use to them, to what it is to us – it does wonders there, but it works miracles here. There it makes the old man younger, but here it makes a child a giant. To us it is river, bridge, road and canal, all one. It saves what we han't got to spare, men, horses, carts, vessels, barges, and what's all in all – time.

Since the creation of the Univarse, I guess it's the greatest invention, arter man. Now this is what I call "cyphering" arter human natur, while figures are cyphering arter "the assistant." These two sorts of cyphering makes idecation – and you may depend on't Squire, there is nothing like folks cyphering, if they want to "go ahead."

III PRE-CONFEDERATION: THE CANADAS

Catharine Parr Traill (1802-1899)

A budding naturalist, Catharine Parr Traill was also a writer of some note in Upper Canada. Fifth daughter of the Stricklands, a family made famous by Agnes and Elizabeth's *Lives of the Queens of England, Lives of the Queens of Scotland* and *Lives of the Bachelor Kings of England*, Catharine Parr Traill was the elder sister of Susannah Moodie and of Samuel Strickland, both of whom also emigrated to Canada and were known on the Canadian literary scene. Catharine published several children's books and three studies of local plant life, as well as her better known works *The Backwoods of Canada* and *The Female Emigrant's Guide*.

Catharine Parr Traill was born in London, England in 1802, the fifth daughter of Thomas Strickland, a London businessman. Shortly after, Thomas retired and bought a country estate, Reydon Hall in Suffolk. The children were educated at home and at Dr. Volpy's School in Norwich. After the end of the Napoleonic Wars, Thomas Strickland encountered business difficulties; following his death in 1818, the family moved to the town house in Norwich. The next ten years the family spent quietly at Norwich and again at Reydon Hall. After the departure of Samuel in 1825 for Canada and of Thomas Junior shortly after for India, the household was all female. In 1831 Susannah married John Dunbar Moodie who introduced Catharine to a regimental brother, Thomas Traill, a widower. Thomas and Catharine were married on May 13, 1832 and on July 7, sailed for Canada, one week later than the Moodies. They arrived at Grosse Isle on August 11 but Catharine came down with cholera in Montreal and it was not until September that they joined Samuel and his family in Douro Township near Peterborough. Here they settled and were joined by John and Susannah in 1834. In 1839 the Traills sold their farm and moved near Peterborough, first to Auburn and then to Scotch village (later Ashburnham). The next few years were hard for the Traills; they moved in 1843 to a farm in Otonabee Township but were forced to sell it to settle a debt incurred by Thomas in aiding a friend. They moved to Ashburnham again in 1845 and to Rice Lake Plains in 1846. In 1851 his creditors took Thomas to court and left the family without a farthing and in 1857 their home itself was destroyed by fire. For the next two years they lived with their son Jamie and the Samuel Stricklands. Following the death of Thomas in 1859, Catharine returned to Lakefield and built a home with a grant of £100 from the British government in honour of her services to the colonies. She also received a grant in 1896 from the British government and Ottawa. She died in 1899 in Lakefield at the age of 97.

Catharine published her first book at the age of sixteen *The Blind Highland Piper and Other Tales*; the manuscript was discovered on the desk by her guardian and sent to a publisher. Before emigrating to Canada, she brought out several children's books including the popular *Adventures of Little Downy, the Field-Mouse*, and *The Young Emigrants*, "pictures of Canada calculated to amuse and instruct the minds of youth" and based on correspondence from friends. *The Backwoods of Canada* appeared in 1836 and *The Female Emigrant's Guide* in 1854 (also titled *The Female Settler's Guide* and *The Canadian Emigrant's Guide*). She continued her books for children with *The Canadian Crusoes* (1852 – also titled *Lost in the Backwoods*), *Lady Mary and Her Nurse: A Peep into the Canadian Forest* (1856) and *Cot and Cradle-Stories* (1895). In addition, she wrote *Rambles in the Canadian Forest* (1859), *Canadian Wild Flowers* (1869) and *Studies of Plant Life in Canada* (1885), the last two illustrated with hand-painted plates by her niece Agnes Moodie Fitzgibbon. *Pearls and Pebbles or Notes of an Old Naturalist* appeared in 1894 when she was 92 years old.

The Backwoods of Canada, subtitled "Letters from the Wife of an emigrant officer, illustrative of the domestic economy of North America", was culled from her letters to her mother and carefully edited to remove personal material. It was immediately popular and went through several editions in the next few years, one in French and one in German. Like Susannah Moodie's *Roughing It in the Bush* it provides an account of her life in the woods, the details of settling, building a home, importing groceries, attending bees and other daily activities of the bush. It is more objective than Susannah's account and shows evidence of Catherine's scientific bent both in the detailed description of the plants and animals of the area and in the style itself. *The Female Settler's Guide,* a Canadian country version of Mrs. Beaton's *Book of Household Management* (1861), was also popular, although one hundred books of this type were published in the same decade. It instructs new settlers on furnishing a house, buying a stove, making rag rugs, and managing servants, and provides a set of hints (in alphabetical order) on such subjects as the ague, beer, bees, borrowing and breadmaking as well as recipes for all needs such as dandelion coffee, black squirrels and baked eel served with a sprig of parsley.

TEXTS:

The Backwoods of Canada. London: Knight, 1836.
The Female Emigrant's Guide. Toronto: Maclear, 1854.

See also:

Audrey Morris. *Gentle Pioneers.* Toronto: Musson, 1968. Hodder & Stoughton, 1968.

Introduction to *The Backwoods of Canada.* ed. Clara Thomas. Toronto: New Canadian Library, 1966.

Introduction to *The Canadian Settler's Guide.* ed. Clara Thomas.
   Toronto: New Canadian Library, 1969.
Sara Eaton. *Lady of the Backwoods.* Toronto: McClelland and Stewart, 1969.

From *The Backwoods of Canada*

LETTER VIII.

Inconveniences of first Settlement. – Difficulty of obtaining Provisions and other
necessaries. – Snow-storm and Hurricane. – Indian Summer, and setting in of
Winter. – Process of clearing the Land.

November the 20th, 1832.

Our log-house is not yet finished, though it is in a state of forwardness. We are still indebted to the hospitable kindness of S_____and
his wife for a home. This being their first settlement on their land they
have as yet many difficulties, in common with all residents in the
backwoods, to put up with this year. They have a fine block of land,
well situated; and S_____ laughs at the present privations, to which he
opposes a spirit of cheerfulness and energy that is admirably calculated
to effect their conquest. They are now about to remove to a larger and
more commodious house that has been put up this fall, leaving us the
use of the old one till our own is ready.

   We begin to get reconciled to our Robinson Crusoe sort of life, and
the consideration that the present evils are but temporary, goes a great
way towards reconciling us to them.

   One of our greatest inconveniences arises from the badness of our
roads, and the distance at which we are placed from any village or
town where provisions are to be procured.

   Till we raise our own grain and fatten our own hogs, sheep, and
poultry, we must be dependent upon the stores for food of every kind.
These supplies have to be brought up at considerable expense and loss
of time, through our beautiful bush roads; which, to use the words of
a poor Irish woman, "can't be no worser." "Och, darlint," she said,
"but they are just bad enough, and can't be no worser. Och, but they
arn't like to our iligant roads in Ireland."

   You may send down a list of groceries to be forwarded when a
team comes up, and when we examine our stores, behold rice, sugar,
currants, pepper, and mustard all jumbled into one mess. What think you
of a rice-pudding seasoned plentifully with pepper, mustard, and may be,

a little rappee or prince's mixture added by way of sauce. I think the recipe would cut quite a figure in the Cook's Oracle or Mrs. Dalgairn's Practice of Cookery, under the original title of a "bush pudding."
quite a figure in the Cook's Oracle or Mrs. Dalgairn's Practice of Cookery, under the original title of a "bush pudding."

And then woe and destruction to the brittle ware that may chance to travel through our roads. Lucky, indeed, are we if, through the superior carefulness of the person who packs them, more than one-half happens to arrive in safety. For such mishaps we have no redress. The storekeeper lays the accident upon the teamster, and the teamster upon the bad roads, wondering that he himself escapes with whole bones after a journey through the bush.

This is now the worst season of the year; – this, and just after the breaking up of the snow. Nothing hardly but an ox-cart can travel along the roads, and even that with difficulty, occupying two days to perform the journey; and the worst of the matter is, that there are times when the most necessary articles of provisions are not to be procured at any price. You see, then, that a settler in the bush requires to hold himself pretty independent, not only of the luxuries and delicacies of the table, but not unfrequently even of the very necessaries.

One time no pork is to be procured; another time there is a scarcity of flour, owing to some accident that has happened to the mill, or for the want of proper supplies of wheat for grinding; or perhaps the weather and bad roads at the same time prevent a team coming up, or people from going down. Then you must have recourse to a neighbour, if you have the good fortune to be near one, or fare the best you can on potatoes. The potatoe is indeed a great blessing here; new settlers would otherwise be often greatly distressed, and the poor man and his family who are without resources, without the potatoe must starve.

Once our stock of tea was exhausted, and we were unable to procure more. In this dilemma milk would have been an excellent substitute, or coffee, if we had possessed it; but we had neither the one nor the other, so we agreed to try the Yankee tea – hemlock sprigs boiled. This proved, to my taste, a vile decoction; though I recognized some herb in the tea that was sold in London at five shillings a pound, which I am certain was nothing better than dried hemlock leaves reduced to a coarse powder.

S———laughed at our wry faces, declaring the potation was excellent; and he set us all an example by drinking six cups of this truly sylvan beverage. His eloquence failed in gaining a single convert; we could not believe it was only second to young hyson. To his assurance that to its other good qualities it united medicinal virtues, we replied that, like all other physic, it was very unpalatable.

"After all," said S———, with a thoughtful air, "the blessings and the evils of this life owe their chief effect to the force of contrast, and are to be estimated by that principally. We should not appreciate the comforts we enjoy half so much did we not occasionally feel the want of them. How we shall value the conveniences of a cleared farm after a few years, when we can realize all the necessaries and many of the luxuries of life."

"And how we shall enjoy green tea after this odious decoction of hemlock," said I.

"Very true; and a comfortable frame-house, and nice garden, and pleasant pastures, after these dark forests, log-houses, and no garden at all."

"And the absence of horrid black stumps," rejoined I. "Yes, and the absence of horrid stumps. Depend upon it, my dear, your Canadian farm will seem to you a perfect paradise by the time it is all under cultivation; and you will look upon it with the more pleasure and pride from the consciousness that it was once a forest wild, which, by the effects of industry and well-applied means, has changed to fruitful fields. Every fresh comfort you realize around you will add to your happiness; every improvement within-doors or without will raise a sensation of gratitude and delight in your mind, to which those that revel in the habitual enjoyment of luxury, and even of the commonest advantages of civilization, must in a great degree be strangers. My pass-words are, 'Hope! Resolution! and Perseverance!' "

"This," said my husband, "is true philosophy; and the more forcible, because you not only recommend the maxim but practise it also." . . .

Hitherto my experience of the climate is favourable. The autumn has been very fine, though the frosts are felt early in the month of September; at first slightly, of a morning, but towards October more severely. Still, though the first part of the day is cold, the middle of it is warm and cheerful.

We already see the stern advances of winter. It commenced very decidedly from the breaking up of the Indian summer. November is not at all like the same month at home. The early part was soft and warm, the latter cold, with keen frosts and occasional falls of snow; but it does not seem to possess the dark, gloomy, damp character of our British Novembers. However, it is not one season's acquaintance with the climate that enables a person to form any correct judgment of its general character, but a close observance of its peculiarities and vicissitudes during many years' residence in the country.

I must now tell you what my husband is doing on our land. He has let out ten acres to some Irish choppers who have established themselves in the shanty for the winter. They are to receive fourteen dollars per acre for chopping, burning, and fencing in that quantity. The ground is to be perfectly cleared of everything but the stumps: these will take from seven to nine or ten years to decay; the pine, hemlock, and fir remain much longer. The process of clearing away the stumps is too expensive for new beginners to venture upon, labour being so high that it cannot be appropriated to any but indispensable work. The working season is very short on account of the length of time the frost remains on the ground. With the exception of chopping trees, very little can be done. Those that understand the proper management of uncleared land, usually underbrush (that is, cut down all the small timbers and brushwood), while the leaf is yet on them; this is piled in heaps, and the windfallen trees are chopped through in lengths, to be logged up in the spring with the winter's chopping. The latter end of the summer and the autumn are the best seasons for this work. The leaves then become quite dry and sear, and greatly assist in the important business of burning off the heavy timbers. Another reason is, that when the snow has fallen to some depth, the light timbers cannot be cut close to the ground, or the dead branches and other incumbrances collected and thrown in heaps.

We shall have about three acres ready for spring-crops, provided we get a good burning of that which is already chopped near the site of the house, – this will be sown with oats, pumpkins, Indian corn, and potatoes: the other ten acres will be ready for putting in a crop of wheat. So you see it will be a long time before we reap a harvest. We could not even get in spring-wheat early enough to come to perfection this year.

We shall try to get two cows in the spring, as they are little expense during the spring, summer, and autumn; and by the winter we shall have pumpkins and oat-straw for them.

LETTER IX.

Loss of a yoke of Oxen. – Construction of a Log-house. – Glaziers' and Carpenters' work. – Description of new Log-house. – Wild Fruits of the Country.

Lake House,
April 18, 1833.

But it is time that I should give you some account of our log-house, into which we moved a few days before Christmas. Many unlooked-for delays having hindered its completion before that time, I began to think it would never be habitable.

The first misfortune that happened was the loss of a fine yoke of oxen that were purchased to draw in the house-logs, that is, the logs for raising the walls of the house. Not regarding the bush as pleasant as their former master's cleared pastures, or perhaps foreseeing some hard work to come, early one morning they took into their heads to ford the lake at the head of the rapids, and march off, leaving no trace of their route excepting their footing at the water's edge. After many days spent in vain search for them, the work was at a stand, and for one month they were gone, and we began to give up all expectation of hearing any news of them. At last we learned they were some twenty miles off, in a distant township, having made their way through bush and swamp, creek and lake, back to their former owner, with an instinct that supplied to them the want of roads and compass.

Oxen have been known to traverse a tract of wild country to a distance of thirty or forty miles going in a direct line for their former haunts by unknown paths, where memory could not avail them. In the dog we consider it is scent as well as memory that guides him to his far-off home; – but how is this conduct of the oxen to be accounted for? They returned home through the mazes of interminable forests, where man, with all his reason and knowledge, would have been bewildered and lost.

It was the latter end of October before even the walls of our house were up. To effect this we called "a bee." Sixteen of our neighbours cheerfully obeyed our summons; and though the day was far from favourable, so faithfully did our hive perform their tasks, that by night the outer walls were raised.

The work went merrily on with the help of plenty of Canadian nectar (whiskey), the honey that our *bees* are solaced with. Some huge joints of salt pork, a peck of potatoes, with a rice-pudding, and a loaf as big as an enormous Cheshire cheese, formed the feast that was to regale them during the raising. This was spread out in the shanty, in *a very rural style.* In short, we laughed, and called it a *pic-nic in the backwoods;* and rude as was the fare, I can assure you, great was the satisfaction expressed by all the guests of every degree, our "bee" being considered as very well conducted. In spite of the difference of rank among those that assisted at the bee, the greatest possible harmony prevailed, and the party separated well pleased with the day's work and entertainment.

The following day I went to survey the newly-raised edifice, but was sorely puzzled, as it presented very little appearance of a house. It was merely an oblong square of logs raised one above the other, with open spaces between every row of logs. The spaces for the doors and windows were not then chopped out, and the rafters were not up. In short, it looked a very queer sort of a place, and I returned home a little disappointed, and wondering that my husband should be so well pleased with the progress that had been made. A day or two after this I again visited it. The *sleepers* were laid to support the floors, and the places for the doors and windows cut out of the solid timbers, so that it had not quite so much the look of a bird-cage as before.

After the roof was shingled, we were again at a stand, as no boards could be procured nearer than Peterborough, a long day's journey through horrible roads. At that time no saw-mill was in progress; now there is a fine one building within a little distance of us. Our flooring-boards were all to be sawn by hand, and it was some time before any one could be found to perform this necessary work, and that at high wages – six-and-sixpence per day. Well, the boards were at length down, but of course of unseasoned timber: this was unavoidable; so as they could not be planed we were obliged to put up with their rough unsightly appearance, for no better were to be had. I began to recall to mind the observation of the old gentleman with whom we travelled from Cobourg to Rice Lake. We console ourselves with the prospect that by next summer the boards will all be seasoned, and then the house is to be turned topsy-turvy, by having the floors all relaid, jointed, and smoothed.

The next misfortune that happened, was, that the mixture of clay and lime that was to plaster the inside and outside of the house between the chinks of the logs was one night frozen to stone. Just as the work was about half completed, the frost suddenly setting in, put a stop to our proceeding for some time, as the frozen plaster yielded neither to fire nor to hot water, the latter freezing before it had any effect on the mass, and rather making bad worse. Then the workman that was hewing the inside walls to make them smooth, wounded himself with the broad axe, and was unable to resume his work for some time.

I state these things merely to show the difficulties that attend us in the fulfilment of our plans, and this accounts in a great measure for the humble dwellings that settlers of the most respectable description are obliged to content themselves with at first coming to this country, – not, you may be assured, from inclination, but necessity: I could give you such narratives of this kind as would astonish you. After all, it serves to make us more satisfied than we should be on casting our eyes around to see few better off than we are, and many not half so comfortable, yet of equal, and, in some instances, superior pretensions as to station and fortune.

Every man in this country is his own glazier; this you will laugh at: but if he does not wish to see and feel the discomfort of broken panes, he must learn to put them in his windows with his own hands. Workmen are not easily to be had in the backwoods when you want them, and it would be preposterous to hire a man at high wages to make two days' journey to and from the nearest town to mend your windows. Boxes of glass of several different sizes are to be bought at a very cheap rate in the stores. My husband amused himself by glazing the windows of the house preparatory to their being fixed in.

To understand the use of carpenter's tools, I assure you, is no despicable or useless kind of knowledge here. I would strongly recommend all young men coming to Canada to acquire a little acquaintance with this valuable art, as they will often be put to great inconvenience for the want of it.

I was once much amused with hearing the remarks made by a very fine lady, the reluctant sharer of her husband's emigration, on seeing the son of a naval officer of some rank in the service busily employed in making an axe-handle out of a piece of rock-elm.

"I wonder that you allow George to degrade himself so," she said, addressing his father.

The captain looked up with surprise. "Degrade himself! In what manner, madam? My boy neither swears, drinks whiskey, steals, nor tells lies."

"But you allow him to perform tasks of the most menial kind. What is he now better than a hedge carpenter; and I suppose you allow him to chop, too?"

"Most assuredly I do. That pile of logs in the cart there was all cut by him after he had left study yesterday," was the reply,

"I would see my boys dead before they should use an axe like common labourers."

"Idleness is the root of all evil," said the captain. "How much worse might my son be employed if he were running wild about streets with bad companions."

"You will allow this is not a country for gentlemen or ladies to live in," said the lady.

"It is the country for gentlemen that will not work and cannot live without, to starve in," replied the captain bluntly; "and for that reason I make my boys early accustom themselves to be usefully and actively employed."

"My boys shall never work like common mechanics," said the lady, indignantly.

"Then, madam, they will be good for nothing as settlers; and it is a pity you dragged them across the Atlantic." . . .

But while I have been recounting these remarks, I have wandered far from my original subject, and left my poor log-house quite in an unfinished state. At last I was told it was in a habitable condition, and I was soon engaged in all the bustle and fatigue attendant on removing our household goods. We received all the assistance we required from_____, who is ever ready and willing to help us. He laughed, and called it a "*moving* bee;" I said it was a "fixing bee;" and my husband said it was a "settling bee;" I know we were unsettled enough till it was over. What a din of desolation is a small house, or any house under such circumstances. The idea of chaos must have been taken from a removal or a setting to rights, for I suppose the ancients had their *flitting*, as the Scotch call it, as well as the moderns.

Various were the valuable articles of crockery-ware that perished in their short but rough journey through the woods. Peace to their manes. I had a good helper in my Irish maid, who soon roused up famous fires, and set the house in order.

We have now got quite comfortably settled, and I shall give you a description of our little dwelling. What is finished is only a part of the original plan; the rest must be added next spring, or fall, as circumstances may suit.

A nice small sitting-room with a store closet, a kitchen, pantry, and bed-chamber form the ground floor; there is a good upper floor that will make three sleeping-rooms.

"What a nut-shell!" I think I hear you exclaim. So it is at present;

but we purpose adding a handsome frame front as soon as we can get boards from the mill, which will give us another parlour, long hall, and good spare bed-room. The windows and glass door of our present sitting-room command pleasant lake-views to the west and south. When the house is completed, we shall have a verandah in front; and at the south side, which forms an agreeable addition in the summer, being used as a sort of outer room in which we can dine, and have the advantage of cool air, protected from the glare of the sunbeams. The Canadians call these verandahs "stoups." Few houses, either log or frame, are without them. The pillars look extremely pretty, wreathed with the luxuriant hop-vine, mixed with the scarlet creeper and "morning glory," the American name for the most splendid of major convulvuluses. These stoups are really a considerable ornament, as they conceal in a great measure the rough logs, and break the barnlike form of the building.

Our parlour is warmed by a handsome Franklin stove with brass gallery, and fender. Our furniture consists of a brass-railed sofa, which serves upon occasion for a bed, Canadian painted chairs, a stained pine table, green and white curtains, and a handsome Indian mat that covers the floor. One side of the room is filled up with our books. Some large maps and a few good prints nearly conceal the rough walls, and form the decoration of our little dwelling. Our bed-chamber is furnished with equal simplicity. We do not, however, lack comfort in our humble home; and though it is not exactly such as we could wish, it is as good as, under existing circumstances, we could have.

I am anxiously looking forward to the spring, that I may get a garden laid out in front of the house; as I mean to cultivate some of the native fruits and flowers, which, I am sure, will improve greatly by culture. The strawberries that grow wild in our pastures, woods, and clearings, are several varieties, and bear abundantly. They make excellent preserves, and I mean to introduce beds of them into my garden. . . .

From *The Canadian Settler's Guide*

FURNISHING LOG HOUSE.

In furnishing a Canadian log-house the main study should be to unite simplicity with cheapness and comfort. It would be strangely out of character to introduce gay, showy, or rich and costly articles of furniture into so rough and homely a dwelling. A log-house is better to be simply furnished. Those who begin with moderation are more likely to abe able to increase their comforts in the course of a few years.

Let us see now what can be done towards making your log parlour comfortable at a small cost. A dozen of painted Canadian chairs, such as are in common use here, will cost you £2 10s. You can get plainer ones for 2s. 9d. or 3s. a chair: of course you may get very excellent articles if you give a higher price; but we are not going to buy drawing-room furniture. You can buy rocking chairs, small, at 7s. 6d.; large, with elbows, 15s.: you can cushion them yourself. A good drugget, which I would advise you to bring with you, or Scotch carpet, will cover your rough floor; when you lay it down, spread straw or hay over the boards; this will save your carpet from cutting. A stained pine table may be had for 12s. or 15s. Walnut or cherry wood costs more; but the pine with a nice cover will answer at first. For a flowered mohair you must give five or six dollars. A piece of chintz of suitable pattern will cost you 16s. the piece of twenty-eight yards. This will curtain your windows: and a common pine sofa stuffed with wool, though many use fine hay for the back and sides, can be bought cheap, if covered by your own hands. If your husband or elder sons are at all skilled in the use of tools, they can make out of common pine boards the frame-work of couches, or sofas, which look when covered and stuffed, as well as what the cabinet-maker will charge several pounds for. A common box or two stuffed so as to form a cushion on the top, and finished with a flounce of chintz, will fill the recess of the windows. A set of book-shelves stained with Spanish brown, to hold your library. – A set of corner shelves, fitted into the angles of the room, one above the other, diminishing in size, form a useful receptacle for any little ornamental matters, or for flowers in the summer, and gives a pleasant finish and an air of taste to the room. A few prints, or pictures, in frames of oak or black walnut, should not be omitted, if you can bring such ornaments with you. These things are sources of pleasure to yourselves, and of interest to others. They are intellectual luxuries, that even the very poorest man regards with delight, and possesses if he can, to adorn his cottage walls, however lowly that cottage may be. . . .

DANDELION COFFEE

Dr. Harrison, of Edinburgh, recommended the use of this root, many years ago. It possesses, he says, all the fine flavour and exhilarating properties of coffee, without any of its deleterious effects. – The plant being of a soporific nature, the coffee made from it, when taken in the evening, produces a tendency to sleep, instead of exciting wakefulness, and may be safely used as a substitute for the Arabian berry, (he adds,) "being equal in substance and flavour to the best Mocha coffee." This is going too far: it is the best substitute that has been found, but certainly not equal in flavour to really fine coffee. I will now give my sister, Mrs. Moodie's, recipe for preparing the dandelion-root, and her method of cooking it. "The roots should be carefully washed, but not so as to remove the fine, brown skin which covers them, and which contains the aromatic flavour. The roots, when dry, should be cut up into small pieces, about the size of a kidney-bean, and roasted either in a Dutch-oven, before the fire, or in the stove, stirring them from time to time, to prevent burning; when they are brown through, and crisp, like freshly-roasted coffee, remove them, and let them cool; grind like coffee. Put a small cupful into the coffee-pot, and pour over it a quart of boiling water, letting it boil again for a few minutes: drunk with sugar and cream, this preparation is very little inferior to good coffee." "Experience," she says, "taught me that the root of this valuable plant was not so good in the Spring as in the Fall. In new clearings this herb abounds, and grows most luxuriantly in the fine new soil. – The best season to collect it is in the month of October, when the potato-crop is being taken up. To persons residing in the bush, to whom tea and coffee may happen to be an expensive article of consumption, the knowledge of this valuable property in a plant spread so abundantly over their fields, may be very useful."

I can speak to the excellence of the dandelion-coffee, having often drunk it, though I do not think I ever succeeded in making it myself, so well as my sister did. I believe that I scraped as well as washed the root, and thus injured instead of improving the flavour. The addition of a small quantity of good coffee would be an improvement, and would be very economical, as the difference would then hardly be detected, between the substitute and the genuine article. . . .

EELS

The eels caught in the Canadian waters are of a very large size, and very rich, but coarse. The best way of cooking them is, first, to parboil them, then open, and carefully remove the oily fat which lines the back-bone; cut out the bone the whole length, and also the tail and head; wash the fish clean, and spread it open; strew over the whole inner surface plenty of chopped parsley and thyme, or summer savory, pepper and salt, with a little allspice; then, beginning at the tail end, roll the fish tight into a bolster, and bind it well with tape or strips of calico; over this fold a piece of clean cloth, and tie it at each end; put it into boiling salt and water; (a handful of salt will be enough;) boil slowly for four or five hours, if your fish be large and the roll thick; do not remove the binders till the fish is quite cold; pour over it half a pint of vinegar, and when served, cut it in slices; garnish with parsley.

BLACK SQUIRRELS

These little animals are often found in great numbers, in the beech and oak-woods in Canada, and are considered very delicate food; being free from any strong flavour. They are roasted like rabbits, or cut in pieces and fried, fricasseed, or made into stews or pies. Some people object to them, simply because they have not been accustomed to see them brought to table, or even to hear of their being used as an article of food, and others consider them as insipid. This last objection is, perhaps, the most weighty; but by seasoning them well, it may be overcome. Nothing can be more cleanly than the habits of these little creatures; their food consisting entirely of grain, or fruits, or vegetables. When fresh meat is scarce, as it often is in the woods, the black and even the red squirrel may be eaten, as a wholesome change of diet. The lumberers and hunters will use the musk-rat, porcupine, and beaver for food, and even the wood-chuck or ground-hog, which is a species of marmot. But though its food is vegetable, it is very fat and oily; and does not make pleasant meat. The bear is also made meat of by the backwoodsman. The meat when cooked, either roasted or boiled, is like coarse beef, and would pass for such, if a person was not told to the contrary. The bear is certainly a more cleanly feeder than the hog. The hams, when well cured, are considered very excellent.

Susannah Moodie (1803-1885)

Susannah Moodie came of a family noted for its literary achievements. Of the six Strickland girls, four wrote poetry, short stories or essays, and Elizabeth edited manuscripts. Agnes and Elizabeth later achieved recognition for their *Lives of the Queens of England, Lives of the Queens of Scotland* and *Lives of the Bachelor Kings of England.* Catharine Parr Traill, a year old than Susannah, wrote *The Backwoods of Canada* and *The Female Emigrant's Guide* as well as several children's books, and their younger brother Samuel published *Twenty-Seven Years in Canada West,* edited by Agnes, in 1853.

Susannah, the sixth Strickland daughter, was born in 1803 at the family home Reydon Hall in Suffolk which her father had bought after retiring from active participation in his London business. Business difficulties which wiped out their fortune led to the early death of Thomas Strickland in 1818, and the family moved to the town house in Norwich to save expenses. In 1825 Samuel emigrated to Canada; soon after, Thomas junior left for India and for several years the household was entirely female. At meetings of the Reform League, Susannah met John Dunbar Moodie, a war veteran who had spent ten years in South Africa, and the couple were married in 1831. As financial prospects in England were not good, they decided to emigrate to Canada, and sailed in July of 1832 with their baby daughter Katie. A week later, Susannah's sister Catharine and her husband Thomas Traill, a regimental brother of John, also set sail. While the Traills went immediately to Rice Lake, Douro Township, where Samuel was settled, the Moodies decided to take up land near Cobourg. After two years of frustration and several accommodations, at least one described as a "hovel," they joined the Traills and the Stricklands at Rice Lake and prepared to clear their grant of land. Here too they were unsuccessful, although Susannah gradually learned the virtues and rewards of simple toil. In 1837 Moodie suffered an accident in the fields, and shortly after, still lame, he was called to assist in the Rebellion of 1837 and its aftermath; although the skirmish with Colonel Moodie at York was brief, John was given military employment in the subsequent months. In 1839 Susannah succeeded in her petition to the Governor for a public appointment for Moodie and in 1840 the family moved to Belleville where he was given the post of sheriff. Despite new problems, they remained here until John's death in 1867; Susannah then moved to Toronto to join her daughter and died here in 1885.

Susannah Moodie's literary career began early. After the death of their father in 1818, the girls turned to writing verse and children's stories for amusement; Catharine was the first to publish at the age of sixteen, but before Susannah emigrated to Canada, she had brought out a book of verse, *Enthusiasm and Other Poems* (1831), and some tales. In Canada, she began writing again while still in the bush, to eke out the family finances. She contributed poems, stories and sketches, first to the *Literary Garland*, and then to the *Victoria Magazine*, published in Belleville and edited by the Moodies until it foundered in 1848 for lack of capital. *Roughing It in the Bush* appeared in 1852 and *Life in the Clearings* in 1853. Susannah also published several novels: *Mark Hurdlestone the Gold Worshipper* (1853), *Geoffrey Monckton* (1853), and *Flora Lyndsay* (1854).

Several selections from *Roughing It in the Bush* first appeared in *The Literary Garland*. The work covers the period from 1832 to 1840 and parts at least were written during this time, in the evenings while the children slept and John was away on military duty. It treats much the same material as Catharine's earlier work *The Backwoods of Canada:* the crossing of the Atlantic, the first view of Quebec, the trip up river, the arrival in the bush, the building of a home, the local bees, the manners of the neighbours, the inevitable fire. But the two works are essentially different. Catharine's is objective, matter-of-fact, and often scientific in its detail of the flora and fauna; Susannah's is more personal, more dramatic and enlivened by a strong sense of comedy. The personal history of the family is interspersed with passages of natural description and anecdotes of other immigrants or acquaintances such as Mad Tom. *Life in the Clearings* is a more systematic account of the new country and describes Canadian traditions, manners, dress and customs in a style intended for the British reader.

TEXTS:

Roughing It in The Bush or Life in Canada. London: Bentley, 1852.
Life in the Clearings Versus the Bush. London: Bentley, 1853 (abridged).

See also:

The introduction in this book to Catharine Parr Traill.
Audrey Morris. *Gentle Pioneers.* Toronto: Musson, 1968. Hodder & Stoughton, 1968.

From *Roughing It in the Bush*

CHAPTER V

OUR FIRST SETTLEMENT, AND THE BORROWING SYSTEM

To lend, or not to lend—is that the question?

"Those who go a-borrowing, go a-sorrowing," saith the old adage; and a wiser saw never came out of the mouth of experience. I have tested the truth of this proverb since my settlement in Canada, many, many times, to my cost; and what emigrant has not? So averse have I ever been to this practice, that I would at all times rather quietly submit to a temporary inconvenience than obtain any thing I wanted in this manner. I verily believe that a demon of mischief presides over borrowed goods, and takes a wicked pleasure in playing off a thousand malicious pranks upon you the moment he enters your dwelling. Plates and dishes, that had been the pride and ornament of their own cupboard for years, no sooner enter upon foreign service than they are broken; wineglasses and tumblers, that have been handled by a hundred careless wenches in safety, scarcely pass into the hands of your servants when they are sure to tumble upon the floor, and the accident turns out a compound fracture. If you borrow a garment of any kind, be sure that you will tear it; a watch, that you will break it; a jewel, that you will lose it; a book, that it will be stolen from you. There is no end to the trouble and vexation arising out of this evil habit. If you borrow a horse, and he has the reputation of being the best-behaved animal in the district, you no sooner become responsible for his conduct than he loses his character. The moment that you attempt to drive him, he shows that he has a will of his own, by taking the reins into his own management, and running away in a contrary direction to the road that you wished him to travel. He never gives over his eccentric capers until he has broken his own knees, and the borrowed carriage and harness. So anxious are you about his safety, that you have not a moment to bestow upon your own. And why? – the beast is borrowed, and you are expected to return him in as good condition as he came to you. But of all evils, to borrow money is perhaps the worst. If of a friend, he ceases to be one the moment you feel that you are bound to him by the heavy clog of obligation. If of a usurer, the interest, in this country, soon doubles the original sum, and you owe an increasing debt, which in time swallows up all you possess.

When we first came to the colony, nothing surprised me more than the extent to which this pernicious custom was carried, both by the native Canadians, the European settlers, and the lower order of Americans. Many of the latter had spied out the goodness of the land, and *borrowed* various portions of it, without so much as asking leave of the absentee owner. Unfortunately, our new home was surrounded by these odious squatters, whom we found as ignorant as savages, without their courtesy and kindness.

The Place we first occupied was purchased of Mr. C_____, a merchant, who took it in payment of sundry large debts which the owner, a New England loyalist, had been unable to settle. Old Joe H_____, the present occupant, had promised to quit it with his family, at the commencement of sleighing; and as the bargain was concluded in the month of September, and we were anxious to plough for fall wheat, it was necessary to be upon the spot. No house was to be found in the immediate neighbourhood, save a small dilapidated log tenement, on an adjoining farm (which was scarcely reclaimed from the bush) that had been some months without an owner. The merchant assured us that this could be made very comfortable until such time as it suited H_____ to remove, and the owner was willing to let us have it for the *moderate* sum of four dollars a month.

Trusting to Mr. C_____'s word, and being strangers in the land, we never took the precaution to examine this delightful summer residence before entering upon it, but thought ourselves very fortunate in obtaining a temporary home so near our own property, the distance not exceeding half a mile. The agreement was drawn up, and we were told that we could take possession whenever it suited us.

The few weeks that I had sojourned in the country had by no means prepossessed me in its favour. The home-sickness was sore upon me, and all my solitary hours were spent in tears. My whole soul yielded itself up to a strong and overpowering grief. One simple word dwelt for ever in my heart, and swelled it to bursting—"Home!" I repeated it waking a thousand times a day, and my last prayer before I sank to sleep was still "Home! Oh, that I could return, if only to die at home!" And nightly I did return; my feet again trod the daisied meadows of England; the song of her birds was in my ears; I wept with delight to find myself once more wandering beneath the fragrant shade of her green hedge-rows; and I awoke to weep in earnest when I found it but a dream. But this is all digression, and has nothing to do with our unseen dwelling. The reader must bear with me in my fits of melancholy, and take me as I am.

It was the 22nd September that we left the steamboat *Natal*, to take possession of our new abode. During the three weeks we had sojourned at _____, I had not seen a drop of rain, and I began to think that the fine weather would last for ever; but this eventful day arose in clouds. Moodie had hired a covered carriage to convey the baby, the servant-maid, and myself to the farm, as our driver prognosticated a wet day; while he followed with Tom Wilson and the teams that conveyed our luggage.

The scenery through which we were passing was so new to me, so unlike any thing that I had ever beheld before, that in spite of its monotonous character, it won me from my melancholy, and I began to look about me with considerable interest. Not so my English servant, who declared that the woods were frightful to look upon; that it was a country only fit for wild beasts; that she hated it with all her heart and soul, and would go back as soon as she was able.

About a mile from the place of our destination the rain began to fall in torrents, and the air, which had been balmy as a spring morning, turned as chilly as that of a November day. Hannah shivered; the baby cried, and I drew my summer shawl as closely round as possible, to protect her from the sudden change in our hitherto delightful temperature. Just then, the carriage turned into a narrow, steep path, overhung with lofty woods, and after labouring up it with considerable difficulty, and at the risk of breaking our necks, it brought us at length to a rocky upland clearing, partially covered with a second growth of timber, and surrounded on all sides by the dark forest.

"I guess," quoth our Yankee driver, "that at the bottom of this 'ere swell, you'll find yourself *to hum*;" and plunging into a short path cut through the wood, he pointed to a miserable hut, at the bottom of a deep descent, and cracking his whip, exclaimed, "'Tis a smart location that. I wish you Britishers may enjoy it."

I gazed upon the place in perfect dismay, for I had never seen such a shed called a house before. "You must be mistaken; that is not a house, but a cattle-shed, or pig-sty."

The man turned his knowing, keen eye upon me, and smiled, half-humorously, half-maliciously, as he said,

"You were raised in the old country, I guess; you have much to learn, and more, perhaps, than you'll like to know, before the winter is over."

I was perfectly bewildered – I could only stare at the place, with my eyes swimming in tears; but as the horses plunged down into the broken hollow, my attention was drawn from my new residence to the perils which endangered life and limb at every step. The driver however, was well used to such roads, and, steering us dexterously between the black stumps, at length drove up, not to the door, for there was none to the house, but to the open space from which that absent but very necessary appendage had been removed. Three young steers and two heifers, which the driver proceeded to drive out, were quietly reposing upon the floor. A few strokes of his whip, and a loud burst of gratuitous curses, soon effected an ejectment; and I dismounted, and took possession of this untenable tenement. Moodie was not yet in sight with the teams. I begged the man to stay until he arrived, as I felt terrified at being left alone in this wild, strange-looking place. He laughed, as well he might, at our fears, and said that he had a long way to go, and must be off; then, cracking his whip, and nodding to the girl, who was crying aloud, he went his way, and Hannah and myself were left standing in the middle of the dirty floor.

The prospect was indeed dreary. Without, pouring rain; within, a fireless hearth; a room with but one window, and that containing only one whole pane of glass; not an article of furniture to be seen, save an old painted pine-wood cradle, which had been left there by some freak of fortune. This, turned upon its side, served us for a seat, and there we impatiently awaited the arrival of Moodie, Wilson, and a man whom the former had hired that morning to assist on the farm. Where they were all to be stowed might have puzzled a more sagacious brain than mine. It is true there was a loft, but I could see no way of reaching it, for ladder there was none, so we amused ourselves, while waiting for the coming of the party, by abusing the place, the country, and our own dear selves, for our folly in coming to it.

Now, when not only reconciled to Canada, but loving it, and feeling a deep interest in its present welfare, and the fair prospect of its future greatness, I often look back and laugh at the feelings with which I then regarded this noble country.

When things come to the worst, they generally mend. The males of our party no sooner arrived than they set about making things more comfortable. James, our servant, pulled up some of the decayed stumps, with which the small clearing that surrounded the shanty was thickly covered, and made a fire, and Hannah roused herself from the stupor of despair, and seized the corn-broom from the top of the loaded wagon, and began to sweep the house, raising such an intolerable cloud of dust that I was glad to throw my cloak over my head, and run out of doors, to avoid suffocation. Then commenced the awful bustle of unloading the two heavily-loaded wagons. The small space within the house was soon entirely blocked up with trunks and packages of all descriptions. There was scarcely room to move, without stumbling over some article of household stuff.

The rain poured in at the open door, beat in at the shattered window, and dropped upon our heads from the holes in the roof. The wind blew keenly through a thousand apertures in the log walls; and nothing could exceed the uncomfortableness of our situation. For a long time the box which contained a hammer and nails was not to be found. At length Hannah discovered it, tied up with some bedding which she was opening out in order to dry. I fortunately spied the door lying among some old boards at the back of the house, and Moodie immediately commenced fitting it to its place. This, once accomplished, was a great addition to our comfort. We then nailed a piece of white cloth entirely over the broken window, which, without diminishing the light, kept out the rain. James constructed a ladder out of the old bits of boards, and Tom Wilson assisted him in stowing the luggage away in the loft.

But what has this picture of misery and discomfort to do with borrowing? Patience, my dear, good friends; I will tell you all about it by and by.

While we were all busily employed – even the poor baby, who was lying upon a pillow in the old cradle, trying the strength of her lungs, and not a little irritated that no one was at leisure to regard her laudable endeavours to make herself heard – the door was suddenly pushed open, and the apparition of a woman squeezed itself into the crowded room. I left off arranging the furniture of a bed, that had been just put up in a corner, to meet my unexpected, and at that moment, not very welcome guest. Her whole appearance was so extraordinary that I felt quite at a loss how to address her.

Imagine a girl of seventeen or eighteen years of age, with sharp, knowing-looking features, a forward, impudent carriage, and a pert, flippant voice, standing upon one of the trunks, and surveying all our proceedings in the most impertinent manner. The creature was dressed in a ragged, dirty purple stuff gown, cut very low in the neck, with an old red cotton handkerchief tied over her head; her uncombed, tangled locks falling over her thin, inquisitive face, in a state of perfect nature. Her legs and feet were bare, and, in her coarse, dirty red hands, she swung to and fro an empty glass decanter.

"What can she want?" I asked myself. "What a strange creature!"

And there she stood, staring at me in the most unceremonious manner, her keen black eyes glancing obliquely to every corner of the room, which she examined with critical exactness.

Before I could speak to her, she commenced the conversation by drawling through her nose,

"Well, I guess you are fixing here."

I thought she had come to offer her services; and I told her that I did not want a girl, for I had brought one out with me.

"How!" responded the creature, "I hope you don't take me for a help. I'd have you to know that I'm as good a lady as yourself. No; I just stepped over to see what was going on. I seed the teams pass our'n about noon, and I says to father, 'Them strangers are cum; I'll go and look arter them.' 'Yes,' says he, 'do – and take the decanter along. Maybe they'll want one to put their whiskey in.' 'I'm goin' to,' says I; so I cum across with it, an' here it is. But, mind – don't break it – 'tis the only one we have to hum; and father says 'tis so mean to drink out of green glass."

My surprise increased every minute. It seemed such an act of disinterested generosity thus to anticipate wants we had never thought of. I was regularly taken in.

"My good girl," I began, "this is really very kind – but – "

"Now, don't go to call me 'gal' – and pass off your English airs on us. We are *genuine* Yankees, and think ourselves as good – yes, a great deal better than you. I am a young lady."

"Indeed!" said I, striving to repress my astonishment. "I am a stranger in the country, and my acquaintance with Canadian ladies and gentlemen is very small. I did not mean to offend you by using the term girl; I was going to assure you that we had no need of the decanter. We have bottles of our own – and we don't drink whiskey."

"How! Not drink whiskey? Why, you don't say! How ignorant you must be! Maybe they have no whiskey in the old country?"

"Yes, we have; but it is not like the Canadian whiskey. But, pray take the decanter home again – I am afraid that it will get broken in this confusion."

"No, no; father told me to leave it – and there it is;" and she planted it resolutely down on the trunk. "You will find a use for it till you have unpacked your own."

Seeing that she was determined to leave the bottle, I said no more about it, but asked her to tell me where the well was to be found.

"The well!" she repeated after me, with a sneer. "Who thinks of digging wells when they can get plenty of water from the creek? There is a fine water-privilege not a stone's-throw from the door," and, jumping off the box, she disappeared as abruptly as she had entered. We all looked at each other; Tom Wilson was highly amused, and laughed until he held his sides.

"What tempted her to bring this empty bottle here?" said Moodie. "It is all an excuse; the visit, Tom, was meant for you."

"You'll know more about it in a few days," said James looking up from his work. "That bottle is not brought here, for naught."

I could not unravel the mystery, and thought no more about it, until it was again brought to my recollection by the damsel herself.

Our united efforts had effected a complete transformation in our uncouth dwelling. Sleeping-berths had been partitioned off for the men; shelves had been put up for the accommodation of books and crockery, a carpet covered the floor, and the chairs and tables we had brought from_____gave an air of comfort to the place, which, on the first view of it, I deemed impossible. My husband, Mr. Wilson, and James, had walked over to inspect the farm, and I was sitting at the table at work, the baby creeping upon the floor, and Hannah preparing dinner. The sun shone warm and bright, and the open door admitted a current of fresh air, which tempered the heat of the fire.

"Well, I guess you look smart," said the Yankee damsel, presenting herself once more before me. "You old country folks are so stiff, you must have every thing nice, or you fret. But, then, you can easily do it; you have *stacks* of money; and you can fix every thing right off with money."

"Pray take a seat," and I offered her a chair, "and be kind enough to tell me your name. I suppose you must live in the neighbourhood, although I cannot perceive any dwelling near us."

"My name! So you want to know my name. I arn't ashamed of my name; 'tis Emily S_____. I am eldest daughter to the *gentleman* who owns this house."

"What must the father be," thought I, "if he resembles the young *lady*, his daughter?"

Imagine a young lady, dressed in ragged petticoats, through whose yawning rents peeped forth, from time to time, her bare red knees, with uncombed elf-locks, and a face and hands that looked as if they had been unwashed for a month—who did not know A from B, and despised those who did. While these reflections, combined with a thousand ludicrous images, were flitting through my mind, my strange visitor suddenly exclaimed.

"Have you done with that 'ere decanter I brought across yesterday?"

"Oh, yes! I have no occasion for it." I rose, took it from the shelf, and placed it in her hand.

"I guess you won't return it empty; that would be mean, father says. He wants it filled with whiskey."

The mystery was solved, the riddle made clear. I could contain my gravity no longer, but burst into a hearty fit of laughter, in which I was joined by Hannah. Our young lady was mortally offended; she tossed the decanter from hand to hand, and glared at us with her tiger-like eyes.

"You think yourselves smart! Why do you laugh in that way?"

"Excuse me—but you have such an odd way of borrowing that I cannot help it. This bottle, it seems, was brought over for your own convenience, not for mine. I am sorry to disappoint you, but I have no whiskey."

"I guess spirits will do as well; I know there is some in that keg, for I smells it."

"It contains rum for the workmen."

"Better still. I calculate when you've been here a few months, you'll be too knowing to give rum to your helps. But old country folks are all fools, and that's the reason they get so easily sucked in, and be so soon wound up. Cum, fill the bottle, and don't be stingy. In this country we all live by borrowing. If you want any thing, why just send and borrow from us."

Thinking that this might be the custom of the country, I hastened to fill the decanter, hoping that I might get a little new milk for the poor weaning child in return; but when I asked my liberal visitor if she kept cows, and would lend me a little new milk for the baby, she burst out into high disdain. "Milk! Lend milk? I guess milk in the fall is worth a York shilling a quart. I cannot sell you a drop under."

This was a wicked piece of extortion, as the same article in the towns, where, of course, it was in greater request, only brought threepence the quart.

"If you'll pay me for it, I'll bring you some to-morrow. But mind—cash down."

"And when do you mean to return the rum?" I said, with some asperity.

"When father goes to the creek." This was the name given by my neighbours to the village of P_____, distant about four miles.

Day after day I was tormented by this importunate creature; she borrowed of me tea, sugar, candles, starch, blueing, irons, pots, bowls,

– in short, every article in common domestic use, – while it was with the utmost diffculty we could get them returned. Articles of food, such as tea and sugar, or of convenience, like candles, starch, and soap, she never dreamed of being required at her hands. This method of living upon their neighbours is a most convenient one to unprincipled people, as it does not involve the penalty of stealing; and they can keep the goods without the unpleasant necessity of returning them, or feel the moral obligation of being grateful for their use. Living eight miles from_____, I found these constant encroachments a heavy burden on our poor purse; and being ignorant of the country, and residing in such a lonely, out-of-the-way place, surrounded by these savages, I was really afraid of denying their requests.

The very day our new plough came home, the father of this bright damsel, who went by the familiar and unenviable title of *Old Satan*, came over to borrow it (though we afterwards found out that he had a good one of his own). The land had never been broken up, and was full of rocks and stumps, and he was anxious to save his own from injury; the consequence was that the borrowed implement came home unfit for use, just at the very time that we wanted to plough for fall wheat. The same happened to a spade and trowel, bought in order to plaster the house. Satan asked the loan of them for *one* hour for the same purpose, and we never saw them again.

The daughter came one morning, as usual, on one of these swindling expeditions, and demanded of me the loan of some *fine slack*. Not knowing what she meant by *fine slack*, and weary of her importunities, I said I had none. She went away in a rage. Shortly after she came again for some pepper. I was at work, and my work-box was open upon the table, well stored with threads and spools of all descriptions. Miss Satan cast her hawk's eye into it, and burst out in her usual rude manner.

"I guess you told me a tarnation big lie the other day."

Unaccustomed to such language, I rose from my seat, and pointing to the door, told her to walk out, as I did not choose to be insulted in my own house.

"Your house! I'm sure it's father's," returned the incorrigible wretch. "You told me that you had no *fine slack*, and you have *stacks* of it."

"What is fine slack?" said I, very pettishly.

"The stuff that's wound upon these 'ere pieces of wood," pouncing as she spoke upon one of my most serviceable spools.

"I cannot give you that; I want it myself."

"I didn't ask you to give it. I only wants to borrow it till father goes to the creek."

"I wish he would make haste, then, as I want a number of things which you have borrowed of me, and which I cannot longer do without."

She gave me a knowing look, and carried off my spool in triumph.

I happened to mention the manner in which I was constantly annoyed by these people, to a worthy English farmer who resided near us; and he fell a-laughing, and told me that I did not know the Canadian Yankees as well as he did, or I should not be troubled with them long.

"The best way," says he, "to get rid of them, is to ask them sharply what they want; and if they give you no satisfactory answer, order them to leave the house; but I believe I can put you in a better way still. Buy some small article of them, and pay them a trifle over the price, and tell them to bring the change. I will lay my life upon it that it will be long before they trouble you again."

I was impatient to test the efficacy of his scheme. That very afternoon Miss Satan brought me a plate of butter for sale. The price was three and ninepence; twice the sum, by the by, that it was worth.

"I have no change," giving her a dollar; "but you can bring it me to-morrow."

Oh, blessed experiment! for the value of one quarter-dollar I got rid of this dishonest girl for ever; rather than pay me, she never entered the house again. About a month after this, I was busy making an apple-pie in the kitchen. A cadaverous-looking woman, very long-faced and witch-like, popped her ill-looking visage into the door, and drawled through her nose,

"Do you want to buy a *rooster?*"

Now, the sucking-pigs with which we had been regaled every day for three weeks at the tavern, were called *roasters*; and not understanding the familiar phrases of the country, I thought she had a sucking-pig to sell.

"Is it a good one?"

"I guess 'tis."

"What do you ask for it?"

"Two Yorkers."

"That is very cheap, if it is any weight. I don't like them under ten or twelve pounds."

"Ten or twelve pounds! Why, woman, what do you mean? Would you expect a rooster to be bigger nor a turkey?"

We stared at each other. There was evidently some misconception on my part.

"Bring the roaster up; and if I like it, I will buy it, though I must confess that I am not very fond of roast pig."

"Do you call this a pig?" said my she-merchant, drawing a fine game-cock from under her cloak.

I laughed heartily at my mistake, as I paid her down the money for the bonny bird. This little matter settled, I thought she would take her departure; but that rooster proved the dearest fowl to me that ever was bought.

"Do you keep backy and snuff here?" says she, sidling close up to me.

"We make no use of those articles."

"How! Not use backy and snuff? That's oncommon."

She paused, then added in a mysterious, confidential tone,

"I want to ask you how your tea-caddy stands?"

"It stands in the cupboard," said I, wondering what all this might mean.

"I know that; but have you any tea to spare?"

I now began to suspect what sort of a customer the stranger was.

"Oh, you want to borrow some? I have none to spare."

"You don't say so. Well, now, that's stingy. I never asked any thing of you before. I am poor, and you are rich; besides, I'm troubled so with the headache, and nothing does me any good but a cup of strong tea."

"The money I have just given you will buy a quarter of a pound of the best."

"I guess that isn't mine. The fowl belonged to my neighbour. She's sick; and I promised to sell it for her to buy some physic. Money!" she added, in a coaxing tone, "Where should I get money? Lord bless you! people in this country have no money; and those who come out with piles of it, soon lose it. But Emily S_____ told me that you are nation rich, and draw your money from the old country. So I guess you can well afford to lend a neighbour a spoonful of tea."

"Neighbour! Where do you live, and what is your name?"

"My name is Betty Fye – old Betty Fye; I live in the log shanty over the creek, at the back of your'n. The farm belongs to my eldest son. I'm a widow with twelve sons; and 'tis _____ hard to scratch along."

"Do you swear?"

"Swear! What harm? It eases one's mind when one's vexed. Every body swears in this country. My boys all swear like Sam Hill; and I used to swear mighty big oaths till about a month ago, when the Methody parson told me that if I did not leave it off I should go to a tarnation bad place; so I dropped some of the worst of them."

"You would do wisely to drop the rest; women never swear in my country."

"Well, you don't say! I always heer'd they were very ignorant. Will you lend me the tea?"

The woman was such an original that I gave her what whe wanted. As she was going off, she took up one of the apples I was peeling.

"I guess you have a fine orchard?"

"They say the best in the district."

"We have no orchard to hum, and I guess you'll want *sarce*."

"Sarce! What is sarce?"

"Not know what sarce is? You are clever! Sarce is apples cut up and dried, to make into pies in the winter. Now do you comprehend?"

I nodded.

"Well, I was going to say that I have no apples, and that you have a tarnation big few of them; and if you'll give me twenty bushels of your best apples, and find me with half a pound of coarse thread to string them upon, I will make you a barrel of sarce on shares – that is, give you one, and keep one for myself."

I had plenty of apples, and I gladly accepted her offer, and Mrs. Betty Fye departed, elated with the success of her expedition. I found to my cost, that, once admitted into the house, there was no keeping her away. She borrowed every thing that she could think of, without once dreaming of restitution. I tried all ways of affronting her, but without success. Winter came, and she was still at her old pranks. Whenever I saw her coming down the lane, I used involuntarily to exclaim, "Betty Fye! Betty Fye! Fye upon Betty Fye! The Lord deliver me from Betty Fye!" The last time I was honoured with a visit from this worthy, she meant to favour me with a very large order upon my goods and chattels.

"Well, Mrs. Fye, what do you want *to-day*?"

"So many things that I scarce know where to begin. Ah, what a thing 'tis to be poor! First, I want you to lend me ten pounds of flour to make some johnnie-cakes."

"I thought they were made of Indian meal?"

"Yes, yes, when you've got the meal. I'm out of it, and this is a new fixing of my own invention. Lend me the flour, woman, and I'll bring you one of the cakes to taste."

This was said very coaxingly.

"Oh, pray don't trouble yourself. What next?" I was anxious to see how far her impudence would go, and determined to affront her if possible.

"I want you to lend me a gown, and a pair of stockings. I have to go to Oswego to see my husband's sister, and I'd like to look decent."

"Mrs. Fye, I never lend my clothes to any one. If I lend them to you, I should never wear them again."

"So much the better for me," (with a knowing grin). "I guess if you won't lend me the gown, you will let me have some black slack to quilt a stuff petticoat, a quarter of a pound of tea and some sugar; and I will bring them back as soon as I can."

"I wonder when that will be. You owe me so many things that it will cost you more than you imagine to repay me."

"Since you're not going to mention what's past, I can't owe you much. But I will let you off the tea and the sugar, if you will lend me a five-dollar bill." This was too much for my patience longer to endure, and I answered sharply,

"Mrs. Fye, it surprises me that such proud people as you Americans should condescend to the meanness of borrowing from those whom you affect to despise. Besides, as you never repay us for what you pretend to borrow, I look upon it as a system of robbery. If strangers unfortunately settle among you, their good-nature is taxed to supply your domestic wants, at a ruinous expense, besides the mortification of finding that they have been deceived and tricked out of their property. If you would come honestly to me and say, 'I want these things, I am too poor to buy them myself, and would be obliged to you to give them to me,' I should then acknowledge you as a common beggar, and treat you accordingly; give or not give, as it suited my convenience. But in the way in which you obtain these articles from me, you are spared even a debt of gratitude; for you well know that the many things which you have borrowed from me will be a debt owing to the day of judgment."

"S'pose they are," quoth Betty, not in the least abashed at my lecture on honesty, "you know what the Scripture saith, 'It is more blessed to give than to receive.'"

"Ay, there is an answer to that in the same book, which doubtless you may have heard," said I, disgusted with her hypocrisy, "'The wicked borroweth, and payeth not again.'"

"Never shall I forget the furious passion into which this too apt quotation threw my unprincipled applicant. She lifted up her voice and cursed me, using some of the big oaths temporarily discarded for *conscience* sake. And so she left me, and I never looked upon her face again.

When I removed to our own house, the history of which, and its former owner, I will give by and by, we had a bony, red-headed, ruffianly American squatter, who had "left his country for his country's good," for an opposite neighbour. I had scarcely time to put my house in order before his family commenced borrowing, or stealing from me. It is even worse than stealing, the things procured from you being obtained on false pretences – adding lying to theft. Not having either an oven or a cooking-stove, which at that period were not so cheap or so common as they are now, I had provided myself with a large bake-kettle as a substitute. In this kettle we always cooked hot cakes for breakfast, preferring that to the trouble of thawing the frozen bread. This man's wife was in the habit of sending over for my kettle whenever she wanted to bake, which, as she had a large family, happened nearly every day, and I found her importunity a great nuisance.

I told the impudent lad so, who was generally sent for it; and asked him what they did to bake their bread before I came.

"I guess we had to eat cakes in the pan; but now we can borrow this kettle of your'n, mother can fix bread."

I told him that he could have the kettle this time; but I must decline letting his mother have it in future, for I wanted it for the same purpose.

The next day passed over. The night was intensely cold, and I did not rise so early as usual in the morning. My servant was away at a quilting bee, and we were still in bed, when I heard the latch of the kitchen-door lifted up, and a step crossed the floor. I jumped out of bed, and began to dress as fast as I could, when Philander called out, in his well-known nasal twang,

"Missus! I'm come for the kettle."

I (*through the partition*): "You can't have it this morning. We cannot get our breakfast without it."

Philander: "Nor more can the old woman to hum," and, snatching up the kettle, which had been left to warm on the hearth, he rushed out of the house, singing, at the top of his voice,

"Hurrah for the Yankee Boys!"

When James came home for his breakfast, I sent him across to demand the kettle, and the dame very coolly told him that when she had done with it I *might* have it, but she defied him to take it out of her house with her bread in it.

One word more about this lad, Philander, before we part with him. Without the least intimation that his company would be agreeable, or even tolerated, he favoured us with it at all hours of the day, opening the door and walking in and out whenever he felt inclined. I had given him many broad hints that his presence was not required, but he paid not the slightest attention to what I said. One morning he marched in with his hat on, and threw himself down in the rocking-chair, just as I was going to dress my baby.

"Philander, I want to attend to the child; I cannot do it with you here. Will you oblige me by going into the kitchen?"

No answer. He seldom spoke during these visits, but wandered about the room, turning over our books and papers, looking at and handling every thing. Nay, I have even known him to take a lid off from the pot on the fire, to examine its contents.

I repeated my request.

Philander: "Well, I guess I sha'n't hurt the young 'un. You can dress her."

I: "But not with you here."

Philander: "Why not? *We* never do anything that we are ashamed of."

I: "So it seems. But I want to sweep the room – you had better get out of the dust."

I took the broom from the corner, and began to sweep; still my visitor did not stir, The dust rose in clouds; he rubbed his eyes, and moved a little nearer to the door. Another sweep, and, to escape its inflictions, he mounted the threshold. I had him now at a fair advantage, and fairly swept him out, and shut the door in his face.

Philander (*looking through the window*): "Well, I guess you did me then; but 'tis deuced hard to outwit a Yankee."

This freed me from his company, and he, too, never repeated his visit; so I found by experience, that once smartly rebuked, they did not like to try their strength with you a second time. When a sufficient time had elapsed for the drying of my twenty bushels of apples, I sent a Cornish lad, in our employ, to Betty Fye's, to inquire if they were ready, and when I should send the cart for them. Dan returned with a yellow, smoke-dried string of pieces, dangling from his arm. Thinking that these were a specimen of the whole, I inquired when we were to send the barrel for the rest.

"Lord, ma'am, this is all there be."

"Impossible! All out of twenty bushels of apples?"

"Yes," said the boy, with a grin. "The old witch told me that this was all that was left of your share; that when they were fixed enough, she put them under her bed for safety, and the mice and the children had eaten them all up but this string."

This ended my dealings with Betty Fye. . . .

From *Life in the Clearings Versus the Bush*

FROM THE CONCLUSION

I know that it would be easier for me to gain the approbation of the Canadian public, by exaggerating the advantages to be derived from a settlement in the colony, by praising all the good qualities of her people, and by throwing a flattering veil over their defects; but this is not my object, and such servile adulation would do them no good, and degrade me in my own eyes. I have written what I consider to be the truth, and as such I hope it may do good, by preparing the minds of emigrants for what they will *really find,* rather than by holding out fallacious hopes that can never be realized.

In "Roughing it in the Bush," I gave an honest personal statement of *facts.* I related nothing but what had really happened; and if illustrations were wanting of persons who had suffered *as much,* and been reduced to the same straits, I could furnish a dozen volumes without having to travel many hundred miles for subjects.

We worked hard and struggled manfully with overwhelming difficulties, yet I have been abused most unjustly by the Canadian papers for revealing some of the mysteries of the Backwoods. Not one word was said *against the country* in my book, as was falsely asserted. It was written as a warning to well-educated persons not to settle in localities for which they were unfitted by their *previous habits and education.* In this I hoped to confer a service both on them and Canada; for the *prosperous* settlement of such persons on cleared farms must prove more beneficial to the colony than their *ruin in the bush.* . . .

The country is not yet in existence that can present us a better government and wiser institutions than the British. Long may Canada recognise her rule, and rejoice in her sway! Should she ever be so unwise as to relinquish the privileges she enjoys under the sovereignty of the mother country, she may seek protection *nearer* and "*fare worse!*" The sorrows and trials that I experienced during my first eight years' residence in Canada, have been more than counterbalanced by the remaining twelve of comfort and peace. I have long felt the deepest interest in her prosperity and improvement. I no longer regard myself as an alien on her shores, but her daughter by adoption, – the happy mother of Canadian children, – rejoicing in the warmth and hospitality of a Canadian Home!

May the blessing of God rest upon the land! and her people ever prosper under a religious, liberal, and free government!

Major John Richardson (1796-1852)

Canada's first native-born novelist of any note, John Richardson established an international reputation for his romances, based on the colourful life of his own time and that of his forebears. He was perhaps the first Canadian to adapt the themes and techniques of the Gothic novelists, Walter Scott and James Fenimore Cooper to the Canadian frontier, and to note the possibilities for fiction in the Canadian past which would later attract such writers as Rosanna Leprohon, William Kirby and Gilbert Parker among others.

Born in Queenston, Upper Canada on October 4, 1796, John Richardson was the son of an assistant surgeon with Simcoe's rangers and his wife Madeleine Askin, daughter of Detroit merchant Colonel John Askin and his Indian wife.[1] In 1802, the family moved to Amherstburg where Dr. Richardson was surgeon to the garrison and here John attended school. At fifteen, he enlisted in the army on the outbreak of the War of 1812 and, as a member of the Guard of Honour, was among those who took possession of the Fort at Detroit. He served in all engagements of the war until his capture at Moraviantown and subsequent imprisonment in Detroit, then in Cincinnati and Frankfort, Kentucky. On his parole he immediately re-enlisted; he joined the 8th King's Regiment and sailed to defeat Napoleon but arrived after Waterloo; when the Regiment disbanded, he joined the Queen's Regiment which sailed to the West Indies in 1816. In 1818 he was transferred to the 92nd Highlanders and placed on half-pay. For the next sixteen years he lived in London and began his writing career. In 1834 he returned to military service and for his aid to Isabella of Spain with the Auxiliary Legion, he was rewarded with the rank of major and a a royal decoration.

In 1838 Richardson returned to Canada but arrived too late to support the crown in the short-lived Rebellion of 1837. He lived first in Toronto, then in Lower Canada and Amherstburg, and awaited recognition and a political appointment from Lord Durham and his successor Lord Sydenham; he even rejected a commission for the London *Times* to write on Canada as the editors opposed Durham. In 1841, disappointed in his hopes, he moved to Brockville where he began a periodical *The New Era* or *Canadian Chronicle* for which he wrote all his own copy; his second periodical *The Canadian Loyalist and Spirit of 1812* was printed in Kingston from 1842-4. He was finally rewarded by an appointment as Superintendent of Police on the Welland Canal in 1845 but the position was abolished in 1846, partly because of some tactlessness on the part of Richardson himself. He spent 1847 and 1848 in Montreal and in 1849 moved to New York, embittered and in search of a wider audience. Here he died in poverty in May, 1852.

Richardson's first publications were a poem in four cantos, "Techumseh" (1828), and a novel *Écarté* or *The Salons of Paris* (1829), a sensational exposé of the evils of gambling. *Wacousta* or *The Prophecy* (1832) deals with the seige of Pontiac on Detroit and a sequel *The Canadian Brothers* or *The Prophecy Fulfilled: A Tale of the late American War* (1840) is drawn from his own experience in the War of 1812 (reprinted in the United States as *Matilda Montgomerie*). Richardson also wrote several pot-boilers: *The Monk Knight of St. John: A Tale of the Crusaders* (1850), *Hardscrabble* or *The Fall of Chicago: A Tale of Indian Warfare* (1850) and a sequel *Wau-nan-gee* or *The Massacre at Chicago* (1852) as well as a novel *Jack Bragg in Spain*, published only in *The New Era*. He also published several political and historical works: "Journal of the Movements of the British Legion" concerning the seige of San Sebastian in two parts (1836 and 1837), "A Trip to Walpole Island and Port Sarnia" for *The Literary Garland* (1842), *The War of 1812* (1842), *Eight Years in Canada* (1847) and its sequel "The Guards in Canada" (1848).

Richardson once remarked bitterly to Lord Sydenham that he was unacknowledged as "the only Author this country has produced, or who has attempted to infuse in it a spirit of literature". Yet he was popular in his day and *Wacousta* saw six printings in its first eight years. In his youth, Richardson had been fascinated by the tales of Pontiac's seige of Detroit in 1763 recounted by his stepgrandmother, and even at that time longed to "grow up to manhood that I might write a book about it". *Wacousta* deals with Pontiac's attempt to wrest the forts of Michilimackinac and Detroit from the British, an episode later made popular by Francis Parkman in his History *The Conspiracy of Pontiac* (1851). In the introduction, Richardson states that only the artifice of Pontiac is real; "all else is imaginary." "Wacousta" is the alias of Reginald Morton who has joined the French forces in league with the Indians to revenge himself upon his rival, Colonel de Haldimar. The novel has been consistently popular since its first publication, and has appeared in twelve different editions, three of these since 1900.

[1] See Desmond Pacey, page 152.

TEXT:

Wacousta. Philadelphia: Kay & Biddle, 1833.

See also:

Introduction to *Wacousta*. ed. Carl F. Klinck. Toronto: New Canadian Library, 1967.

Ray Palmer Baker. *A History of English Canadian Literature*. Cambridge: University Press, 1920.

Desmond Pacey. "John Richardson: A Colonial Romantic" in *Essays in Canadian Criticism*. Toronto: Ryerson, 1969.

William Renwick Ridell. *John Richardson*. Toronto: Ryerson, 1923.

From *Wacousta*

CHAPTER XV

[*A week has passed between the visit of Pontiac and his chiefs to the fort at Detroit and the day they have appointed for their second meeting in council. In the meantime, the garrison has collected supplies of venison and Indian corn which will last them for over six weeks. At length the day dawns in the full glory of autumn.*]

MEANWHILE the white flag had again been raised by the Indians upon the bomb-proof; and this having been readily met by a corresponding signal from the fort, a numerous band of savages now issued from the cover with which their dark forms had hitherto been identified, and spread themselves far and near upon the common. On this occasion they were without arms, offensive or defensive, of any kind, if we may except the knife which was always carried at the girdle, and which constituted a part rather of their necessary dress than of their warlike equipment. These warriors might have been about five hundred in number, and were composed chiefly of picked men from the nations of the Ottawas, the Delawares, and the Shawanees; each race being distinctly recognisable from the others by certain peculiarities of form and feature which individualised, if we may so term it, the several tribes. Their only covering was the legging before described, composed in some instances of cloth, but principally of smoked deerskin, and the flap that passed through the girdle around the loins, by which the straps attached to the leggings were secured. Their bodies, necks, and arms were, with the exception of a few slight ornaments, entirely naked; and even the blanket, that served them as a couch by night and a covering by day, had, with one single exception, been dispensed with, apparently with a view to avoid anything like encumbrance in their approaching sport. Each individual was provided with a stout sapling of about three feet in length, curved, and flattened at the root extremity, like that used at the Irish hurdle; which game, in fact, the manner of ball-playing among the Indians in every way resembled.

Interspersed among these warriors were a nearly equal number of squaws. These were to be seen lounging carelessly about in small groups, and were of all ages; from the hoary-headed, shrivelled-up hag, whose eyes still sparkled with a fire that her lank and attenuated frame denied, to the young girl of twelve, whose dark and glowing cheek, rounded bust, and penetrating glance, bore striking evidence of the precociousness of Indian beauty. These latter looked with evident interest on the sports of the young warriors, who, throwing down their hurdles, either vied with each other in the short but incredibly swift foot-race, or indulged themselves in wrestling and leaping; while their companions, abandoned to the full security they felt to be attached to the white flag waving on the fort, lay at their lazy length upon the sward, ostensibly following the movements of the several competitors in these sports, but in reality with heart and eye directed solely to the fortification that lay beyond. Each of these females, in addition to the machecoti, or petticoat, which in one solid square of broad-cloth was tightly wrapped around the loins, also carried a blanket loosely thrown around the person, but closely confined over the shoulders in front, and reaching below the knee. There was an air of constraint in their movements, which accorded ill with the occasion of festivity for which they were assembled; and it was remarkable, whether it arose from deference to those to whom they were slaves, as well as wives and daughters, or from whatever other cause it might be, none of them ventured to recline themselves upon the sward in imitation of the warriors.

When it had been made known to the governor that the Indians had begun to develope themselves in force upon the common unarmed, yet redolent with the spirit that was to direct their meditated sports, the soldiers were dismissed from their respective companies to the ramparts; where they were now to be seen, not drawn up in formidable and hostile array, but collected together in careless groups, and simply in their side-arms. This reciprocation of confidence on the part of the garrison was acknowledged by the Indians by marks of approbation, expressed as much by the sudden and classic disposition of their fine forms into attitudes strikingly illustrative of their admiration and pleasure, as by the interjectional sounds that passed from one to the other of the throng. From the increased alacrity with which they now lent themselves to the preparatory and inferior amusements of the day, it was evident their satisfaction was complete.

Hitherto the principal chiefs had, as on the previous occasion, occupied the bomb-proof; and now, as then, they appeared to be deliberating among themselves, but evidently in a more energetic and serious manner. At length they separated, when Ponteac, accompanied by the chiefs who had attended him on the former day, once more led in the direction of the fort. The moment of his advance was the signal for the commencement of the principal game. In an instant those of the warriors who lay reclining on the sward sprang to their feet, while

the wrestlers and racers resumed their hurdles, and prepared themselves for the trial of mingled skill and swiftness. At first they formed
a dense group in the centre of the common; and then, diverging in
two equal files both to the right and to the left of the immediate
centre, where the large ball was placed, formed an open chain, extending from the skirt of the forest to the commencement of the village.
On the one side were ranged the Delawares and Shawanees, and on
the other the more numerous nations of the Ottawas. The women of
these several tribes, apparently much interested in the issue of an
amusement in which the manliness and activity of their respective
friends were staked, had gradually and imperceptibly gained the front
of the fort, where they were now huddled in groups, at about twenty
paces from the drawbridge, and bending eagerly forward to command
the movements of the ball-players.

In his circuit round the walls, Ponteac was seen to remark the
confiding appearance of the unarmed soldiery with a satisfaction that
was not sought to be disguised; and from the manner in which he
threw his glance along each face of the rampart, it was evident his
object was to embrace the numerical strength collected there. It was
moreover observed, when he passed the groups of squaws on his way
to the gate, he addressed some words in a strange tongue to the elder
matrons of each.

Once more the dark warriors were received at the gate, by Major
Blackwater; and, as with firm but elastic tread, they moved across the
square, each threw his eyes rapidly and anxiously around, and with
less of concealment in his manner than had been manifested on the
former occasion. On every hand the same air of nakedness and desertion met their gaze. Not even a soldier of the guard was to be seen;
and when they cast their eyes upwards to the windows of the block-
houses, they were found to be tenantless as the area through which
they passed. A gleam of fierce satisfaction pervaded the swarthy
countenances of the Indians; and the features of Ponteac, in particular,
expressed the deepest exultation. Instead of leading his party, he now
brought up the rear; and when arrived in the centre of the fort, he,
without any visible cause for the accident, stumbled, and fell to the
earth. The other chiefs for the moment lost sight of their ordinary
gravity, and marked their sense of the circumstance by a prolonged
sound, partaking of the mingled character of a laugh and a yell.
Startled at the cry, Major Blackwater, who was in front, turned to
ascertain the cause. At that moment Ponteac sprang lightly again to
his feet, responding to the yell of his confederates by another even
more startling, fierce, and prolonged than their own. He then stalked
proudly to the head of the party, and even preceded Major Blackwater
into the council room.

In this rude theatre of conference some changes had been made
since their recent visit, which escaped not the observation of the

quick-sighted chiefs. Their mats lay in the position they had previously occupied, and the chairs of the officers were placed as before, but the room itself had been considerably enlarged. The slight partition terminating the interior extremity of the mess-room, and dividing it from that of one of the officers, had been removed; and midway through this, extending entirely across, was drawn a curtain of scarlet cloth, against which the imposing figure of the governor, elevated as his seat was above those of the other officers, was thrown into strong relief. There was another change, that escaped not the observation of the Indians, and that was, not more than one half of the officers who had been present at the first conference were now in the room. Of these latter, one had, moreover, been sent away by the governor the moment the chiefs were ushered in.

"Ugh!" ejaculated the proud leader, as he took his seat unceremoniously, and yet not without reluctance, upon the mat. "The council-room of my father, is bigger than when the Ottawa was here before, yet the number of his chiefs is not so many."

"The great chief of the Ottawas knows that the Saganaw has promised the red skins a feast," returned the governor. "Were he to leave it to his young warriors to provide it, he would not be able to receive the Ottawa like a great chief, and to make peace with him as he could wish."

"My father has a great deal of cloth, red, like the blood of a pale face," pursued the Indian, rather in demand than in observation, as he pointed with his finger to the opposite end of the room. "When the Ottawa was here last, he did not see it."

"The great chief of the Ottawas knows that the great father of the Saganaw has a big heart to make presents to the red skins. The cloth the Ottawa sees there is sufficient to make leggings for the chiefs of all the nations."

Apparently satisfied with this reply, the fierce Indian uttered one of his strong guttural and assentient "ughs," and then commenced filling the pipe of peace, correct on the present occasion in all its ornaments, which was handed to him by the Delaware chief. It was remarked by the officers this operation took up an unusually long portion of his time, and that he frequently turned his ear, like a horse stirred by the huntsman's horn, with quick and irrepressible eagerness towards the door.

"The pale warrior, the friend of the Ottawa chief, is not here," said the governor, as he glanced his eye along the semicircle of Indians. "How is this? Is his voice still sick, that he cannot come; or has the great chief of the Ottawas forgotten to tell him?"

"The voice of the pale warrior is still sick, and he cannot speak," replied the Indian. "The Ottawa chief is very sorry; for the tongue of his friend the pale face is full of wisdom."

Scarcely had the last words escaped his lips, when a wild shrill cry from without the fort rang on the ears of the assembled council, and caused a momentary commotion among the officers. It arose from a single voice, and that voice could not be mistaken by any who had heard it once before. A second or two, during which the officers and chiefs kept their eyes intently fixed on each other, passed anxiously away, and then nearer to the gate, apparently on the very drawbridge itself, was pealed forth the wild and deafening yell of a legion of devilish voices. At that sound, the Ottawa and the other chiefs sprang to their feet, and their own fierce cry responded to that yet vibrating on the ears of all. Already were their gleaming tomahawks brandished wildly over their heads, and Pontéac had even bounded a pace forward to reach the governor with the deadly weapon, when at the sudden stamping of the foot of the latter upon the floor, the scarlet cloth in the rear was thrown aside, and twenty soldiers, their eyes glancing along the barrels of their levelled muskets, met the startled gaze of the astonished Indians.

An instant was enough to satisfy the keen chief of the true state of the case. The calm composed mien of the officers, not one of whom had even attempted to quit his seat, amid the din by which his ears were so alarmingly assailed, – the triumphant, yet dignified, and even severe expression of the governor's countenance; and above all, the unexpected presence of the prepared soldiery, – all these at once assured him of the discovery of his treachery, and the danger that awaited him. The necessity for an immediate attempt to join his warriors without, was now obvious to the Ottawa; and scarcely had he conceived the idea before it was sought to be executed. In a single spring he gained the door of the mess-room, and, followed eagerly and tumultuously by the other chiefs, to whose departure no opposition was offered, in the next moment stood on the steps of the piazza that ran along the front of the building whence he had issued.

The surprise of the Indians on reaching this point was now too powerful to be dissembled; and, incapable either of advancing or receding, they remained gazing on the scene before them with an air of mingled stupefaction, rage, and alarm. Scarcely ten minutes had elapsed since they had proudly strode through the naked area of the fort, and yet, even in that short space of time, its appearance had been entirely changed. Not a part was there now of the surrounding buildings that was not redolent with human life, and hostile preparation. Through every window of the officers' low rooms, was to be seen the dark and frowning muzzle of a field-piece, bearing upon the gateway; and behind these were artillerymen, holding their lighted matches, supported again by files of bayonets, that glittered in their rear. In the block-houses the same formidable array of field-pieces and muskets was visible; while from the four angles of the square, as many heavy guns, that had been artfully masked at the entrance of the chiefs, seemed ready to sweep away every thing that should come before them. The guard-room near the gate presented the same hostile front. The doors of this, as well as of the other buildings, had been firmly secured within; but from every window affording cover to the troops, gleamed a line of bayonets rising above the threatening field-pieces, pointed, at a distance of little more than twelve feet, directly upon the gateway. In addition to his musket, each man of the guard moreover held a hand grenade, provided with a short fuze that could be ignited in a moment from the matches of the gunners, and with immediate effect. The soldiers in the block-houses were similarly provided.

Almost magical as was the change thus suddenly effected in the appearance of the garrison, it was not the most interesting feature in the exciting scene. Choking up the gateway, in which they were completely wedged, and crowding the drawbridge, a dense mass of dusky Indians were to be seen casting their fierce glances around; yet paralysed in their movements by the unlooked for display of a resisting force, threatening instant annihilation to those who should attempt either to advance or to recede. Never, perhaps, was astonishment and disappointment more forcibly depicted on the human countenance, than as they were now exhibited by these men, who had already, in imagination, secured to themselves an easy conquest. They were the warriors who had so recently been engaged in the manly yet innocent exercise of the ball; but, instead of the harmless hurdle, each now carried a short gun in one hand and a gleaming tomahawk in the other. After the first general yelling heard in the council-room not a sound was uttered. Their burst of rage and triumph had evidently been checked by the unexpected manner of their reception, and they now stood on the spot on which the further advance of each had been arrested, so silent and motionless, that, but for the rolling of their dark eyes, as they keenly measured the insurmountable barriers that were opposed to their progress, they might almost have been taken for a wild group of statuary.

Conspicuous at the head of these was he who wore the blanket; a tall warrior, on whom rested the startled eye of every officer and soldier who was so situated as to behold him. His face was painted black as death; and as he stood under the arch of the gateway, with his white turbaned head towering far above those of his companions, this formidable and mysterious enemy might have been likened to the spirit of darkness presiding over his terrible legions.

In order to account for the extraordinary appearance of the Indians, armed in every way for death, at a moment when neither gun nor tomahawk was apparently within miles of their reach, it will be necessary to revert to the first entrance of the chiefs into the fort. The fall of Ponteac had been the effect of design; and the yell pealed forth by him, on recovering his feet, as if in taunting reply to the laugh of his comrades, was in reality a signal intended for the guidance of the Indians without. These, now following up their game with increasing spirit, at once changed the direction of their line, bringing the ball nearer to the fort. In the eagerness to effect this object, they had overlooked the gradual secession of the unarmed troops, spectators of their sport, from the ramparts, until scarcely more than twenty stragglers were left. As they neared the gate, the squaws broke up their several groups, and, forming a line on either hand of the road leading to the drawbridge, appeared to separate solely with a view not to impede the action of the players. For an instant a dense group collected around the ball, which had been driven to within a hundred yards of the gate, and fifty hurdles were crossed in their endeavors to secure it, when the warrior, who formed the solitary exception to the multitude, in his blanket covering, and who had been lingering in the extreme rear of the party, came rapidly up to the spot where the well-affected struggle was maintained. At his approach, the hurdles of the other players were withdrawn, when, at a single blow of his powerful arm, the ball was seen flying into the air in an oblique direction, and was for a moment lost altogether to the view. When it again met the eye, it was descending perpendicularly into the very centre of the fort.

With the fleetness of thought now commenced a race that had ostensibly for its object the recovery of the lost ball; and in which, he who had driven it with such resistless force, outstripped them all. Their course lay between the two lines of squaws; and scarcely had the heads of the bounding Indians reached the opposite extremity of those lines, when the women suddenly threw back their blankets, and disclosed each a short gun and a tomahawk. To throw away their hurdles and seize upon these, was the work of an instant. Already, in imagination, was the fort their own; and, such was the peculiar exultation of the black and turbaned warrior, when he felt the planks of the drawbridge bending beneath his feet, all the ferocious joy of his soul was pealed forth in the terrible cry which, rapidly succeeded by that of the other Indians, had resounded so fearfully through the council room. What their disappointment was, when, on gaining the interior, they found the garrison prepared for their reception, has already been shown.

"Secure that traitor, men!" exclaimed the governor, advancing into the square, and pointing to the black warrior, whose quick eye was now glancing on every side, to discover some assailable point in the formidable defences of the troops.

A laugh of scorn and derision escaped the lips of the warrior. "Is there a man – are there any ten men, even with Governor de Haldimar at their head, who will be bold enough to attempt it?" he asked. "Nay!" he pursued, stepping boldly a pace or two in front of the wondering savages, – "here I stand singly, and defy your whole garrison!"

A sudden movement among the soldiers in the guard-room announced they were preparing to execute the order of their chief. The eye of the black warrior sparkled with ferocious pleasure; and he made a gesture to his followers, which was replied to by the sudden tension of their hitherto relaxed forms into attitudes of expectance and preparation.

"Stay, men; quit not your cover for your lives!" commanded the governor, in a loud deep voice: – "keep the barricades fast, and move not."

A cloud of anger and disappointment passed over the features of the black warrior. It was evident the object of his bravado was to draw the troops from their defences, that they might be so mingled with their enemies as to render the cannon useless, unless friends and foes (which was by no means probable) should alike be sacrificed. The governor had penetrated the design in time to prevent the mischief.

In a moment of uncontrollable rage, the savage warrior aimed his tomahawk at the head of the governor. The latter stepped lightly aside, and the steel sank with such force into one of the posts supporting the piazza, that the quivering handle snapped close off at its head. At that moment, a single shot, fired from the guard-house, was drowned in the yell of approbation which burst from the lips of the dark crowd. The turban of the warrior was, however, seen flying through the air, carried away by the force of the bullet which had torn it from his head. He himself was unharmed.

"A narrow escape for us both, Colonel de Haldimar," he observed, as soon as the yell had subsided, and with an air of the most perfect unconcern. "Had my tomahawk obeyed the first impulse of my heart, I should have cursed myself and died: as it is, I have reason to avoid all useless exposure of my own life, at present. A second bullet may be better directed; and to die, robbed of my revenge, would ill answer the purpose of a life devoted to its attainment. Remember my pledge!"

At the hasty command of the governor, a hundred muskets were raised to the shoulders of his men; but, before a single eye could glance along the barrel, the formidable and active warrior had bounded over the heads of the nearest Indians into a small space that was left unoccupied; when, stooping suddenly to the earth, he disappeared altogether from the view of his enemies. A slight moving in the centre of the numerous band crowding the gateway, and extending even beyond the bridge, was now discernible: it was like the waving of a field of standing corn, through which some animal rapidly winds its tortuous course, bending aside as the object advances, and closing again when it has passed. After the lapse of a minute, the terrible warrior was seen to spring again to his feet, far in the rear of the band; and then, uttering a fierce shout of exultation, to make good his retreat towards the forest.

Meanwhile, Ponteac and the other chiefs of the council continued rooted to the piazza on which they had rushed at the unexpected display of the armed men behind the scarlet curtain. The loud "Waugh" that burst from the lips of all, on finding themselves thus foiled in their schemes of massacre, had been succeeded, the instant afterwards, by feelings of personal apprehension, which each, however, had collectedness enough to disguise. Once the Ottawa made a movement as if he would have cleared the space that kept him from his warriors; but the emphatical pointing of the finger of Colonel de Haldimar to the levelled muskets of the men in the block-houses prevented him, and the attempt was not repeated. It was remarked by the officers, who also stood on the piazza, close behind the chiefs, when the black warrior threw his tomahawk at the governor, a shade of displeasure passed over the features of the Ottawa; and that, when he found the daring attempt was not retaliated on his people, his countenance had been momentarily lighted up with a satisfied expression, apparently marking his sense of forbearance so unexpectedly shown.

"What says the great chief of the Ottawas now?" asked the governor, calmly, and breaking a profound silence that had succeeded to the last fierce yell of the formidable being just departed. "Was the Saganaw not right when he said the Ottawa came with guile in his heart, and a lie upon his lips? But the Saganaw is not a fool, and he can read the thoughts of his enemies upon their faces, and long before their lips have spoken."

"Ugh!" ejaculated the Indian; "my father is a great chief, and his head is full of wisdom. Had he been feeble, like the other chiefs of the Saganaw, the stronghold of the Detroit must have fallen, and the red skins would have danced their war dance round the scalps of his young men, even in the council room where they came to talk of peace."

"Does the great chief of the Ottawas see the big thunder of the Saganaw?" pursued the governor: "if not, let him open his eyes and look. The Saganaw has but to move his lips, and swifter than the lightning would the pale faces sweep away the warriors of the Ottawa, even where they now stand: in less time than the Saganaw is now speaking, would they mow them down like the grass of the prairie."

"Ugh!" again exclaimed the chief, with mixed doggedness and fierceness: "if what my father says is true, why does he not pour out his anger upon the red skins?"

"Let the great chief of the Ottawas listen," replied the governor with dignity. "When the great chiefs of all the nations that are in league with the Ottawas came last to the council, the Saganaw knew that they carried deceit in their hearts, and that they never meant to smoke the pipe of peace, or to bury the hatchet in the ground. The Saganaw might have kept them prisoners, that their warriors might be without a head; but he had given his word to the great chief of the Ottawas, and the word of the Saganaw is never broken. Even now, while both the chiefs and the warriors are in his power, he will not slay them, for he wishes to show the Ottawa the desire of the Saganaw is to be friendly with the red skins, and not to destroy them. Wicked men from the Canadas have whispered lies in the ear of the Ottawa; but a great chief should judge for himself, and take council only from the wisdom of his own heart. The Ottawa and his warriors may go," he resumed, after a short pause; "the path by which they came is again open to them. Let them depart in peace; the big thunder of the Saganaw shall not harm them."

The countenance of the Indian, who had clearly seen the danger of his position, wore an expression of surprise which could not be dissembled; low exclamations passed between him and his companions; and, then pointing to the tomahawk that lay half buried in the wood, he said, doubtingly, –

"It was the pale face, the friend of the great chief of the Ottawas, who struck the hatchet at my father. The Ottawa is not a fool to believe the Saganaw can sleep without revenge."

"The great chief of the Ottawas shall know us better," was the reply. "The young warriors of the Saganaw might destroy their enemies where they now stand, but they seek not their blood. When the Ottawa chief takes council from his own heart, and not from the lips of a cowardly dog of a pale face, who strikes his tomahawk and then flies, his wisdom will tell him to make peace with the Saganaw, whose warriors are without treachery, even as they are without fear."

Another of those deep interjectional "ughs" escaped the chest of the proud Indian.

"What my father says is good," he returned; "but the pale face is a great warrior, and the Ottawa chief is his friend. The Ottawa will go."

He then addressed a few sentences, in a tongue unknown to the officers, to the swarthy and anxious crowd in front. These were answered by a low, sullen, yet assentient grunt, from the united band, who now turned, though with justifiable caution and distrust, and recrossed the drawbridge without hinderance from the troops. Ponteac waited until the last Indian had departed, and then making a movement to the governor, which, with all its haughtiness, was meant to mark his sense of the forbearance and good faith that had been manifested, once more stalked proudly and calmly across the area, followed by the remainder of the chiefs. The officers who were with the governor ascended to the ramparts, to follow their movements; and it was not before their report had been made that the Indians were immerging once more into the heart of the forest, the troops were withdrawn from their formidable defences, and the gate of the fort again firmly secured.

Alexander McLachlan (1818-1896)

"The Burns of Canada" as he was called, Alexander McLachlan was one of the few Canadian poets writing before Confederation whose name is still known today. Although he is remembered for his popular verse celebrating the cause of the working man, McLachlan was also a link between the early verse of Goldsmith and Howe and the more authentically Candian poetry of Sangster and his successors. In his *Selection from Canadian Poets* E. H. Dewart refers to McLachlan as "one of the pioneer bards of British Canada who have laid the foundations of our poetic literature in the face of many discouragements".

Alexander McLachlan was born in 1818 in Johnston, Renfrewshire, Scotland. His father and an uncle went to Upper Canda in the thirties where they bought farms in Caledon, Peel County. But Charles McLachlan died before he could return home for his family, and Alexander remained in Scotland where he worked to help support his mother and sisters, first in a cotton factory and later as an apprentice to a tailor in Glasgow. In 1840 he emigrated to Canada and settled on his father's farm in Peel County, where he met and married his uncle's daughter Clamina. A year later he sold the farm, and in 1844 took up a bush farm in Downie Township and in 1847 another in North Easthope, both in Perth County. Finally he abandoned attempts to live by farming and moved to Erin Township, Wellington County, where he did some tailoring, lectured for the Mechanics' Institute, and devoted himself to reading and writing. Through the influence of his friend Thomas D'Arcy McGee, he was appointed government lecturer and emigration agent for Canada in Scotland in 1862. In 1877 he returned to country life, settling in Amaranth Township west of Orangeville where his son Malcolm and later Alexander junior managed the farm. After the death of Alexander in 1895, he moved to Orangeville where he died a few months later.

He printed a number of books during his lifetime at his own cost: *The Spirit of Love and Other Poems* (1846) *Poems* (1856), *Lyrics* (1858), and *The Emigrant and Other Poems* (1861). *Poems and Songs* was published in 1874 at the expense of a loyal group of subscribers, and reprinted in 1888. *The Poetical Works of Alexander McLachlan* did not appear until 1900, several years after his death.

McLachlan is best known to-day for his popular pieces such as "Jack's as Good as His Master" and '"The Man Who Rose from Nothing" which reflect the strong feeling of the labouring classes as opposed to those of the gentry expressed by such writers as Susannah

Moodie. But McLachlan's poetry has many facets. "The Emigrant", a long narrative published in part in 1861, and never completed describes in rhyming couplets with occasional quatrains the response of the immigrant to the experience of a new land, his nostalgia for home, his daily discouragements, and his optimism for the future. McLachlan's range is much wider than is commonly recognized, and he has been called by Dewart "the sweetest and most intensely human of all our bards". His natural descriptions and his preference for a rural to an urban environment look forward to Sangster and the Confederation Poets, in particular Lampman. Some of the personal poems are effective, and the dialect poems and narratives such as "Auld Hawkie's Dream" suggest his master Burns in their simplicity and satiric wit.

TEXTS:

Where possible, works have been chosen from *Poems and Songs*, Toronto: Hunter and Rose, 1884. The *Poetical Works*, (Toronto: Briggs 1900) edited by McLachlan's daughter Mary and his literary executor, have adopted a number of readings which vary from minor changes in punctuation to major alteration of the lines and stanzas. The dates of the poems indicate which text been used.

See also:

Introduction to *The Poetical Works*
Nineteenth Century Narrative Poetry. ed. David Sinclair. Toronto: New Canadian Library, 1972.

Young Canada, or Jack's as Good as his Master

I love this land of forest grand!
    The land where labour's free;
Let others roam away from home,
    Be this the land for me!
Where no one moils, and strains and toils,
    That snobs may thrive the faster;
And all are free, as men should be,
    And Jack's as good's his master!

Where none are slaves, that lordly knaves
  May idle all the year;
For rank and caste are of the past, –
  They'll never flourish here!
And Jew or Turk if he'll but work,
  ` Need never fear disaster;
He reaps the crop he sowed in hope,
  For Jack's as good's his master.

Our aristocracy of toil
  Have made us what you see –
The nobles of the forge and soil,
  With ne'er a pedigree!
It makes one feel himself a man,
  His very blood leaps faster,
Where wit or worth's preferred to birth,
  And Jack's as good's his master!

Here's to the land of forests grand!
  The land where labour's free;
Let others roam away from home,
  Be this the land for me!
For here 'tis plain, the heart and brain,
  The very soul grows vaster!
Where men are free, as they should be,
  And Jack's as good's his master!

(1874)

The Man Who Rose from Nothing

Around the world the fame is blown
  Of fighting heroes, dead and gone;
But we've a hero of our own –
  The man who rose from nothing.

He's a magician great and grand;
The forests fled at his command;
And here he said, "let cities stand!" –
  The man who rose from nothing.

And in our legislative hall
He towering stands alone, like Saul,
"A head and shoulders over all," –
   The man who rose from nothing.

His efforts he will ne'er relax,
Has faith in figures and in facts,
And always calls an axe an axe, –
   The man who rose from nothing.

The gentleman in word and deed;
And short and simple is his creed;
"Fear God and help the soul in need!" –
   The man who rose from nothing.

In other lands he's hardly known,
For he's a product of our own;
Could grace a shanty or a throne, –
   The man who rose from nothing.

Here's to the land of lakes and pines,
On which the sun of freedom shines,
Because we meet on all our lines
   The man who rose from nothing.

(1874)

Whip-Poor-Will

There is a lonely spirit,
   Which wanders through the wood,
And tells its mournful story,
   In every solitude.
It comes abroad at eventide,
   And hangs beside the rill,
And murmurs to the passer by –
   "Whip-poor-will."

O, 'tis a hapless spirit,
    In likeness of a bird!
A grief, that cannot utter
    Another woful word.
A soul that seeks for sympathy,
    A woe that won't be still;
A wandering sorrow murmuring –
    "Whip-poor-whill!"

(1858)

Autumn

The flowers of the summer have faded away,
And Autumn is here with her mantle of grey;
The sear leaves are falling, the woodlands are mute,
And the sound of brooks wailing ascends like a lute;
The bow'r is forsaken, its beauty is gone –
One poor little robin is chirping alone –
And the winds wi' their soughing how sadly they say,
"All things that are lovely are passing away!"

The blackbird is silent beside the lone spring,
The lav'rock is folding her weary, wet wing;
Afar in the dell of the desolate yew
Is heard the deep wail of the lonely curlew;
The cuckoo is off and away with the spring,
And the heart vainly seeks for some beautiful thing,
While the winds with their soughing, how sadly they say,
"All things that are lovely are passing away!"

So dark and unlovely's the Autumn of life,
For grey hair and mem'ry with joys are at strife;
The bright past has perish'd, the future is black,
The heart's only pleasure's a long looking back –
A long looking back to life's early spring,
To hearts that have wither'd, to hopes taken wing;
While forms of the lost ones come sadly and say,
"All things that are lovely are passing away!"

And were they but shadows, false, fleeting, and vain?
And shall I ne'er meet them in gladness again?
Bright meteors that came but to dazzle the sight,
And then fade away in the bosom of night?
Came they but to leave us in darkness and woe,
Aweary of all fleeting things here below?
"They've gone and we'll follow," Hope sweetly doth say,
"Where nothing that's lovely shall e'er pass away."

(1900)

Sighs in the City

Wearily my days are past;
For my heavy lot is cast
In the crowded city vast.

How my spirit longs to be
From this dreary prison free –
Oh, the laughing meads for me!

Oh! to follow the cuckoo,
While the glades are drapt wi' dew,
And the lark is in the blue!

Oh, to tread the flowery sod,
Free from all this heavy load –
One with Nature and with God!

Spring is forth with joyous air,
Strewing gems so rich and rare,
Showering gowans everywhere.

I will go where'er she goes,
Pausing often where she throws
The vi'let, and the red, red rose.

And we'll seek the glades of green,
Where the honeysuckles lean,
And the bluwarts ope their een;

Where the auld witch hazels hing,
And the woodbines creep and cling,
Round about the lonely spring;

Where the birds are blithe aboon,
And the laughing runnels rin
Onward in their merry din,

Treading paths the wild bee knows;
Where the grass the greenest grows,
In the haunts of the primrose.

Where the foxglove, fair and tall,
Leans against the rocky wall,
List'ning to the waterfall;

Where the bonnie hawthorn hings,
And the wee gray lintie sings
Of unutterable things:

And half hidden by the weeds,
Bonnie bluebells hing their heads,
Drapt wi' dew, like siller beads.

And the lily, meek and mild,
Blooming in the lonely wild,
That I lov'd so when a child!

Little wildlings, pure and bright,
Still, as to my childhood's sight,
Ye're a rapture, a delight!

Far from those who buy and sell,
I will seek the quiet dell –
Lonely ones with you to dwell!

Where no worldling soils the sod,
I'll live in your green abode,
One with Nature and with God.

(1874)

Lovely Alice

Awake, lovely Alice, the dawn's on the hill,
The voice of the mavis is heard by the rill,
The blackbird is singing his song in the brake,
And the green woods are ringing – awake, love, awake!

The wild rose is blushing, the pea is in bloom,
The zephyr is brushing the long yellow broom;
But thy voice is far sweeter than bird's on the tree,
And joy is far deeper, sweet Alice, with thee.

The voice of lone Locher comes mellow and sweet,
But sweeter to me were the fa' o' thy feet;
The hawthorn is hoary and rich with perfume,
But thou art the glory of nature in bloom.

Far deeper the joy, love, would nature impart
Were I but the lord of thine innocent heart;
And 'neath fortune's malice I ne'er would repine,
Wert thou, lovely Alice, oh, wert thou but mine!

(1861, 1900)

My Love Is Like the Lily Flower

My love is like the lily flower
   That blooms upon the lea:
I wadna gie ae blink o' her
   For a' the maids I see.

Her voice is like the bonnie bird's,
   That warbles 'mang the bow'rs,
Her breath is like the hawthorn when
   It's wat wi' morning show'rs.

And frae the gowans o' the glen
` She's caught her modest grace,
And a' the blushes o' the rose
    Hae leapt into her face.

She bears aboot, I kenna hoo,
    The joy o' simmer days,
The voice o' streams, and happy dreams
    Amang the broomy braes.

And when the bonnie lassie smiles
    Sae sweetly upon me,
Nae human tongue can ever tell
    The heav'n that's in her e'e.

And a' the lee-lang simmer day
    I'm in a dream divine,
And aye I wauken but to wish,
    Oh, were the lassie mine!

(1861)

Wilson's Grave[1]

They should not have buried thee here!
    O! they should have made thee a bed,
Where the flowers at thy feet would appear,
    And the birds would sing over thy head.

O! They should have laid thee to rest,
    From the smoke of the city, away
Where the dew would fall bright on thy breast,
    And the green turf would cover thy clay.

Afar in the forest's green shade,
    The tall pine above thee should wave,
Where the "Blue-bird" would perch o'er thy head,
    And the "Whip-poor-Will" sit on thy grave.

[1] Alexander Wilson, the Scottish poet and American ornithologist. He is buried in South-
wark, Philadelphia, near the wharves and the Navy-yard refreshment rooms.

Where Spring would come forth with her smiles,
    And the birds that to thee were so dear;
And sing 'mong the green leafy aisles,
    The songs you delighted to hear.

And the red man would marvel to meet
    A grave in the green forest shade;
And the hunter at evening would sit,
    And weep where thine ashes are laid.

They should not have buried thee here,
    For the forest above thee should wave,
But have borne thee away on thy bier,
    Where the birds would sing over thy grave.

(1874)

Auld Hawkie's Dream

'Tween midnicht an' mornin', that eerie hour when,
As Scripture says, "Deep sleep fa's doun upon men,"
When the wild winds are a' lockit up in their caves,
An' the ghosts o' the deid venture oot o' their graves,
To dauner aboot 'neath the bonnie muneshine,
Or bide aroun' places they likit lang syne.
Then, somehoo' or ither, I dreamed I was deid –
Guid kens what could put sie a thocht in my heid!
I was borne thro' the lift, an' awa' 'yont the mune,
And a' the wee stars that were rowin' abune.
At last I was loutit richt down at the gate,
Where holy Saint Peter's appointed to wait;
But tied on my back was a burden o' sin,
Sae I thocht I'd hae trouble ere I could get in.
There were things on my conscience that heavily sat,
Sic as dribblin' an' drinkin', an' waur things than that.
Ah! ye may believe me, I felt unco blate,
An' couldna tak' courage to rap at the gate.
Sae I crept in a corner to watch for a chance,
Whan wha does I see like a trooper advance,
But Granny McNab! Haith! I trummelt wi' fear!

What the deevil, thinks I, brings the auld viper here?
I dootna she comes just to clype upon me,
An' feth, the auld lass winna stick at a lee!
I only could mutter, "Guid guide us frae skaith,
A lost sowl am I if it's left to her aith!"
Oot at her I keekit, a' sweetin' wi' fricht,
An' thankfu' was I to be oot o' her sicht;
But up she comes bauldly, an' raps at the gate,
An' cries, "Open quickly, for I canna wait!"
Says I to mysel', "Lass, if they'll tak' you in
There's hope for me yet wi' my burden o' sin."

Then oot cam' Saint Peter – an' there did he stan',
The keys at his girdle, a sword in his han' –
An' says, rather snelly, "Wife, wha may ye be?"
When Granny says, smilin', "Ye suirly ken me?
I'm Mistress McNab, frae the East Neuk o' Fife –
Ye'll fin' my name's doun in the Lamb's Book o' Life.
I've focht the guid fecht, an' the battle I've won,
Sae lead me in-by to the Faither and Son.
I claim the reward – naething less than the croun,
Wi' the gems and the jewels a' buskit aroun'!
Upon His ain shoulders I laid a' my sin,
Sae stan' here nae langer, but juist tak' me in.
I can say a' my questions, I've lines frae the Session,
For ne'er was I catcht, sir, in ony transgression;
I believ'd the haill Book frae beginnin' to en',
Its' a' richt wi' me, Saint, sae juist tak' me ben."
"Hoot, hoot!" quo' the Saint, and he seem'd unco brief,
"We carena a bodle aboot your belief;
But juist let me hear o' some guid ye hae dune,
For it's only by guid works ye'll ever get in."

"The guid works I've done?" quo' she, "hear to the man!
I'm tellin' ye o' them as fast as I can.
The foremaist was I, man, in ev'ry guid work –
The pillar an' prop o' the auld Burgher Kirk.
I ne'er could put up wi' the claver an' clash
O' the Baptists an' a' the mere Methody trash:
Wi' their wun' an' their water, I haena a doot,
If there's licht amang them they'll sune put it oot.
An' then wi' new notions I ne'er could agree,
I stuck to the auld anes, whate'er they might be.
Jean Tamson insisted on common Salvation,
But, heth! I preferr'd universal Damnation.
Jean gangs to nae kirk, an' she tell't me atweel
Sectarianism's the wark o' the deil!

'Ah, Granny,' says she, 'when we leave this auld frame,
An' the spirit, unfetter'd, mak's aff for its hame,
We'll never be speert to which kirk did we go,
Were we sprinkled, or plowtit, – ah, no, Granny, no!
It's the lives we hae led, the guid or ill we hae dune,
That mak's us or mars us wi' them up abune.'

"She tried to convert me to Mercy an' Grace,
An' the natural guidness o' a' Adam's race,
An' spak' o' the caum o' the bonnie blue sky,
An' the fountain o' Mercy that never rins dry.
Noo, Saint, did ye e'er hear sic havers as thae?
Should she be alloo'd to lead young anes astray?
They're awfu', the doctrines that she does advance –
Thinks swearers and cut-throats may a' hae a chance;
She couldna catch me! for I threw in her mouth
'An e'e for an e'e, an' a tooth for a tooth.'"

The Saint shook his heid, and said, "Woman, begin
And tell me at last o' some guid ye hae dune!"

"But still," she continued, "od! am I no sayin',
'Tween huntin' down heresy, plottin' and prayin',
An' haulin' the ne'er-do-weel backsliders up,
An' them wha unworthily drank o' the cup,
I had a big han'fu' o' wark to get thro'.
Oh, wha's to look after the licht limmers noo?"

"Hoot! hoot!" quo' the Saint, "wife, for guidsake begin
An' tell me at last o' some guid ye hae dune!"

"Do ye mean to tell me, sir, I did nae guid,
When I for the kirk an' the cutty-stool stuid?
When I was reviled by the licht an' profane,
And bore the haill brunt o' the parish my lane,
An' focht wi' Auld Hawkie – the warst o' a' men –
Wha said 'twas a farce frae beginnin' to en'.
Oh, he's an auld blackguard, an' has a vile tongue!
His words aye fell on me like strokes frae a rung.
He said my religion was a' a mere sham;
Tell't me to my face, sir, I likit a dram;
An' tho' I had gotten the faith o' assurance,
That I was a Jezebel past a' endurance;
Tell't me to my face, in my auld flannen mutch,
In the days of lang syne, I'd been burnt for a wutch.

'Ye're juist Mistress Grundy,' quo' he – the auld rake!
I'm sorry there isna a hell for his sake!
Ye'll min' when he comes here o' what he has dune,
An' ye'll no let the wicked auld blasphemer in."

"Whisht! whisht!" said the Saint, "wife, I've hearken'd
    owre lang;
That ane ye ca' Hawkie was hardly far wrang.
Ye've come to the wrang place, my woman, I fear;
Your kind o' religion's o' nae accoont here.
Ye ne'er were the woman to lichten the load
O' ony puir wretch on life's wearisome road;
And, by your ain story, ye lived but a life
O' pious pretension, backbiting, and strife.
On mony a tender affection ye trod,
Tell't mony a lee for the glory o' God;
Ye've weel earned your place in the great lowin' heuch.
Speak nae ither word, I've heard mair than eneuch!
To a' honest folk ye're a terrible fricht,
Sae aff, ye auld bissom, an' oot o' my sicht!"

Dumbfounded, a moment the auld hizzie stan's,
Then up she rins at him, aclappin' her han's.
"A pretty-like story! Is't you, sir," says she,
"Wha daurs to keep oot sic a woman as me?
Ye were but a cooart, man, whan ye were tried!
I'm thinkin' the Maister I never denied.
Ye cursin' auld scunner! ye leein' auld lout!
An' ye'd be for keepin' the like o' me oot!
Na, na! Maister Peter, ere I gang to hell,
I'll hae twa-rhee words wi' the Faither himsel'."

For mair o' her clatter the Saint didna wait,
But in he slipt quickly an' bolted the gate.
An' oh! sic a pictur' was auld Granny's face,
O' impidence baffled, o' shame, an' disgrace,
I burst oot a lauchin'! – I fairly did scream –
Which startled me out o' my won'erfu' dream.

(1900)

Charles Heavysege (1816-1876)

An immigrant from England, Charles Heavysege came to Canada at the age of thirty-seven. His literary works were heavily influenced by Shakespeare, Milton and the King James version of the Bible, and dealt almost exclusively with Biblical or Continental subjects. Yet Heavysege was nevertheless accepted in his day as a writer of note from Canada. Indeed Coventry Patmore declared his *Saul* to be the greatest English poem published outside Great Britain, and Longfellow called the writer "the greatest dramatist since Shakespeare".

Charles Heavysege was born in Huddersfield, Yorkshire, England on May 2, 1816. From the age of nine, he was employed as a wood-carver in a furniture factory, working six days a week and ten to twelve hours a day. He was essentially self-educated; while still a youth, he saw a production of *Macbeth* and subsequently bought for himself a complete set of Shakespeare's works. His style also shows the influence of Milton and the Bible. Many early poems were destroyed and in 1852, he published his first work, *The Revolt of Tartarus*, a rhetorical poem which appeared anonymously and was reprinted in revised form in Montreal (1855). The following year, in 1853, he emigrated with his wife to Canada and settled in Montreal, where he took up his trade of wood-carver in the factory of J. and W. Hilton. His first Canadian work was a series of sonnets, circulated among his friends in 1854 and published anonymously in 1855; some of these were revised and appended to a later work *Jepthah's Daughter*. In 1857 Heavysege brought out his best-known work, *Saul*, a drama in three parts; it received a chill reception in Canada although it was reviewed favourably by Hawthorne, and by the *Northern British Review* and was approved by Coventry Patmore, Longfellow and Emerson. A slightly revised edition appeared in 1859. In 1860, Heavysege gave up his trade for a position as reporter on the Montreal *Transcript* and later as reporter and proof-reader on the *Daily Witness*. Another verse drama *Count Filippo or the Unequal Marriage* was published in 1860 and was followed by three long narratives: *The Owl* (1864), *Jepthah's Daughter* (1865) and *Jezebel (The New Dominion Monthly,* 1867). No copy of *The Dark Huntsman (A Dream)* (1865) is extant. His one novel, *The Advocate*, has been called by Ray Palmer Baker "the worst of the notoriously bad novels written in the Dominion." Heavysege died in 1876, at the age of sixty.

Little of the poetry of Heavysege is Canadian in setting, theme or style, although the sonnets do touch on the physical environment which is central to most of his contemporaries of the period. The plays, despite their length and rhetoric, are frequently impressive. *Saul*, a closet drama of one hundred and thirty-five scenes, approaches a Biblical subject in a novel manner. In his introduction, Heavysege comments on his choice of theme: "The reader of *Saul* must have been struck by its picturesque grandeur, its sadness and tragic issue. First of the Hebrew Kings, his reign far surpasses in dramatic interest every other in the long line of his successors". The central appeal for Heavysege seems to be Saul's illustration of the principle of the Shakespearean hero. "How are the mighty fallen!", he quotes, and Saul rises from humble life to the possession of a throne and then is destroyed by his own weakness, finally bringing defeat to his army and death to himself and his sons. Saul's visit to the Witch of Endor marks the dramatic crisis of the work.

TEXT:

Saul, A Drama in Three Parts. Second Edition revised. Montreal: Lovell, 1859.
Jepthah's Daughter. Montreal: Dawson, 1865.

See also:

Ray Palmer Baker. *A History of English-Canadian Literature to the Confederation*. Cambridge: Harvard University Press, 1920.
Lawrence J. Burpee in *Transactions of the Royal Society of Canada*. Second Series, 7: 19-60.
Daniel Clark in *The Canadian Monthly and National Review* 10: 127-34 (August 1876).
M. J. Montgomery in *The Canadian Poetry Magazine* 5: 5-12 (September 1940).

Sonnets

XIV

The stars are glittering in the frosty sky,
Frequent as pebbles on a broad sea-coast;
And o'er the vault the cloud-like galaxy
Has marshalled its innumerable host.
Alive all heaven seems! with wondrous glow
Tenfold refulgent every star appears,
As if some wide, celestial gale did blow,
And thrice illume the ever-kindled spheres.
Orbs, with glad orbs rejoicing, burning, beam,
Ray-crowned, with lambent lustre in their zones,
Till o'er the blue, bespangled spaces seem
Angels and great archangels on their thrones;
A host divine, whose eyes are sparkling gems,
And forms more bright than diamond diadems.

XVIII

How great unto the living seem the dead!
How sacred, solemn; how heroic grown;
How vast and vague, as they obscurely tread
The shadowy confines of the dim unknown! —
For they have met the monster that we dread,
Have learned the secret not to mortal shown.
E'en as gigantic shadows on the wall
The spirit of the daunted child amaze,
So on us thoughts of the departed fall,
And with phantasma fill our gloomy gaze.
Awe and deep wonder lend the living lines,
And hope and ecstasy the borrowed beams;
While fitful fancy the full form divines,
And all is what imagination dreams.

(1865)

From *Saul*

SCENE II

Country near Gibeah. Cattle grazing at a distance. SAUL, *after being anointed king by Samuel, has returned home to Gibeah, and is there occupied as formerly.*

SAUL, *musing.*

How tame now seems to me this herdsman life!
Unprofitable too: I naught do here,
Naught that can serve good purpose; I am like
A taper that is left to burn to waste
Within an empty house. Why do I stay?
Others could tend these herds as well as I, –
And haply better, for my thoughts are far
From meads and kine, and all the servile round
Of household duties, same from year to year, –
Alike far from the rural dull routine,
And traffic of the town, when I it visit
To exchange my herds and corn for silver shekels.
Yet I will wait my time: – and yet the steer
Puts forth his horns when his due months arrive,
And pushes with them though they be but tender;
The blade starts through the clod in spring; the leaf
Then on the bough sits in its pride of green:
The blossom, punctual to its season, comes,
Milk-white or ruddy; and the perfect fruit
Appears with autumn; nor the snow doth fail
The hoary winter. Doth the snake not shed
Its slough? the fledgling leave its natal nest?
Twice what I once was now I feel to be!
Down, proud imagination; quiet keep,
Thou rash impatience: – and yet Samuel said,
"Now God is with tnee, act as thou seest fit."
What should I do? Deem this less zeal than pride,
And here in all tranquillity abide.

[Exit.

ACT VI, SCENE VIII.

Endor. Outside of the WITCH'S *house. Time, night.*
Enter SAUL *in plain garments, and two* SOLDIERS *attending him, but disguised as his companions.*

SAUL

By the description, this must be the dwelling.
It stands alone, is ample, yet a hovel;
With only one small window, that can scarcely
Admit sufficient light, even at noonday,
To chase thence darkness. Doubtless 'tis the place:
It seems fit habitation for dark rites.
Decay seems to possess it, and around
Mute in the dimness looms dilapidation.
Knock thou, and make inquiry of who comes.

[*The first* ATTENDANT *knocks gently.*

She comes not. Knock again; and louder this time.

[*The* ATTENDANT *knocks a second time.*
[*Aside.*

Danger hath made the creature cautious; and as I
Seek, in the darkness of my present plight,
To peer through her skill's medium, and learn
What were the best that I should do, so she,
Perchance, is, from the darkness of her dwelling,
Noting us through the casement, so that she
May know if to admit us. Some one comes.
The door is slowly and partially opened by the WITCH, *who stands
timorously within, with her hand upon the latch.*

FIRST ATTENDANT.

Lives here the Wisewoman?

WITCH.

What Wisewoman, stranger?
There lives a woman here both poor and lonely.

FIRST ATTENDANT.

And is she now alone, and art thou she?

WITCH.

I am the only woman dwelling here. –
You surely have not hither come to rob me!
Alas, what is there in this place forlorn?

FIRST ATTENDANT.

Art thou the Witch and art thou now alone?
Tell us, for we are seeking to consult her.

WITCH.

And were I both, pray what would you want with me?
To inquire of such were now a misdemeanour,

SAUL.

Did any such survive beneath Saul's rigor.
Witches are none in Israel now thou knowest.

SECOND ATTENDANT.

Fear not: we are honest men. Art thou the witch?
For we are told that hereabouts there dwells one.

WITCH.

Art thou not mad to ask me such a question,
When such are now not to be found in Israel?
Then how darest use that dangerous name towards me?
Why come ye laying snares for a lone woman?

SECOND ATTENDANT.

We lay no snares; but art thou not the witch?

WITCH.

What, I?

SECOND ATTENDANT.

　　　　　Yes thou thyself. Do not to thee
The love-crossed wights and pining maids repair,
To learn their fate, or purchase from thee charms?
Canst thou not tell where missing treasure is?
Dost thou not prophesy who shall grow rich,
Who shall have fruitful wives, who disobedient
Children; who early die, who live to see
Four generations and be called great-grandsire?

SAUL.

Speak fearlessly. Art thou not one of those,
Who, in the weird sagacity of their art,
Foretell which course shall prosper and which not;
What critical and pregnant enterprise
Succeed, and what result in black disaster?
Art thou not one of those proud sorceresses
Who have prevision, and the power to summon
Back to the world the spirits of the dead?

WITCH

The wind blows cool: come in
　　　　　[*They go in, and the* WITCH *closes the door.*

WITCH

Enter this inner room; for I to none
Give entertainment in the outer one,
That the rude winds do enter, and, for aught
I know, where stands now at the door a wolf,
Which may to-morrow howl among the hills
That I to-night was hospitable to you.
How know I you're sincere! How do I know
But that you come to pry, and see if I
Be she who here (as goes, you say, report)
Follows the witch's now illegal art!
Ah, I suspect you; strongly I suspect you!
I like not thee, tall stranger: – thou'rt a spy,
And these men are thy witnesses. Ah, base
And cruel witnesses; for ye know well,
Full well ye know all three, what Saul hath done, –
How he hath put to death all female kind
Who had familiar spirits, also male
That dared commune with goblin, or foul fiend,
Spirit, or power of the invisible world,
'Till not a wizard is left in all the land!
Then wherefore come ye three men unto me,
As though I were to conjurations given?
Why lay a snare for me, that ye may hale
Me hence to execution?

SAUL.

Peace, I swear –

WITCH.

What dost thou swear by?

SAUL.

By what'er thou wilt: –
By hell, for thou'st no interest in heaven.

WITCH.

How much hast thou? Swear to me by the moon,
That is the witch's workshop and areanum,
From whence they cast on those who persecute them
All woes that body and that mind can bear,
Pain, horror. Swear, then, to me by the moon.

SAUL.

I will not swear unto thee by the moon,
But by the moon's Creator. As God lives,
There shall no mischief unto thee occur
For doing what I bid thee.

WITCH.
Thou hast sworn.

SAUL.

And I will keep mine oath.

WITCH.

I tell thee, stranger;
That thou hadst better; for I shall have given
To me thy soul in endless slavery,
If thou prove treacherous. Remember: and
Now say what I must do.

SAUL.
Divine to me
By thy familiar spirit, since thou hast one,
And bring up him whom I shall name to thee.
Begin thine incantations; for the moments
Fly, and I've far to go and much to do
Or ere the dawn.

WITCH
Whom wouldst thou I should shew thee?

SAUL.

Shew to me Samuel.

WITCH.
Samuel! Thinkest thou
That he'd appear for such as thou art? No,
He would not come for any less than Saul: –
No, nor for him; for he is now abandoned,
And we whom he tormented are revenged.
Long have they said that God has left him. – Well
Others have lost their souls beyond redemption.
They say he has a demon – so have others –
But come, I'll disappoint thee; for, remember,
Samuel will not be roused for thee, although
I'll knock with thunder at his resting-place,
And send my piercing spirit (who, like frost,
Can penetrate a rocky sepulchre)
To project molten lightning through his bones.
Prostrate yourselves; nor, till I bid you, look
At what shall lie before you soon agape,
The yawn of hades, the dark mouth of hell.
                    [SAUL *and his companions fall prostrate.*

Ha hee! ha hee! ho! Adramuel,
Adramuel, Adramuel, thee shew,
From sunny height or gloom below!
Adramuel, why is it so?
Dost thou not thy mistress know?

       [A strange sound heard. Appear ADRAMUEL.

Oh, my sweet slave, oh, my dear friend and master,
Still, still so faithful to me! Now go faster
Than do the fabulous coursers of the wind,
To Ramah, or to Hades, and bring Samuel.

         [ADRAMUEL *vanishes.*

      [Aside.

Whither would not Adramuel go? Brave spirit!
If I command him, he would wind his way
Into the presence of the sons of God,
And there, although in vain, demand the prophet.
It cannot be; for Samuel may not come
From Abraham's arms. I mock my mighty demon.
But whence this tremor creeping through my frame?
Ah, I am strangely warped! I have a loom
That he I've sent for, will arise and come.
Be still, ye tottering limbs. Adramuel hastes; —

         [Listening.

Adramuel nearer comes. I hear a mourning,
As if he bore within his arms
A soul that came unwillingly to my charms.

     [Bending forward as if to see something.

Roll, roll away, thou stygian smoke,
And let me into the abysm look.   *[Shrieks.*

      [Crying with a loud voice

Ah, why has thou deceived me? — Thou art Saul.

SAUL.

Calm thee. What hast thou seen?

WITCH.
Oh, gods ascending.

Angels I saw or gods — I know not which —
Out of the earth ascending, and another
Borne up amidst them careful.

SAUL.
Of what form?

WITCH.

An old man, and upcovered with a mantle.

SAUL *(aside)*.

'Tis Samuel here again!
  [SAUL *bows his face to the ground, and the ghost of* SAMUEL *rises.*

GHOST *(inaudible except to* SAUL*)*.

Unhappy king, why hast thou summoned me,
Out of the tranquil ecstacy of death? –
Why has thou troubled me to bring me hither?

SAUL.

I am in great distress, for the Philistines
Again are making war against me, and
Invade my kingdom; whilst the Lord hath left me,
And answers me no more by dreams or prophets,
Neither by Urim's light nor kindling Thummim's:
Therefore I've called on thee that thou mayest shew me
What I shall do.

GHOST.

Forsaken by Jehovah,
Why hast thou thus resorted unto me?
God now performs that which, by me, He promised
To David, and now finally ends thy reign;
The kingdom being no longer thine but David's,
Because thou hast been disobedient,
Nor didst God's vengeance upon Amalek.
Therefore God leaveth thee this hour in darkness.
Yet, not obedient to charm or spell,
Which thou hast wickedly employed, I come
Declare, He will thee and thy host surrender
Into the power of the Philistines; tell thee
Thou and thy sons shall be with me to-morrow.
SAUL *faints away, and the* GHOST *and all supernatural phenomena
    disappear with a dull sound.*

SECOND ATTENDANT.

'Tis thunder, and it shakes to its foundations
This crazy dwelling. Lo, the witch's form
Trembles like it, and is as pale as moonlight,
As, like to a detected culprit, she
Stands with clasped hands, aghast at her own doing.

FIRST ATTENDANT.

Now may I ne'er again assist at magic!

*   *   *

SAUL (*awakening*)

What hour is it? Have I slept long?
Bring me some food, woman, quickly.

[*Exit* WITCH.
Ere the morn

Shall tint the orient with the soldier's color,
We must be at the camp. What watch is it? –
Bring the food hither quickly. Hath the moon
Yet risen? Look out and tell me; look out at th' window.
               [*The* FIRST ATTENDANT *looks out at the window.*
                    [*Aside.*
The last outlook has come, and drear it is!
                    [*Aloud.*
Well, what's the moon a-doing?

FIRST ATTENDANT.
Your majesty,

With visionary dawn she is advancing
Unto the whitening frontier of the east.

SAUL.

And yet she rises late to-night: she's old.
We must begone, we must begone. Poor moon,
She is old, and so am I! – Is the food coming?
Bring food here with dispatch; or th' moon up heaven,
Will, with her ancient, silver feet, be treading
Ere we upon our road. – How old is the
Moon now?

SECOND ATTENDANT.
She is in her last quarter.

SAUL.
Then

I shall behold her this last time when she's
An emblem of myself. Yet she'll return
And rule the night; but I shall from my shade
Come up no more! – Say, is the food a-coming?
I have heard tell of culprits who have ravened
Upon the margin of their execution, and myself
Begin to feel an hungered. – Comrades, comrades,
You'll butchers be to-morrow, and can fatten you.
To-morrow – oh, come thou dreadful morrow!

FIRST ATTENDANT (*to his companion*).
Mark.

SECOND ATTENDANT.

His mind is wandering.

FIRST ATTENDANT.

I know not that.
He has been warned of some dire mischief coming.

SECOND ATTENDANT.

And yet I'm sure he wanders. – Oh, see, see,
How thought-fixed are his eyes, rigid his muscles!
His soul is toward the camp: it is not here.
He wanders homeward, like to a lost creature
That through foul roads still drags its mirèd limbs.
Your majesty, lie down, and rest whilst waiting.
The witch is making haste: I hear her busy.

SAUL.

No no, not yet: there'll be a long lie down
Anon. Yes, presently there'll be a sleep
With time enough to dream in. [*Aside.*] Oh, how all
Like to a dream seems my career now closing!
How like a troubled April day it seems!
How like a famine-smit, disastrous year! –
Will that foul witch be long?

SECOND ATTENDANT.
Your majesty, no.

SAUL.

'Tis well. [*Aside.*] As round some spent, delirious one,
Fallen, at last, asleep, the hand of friendship
Draws the thin curtains, who shall draw around
My memory apologetic shade?
For Ahinoam is dead; and Jonathan,
And Melchi-shuah, and Abinadab,
Shall go to morrow with me, and the rest
Are all too young. – Yet Abner may remain
And vindicate me somewhat. But if he,
Too, die, (for David will not curb the priesthood,)
Then I must leave a blotted name behind me,
And enemies whose pens shall slander me
On biding parchment. No, not slander, surely:
I would not abdicate. Oh, love of rule,
For thee I may have damned my soul to hell,
Murdering for thee the sacred priests of heaven!
It was the fiend, – yet will the fiend for 't suffer?
Shall I not be beneath with him to-morrow? –
How now? The food, the food!

[*Enter the* WITCH *with viands.*
Thou'rt here. Woman,
Are these your sorcerer's victuals?

WITCH.
Your majesty,
Although these hands of mine prepared them, they
Are pure as any that, by hands of priests,
E'er did on altar smoke in holy rites.

SAUL *(aside).*

The priests! the priests! – 'twas Doeg's hands, not mine:
Mine are not red with Aaron's blood. – Oh, but
My heart is black with blood that rage then caused
To overflow it, and which still it wears;
Even as earth is covered to this hour
With relics of the angry Deluge' wave.
The priests! the priests! the priests! [*Aloud.*] Why eat ye not?
Fall on: from ceremony I absolve you.
Nay, nay: no more request me to partake.

[*The men begin to eat.*
[*Aside.*
Why should a dead man eat! – Oh, that the dead
Could come again and live! – that Aaron's sons,
While I in death put off my royal robes,
Revived, could fill again their sacred vestments!
Cannot the spirit live again in clay,
E'en as old tenants to old homes return? –
Return to life, ye murdered priestly shades;
Live in the sanctuaries of your ancient forms!
Oh, Life, how delicate a thing thou art,
Crushed with the feathery edge of a thin blade!
Frail! – why wert thou not made inviolable?
Why art thou irrecoverable as frail?
Thou, noblest guest, art all as much exposed
To foul ejectment from the flesh, as is
The spider from its web by maiden's broom.
Yea, with a little wielded iron, any
Can drive thee forth from thy recesses' walls,
Which thou wilt not repair; for thou, weak fool,
At voice of death, from thine old banquet-room
Start'st like a haughty noble that, in huff,
Leaves his convives, and will return no more. –
Why should I cherish thee, why feed thee now!
Yet I, a breathing corse, must mumble, – I,
A shadow, raise my sunken, phantom maw
With the refection of this solid world.

[*Rising, after having eaten a little.*

Now let us go. Here take these shekels, woman:
I pay thee for the evil thou hast shewn me.
Live and repent of thy black arts, ere death
Shall send thee where there may not be a whitening.
                              [*Aside.*
She may still live and bleach by pious sighs,
And showers of tears, and dews of holy deeds;
But I must due, with foul sins on my head,
Betake me to the region of the dead
                              [*Aloud.*
Lead, and unbar the door; – and see thou sellest
Amulets no more while on the earth thou dwellest.
What I have given thee will thy wants supply.
Amend thy life; for thou, too, shalt soon die.

                                        [*Exeunt.*

Thomas D'Arcy McGee (1825-1868)

One of the more colourful Fathers of Confederation who prophesied as early as 1860 the constitution of the Dominion of Canada, Thomas D'Arcy McGee was a statesman, a poet and an orator of international reputation. After his assassination in 1868, the *Toronto Globe* paid tribute to his eloquence: "His words were fitly chosen. . . . His wit – his power of sarcasm – his readiness in reply – his aptness in quotation – his pathos which melted into tears, and his broad humour which convulsed with laughter – were all undoubtedly of a very high order."

Thomas D'Arcy McGee was born in Carlingford, County Louth, Ireland in 1825. When he was eight, the family moved to Wrexford and here, before he was fifteen, Tommy McGee was drawing large crowds to the meetings of the juvenile temperance society with his oratory. With the death of his mother and his father's re-marriage in 1842, McGee and his sister emigrated to the United States. Offered a job on the *Boston Pilot* as a result of an impromptu fourth of July speech overheard by the editor, he moved rapidly upwards from clerk to travelling agent, special correspondent and finally joint editor in 1844. In 1845 he went to London as the political correspondent for the Dublin *Freeman's Journal*; here he joined the Young Ireland Party advocating political freedom from Britain, and wrote for their organ *The Nation*. In 1848 when their abortive rebellion failed and the leaders were imprisoned, McGee escaped to America in the guise of a priest. He established the *New York Nation* in Philadelphia and in 1850 the *American Celt*, championing the rights of Irish immigrants in America. But opposition to the Know-Nothing Party, which sought to exclude immigrants from political rights, left him disillusioned with the American system, and in May of 1857 he moved to Montreal at the invitation of a group of Irishmen to become their leader.

In Canada, McGee quickly rose to national prominence. He established the *New Era*, the first newspaper to forward the union of British North America, and here he introduced ideas later put forward in the Charlottetown Conference. After a speech in Ottawa proposing a new constitution to balance local autonomy with a strong national government, he was chosen to run as an Independent in the coming election. In 1858, he entered parliament, first as a member of the Opposition Party of George Brown and Dorian, then in 1862 in the cabinet; in 1863 he joined the opposition party of John A. Macdonald and was briefly in power as minister of agriculture in 1864. When the government fell again, McGee and George Brown recommended Canadian Union as the only solution to the country's dilemma. He attended the Charlottetown Conference in September of 1864 and the following Quebec Conference, and was chosen by John A. Macdonald for the first Canadian cabinet in 1867, although he and Tupper declined in order to prevent too unwieldy a body. On the evening of April 6, 1868 he gave his last speech in parliament, an impassioned plea to Nova Scotia to support Confederation. On the way home in the early morning, he was shot by an assassin; a young Fenian Canadian, member of an Irish-American society whose ire he had aroused, was tried and executed for the deed.

McGee wrote continuously from his first arrival in America and his first book, a eulogy for the Irish agitator O'Connel, appeared in 1845. Most of his books are histories such as the *Catholic History of North America* [1855] and *The Popular History of Ireland* [1863] or biographies such as *The Life of Bishop Maginn* [1857] and *Irish Writers of the Seventeenth Century* [1863]. He published a collection of speeches on British-American Union [1865] and a small volume of poems, *Canadian Ballads and Occasional Verses* [*1858*]. His *Collected Poems* appeared in 1869, a year after his death.

As late as 1867, McGee intended to withdraw from politics and devote himself to literature but his sudden death prevented this. Much of his verse is of little interest today although a few pieces such as "Jacques Cartier" and "The Arctic Indian's Faith" are well-known and appear in many anthologies. It is for his prose rather than his poetry that his name is remembered in literary circles. His vision of Canada in 1860 is a prophecy not only of Confederation but also of the Canadian concept of the mosaic as opposed to the American melting-pot. "The Mental Outfit of the New Dominion" was addressed to the people on November 4, 1867. A plea for mental self-reliance, it argues convincingly the need for a distinctive intellectual and cultural life for the new nation twenty-four years before Lampman's lecture, "Two Canadian Poets". Both of McGee's speeches reveal the rhetorical powers which established him as one of the most important orators of the nineteenth century.

TEXT:

The Poems of Thomas D'Arcy McGee. ed. Mrs. J. Sadlier. New York: Sadlier, 1869.
1825 D'Arcy McGee – 1927: A Collection of Speeches and Addresses. ed. Charles Murphy. Toronto: Macmillan, 1937. (abridged)

See also:

Alexander Brady. *Thomas D'Arcy McGee*. Toronto: Macmillan, 1925.
Josephine Phelan. *The Ardent Exile: The Life and Times of Thomas D'Arcy McGee.* Toronto: Macmillan, 1951.
Isabel Skelton. *The Life and Times of Thomas D'Arcy McGee.* Gardenvale, P.Q.: Garden City Press, 1925.

The Arctic Indian's Faith.

I.

We worship the Spirit that walks, unseen,
  Through our land of ice and snow:
We know not His face, we know not His place,
  But his presence and power we know.

II.

Does the buffalo need the pale-face' word
  To find his pathway far?
What guide has he to the hidden ford,
  Or where the green pastures are?
Who teacheth the moose that the hunter's gun
  Is peering out of the shade?
Who teacheth the doe and the fawn to run
  In the track the moose has made?

III.

Him do we follow, Him do we fear —
  The spirit of earth and sky;
Who hears with the *Wapiti's** eager ear
  His poor red children's cry.

Whose whisper we note in every breeze
  That stirs the birch canoe,
Who hangs the reindeer moss on the trees
  For the food of the *Caribou.*

IV.

That Spirit we worship who walks, unseen,
  Through our land of ice and snow:
We know not His face, we know not His place,
  But His presence and power we know.

(1869)

* *Wapiti* – the elk.

A Prophetic Vision

From a speech of Hon. Thomas D'Arcy McGee
in the Legislative Assembly, May 2nd, 1860

"I conclude, Sir, as I began, by entreating the House to believe that I have spoken without respect of persons, and with a sole single desire for the increase, prosperity, freedom and honour of this incipient Northern Nation. I call it a Northern Nation – for such it must become, if all of us do our duty to the last. Men do not talk on this continent of changes wrought by centuries, but of the events of years. Men do not vegetate in this age, as they did formerly in one spot – occupying one position. Thought outruns the steam car, and hope outflies the telegraph. We live more in ten years in this era than the patriarchs did in a thousand. The patriarch might outlive the palm tree which was planted to commemorate his birth, and yet not see so many wonders as we have witnessed since the constitution we are now discussing was formed. What marvels have not been wrought in Europe and America from 1840 to 1860? – and who can say the world, or our own portion of it more particularly, is incapable of maintaining to the end of the century the ratio of the past progress? I, for one, cannot presume to say so. I look to the future of my adopted country with hope, though not without anxiety; I see in the not remote distance one great nationality bound, like the shield of Achilles, by the blue rim of Ocean. I see it quartered into many communities, each disposing of its internal affairs, but all bound together by free institutions, free intercoruse, and free commerce; I see within the round of that shield the peaks of the Western Mountains and the crests of the Eastern waves – the winding Assiniboine, the five-fold lakes, the St. Lawrence, the Ottawa, the Saguenay, the St. John, and the Basin of Minas – by all these flowing waters, in all the valleys they fertilize, in all the cities they visit in their courses, I see a generation of industrious, contented, moral men, free in name and in fact, – men capable of maintaining, in peace and in war, a Constitution worthy of such a country."

The Mental Outfit of the New Dominion

*Before the Montreal Literary
Club, November 4th, 1867*

Mr. President and Gentlemen:

I propose to offer the Club a short paper, on "The Mental Outfit of the new Dominion".

Concerning the physical resources of the united provinces – their military and maritime interests – the changes and improvements in their means of intercourse – their most urgent necessities in the way of legislation: of all these there will be occasions enough to speak elsewhere. For the present subject, the present time would seem most suitable, and this Club the natural audience, to which to address whatever is to be said. It is true some mere politician may say, "Let us look to Ottawa," as to the best collection of our mental productions; or some much occupied citizen here (in Montreal) may interpose with, "patience, friend, we are building our city." I know the city must be built, and I hope it will be wisely and well built; I know the country must be governed, and I trust it will be well and wisely governed; but it can neither hinder the growth of the city, nor distract the councils of the country, to consider now, on the eye of our first Dominion Parliament with what intellectual forces and appliances, with what quantity and kind of mental common stock, we are about to set up for ourselves a distinct national existence in North America.

All political observers are, I believe, now agreed that all the forces of a nation may be classed under three heads: of moral, mental and physical force. It needs no argument to prove that in this reading and writing age, "the age of the press" as it has been called, power must be wherever true intelligence is, and, where most intelligence, most power. . . .

Regarding the New Dominion as an incipient new nation, it seems to me that our mental self-reliance is an essential condition of our political independence; I do not mean a state of public mind puffed up on small things; an exaggerated opinion of ourselves and a barbarian depreciation of foreigners; a controversial state of mind; or a merely imitative apish civilization. I mean a mental condition, thoughtful and true; national in its preferences, but catholic in its sympathies; gravitating inward, not outward; ready to learn from every other people on one sole condition, that the lesson when learned has been worth acquiring. In short, I would desire to see, Gentlemen, our new national character distinguished by a manly modesty as much as by mental independence; by the conscientious exercise of the critical faculties, as well as by the zeal of the inquirer.

"Patience, friend, we are building our city!" With all my heart –

build away. God speed the trowel and the plumb-line, as well as the loom, the plough and the anvil. But dream not, my dear neighbour, that great cities are built chiefly by stone-masons. Let me give you an illustration of the contrary fact. Take Boston and Montreal, for example, in their actual relations. Boston has some advantages in size and wealth, but it has another and a nobler sort of superiority; it is the vicinage of native poets like Longfellow and Lowell; of orators like Wendell Phillips; of a sort of Leipsic commerce in books, if not the largest in quantity, the most valuable in quality, of any carried on in the New World. Take a thousand of the most intelligent of our citizens, and you will find that Boston books and Boston utterances sway the minds of one-half of them; while Montreal is, I fear, absolutely unknown and unfelt, as an intellecutal community in Boston and elsewhere. Far be it from me to disparage our own city; I cordially concur in the honest pride of every inhabitant, in the strong masonry and fine style of our new edifices. But if "stone walls do not a prison make", still less do they make a capital – a ruling city – a seat of light and guidance, and authority, to a nation or a generation. . . .

Our reading supplies are, as you know, drawn chiefly from two sources; first, books, which are imported from the United States, England and France – a foreign supply likely long to continue foreign. The second source is our newspaper literature, chiefly supplied, as we have seen, from among ourselves, but largely supplemented by English and American journals. . . .

This newspaper literature forms by much the largest part of our general reading. There are in the four united provinces about one hundred and thirty journals, of which thirty at least are published daily. Of the total number of habitual readers it is not possible to form a close estimate, but they are probably represented by one-half of the male adults of the population – say 400,000 souls. However ephemeral the form of this literature, the effect must be lasting; and men of one newspaper, especially, are pretty much what their favourite editors make them The responsibility of the editor is, therefore, in the precise proportion to the number and confidence of his readers. If they are 500, or 5,000 or 50,000, so is the moral responsibility multiplied upon him. He stands to hundreds of thousands, in relation as intimate as that of the physician to his patient, or the lawyer to his client; and only in a degree less sacred, than that of the pastor to his people.

. . . The best English and American journals are now written in a style not inferior in finish to the best books, and though ours is the limited patronage of a Province, it is not unreasonable that in our principal cities we should look for a high-toned, thoughtful, and scholarly newspaper style of writing. . . .

As to the other branch of supply I believe our booksellers have nothing to complain of. The sale of books is on the increase, though not at all so largely as the sale of newspapers. Our books are mainly

184/*Canadian Literature*

English or American reprints of English originals. In point of price the editions are not so far apart as they were on the other side of the Civil War. As to the classes of books most in request, I have been informed by one of our members well informed on the matter, that the sales may be divided somewhat in these proportions: religious books, 18 per cent.; poetical works, 10 per cent.; books on historical, scientific and literary subjects 28 per cent.; and works of fiction 44 per cent. My obliging informant (Mr. Samuel Dawson) adds in relation to the comparative money value of the several classes of books most in demand, the historical, scientific and literary works would represent about 45 per cent., the works of fiction 22, the poetical 15, and the religious 18 per cent. of the whole. We thus have this striking result that, whereas the works of fiction are, in volume, nearly one-half of all the reading done among us, in cost they come to less than one-fourth what is expended for other and better books. An accurate analysis of these books would be a valuable index to what it much concerns us to know whether *Thomas à Kempis* is still the book most read next to the Bible; how many of Shakespeare and how many of Tupper go the hundred; whether *The Pilgrim's Progress* is bought chiefly as a child's book, and whether Keble's *Christian Year* sells as well or better than *Don Juan*? "The demand for novels," says my informant, "is not nearly so great as it was," and this he traces to the growing preference for newspapers and periodicals containing serial stories and romances in chapters.

On the general subject of reading fictitious works, I hold a *juste milieu* opinion. I hold that a bad novel is a bad thing, and a good one a good thing. That we have many bad novels ushered from the press every day is a lamentable fact; books just as vile and flagitious in spirit as any of Mrs. Behn's abominations of a former century. The very facility with which these books are got together by their author, might itself be taken as evidence of their worthlessness; for what mortal genius ever threw off works of thought or of art worthy of the name with such steam-engine rapidity? It is true Lopez de Vega could compose a comedy at a sitting, and Lafontaine, after writing 150 sentimental stories, was obliged to restrain himself to two days' writing in the week, otherwise he would have drowned out his publisher. But you know what has been said of "easy writing" generally. For my own part, though no enemy to a good novel, I feel that I would fail of my duty if I did not raise a warning voice against the promiscuous and exclusive reading of sensational and sensual books, many of them written by women, who are the disgrace of their sex, and read with avidity by those who want only the opportunity equally to disgrace it.

We must battle bad books with good books. As our young people in this material age will hunger and thirst for romantic relations, there is no better corrective for an excess of imaginative reading than the actual lives and books of travel of such men as Hodgson, Burton, Speke, Kane, Du Chaillu, Huc, and Livingstone. These books lead us through strange scenes, among strange people, are full of genuine romance, proving the aphorism "Truth is strange – stranger than fiction". But these are books which enlarge our sympathies; and do not pervert them; which excite our curiosity, and satisfy it, but not at the expense of morals; which give certainty and population to the geographical and historical dreams of our youthful days; which build up the gaps and spaces in our knowledge with new truths, certain to harmonize speedily with all old truth. . . .

Mention must be made, Gentlemen, of those institutions of learning, and those learned professional classes which ought, and doubtless do, leaven the whole lump of our material progress. We have already twelve Universities in the Dominion – perhaps more than enough, though dispersed at long distances – as from Windsor and Fredericton to Cobourg and Toronto. The charters of these institutions, up to the last decade, were Royal charters, granted directly by the Crown, with the concurrence, of course, of the Colonial authorities for the time being. In the order of time, they range thus: King's College, Windsor, Nova Scotia, 1802; McGill College, Montreal, chartered in 1821, actually commenced only in 1829; King's College, Fredericton, 1823; Laval, 1852; Lennoxville, 1853; St. Mary's, Montreal, 1859; Queen's College, Kingston, 1841; Victoria College, Cobourg, 1841; Trinity College (formerly King's), Toronto, 1842; Toronto University, 1860; Ottawa, 1866; Regiopolis, 1866. All these institutions possess and exercise University powers in granting degrees both to graduates and "honoris causa", though some of them have never had organized classes in more than two faculties – Divinity and Arts; Nova Scotia has, I believe, no native medical school; New Brunswick, I believe, is in a similar position; and some of our Ontario and Quebec Universities have been always deficient in one or other of the four faculties. In the ancient sense, therefore, of a University being the seat of universal knowledge, we have no such institutions, but it cannot be supposed for a moment that the existence at twelve different points of our territory, of classes even in the single Faculty of Arts, is not, in itself, a cause of thankfulness.

Of public libraries I grieve to say that we have not, so far as I know, a single one in the whole Dominion. There is a Society Library, containing some good books, at Quebec; there are, of course, college libraries, more or less incomplete; there are law libraries at Osgoode Hall, and elsewhere; there is our own excellent Parliamentary Library (some 60,000 chosen volumes); but no public library in any of our chief towns. To Montreal I certainly must always consider this a shameful reproach; but I have spoken so often of it elsewhere, that I shall not dwell upon it again.

From all these sources – our numerous reading classes – our colleges – our learned professions – we ought to be able to give a good account of the mental outfit of the new Dominion. Well, then, for one of those expected to say what he thinks in these matters, I must give it as my opinion that we have as yet but few possessions in this sort that we can call our own. We have not produced in our Colonial era any thinker of the reputation of Jonathan Edwards, or Benjamin Franklin; nor any native poet of the rank of Garcilaso de la Vega – the Spanish American. The only sustained poems we have of which the scenes are laid within the Dominion are both by Americans, Longfellow's "Evangeline" and Mr. Streets's "Frontenac" – the latter much less read than it deserves. One original humourist we have had, hardly of the highest order, however, in the late Judge Haliburton; one historian of an undoubtedly high order, in the late Mr. Garneau; one geologist, Sir William Logan; but, as yet, no poet, no orator, no critic, of either American or European reputation.

About a century ago an eminent French writer raised a doubt as to whether any German could be a literary man. Not, indeed, to answer that, but many others, arose as a golden cloud that gifted succession of poets, critics, and scholars, whose works have placed the German language in the vanguard of every department of human thought. Thirty years ago a *British Quarterly Review* asked: "Who reads an American book?" Irving had answered that long ago; but Longfellow, Cooper, Emerson, Prescott, Hawthorne, Holmes, and many another, has answered the taunt triumphantly since. Those Americans might, in turn, taunt us to-day with "Who reads a Canadian book?" I should answer frankly, very few, for Canadian books are exceedingly scarce. Still, we are not entirely destitute of resident writers. Dr. Dawson has given the world a work on his favourite science, which has established his name as an authority; Dr. Daniel Wilson's speculations and re-[search on] historic Man have received the approval of high names; Mr. Alpheus Todd has given us a masterly and original treatise on Parliamentary Government, which will be read and quoted wherever there is constitutional government in the world: Hevysedge, Sangster, and McLaughlin, are not without honour. An amiable friend of mine, Mr. J. LeMoine of Quebec, has given to the world many "Maple Leaves" worthy of all praise – the only thoroughly Canadian book in point of subject which has appeared of late days, and for which, I am ashamed to say, the author has not received that encouragement his labours deserve. If he were not an enthusiast he might well have become a misanthrope, as to native literature, at least. Another most deserving man in a different walk – a younger man – but a man of very untired industry and laudable ambition – Mr. Henry J. Morgan, now of Ottawa, announces a new book of reference, *The Bibliotheca Canadensis*, which I trust will repay him for the enormous labour of such a compilation.

These are, it is true, but streaks on the horizon, yet even as we watch, others may arise; but be they more or less, I trust every such book will be received by our public less censoriously than is sometimes the case; that if a native book should lack the finish of a foreign one, as a novice may well be less expert than an old hand, yet if the book be honestly designed, and conscientiously worked up, the author shall be encouraged, not only for his own sake, but for the sake of the better things which we look forward to with hopefulness. I make this plea on behalf of those who venture upon authorship among us, because I believe the existence of a recognized literary class will by and by be felt as a state and social necessity. The books that are made elsewhere, even in England, are not always the best fitted for us; they do not always run on the same mental gauge, nor connect with our trains of thought; they do not take us up at the by-stages of cultivation at which we have arrived, and where we are emptied forth as on a barren, pathless, habitationless heath. They are books of another state of society, bearing traces of controversies, or directed against errors or evils which for us hardly exist, except in the pages of these exotic books. Observe, I do not object to such books, especially when truthfully written: but it seems to me we do much need several other books calculated to our own meridian, and hitting home to our own society, either where it is sluggish or priggish, or wholly defective in its present style of culture.

If English-made books do not mortice closely with our Colonial deficiencies, still less do American national books. I speak not here of such literary universalists as Irving, Emerson and Longfellow; but of such American nationalists as Hawthorne, Bancroft, Brownson. Draper, and their latter prose writers generally. Within the last few years, especially since the era of the Civil War, there has been a craving desire to assert the mental independence of America as against England; to infuse an American philosophy of life, and philosophy of government, into every American writing and work of art.

It is quite clear to me that if we are to succeed with our new Dominion, it can never be by accepting a ready-made easy literature, which assumes Bostonian culture to be the worship of the future, and the American democratic system to be the manifestly destined form of government for all the civilized world, new as well as old. While one can see well enough that mental culture must become more and more to many classes what religion alone once was to all our ancestors in individual and family government – while the onward march of political democracy is a fact, equally apparent – it is by no means clear to myself, for one, that religion will wield diminished power in the presence of a genuine, modest, deep-seated culture; or that the aristocratic inequalities inherent in men from their mothers' womb will not assert themselves successfully in any really free State. In other words, I rely upon Nature and Revelation against levelling and system-mongering of the American, or any other kind. In Nature and in Revelation we should lay the basis of our political, mental and moral philosophy as a people; and once so laid, those foundations will stand as firmly set and rooted, as any rocks in the Huronian or Laurentian range.

It is usual to say of ourselves, Gentlemen, that we are entering on a new era. It may be so, or it may be only the mirage of an era painted on an exhalation of self-opinion. Such eras, however, have come for other civilized States, why not for us also? There came for Germany the Swabian era, the era of Luther, and the era of Goethe; for modern Italy the age of Leo. X; for France the age of Louis XIV; in our own history there have been an Elizabethan and a Georgian era; and perhaps there is at hand an American era, in ideas, in manners, and in politics. How far we, who are to represent British ethics and British culture in America – we, whose new Constitution solemnly proclaims "the well-understood principles of the British Constitution"; how far we are to make this probable next era our own – either by adhesion or resistance – is what, Gentlemen, we must all determine for ourselves, and so fare forth, for the Dominion.

I shall venture in concluding this merely tentative and preliminary paper, to address myself directly to the educated young men of Canada, as it now exists. I invite them, as a true friend, not to shrink from confronting the great problems presented by America to the world, whether in morals or in government. I propose to them that they should hold their own, and their own soil, sacrificing nothing of their originality; but rejecting nothing, nor yet accepting anything, merely because it comes out of an older, or richer, or greater country. That it should always remain a greater country is, partly, for us, also, to determine; for, at least to our notions, ancient Greece was a greater country than the Persian empire, as at this day England proper may be considered a greater country than Russia. But North America is emerging; and why should not our one-third of the North rise to an equal, even if an opposing altitude, with the land conterminous? Why not? I see no reason why not. What we need are the three levers – moral power, mental power and physical power. We know tolerably well what our physical resources are, and by that knowledge we are cheered on; questions of purely moral strength or weakness we may leave to their appointed professors, the reverend clergy; of our existing mental ways and means, I have given a rapid résumé.

To supply a list of our deficiencies, I have not undertaken. Yet, as the object of all intellectual pursuits worthy of the name is the attainment of Truth; as this is the sacred temple to be built or re-built; as this is the Ithaca of every Ulysses really wise; I venture humbly to suggest that we need more active conscientiousness in our choice of books and periodicals, for ourselves and for our young people; that the reading acquirement which moves, and embraces and modifies, every faculty of our immortal souls, is too fearful an agent to be employed capriciously, or wantonly, much less wickedly, to the peril of interests which will not be covered up forever, by the sexton's last shovel of church-yard clay. I venture to suggest that we should look abroad, and see with the aid of this all-powerful agent or acquirement, what other nations are doing as intellectual forces in the world; not limiting our vision to America, or England, or France, but extending eager, honest, inquiries, beyond the Rhine, and beyond the Alps. From Germany the export of ideas, systems, and standards of philosophy, criticism, and belief, has not yet ceased; and from re-constructed Italy – so ripe in all intelligence – a new mental kingdom must come forth; if the new political kingdom is to stand. I venture to invite the younger minds of the Dominion to the study of the inner life of other nations, not to inspire them with a weak affectation of imitating foreign models, but rather with a wholesome and hearty zeal for doing something in their own right, on their own soil. From a population of four millions we ought to yield in every generation forty eminent, if not illustrious men; that is to say, one man to every 100,000 souls. And favoured as we are, we should certainly do so, if the cultivation of the mind was pursued with the same zeal as the good of the body; if wisdom were valued only as high as mere material wealth, and sought as strenuously day by day.

I am well convinced that there do exist, in the ample memories, the northern energy, and the quick apprehension of our young men, resources all unwrought, of inestimable value to society. I would beseech of that most important class, therefore, to use their time; to exercise their powers of mind as well as body; to acquire the mental drill and discipline, which will enable them to bear the arms of a civilized state in times of peace, with honour and advantage. If they will pardon me the liberty I take, I venture to address to them an apostrophe of a poet of another country, slightly altered to suit the case of Canada:

Oh brave young men, our hope, our pride, our promise,
    On you our hearts are set,
In manliness, in kindness, in justice,
    To make Canada a nation yet!

Charles Sangster (1822-1893)

As the literary heir of Goldsmith and Howe, and the predecessor of the Confederation Poets, Charles Sangster stands in a key position in Canadian literary tradition. In his own time, Sangster established his reputation as "Canada's national bard", as his obituary in the Toronto *Globe* pronounced. W. D. Lighthall in his introduction to *Songs of the Great Dominion* refers to him as our "first important national poet . . . a born son of the Muses, and . . . long the people's favourite", and Susannah Moodie wrote to him from Belleville: "your name will rank high among the gifted Sons of Song . . . her Bard who has sung in such lofty strains the beauties of his native land".

Born in Kingston, Upper Canada, on July 16, 1822, Sangster was the son of a shipbuilder in the Royal Navy and grandson of a United Empire Loyalist who fought under General Burgoyne in the American Revolution. A twin sister died in infancy. The death of Charles' father before he was two forced him to become self-supporting as early as possible, and at fifteen he was employed at Fort Henry where he made cartridges for the rebellion of 1837. From 1839-49 he was a clerk in the Ordnance Office at "the rank of a messenger and the pay of a labourer", as he later remarked. During this period he also contributed to the *British Whig*. In 1849 he moved to Amherstburg as editor of the *Courier,* but with the death of the publisher a few months later, he returned to Kingston as bookkeeper and proof-reader of the *British Whig* and remained here until 1864. Separation from other poets, uncongenial work and the death of his young wife eighteen months after their marriage increased his tendency to melancholy during this period, and in 1859 a phrenologist whom he visited described him as nervous and sensitive. He remarried in 1860 and about 1864 he became a reporter for the *Kingston Daily News.* In 1868 he moved to Ottawa as a second-class clerk with the Post Office Department where he was joined in 1882 by Archibald Lampman. In 1886 Sangster retired to Kingston where he hoped to find time for further writing and to publish two more volumes but ill health prevented the completion of his work and he died in 1893.

Sangster's first volume *The St. Lawrence and the Saguenay and Other Poems* was printed in New York in 1856 by subscription. It was followed by *Hesperus and Other Poems and Lyrics* (1860), published in Montreal at Sangster's own expense. A letter dated in 1889 indicates plans for two later volumes *Norland Echoes and Other Strains* and *The Angel Guest and Other Poems* but these were never completed. Despite these difficulties, he did receive considerable encouragement and was represented in such contemporary publications as *The Literary Garland,* Dewart's *Selections from Canadian Poets* and Lighthall's *Songs of the Great Dominion.* As unofficial poet laureate, he contributed the dedication to the second Brock monument at Queenston in 1859; in 1882 he was elected as a charter member of the Royal Society of Canada, and in 1890 he was declared an honorary member of the Society of Canadian Literature, inaugurated in Montreal by Lighthall.

In his *Handbook of Canadian Literature,* Archibald MacMurchy notes that Sangster is "the first poet who made appreciative use of Canadian subjects". His best-known work, the title poem of his first volume "The St. Lawrence and the Saguenay", is a sequence of one hundred and ten Spenserian stanzas describing a canoe trip through the Thousand Islands and along the great Eastern waterways; like his "Sonnets Written in the Orillia Woods", it records a sensitive response to the distinctive qualities of the Canadian scene. The sonnets in particular show an awareness of North American history and of the process of evolution which was advanced in Sangster's day and is common to the modern works of E. J. Pratt, F. R. Scott and Birney. Sangster also treats the themes of patriotism and love, and his "Lament of Shingwakonce" looks forward to the Indian poems of Pauline Johnson and Duncan Campbell Scott.

TEXT:

The St. Lawrence and the Saguenay, and Other Poems. Kingston: Creighton & Duff, 1856.
Hesperus and Other Poems and Lyrics. Montreal: Lovell, 1860.

See also:

Desmond Pacey. *Ten Canadian Poets.* Toronto: Ryerson, 1958.
W. D. Hamilton. *Charles Sangster.* New York: Twayne, 1971.

Brock

OCTOBER 13TH, 1859.*

One voice, one people, one in heart
  And soul, and feeling, and desire!
  Re-light the smouldering martial fire,
  Sound the mute trumpet, strike the lyre,
  The hero deed can not expire,
    The dead still play their part.

Raise high the monumental stone!
  A nation's fealty is theirs,
  And we are the rejoicing heirs,
  The honored sons of sires whose cares
  We take upon us unawares,
    As freely as our own.

We boast not of the victory,
  But render homage, deep and just,
  To his – to their – immortal dust,
  Who proved so worthy of their trust
  No lofty pile nor sculptured bust
    Can herald their degree.

No tongue need blazon forth their fame –
  The cheers that stir the sacred hill
  Are but mere promptings of the will
  That conquered then, that conquers still;
  And generations yet shall thrill
    At Brock's remembered name.

Some souls are the Hesperides
  Heaven sends to guard the golden age,
  Illuming the historic page
  With records of their pilgrimage;
  True Martyr, Hero, Poet, Sage:
    And he was one of these.

* The day of the inauguration of the new Monument on Queenston Heights.

Each in his lofty sphere sublime
   Sits crowned above the common throng,
   Wrestling with some Pythonic wrong,
   In prayer, in thunder, thought, or song;
   Briareus-limbed, they sweep along,
     The Typhons of the time.

(1860)

A Thought For Spring

I am happier for the Spring;
   For my heart is like a bird
That has many songs to sing,
   But whose voice is never heard
Till the happy year is caroling
   To the daisies on the sward.

I'd be happier for the Spring,
   Though my heart had grown so old
Like a crone 'twould sit and sing
   Its shrill runes of wintry cold;
For I'd know the year was caroling
   To the daisies on the wold.

(1860)

The Whirlwind

It comes with its swift, destructive tread,
   It tosses the waves on high,
And it hurries away where the lightnings play,
   Through the black and frowning sky;
And the weeping clouds are madly driven
By its violent breath, o'er the face of heaven.

It leaps through the woods in its fearless flight,
   Uprooting the firm-set trees;
And it shivers the trunk of the kingly oak,
   That had long defied the breeze;
Hurling down, in its furious mirth,
These tough and sturdy limbs to earth.

Away it flies, with a maniac howl,
   To the mountains' dismal height,
And it lifts the rocks from their granite beds,
   By the force of its giant might;
Waking the birds from their brief repose,
And spreading dismay where'er it goes!

(1860)

The Indian Summer

It is not like the Spring-time, bright
   With budding leaves and opening flowers,
But there's a glory in its light,
Softer than that which falls by night
   On lovers' bowers.
There is a mellow tint on every tree,
And nature's breath is sweet, and all is harmony.

It is not like the Summer time,
   Enlivened by a brilliant sun,
It savors of a purer clime
Than Summer, in its earliest prime,
   E'er smiled upon.
There is a light serene on everything,
Half veiled, and blushing, like a Bride in Spring.

Thou com'st in Autumn, when the trees
   Have doff'd their florid livery,
Ere Winter sweeps, with blighting breeze,
And fetters strong, to bind the seas –
   All hail to thee!
To thee, whose subtle charms no pen can trace,
To whom the artist's skill imparts no flattering grace.

(1856)

Sonnets in The Orillia Woods

IV.

    The birds are singing merrily, and here
A squirrel claims the lordship of the woods,
And scolds me for intruding. At my feet
The tireless ants all silently proclaim
The dignity of labour. In my ear
The bee hums drowsily; from sweet to sweet
Careering, like a lover weak in aim.
I hear faint music in the solitudes;
A dreamlike melody that whispers peace
Imbues the calmy forest, and sweet rills
Of pensive feeling murmur through my brain,
Like ripplings of pure water down the hills
That slumber in the moonlight. Cease, oh, cease!
Some day my weary heart will coin these into pain.

VIII.

    Above where I am sitting, o'er these stones,
The ocean waves once heaved their mighty forms;
And vengeful tempests and appalling storms
Wrung from the stricken sea portentous moans,
The rent stupendous icebergs, whose huge heights
Crashed down in fragments through the startled
    nights.
Change, change, eternal change in all but God!
Mysterious nature! thrice mysterious state
Of body, soul, and spirit! Man is awed,
But triumphs in his littleness. A mote,
He specks the eye of the age and turns to dust,
And is the sport of centuries. We note
More surely nature's ever-changing fate;
Her fossil records tell how she performs her trust.

XVI.

> My footsteps press where, centuries ago,
> The Red Men fought and conquered; lost and won.
> Whole tribes and races, gone like last year's snow,
> Have found the Eternal Hunting-Grounds, and run
> The fiery gauntlet of their active days,
> Till few are left to tell the mournful tale:
> And these inspire us with such wild amaze
> They seem like spectres passing down a vale
> Steeped in uncertain moonlight, on their way
> Towards some bourn where darkness blinds the day,
> And night is wrapped in mystery profound.
> We cannot lift the mantle of the past:
> We seem to wander over hallowed ground:
> We scan the trail of Thought, but all is overcast.

(1860)

The Impatient Lover

Haste hither, my love, the river
  Is tinged with the pale moonlight,
The leaves of the dark trees quiver,
  And throb in the parting night.
Why linger, my love, why linger?
  Swift fly the hours away,
And soon will Aurora's finger
  Point to the dawning day.

The Spirit of Morn doth hover
  Above the horizon dark,
'Tis time that both Maid and Lover
  Were safe in their waiting bark;
Then hasten to meet me, dearest,
  Why does my true-love stay?
Oh! haste, and your loved-one nearest,
  We'll leave ere the dawn of day.

As the Spring-time awaits the Summer,
  With longing I wait for thee;
All graceful the gay new comer
  Trips smilingly o'er the lea;
As Summer the Spring embraces,
  So chide I thy long delay;
Now we'll leave ere Aurora chases
  The mists from the waking day.

(1860)

Song. – Love While You May

Day by day, with startling fleetness,
  Life speeds away;
Love, alone, can glean its sweetness,
  Love while you may.
While the soul is strong and fearless,
While the eye is bright and tearless,
Ere the heart is chilled and cheerless –
  Love while you may.

Life may pass, but love, undying,
  Dreads no decay;
Even from the grave replying,
  "Love while you may."
Love's the fruit, as life's the flower;
Love is heaven's rarest dower;
Love gives love its quick'ning power –
  Love while you may.

(1860)

Lament Of Shingwakonce

In the year 1849 some difficulty occurred between the Provincial Government, and the Indians on Lake Superior, in consequence of the sale of the lands in that region, to a certain Mining Company, by which the Indians were most unfairly dealt with, and almost driven from the occupation of lands to which they had the strongest possible claim. The chiefs of the Chippewas, headed by Shingwakonce, despatched a very strong remonstrance to the Government, in view of which these lines were written. They do not however, contain a particle of the address, but grew out of the occasion, as it were.

I.

Where are the Hunting Grounds,
 O'er which we chased
The wild deer and buffalo?
 All laid waste!
By the White Man made desolate,
 Where shall we go
To hunt down the bison,
 Or the wild roe?
Away from the sacred mounds,
 To the far west,
From the graves of our fathers,
 We travel, oppress'd.
Back, back to the desert,
 Where the Pale Face has never
Set the print of his footsteps:
 Thus shall it be ever!

II.

Far from the tangled brakes,
Far from the sunny lakes,
Where the Red Man's rifle wakes
 The wild bird at morn:
Far from our chosen home,
Friendless, unfed, we roam,
 Hungered – forlorn!
 Far from the lands
Which the Great Spirit gave us,
 Driven by hands
That should stretch out to save us;

Far from our Wigwams rude,
To the deep solitude
Of the untrodden wood,
  Evermore driven!
  Hear it Oh! Heaven!
  Witness, ye Sun,
  That lights us at noon,
  And thou, restless Moon;
Ye witnesses all
  Of the Great Unseen Spirit,
When shall the Red Man
  His lost rights inherit?
Shall he be driven thus,
  Backward, forever?
  Never – Oh! never!

III.

Why, then, do we suffer
  The wrongs that surround us?
Why this barefaced injustice
  Submit to for aye?
Why? Because we believed them,
  When they promised to own us
For Friends and for Brothers –
For such they have found us
  In battle and fray.
  But, alas! for the day
When we kindly received them!
  Alas! for the day
When our weapons retrieved them
From destruction and danger;
  From threatening foes,
Who harassed their ranks,
  Till the Red Man arose!
  A curse on the day!
If this be their boasted
  Support and protection;
To suffer marauding bands
  To hold in subjection
Our hard-fought-for lands –
Bands of Long Knives, who never
  Befriended, or served us,
But who would have scattered,
  Destroyed us – unnerved us,
  At once and forever!

IV.

Oh! for the time, when we
Could dot the stormy sea
    With our birchen fleet!
Then we were strong and proud,
With a nation's strength endowed;
Then we roved the prairie vast,
Thinking it would ever last;
Then we were united all,
Mustering at the Great Chief's call:
    Then we had the feet
Of the bounding antelope,
Full of buoyant life and hope;
Then we were determined,
    As brave men should be;
As the oaks we stood firmly,
    As the winds we were free;
We had food in abundance,
    And fish from the sea;
We warred not for others,
    Of woes, we had none,
And we rested securely
    When our hunting was done.

V.

But the Pale Faces saw us,
    They envied the lot
Of the Sons of the Forest,
    Who doubted them not;
They came with professions
    Of kindness and love,
And the Red Men believed
    They were sent from above;
They came to despoil us
    Of every right
Which we long had enjoyed,
    Came, disputing our might;
They came to divide us,
    They sought to enslave
A race, that, when injured,
    Could learn to be brave!
We fought – we were victors,
    But more Pale Faces came,
And murdered our Nations
    With thunder and flame;
We fought – we were scattered
    Abroad through the land,
To seek a new shelter
    On some distant strand.

VI.

More Pale Faces came,
   From a far-foreign isle,
They came not to waste us,
   Came not to revile;
But by their broad banner,
   The Red Cross they bore,
They vowed to protect us –
   What could they do more?
Their battles we fought,
   When the Long Knives oppress'd them,
Their battles we won,
   When the Great Spirit bless'd them;
Our rights they respected,
   As brothers we shared
The bountiful country,
   With faith unimpaired.
For this we have loved them,
   For this we have stood
Battling danger and death,
   Both by land and by flood;
For this, when the terrible
   War-cry uprose,
Did we bare our breasts
   To the stroke of their foes!

VII.

And shall they who have owned us
   For brothers so long –
Shall they break their promise?
   Shall they do us wrong?
No! by that sacred Banner
   We looked on of yore,
When our friendly White Brothers
   First stood on our shore;
By the faith we then pledged,
   By their prowess and might!
We know they are willing
   To serve us aright.
Why, then, do they barter
   Our rich lands away
To the Long Knives, who hate us,
   As thieves hate the day?
Why suffer us backward
   By our foes to be driven?
The wrong calls for mercy,
   For justice from heaven!

VIII.

Rise, then, my Red Brothers!
  Speak aloud for your own,
For the Right has a voice,
  Like the thunder's loud tone;
Rise, not in deep anger,
  But firmly demand
That your White Brothers purchase
  Their right to our land:
Then, though we must wander
  Through forests unknown,
'Twere better than famish
  On lands not our own.
Rise! Sons of Tecumseh!
  Ojibwas, arise!
Let the voice of the Mohawks
  Ascend to the skies!
Rise! tell our Great Father
  The wrongs we sustain,
And He, who loves Justice,
  Will heal them again.

IX.

Where are our mighty Chiefs,
  Whose deeds of war
Spread from this fertile land
  To climes afar?
Where are our stalwart sons,
  Our nations strong,
Who in our memories live,
  And in the White Man's song?
Spread like the autumn leaves
  Before the blast
Of the cold winds of winter –
  Their day has pass'd!
Behold! how few survive
  Of that countless host
Of brave and stern-faced warriors
  We once could boast!
Some perished by the White Man's hand,
  In mortal strife,
When the war whoop rose and fell
  With each chieftain's life!
Others, in peace were borne
  To the blest Hunting Grounds,
Where the Red Men's spirits live,
  Where the war cry never sounds.

X.

Come, then, my brothers few,
    Let us depart,
Though we leave the wilds we love,
    With a heavy heart.
There are lands where the White Man's feet
    May never press,
Where the wild fowl still abound –
    In the deep wilderness;
There are rivers wide,
    Where the birch canoe,
As of old, can glide
    O'er the waters blue;
There are forests deep,
    Where the deer are found,
There are lands untrod –
    These are Freedom's ground,
Where we can live, till the Great Spirit calls
    The last of our tribes away,
    To hunt from day to day,
    From year to happier year,
In the blest Hunting Grounds
    Which the Red Men revere;
There to live evermore,
    Where death shall not sever
The loved from the loving,
    Through ages, whose vistas
    Stretch onward forever,
Where the White Man's unholy oppression shall cease,
And strife be unknown in those regions of Peace.

(1856)

Charles Mair (1838-1927)

An ardent nationalist and patriot, Charles Mair led a stirring and colourful career which is in many ways more interesting than his literary works. Yet he was the forerunner of the poets of the Confederation, publishing his first volume in 1868, and as a member of the Canada First Movement, was one of the forces behind the literary awakening of the eighties and nineties. The Toronto *Globe* greeted his *Dreamland and Other Poems* as "unquestionably the best collection of poems by a Canadian that has yet appeared" and "only surpassed by some among the best known living English and American poets," and his *Tecumseh*, Charles G. D. Roberts described as "by far the finest thing Canada has produced."

Son of a Scots immigrant who brought his family to Canada in 1831, Charles Mair was born in Lanark-on-Clyde where his father owned a store and warehouse. He was educated locally in Perth and attended Queen's University in 1857-8 and again in 1867-8, after an interval in the family business. He intended to pursue a career in medicine but a trip to Ottawa in 1868 with a manuscript of poems changed his life. There he met several young men: George Taylor Denison, William Alexander Foster, Henry James Morgan and Robert Grant Haliburton, son of Thomas, and they formed the Canada First Group. Here also he met William McDougall, who engaged Mair to research documents in the Parliamentary Library in connection with the transfer to Canada of Hudson's Bay Territory in the North West, and subsequently to proceed to Fort Garry to supervise road operations. Mair travelled west to Chicago by rail and then north to Winnipeg by steamer, stagecoach, and horse-and-buggy. Here he became the centre of controversy as a delegate of the new government feared by both Indians and Métis, as a friend of the unpopular Dr. Schultz, and as author of several unfavourable accounts of Western society.

After his marriage to Eliza, a niece of Schultz, Mair set off to meet William McDougall, arriving as Lieutenant-Governor designate of Manitoba, but was imprisoned by Louis Riel and his supporters, first in December and again in January in an attempt to retake Fort Garry. Escaping a second time he set off for Toronto, much of the way on foot and by dogsled, to raise a militia. In July of 1870, after an army of British regulars and Ontario militia had ousted Riel, John A. Macdonald proclaimed Manitoba a province and appointed a new Lieutenant-Governor. Mair returned west in the summer and settled with his wife in

Portage La Prairie where he established a store, a land-sales office and a fur-trade, and came into prominence socially. In 1877 he moved to Prince Albert Mission, where he established the *Prince Albert Times,* headed the telegraph committee, acted as postmaster and as agent for insurance, and wrote advertising propaganda for the North West Council. He remained here until 1892 except for a brief period in Windsor, and in the following years, attempted to establish general stores in Kelowna and Benvoulin, British Columbia, and a book and stationery store in Fort Steele to profit from the Klondike gold-rush. In 1898, he began a career with the Immigration Service of the Interior which was to last for twenty-five years. He lived in Winnipeg until 1903, then in Lethbridge, Alberta, and Coutts and Fort Steele, British Columbia, from which bases he escorted new settlers to homes in the Western Provinces. He lived with a daughter in Calgary from 1921 to 1924 and died in Victoria in 1927 at the age of eighty-nine.

Mair's first work *Dreamland and Other Poems* was published in 1868. In 1886, he brought out *Tecumseh: A Drama*, reprinted in *Tecumseh and Canadian Poems* in 1901. A prose work *Through the Mackenzie Basin* (1908) recounts his travels with the scrip commission negotiating transfer of the Athabasca and Peace Basins into government hands. Mair received recognition in his day. He was elected to the Royal Society of Canada in 1899, and his address on the American bison to the Society aroused the government to preserve the species through the establishment of a herd brought from Montana to Wainwright Park, Alberta, a site chosen by Mair. In 1924 he was given an LL.D. by Queen's University and in 1927, a few months before his death, John Garvin brought out an edition of his collected writings and paid tribute to his career.

Dreamland and Other Poems appeared when Mair was thirty years of age and Canada as a nation was barely a year old. A young man's work, it shows the influence of Wordsworth, Keats and Tennyson. Later poems anticipate the work of Roberts and Lampman in their sensitive recording of the landscape around Lanark. Mair's most ambitious work, *Tecumseh,* is a closet or literary drama of five acts and twenty-four scenes. Requiring four hours on stage, it has never been performed in full. The War of 1812 Mair saw as "the turning-point of Canada's destiny", and the heroes Brock and Tecumseh as "men of transcendent ability, to whose genius and self-sacrifice at the most critical period in her history is due the preservation of Canada to the Empire". His early fascination with this subject is indicated in his "Prologue to Tecumseh" published in 1868. To the historic figures Brock, Hull, Harrison, Proctor, Tecumseh and his brother the Prophet, Mair added a pair of young lovers for romance, and a set of Yankee ruffians to provide comic relief. One of the first works to sucessfully employ Canadian historic material in drama, *Tecumseh* has a grandeur and a dignity which is still impressive today.

TEXT:

Tecumseh: A Drama and Canadian Poems. Toronto: Briggs, 1901.

See also:

Norman Shrive. *Charles Mair: Literary Nationalist*. Toronto: University of Toronto Press, 1965.

The Fire-flies.

I SEE them glimmer where the waters lag
By winding bays, and to the willows sing;
And, far away, where stands the forest dim,
Huge-built of old, their tremulous lights are seen.
High overhead they gleam like trailing stars,
Then sink adown, until their emerald sheen
Dies in the darkness like an evening hymn, –
Anon to float again in glorious bars
Of streaming rapture, such as man may hear
When the soul casts its slough of mortal fear.
And now they make rich spangles in the grass,
Gilding the night-dew on the tender blade;
Then hover o'er the meadow-pools, to gaze
At their bright forms shrined in the dreamy glass
Which earth, and air, and bounteous rain have made.
One moment, and the thicket is ablaze
With twinkling lamps, which swing from bough to bough;
Another, and like sylphids they descend
To cheer the brook-side where the bell-flowers grow.
Near, and more near, they softly come, until
Their little life is busy at my feet;
They glow around me, and my fancies blend
Capriciously with their delight, and fill
My wakeful bosom with unwonted heat.
One lights upon my hand, and there I clutch
With an alarming finger its quick wing;
Erstwhile so free, it pants, the tender thing!
And dreads its captor and his handsel touch.

Where is thy home? On what strange food dost feed,
Thou fairy hunter of the moonless night?
From what far nectar'd fount, or flow'ry mead,
Glean'st thou, by witching spells, thy sluicy light?

(text as abridged in E. H. Dewart's *SELECTIONS FROM CANA-
DIAN POETS*, 1864)

Love's Land.

When those unfathomable eyes of thine,
O Love, are closed no longer can I see!
There are no looks to take the gloom from mine,
No soarings from the sordid earth for me.
But, when they gaze on mine, methinks I rise,
On spirit wings, to some enchanted land
Where mystic seas take colour from the skies,
And voiceless on a mountain-top I stand.

(1901)

From *Tecumseh*

ACT II, SCENE IV

*Servants and soldiers carry chairs and benches to the grove, followed
by* GENERAL HARRISON *and others, who seat themselves –* TECUMSEH
and his followers still standing in the lower part of the grove.

    HARRISON. We have not met to bury our respect,
Or mar our plea with lack of courtesy.
The Great Chief knows it is his father's wish
That he should sit by him.
    TECUMSEH.   My father's wish!
My father is the sun; the earth my mother,
                            [*Pointing to each in turn.*
And on her mighty bosom I shall rest.

[TECUMSEH *and his followers seat themselves on the grass.*
HARRISON. (*Rising.*) I asked Tecumseh to confer with me,
Not in war's hue, but for the ends of peace.
Our own intent – witness our presence here,
Unarmed save those few muskets and our swords.
How comes it, then, that he descends on us
With this o'erbearing and untimely strength?
Tecumseh's virtues are the theme of all;
Wisdom and courage, frankness and good faith –
To speak of these things is to think of him!
Yet, as one theft makes men suspect the thief –
Be all his life else spent in honesty –
So does one breach of faithfulness in man
Wound all his after deeds. There is a pause
In some men's goodness like the barren time
Of those sweet trees which yield each second year,
Wherein what seems a niggardness in nature
Is but good husbandry for future gifts.
But this tree bears, and bears most treacherous fruit!
Here is a gross infringement of all laws
That shelter men in council, where should sit
No disproportioned force save that of reason –
Our strong dependence still, and argument,
Of better consequence than that of arms,
If great Tecumsen should give ear to it.
   TECUMSEH. (*Rising.*) You called upon Tecumseh and
     he came!
You sent your messenger, asked us to bring
Our wide complaint to you – and it is here!

[*Pointing to his followers.*

Why is our brother angry at our force,
Since every man but represents a wrong?
Nay! rather should our force be multiplied!
Fill up your streets and overflow your fields,
And crowd upon the earth for standing room;
Still would our wrongs outweigh our witnesses,
And scant recital for the lack of tongues.
I know your reason, and its bitter heart,
Its form of justice, clad with promises –
The cloaks of death! That reason was the snare
Which tripped our ancestors in days of yore –
Who knew not falsehood and so feared it not:
Men who mistook your fathers' vows for truth,
And took them, cold and hungry, to their hearts,
Filled them with food, and shared with them their homes,
With such return as might make baseness blush.
What tree e'er bore such treacherous fruit as this?

But let it pass! let wrongs die with the wronged!
The red man's memory is full of graves.
But wrongs live with the living, who are here –
Inheritors of all our fathers' sighs,
And tears, and garments wringing wet with blood.
The injuries which you have done to us
Cry out for remedy, or wide revenge.
Restore the forests you have robbed us of –
Our stolen homes and vales of plenteous corn!
Give back the boundaries, which are our lives,
Ere the axe rise! aught else is reasonless.
   HARRISON. Tecumseh's passion is a dangerous flood
Which sweeps away his judgment. Let him lift
His threatened axe to hit defenceless heads!
It cannot mar the body of our right,
Nor graze the even justice of our claim:
These still would live, uncancelled by our death.
Let reason rule us, in whose sober light
We read those treaties which offend him thus:
Settled for centuries, with title sound?
You know that people, the Miami, well.
Long ere the white man tripped his anchors cold,
To cast them by the glowing western isles,
They lived upon these lands in peace, and none
Dared cavil at their claim. We bought from them,
For such equivalent to largess joined,
That every man was hampered with our goods,
And stumbled on profusion. But give ear!
Jealous lest aught might fail of honesty –
Lest one lean interest or poor shade of right
Should point at us – we made the Kickapoo
And Delaware the sharer of our gifts,
And stretched the arms of bounty over heads
Which held but by Miami sufferance.
But, you! whence came you? and what rights have you?
The Shawanoes are interlopers here –
Witness their name! mere wanderers from the South!
Spurned thence by angry Creek and Yamasee –
Now here to stir up strife, and tempt the tribes
To break the seals of faith. I am surprised
That they should be so led, and more than grieved
Tecumseh has such ingrates at his back.
   TECUMSEH. Call you those ingrates who but claim their
     own,
And owe you nothing but revenge? Those men
Are here to answer and confront your lies.
                       [Turning to his followers.

Miami, Delaware and Kickapoo!
Ye are alleged as signers of those deeds –
Those dark and treble treacheries of Fort Wayne.
Ye chiefs, whose cheeks are tanned with battle-smoke,
Stand forward, then, and answer if you did it!
    KICKAPOO CHIEF. (*Rising*.) Not I! I disavow them!
      They were made
By village chiefs whose vanity o'ercame
Their judgment, and their duty to our race.
    DELAWARE CHIEF. (*Rising*.) And I reject the treaties in
      the name
Of all our noted braves and warriors.
They have no weight save with the palsied heads
Which dote on friendly compacts in the past.
    MIAMI CHIEF. (*Rising*.) And I renounce them also.
      They were signed
By sottish braves – the Long-Knife's tavern chiefs –
Who sell their honour like a pack of fur,
Make favour with the pale-face for his fee,
And caper with the hatchet for his sport.
I am a chief by right of blood, and fling
Your false and flimsey treaties in your face.
I am my nation's head, and own but one
As greater than myself, and he is here!
                   [*Pointing to* TECUMSEH.
    TECUMSEH. You have your answer, and from those
      whose rights
Stand in your own admission. But from me –
The Shawanoe – the interloper here –
Take the full draught of meaning, and wash down
Their dry and bitter truths. Yes! from the South
My people came – fall'n from their wide estate
Where Altamaha's uncongealing springs
Kept a perpetual summer in their sight,
Sweet with magnolia blooms, and dropping balm,
And scented breath of orange and of pine.
And from the East the hunted Delawares came,
Flushed from their coverts and their native streams;
Your old allies, men ever true to you,
Who, resting after long and weary flight,
Are by your bands shot sitting on the ground.
    HARRISON. Those men got ample payment for their
      land,
Full recompense, and just equivalent.
    TECUMSEH. They flew from death to light upon it here!
And many a tribe comes pouring from the East,
Smitten with fire – their outraged women, maimed,

Screaming in horror o'er their murdered babes,
Whose sinless souls, slashed out by white men's swords,
Whimper in Heaven for revenge. O God!
'Tis thus the pale-face prays, then cries "Amen"; –
He clamours, and his Maker answers him,
Whilst our Great Spirit sleeps! Oh, no, no, no –
He does not sleep! He will avenge our wrongs!
That Christ the white men murdered, and thought dead –
Who, if He died for mankind, died for us –
He is alive, and looks from heaven on this!
Oh, we have seen your baseness and your guile;
Our eyes are opened and we know your ways!
No longer shall you hoax us with your pleas,
Or with the serpent's cunning wake distrust,
Range tribe 'gainst tribe – then shoot the remnant down,
And in the red man's empty cabin grin,
And shake with laughter o'er his desolate hearth.
No, we are one! the red men all are one
In colour as in love, in lands and fate!

HARRISON. Still, with the voice of wrath Tecumseh speaks,
And not with reason's tongue.

TECUMSEH.   Oh, keep your reason!
It is a thief which steals away our lands.
Your reason is our deadly foe, and writes
The jeering epitaphs for our poor graves.
It is the lying maker of your books,
Wherein our people's vengeance is set down,
But not a word of crimes which led to it.
These are hushed up and hid, whilst all our deeds,
Even in self-defence, are marked as wrongs
Heaped on your blameless heads.
                              But to the point!
Just as our brother's Seventeen Council Fires
Unite for self-protection, so do we.
How can you blame us, since your own example
Is but our model and fair precedent?
The Long-Knife's craft has kept our tribes apart,
Nourished dissensions, raised distinctions up,
Forced us to injuries which, soon as done,
Are made your vile pretexts for bloody war.
But this is past. Our nations now are one –
Ready to rise in their imbanded strength.
You promised to restore our ravaged lands
On proof that they are ours – that proof is here,
And by the tongues of truth has answered you.
Redeem your sacred pledges, and no more

Our "leaden birds" will sing amongst your corn;
But love will shine on you, and startled peace
Will come again, and build by every hearth.
Refuse – and we shall strike you to the ground!
Pour flame and slaughter on your confines wide,
Till the charred earth, up to the cope of Heaven,
Reeks with the smoke of smouldering villages,
And steam of awful fires half quenched with blood.

TWANG. Did you ever hear the like? If I hed my
shootin'-iron, darn me if I wouldn't draw a bead on that
barkin' savage. The hungry devil gits under-holts on our
Guvner every time.

SLAUGH. You bet! I reckon he'd better put a lump o'
bacon in his mouth to keep his bilin' sap o' passion down.

BLOAT. That's mor'n I'd do. This is jest what we git
for allowin' the skulkin' devils to live. I'd vittle 'em on
lead pills if I was Guvner.

TWANG. That's so! Our civilizashun is jest this – we
know what's what. If I hed *my* way –

HARRISON. Silence, you fools! If you provoke him
here your blood be on your heads.

GERKIN. Right you air, Guvner! We'll close our
dampers.

TECUMSEH. My brother's ears have heard. Where is
his tongue?

HARRISON. My honest ears ache in default of reason.
Tecumseh is reputed wise, yet now
His fuming passions from his judgment fly,
Like roving steeds which gallop from the catch,
And kick the air, wasting in wantonness
More strength than in submission. His threats fall
On fearless ears. Knows he not of our force,
Which in the East swarms like mosquitoes here?
Our great Kentucky and Virginia fires?
Our mounted men and soldier-citizens?
These all have stings – let him beware of them!

TECUMSEH. Who does not know your vaunting citizens!
Well drilled in fraud and disciplined in crime;
But in aught else – as honour, justice, truth –
A rabble, and a base disordered herd.
We know them; and our nations, knit in one,
Will challenge them, should this, our last appeal,
Fall on unheeding ears. My brother, hearken!
East of Ohio you possess our lands,
Thrice greater than your needs, but west of it
We claim them all; then, let us make its flood
A common frontier, and a sacred stream

Of which our nations both may drink in peace.

    HARRISON. Absurd! The treaties of Fort Wayne must
      stand.

You village chiefs are heads of civil rule,
Whose powers you seek to centre in yourself,
Or vest in warriors whose trade is blood.
We bought from those, and from your peaceful men –
Your wiser brothers – who had faith in us.

    TECUMSEH. Poor, ruined brothers, weaned from honest
      lives!

    HARRISON. They knew our wisdom, and preferred to
      sell

Their cabins, fields, and wilds of unused lands
For rich reserves and ripe annuities.
As for your nations being one like ours –
'Tis false – else would they speak one common tongue.
Nay, more! your own traditions trace you here –
Widespread in lapse of ages through the land –
From o'er the mighty ocean of the West.
What better title have you than ourselves,
Who came from o'er the ocean of the East,
And meet with you on free and common ground?
Be reasonable, and let wisdom's words
Displace your passion, and give judgment vent.
Think more of bounty, and talk less of rights –
Our hands are full of gifts, our hearts of love.

    TECUMSEH. My brother's love is like the trader's
      warmth –

O'er with the purchase. Oh, unhappy lives –
Our gifts which go for yours! Once we were strong.
Once all this mighty continent was ours,
And the Great Spirit made it for our use.
He knew no boundaries, so had we peace
In the vast shelter of His handiwork,
And, happy here, we cared not whence we came.
We brought no evils thence – no treasured hate,
No greed of gold, no quarrels over God;
And so our broils, to narrow issues joined,
Were soon composed, and touched the ground of peace.
Our very ailments, rising from the earth,
And not from any foul abuse in us,
Drew back, and let age ripen to death's hand.
Thus flowed our lives until your people came,
Till from the East our matchless misery came!
Since then our tale is crowded with your crimes,
With broken faith, with plunder of reserves –
The sacred remnants of our wide domain –

With tamp'rings, and delirious feasts of fire,
The fruit of your thrice-cursèd stills of death,
Which make our good men bad, our bad men worse,
Ay! blind them till they grope in open day,
And stumble into miserable graves.
Oh, it is piteous, for none will hear!
There is no hand to help, no heart to feel,
No tongue to plead for us in all your land.
But every hand aims death, and every heart,
Ulcered with hate, resents our presence here;
And every tongue cries for our children's land
To expiate their crime of being born.
Oh, we have ever yielded in the past,
But we shall yield no more! Those plains are ours!
Those forests are our birth-right and our home!
Let not the Long-Knife build one cabin there –
Or fire from it will spread to every roof,
To compass you, and light your souls to death!
    HARRISON. Dreams he of closing up our empty plains?
Our mighty forests waiting for the axe?
Our mountain steeps engrailed with iron and gold?
There's no asylumed madness like to this!
Mankind shall have its wide possession here;
And these rough assets of a virgin world
Stand for its coming, and await its hand.
The poor of every land shall come to this,
Heart-full of sorrows, and shall lay them down.
    LEFROY. (*Springing to his feet.*) The poor! What care
      your rich thieves for the poor?
Those graspers hate the poor, from whom they spring,
More deeply than they hate this injured race.
Much have they taken from it – let them now
Take this prediction, with the red man's curse!
The time will come when that dread power – the Poor –
Whom, in their greed and pride of wealth, they spurn –
Will rise on them, and tear them from their seats;
Drag all their vulgar splendours down, and pluck
Their shallow women from their lawless beds,
Yea, seize their puling and unhealthy babes,
And fling them as foul pavement to the streets.
In all the dreaming of the Universe
There is no darker vision of despairs!
    1ST OFFICER. What man is this? 'Tis not an Indian.
    HARRISON. Madman, you rave! – you know not what
      you say.

TECUMSEH. Master of guile, this axe should speak for
  him!
  [*Drawing his hatchet as if to hurl it at* HARRISON.

2ND OFFICER. This man means mischief! Quick! Bring up the guard!
  [GENERAL HARRISON *and officers draw their swords. The warriors
  spring to their feet and cluster about* TECUMSEH, *their eyes fixed
  intently upon* HARRISON, *who stands unmoved.* TWANG *and his
  friends disappear. The soldiers rush forward and take aim, but are
  ordered not to fire.*

[END OF SECOND ACT]

(1886)

IV THE NEW DOMINION

Edward Hartley Dewart (1828-1903)

One of the first literary critics in Canada and a proponent of a native Canadian literature, Edward Hartley Dewart is known chiefly to-day for his *Selections from Canadian Poets*, the first extensive anthology of poetry in Canada and published in 1864, three years before Confederation. Written midway in a busy career devoted largely to theological pursuits, Dewart's introduction to his anthology is an important document in Canadian literary criticism and its comments on the state of Canadian poetry are still relevant today over a century later.

Edward Hartley Dewart was born in Stradone, County Cavar, Ireland in 1828 of Scottish and English origins. In 1834, the family emigrated to Canada and settled on a farm near Peterborough, Ontario; Dewart was educated in Peterborough and at the Provincial Normal School, Toronto and taught for a short period. He became a Methodist minister in 1851 and was junior preacher in St. Thomas circuit; after his ordination in 1855 he was situated in Dundas, then in St. Andrews, New Brunswick; Odelltown, Quebec; Montreal West; St. John's, Newfoundland; Collingwood and Ingersoll. In 1869 he became editor of the *Christian Guardian*, the organ of the Methodist church, and retained this position till 1894. In 1873 he negotiated the union of the Wesleyans, Methodists and New Connections; he attended the Ecumenical Methodist Conference in London in 1881 and in Washington in 1891. He advocated Methodism in the Guardian, and as one of the regents of Victoria University, he urged the federation of Victoria University with the University of Toronto. He received a D.D. from Victoria University in 1879. In 1880 he was Ontario President of the Dominion Alliance for Prohibition and in 1889 became President of The Canadian Press Association. He died in Toronto in June 1903.

Dewart's publications are largely theological. *Selections from Canadian Poets* (1864) was followed by *Songs of Life: A Collection of Poems* (1869), *Additional Poems* (1892?) and *Essays for the Times: Studies of Eminent Men and Important Living Questions* (1898). He compiled and edited a new hymnal for the Methodist Church, and *The Canadian Speaker and Evolutionary Reader* (1868). He was also author of several pamphlets: "Broken Reeds: The Heresies of the Plymouth Brethren" (1869), "High Church Pretensions Disproved" (1879), and "Brief Outline of Christian Doctrine" (1898), and of three books: *Living Epistles: Christ's Witnesses in the World* (1878), *Jesus the Messiah in Prophecy and Fulfilment* (1890), and *The Bible Under Higher Criticism: A Review of Current Evolutionary Theories about the Old Testament* (1900).

Dewart's *Selections from Canadian Poets* is an important work not only as a historical record of the culture of the period, but also as literature. The anthology brings together in one volume most of the important poets in Canada to that date. The introduction is concerned in part with assumptions on poetry and the role of the poet in society, assumptions which belong more properly to their own century, but the key passages which examine the state of Canada's culture sound a contemporary note today. Indeed E. K. Brown in his *Canadian Poetry* of 1944 reasserts many of these very arguments. Dewart's introduction, along with McGee's "The Mental Outfit of the New Dominion" and Howe's "Local Patriotism", marks the beginnings of modern cultural and literary criticism in Canada.

TEXT:

Selections from Canadian Poets. Montreal: Lovell, 1864.

Introductory Essay to *Selections from Canadian Poets*

ONLY the illiterate and unreflecting adopt the sentiment, that, because more books have been already produced than can possibly be read in the compass of the longest life, to increase the number of books or the quantity of literature, is undesirable and unnecessary. The literature of the world is the foot-prints of human progress; and unless all progress should cease, and mental paralysis arrest all human activity, these way-marks shall continue to be erected along the pathway of the vanishing years. Whatever is discovered as new in the records of creation, in the capacities and relations of things, in the history of the mind's operations, or in the forms of thought and imagery by which in its higher moods soul speaks to soul, will always demand some suitable embodiment in literature.

Equally shallow and reprehensible is the idea, very widely entertained, that, because we can procure sufficient quantities of mental aliment from other lands, it is superfluous to make any attempt to build up a literature of our own. A national literature is an essential element in the formation of national character. It is not merely the record of a country's mental progress: it is the expression of its intellectual life, the bond of national unity, and the guide of national energy. It may be fairly questioned, whether the whole range of history presents the spectacle of a people firmly united politically, without the subtle but powerful cement of a patriotic literature. On the other hand, it is easy to show, that, in the older countries of the world, the names of distinguished poets, enshrined in the national heart, are the watchwords of national union; and it has become a part of the patriotism of the people to honor and love their memory. To mention the names of Shakspere and Burns, alone justifies this assertion. It is to be regretted that the tendency to sectionalism and disintegration, which is the political weakness of Canada, meets no counterpoise in the literature of the country. Our French fellowcountrymen are much more firmly united than the English colonists; though their literature is more French than Canadian, and their bond of union is more religious than literary or political. Besides, if the conditions of human existence and progress are changed, by the lapse of time, the advances of physical and mental science, difference of social and political institutions, and geographical situation, it would be absurd to suppose that such changes demanded no corresponding modifications in the teachings of literature.

There is probably no country in the world, making equal pretensions to intelligence and progress, where the claims of native literature are so little felt, and where every effort in poetry has been met with so much coldness and indifference, as in Canada. And what is more to be deprecated than neglect of our most meritorious authors, is the almost universal absence of interest and faith in all indigenous literary productions, and the undisturbed satisfaction with a state of things, that, rightly viewed, should be regarded as a national reproach. The common method of accounting for this by the fact that almost the whole community is engaged in the pursuit of the necessaries and comforts of life, and that comparatively few possess wealth and leisure, to enable them to give much time or thought to the study of poetry and kindred subjects, is by no means satisfactory. This state of things is doubtless unfavorable to the growth of poetry; but there are other causes less palpable, which exert a more subtle and powerful antagonism.

Nothing so seriously militates against the growth and extension of our poetic literature, as the low and false conceptions which extensively prevail respecting the nature and influence of poetry itself. Many regard it as a tissue of misleading fancies, appealing chiefly to superstitious credulity, a silly and trifling thing, the product of the imagination when loosed from the control and direction of reason. These misconceptions may have arisen from a natural incapacity for appreciating the truths which find their highest embodiment in poetry, from familiarity with low styles, or from the frequency with which verse has been degraded to be the vehicle of low and debasing thought. But whatever be their origin, they are false and misleading. They ignore the essential unity of the mind. Poetry is not the product of any one faculty of the mind: it is the offspring of the whole mind, in the full exercise of all its faculties, and in its highest moods of sympathy, with the truths of the worlds of mind and matter. It is not some artificial distortion of thought and language by a capricious fancy: it has its foundation in the mental constitution which our Creator has given us. As fragrance to the sense of smell, music to the ear, or beauty to the eye, so is poetry to the sensibilities of the heart. It ministers to a want of our intellectual nature. This is the secret of its power; and the pledge of its perpetuity. An able American writer observes with great truth and beauty: "It was spontaneous in its growth, and native in its origin. It arose from those immutable principles of harmony, established originally by Him who strung that invisible harp in the nature of man, and tuned accordant the mightier instruments of the universe around him. It is not therefore dependent on the mutations of human caprice and fashion; nor is it superseded by the discoveries and improvements in society." Poetry is the medium by which the emotions of beauty, joy, admiration, reverence, harmony, or tenderness kindled in the poet-soul, in communion with Nature and God, is conveyed to the souls of others. As there are rhymesters who have no true poetic feeling, so there are many who are not gifted with the power of giving expression to the emotions which throb for utterance at the heart. The influence of beauty or grandeur, moral and physical, "they feel, but cannot speak." To this feeling, which exists in a stronger or weaker degree in all minds, Poetry appeals. Where this tongueless poetry of the heart has no existence, or exists in a very feeble degree, the conditions for appreciating poetic excellence are wanting. As well might the blind judge of beauty, or the deaf of music, as such to judge of poetry. Let no one therefore speak of their disregard for poetry as if it indicated a superiority to ordinary weakness: it is an imperfection, that may be endured as a misfortune, but should never be flaunted as a virtue.

Persons of this class often assume, that because poetry has not a low tangible utility, capable of being comprehended by sordid minds, it is vain and useless. But there are many things in nature to which God has given the power of increasing human happiness and well-being, though they do not impart what may be called tangible benefits or gross enjoyment. Of this character is the pleasure received from the beauty and fragrance of a flower-garden; the murmur and sparkle of a pebbly stream; a mountain-lake sleeping among the hills; a tranquil evening, when the sunset-flush of departing day gilds every object with golden lustre; or the soul-soothing strains of melodious music. It is not without design that God has spread these sources of pleasure so thickly around us. To persons of sensibility, they yield a deep and speechless joy, vastly purer and more elevating than any form of sordid or sensual gratification. Now, poetry may be regarded as occupying in the world of mind, a place and a purpose analogous to scenes of beauty or grandeur in the material world. The useful and the beautiful are both from God. Each has its appropriate sphere. They are not antagonistic: the one is the complement of the other. And although poetry may not be the vehicle of hard jagged facts, it may convey truths of greater depth and power than are embodied in granite syllogisms or definitions. The greatest truths are not those that are most readily and flippantly expressed in words. In the language of an eminent English divine, "what is gained in clearness is lost in breadth." When we fancy we have compressed a truth into some very clear and definite form of words, some of its deeper meanings have escaped: like pressed-grapes, the substance may be there, but the wine is gone.

If the indefiniteness of poetic language and thought be urged as an objection, it is easy to show that this indefiniteness belongs essentially to the subjects with which it converses. Beauty, truth, the human soul, the works of God, the mystery of life, – are not themes whose significance can be easily compressed into rigid and superficial forms of speech. Let it not therefore be supposed, that because poetry is not fruitful in direct and palpable results, that its influence is small or its mission unimportant. Its soothes human sorrow. It ministers to human happiness. It fires the soul with noble and holy purpose. It expands and quickens. It refines the taste. It opens to us the treasures of the universe, and brings us into closer sympathy with all that is beautiful, and grand, and true. It sheds a new charm around common objects; because it unveils their spiritual relations, and higher and deeper typical meanings. And it educates the mind to a quicker perception of the harmony, grandeur, and truth disclosed in the works of the Creator. The history of poetry is a sufficient rebuke to those who speak slightingly of its influence. We know of no period in the world's history where it was not a power either for good or evil. It has exerted a mighty influence on some of the leading minds of every age; to say nothing of the "hymns of faith and hope," that have, in every period and sphere in the history of the church, proved, in life and in death, a source of strength and consolation to its members. If, in many instances, this sacred gift has been linked with folly, scepticism, and licentiousness, this did not arise from any native tendency of poetry itself. In such instances, Poetry is false to her mission; and gifted men are wicked in spite of their gifts. But this is not her native sphere. It is the beloved son, far from his true home, feeding swine. And even in those melancholy cases where poetic gifts are perverted and degraded, there are seen, like grains of gold amid the dross, outbursts of indignation against wrong, gleams of admiration for virtue, and gushes of tender sympathy for human suffering, that seem like the protest of Poesie, in her thraldom, against a forced and unnatural divorcement from beauty, purity, and truth.

These views respecting the dignity of poetry will enable us to take higher and truer views of the work and mission of him to whom God has given this "vision and faculty divine." How low and unworthy are the popular conceptions of the Poet's work and character! The many have thought of him as a mere rhymer of idle and foolish fancies, deserving censure because not better employed. Of course those who cherished false and degrading views of poetry, had equally false and unworthy views of the character of a Poet. But the Poet's work is a lofty and sacred work. It is not merely to wreath garlands around the brow of Beauty, to cover Vice with graceful drapery, or to sing the praise of Bacchus and Venus in Anacreontic ditties: but to refine and elevate the spiritual in our nature; to sing of earth's woes and sufferings, and pour the balm of a tender sympathy into sorrow-stricken hearts; to unveil, in its true deformity, the selfish cruelty of man to his fellow-man; and to portray the loveliness of unselfish benevolence, piety, and truth. The true Poet does for us what the eagle is said to do for her young, bears us aloft, and teaches us to fly. On the wings of his soaring spirit, we are borne into higher and more ethereal regions of thought, than our own unaided pinions could attain; where the silent forms of inanimate Nature awake to life, and pour their melodious eloquence upon the soul. He stands as a priest at Nature's high altars to expound her symbolic language, to unveil her hidden beauty, to dispense her sacred lessons, and to lead the mind up from the tokens of his presence on earth to the Great Father of all in heaven.

Our colonial position, whatever may be its political advantages, is not favorable to the growth of an indigenous literature. Not only are our mental wants supplied by the brain of the Mother Country, under circumstances that utterly preclude competition; but the majority of persons of taste and education in Canada are emigrants from the Old Country, whose tenderest affections cling around the land they have left. The memory of the associations of youth, and of the honored names that have won distinction in every department of human activity, throws a charm around everything that comes from their native land, to which the productions of our young and unromantic country can put forth no claim.

When the poets of other countries sing of the birds and flowers, the mountains and streams, of those lands, whose history is starred with deathless names, and rich with the mellow and hazy light of romance, every reference to those immortal types of beauty or grandeur commands sympathy and admiration. But let any Canadian bard presume to think that the wild-flowers which formed the garlands of his sunny childhood, the sweet song-birds that sang him to sleep in infancy, or the magnificent lakes, forests, and rivers of his native land, are as worthy of being enshrined in lyric numbers, and capable of awaking memories of days as bright, associations as tender, and scenery as beautiful, as ever was sung by hoary harper of the olden time, and he is more likely to secure contempt than sympathy or admiration. Things that are hoary with age, and dim in their distance, from us, are more likely to win veneration and approval, while whatever is near and familiar loses in interest and attraction. There is a large class of persons who could scarcely conceive it possible that a Canadian lyric might have as deep and true feeling as those they have most admired; or that a Canadian Poet might be as highly gifted as some of the favourite names, who are crowned with the wreaths of unfading fame. And yet such things are not altogether inconceivable. But if a Milton or a Shakspere, was to arise among us, it is far from certain that his merit would be recognized. The mass of readers find it easier and safer to re-echo the approbation of others, – to praise those whom all praise, – than to form an intelligent and independent judgment of their own.

Other antagonistic influences have not been wanting. Religious intolerance is always unjust to talent that does not belong to its party, and pronounce its watchwords. There are many who take great credit for liberality, so blinded by bigotry, that with them it would be enough to condemn the most meritorious work, that it sprung from any quarter, from which it was not in accordance with their canonized prejudices to believe anything good could come.

The indiscriminate praise, by the press, of some writers, in which, whatever their merit, the dross was largely mixed with the pure ore, has tended to mislead the public, and to give the authors false notions of their talents and achievements. Booksellers, too, because they make surer sales and large profits on British and American works, which have already obtained popularity, seldom take the trouble to judge of a Canadian book on its merits, or use their influence to promote its sale. The chances are, that, whatever its merit, the author will be left to send his work around to the bookstores at his own expense, and leave it to be sold at his own risk, paying a liberal percentage for any copies that may be sold.

In pronouncing judgment on the character of our native poetry, the most partial critic must confess that it is extensively marked by crudity and imperfection. This is to some extent accounted for by the want of educational advantages incident to a new country. Many writers of undoubted genius have been deficient in that thorough literary culture essential to high artistic excellence. But in many instances this want of finish may be traced to want of application, resulting from a low estimate of poetry as an art. The adage, that "whatever is worth doing at all is worth doing well," has a special application here. There is no such dearth of poetry, as to warrant every unfledged bantling being thrust upon the public as a bird of Paradise. It would be well, if all who have contracted the habit of turning commonplace puerilities into rhyme "for their own amusement," would sacredly devote them to that purpose. Poesie, like Truth, will unveil her beauty and dispense her honors, only to those who love her with deep and reverential affection. Because no rules nor study can make a man a poet with genius, it does not follow that the most gifted may not be profited by a study of those principles that are illustrated in the works of the great masters of lyric harmony. Every true conception of poetry must regard it both as a sentiment and an art. The essence of poetry lies in the character of the thought. No dexterity of art can galvanize into poetry, low, puerile thought, destitute of pathos, beauty, and grandeur. But it is an error to infer from this that the character of the thought is everything, and the form in which it is expressed of little consequence. The difference between prose and poetry consists more in the form than in the essential nature of the thought. Every reader knows that noble and good sentiments may be so tamely expressed, as to produce aversion rather than pleasure. Much "religious poetry" and "hymns" painfully illustrate this. Themes which require the most masterly genius, are most frequently travestied by feeble incompetence. The careful selection of unhackneyed, elegant, and expressive words, and their arrangement in such forms as will produce musical harmony, are elements of success with which no genius can dispense.

If, as we have seen, the object of poetry is to convey to others the emotions and conceptions which thrill the poet's own soul, in his highest mental moods, it follows that the perfection of the medium to which these thoughts are committed, is a matter of essential importance. Poetry bears a close analogy to music, and appeals to the sense of harmony, as well as to the understanding. No really good poetry is deficient in metrical harmony. Hence we see the folly of the objection, sometimes urged against poetry, "that generally on being translated into prose it does not seem to contain much." This is assuming that the object of poetry is to convey knowledge of positive facts, and consequently judging it by a wrong standard. As well might we deny the beauty of a sparkling dew-drop, because on examination it is found to consist of common water; or the merit of a beautiful painting, because the colors to which it owes its fine effect, might be so mixed or arranged as to possess no charm or beauty.

To those who are best acquainted with the poetry of Canada, the wonder is, not that so little has been achieved, but that so much true poetry has been written, in spite of such unpropitious circumstances. For poetic fire, like its earthly type, requires vent in order to burn brightly. Some of our most gifted poets, after ineffectual efforts to gain the attention and approval of of the public, have despairingly turned to more hopeful, though less congenial labors, feeling that their choicest strains fell on listless ears, and unsympathetic hearts.

Among those who have most courageously appealed to the reading public, and most largely enriched the poetic literature of Canada, the first place is due to CHARLES SANGSTER. The richness and extent of his contributions, the originality and descriptive power he displays, the variety of Canadian themes on which he has written with force and elegance, his passionate sympathy with the beautiful in Nature, and the chivalrous and manly patriotism which finds an utterance in his poems, fully vindicate his claim to a higher place in the regard of his countrymen, than he has yet obtained. ALEXANDER MCLACHLAN has also evinced that he possesses in a high degree the gift of song. In the opinion of many, he is the sweetest and most intensely human of all our Canadian bards. As Sangster and McLachlan are quite unlike, and each possesses a strongly marked individuality of his own, any comparison between them is inappropriate, and might be unfair to both. In elaborate elegance and wealth of descriptive power, in the success with which he has treated Canadian themes, and in something of Miltonic stateliness and originality of style, Sangster has certainly no equal in this country. But in strong human sympathy, in subtle appreciation of character, in deep natural pathos, and in those gushes of noble and manly feeling which awaken the responsive echoes of every true heart, McLachlan is equally peerless. That they should both be so little known to the reading public of Canada, is a matter of sincere regret. Taking into consideration the subtle delicacy of thought and elevation of style which distinguishes much of his poetry, it is not so difficult to understand why Sangster should be comparatively unappreciated by the great mass of readers; but that the sentiments of sympathy with humanity in all conditions, and the protests against every form of injustice and pretension, so simply and earnestly expressed in McLachlan's poetry, should secure so few admirers, is a fact that, in spite of all possible explanations, is by no means creditable to the taste or intelligence of Canada.

Enough however has already been achieved, to be an earnest of better things for the future. The philosophic subtlety and creative imagination of HEAVYSEGE, – the profound sensibility and exquisite musical harmony of MISS VINING, – the lofty aspirations and ringing energy of MISS HAIGHT, – the delicate perception of beauty which breathes forth in the lyrics of ASCHER, – the ardent human sympathy and tenderness of MRS. LEPROHON, – the calm beauty and attractive grace of PROF. CHAPMAN, – the simple and graphic truthfulness of MRS. MOODIE, – the intense communion with Nature in her moods of quiet loveliness, which soothes and charms, in the musical strains of J. F. McDONNELL, – the simple melodies of MISS JOHNSON, full of earnestness and deep religious feeling, – and many other names worthy of honorable mention, give a pledge to futurity that it will not always be Winter with Canadian poetry. Should the soft Spring breath of kindly appreciation warm the chilly atmosphere, flowers of greater luxuriance and beauty would soon blossom forth, to beautify and enrich our literature.

If these anticipations are not realized, it is not because there is anything in the country itself uncongenial to poetry. If we are deprived of many of the advantages of older countries, we have ample compensation in more unshackled freedom of thought, and broader spheres of action. Though poor in historic interest, our past is not altogether devoid of events capable of poetic treatment. But if Memory cannot draw rich materials for poetry from treasures consecrated to fame, Hope unfolds the loftier inspiration of a future bright with promise. If we cannot point to a past rich with historic names, we have the inspiring spectacle of a great country, in her youthful might, girding herself for a race for an honorable place among the nations of the world. In our grand and gloomy forests – in our brilliant skies and varied seasons – in our magnificent lakes and rivers – in our hoary mountains and fruitful valleys, external Nature unveils her most majestic forms to exalt and inspire the truly poetic soul; while human nature – especially human nature in its relation to the spiritual and divine – still presents an exhaustless mine of richest ore, worthy of the most exalted genius, and of the deepest human and spiritual knowledge.

William Douw Lighthall (1857-1946)

A poet and novelist in his own right, William Douw Lighthall is notable today chiefly for his anthology *Songs of the Great Dominion* rather than for his creative work, and for his encouragement of new young writers across the Dominion whom he attempted to bring together through his organization The Society of Canadian Literature, a forerunner of the Canadian Authors' Association.

Born of Loyalist stock in Hamilton, Ontario on December 27, 1857, Lighthall moved at an early age to Montreal where his father was Dean of Notaries and here he attended high school. He continued on to McGill University where he took the Shakespeare gold medal in English Literature and graduated with a B.A. in 1879. After a year in medical studies, he decided to enter the profession of law and received his B.C.L. in 1881 and his M.A. in 1885. He practised law in Montreal from 1891 until 1944, becoming a King's Counsel in 1906. He also played a leading role in local politics and business. As mayor of Westmount from 1900 to 1902, he founded in 1901 the Union of Canadian Municipalities. For several years he was counsel for the Indian Department and for his services he was made Iroquois Chief "Ticonderoga" in 1909. During the First World War he served in the Victoria Rifles and founded the Great War Veterans' Association, now the Canadian Legion. He also founded the Society of Canadian Literature, the Canadian National League, and the Westmount Liberal Club. Interested in the preservation of Montreal, he founded the Chateau de Ramezay Museum in 1895 and also the Westmount Tourist Association, and was influential in preserving the Maisonneuve Mansion. He was made president of the Antiquarian Society in 1912 and at his death he was Honorary President. Lighthall was elected to the Royal Society of Canada in 1905 and became its president in 1918. In 1921 he received a D.C.L. from his alma mater, McGill University.

In the midst of this busy career, Lighthall found time to devote to writing. His first volume of poetry *Thoughts, Moods and Ideals* was published in 1887 with the sub-title *Crimes of Leisure*; several of these poems had already appeared in *The Week* and he printed a selection in his *Songs from the Great Dominion*. His *Collected Poems* appearing in 1922 included both his early historic and patriotic poems and later war verses. He published three novels, *The Young Seigneur or Nation-Making*, a fictional romance of a Quebec by-election which appeared in 1888 under the pseudonym Wilfred Chateauclair, *The False Chevalier*; or *The Lifeguard of Marie Antoinette* depicting

France during the reign of Terror before the Revolution, and *The Master of Life: A Romance of the Five Nations and of Prehistoric Montreal* (1908), a romantic treatment of the life of Hiawatha and the founding of the Iroquois Confederacy in 1570. He also wrote a guide-book to the sights and shrines of Montreal (1899) and, for the two hundred and fiftieth anniversary of Montreal, a historic sketch of the city (1892), as well as two Imperialist works, *Canada: A Modern Nation* (1904) and *The Governance of Empire* (1910).

Songs of the Great Dominion, published in London in 1889, was inspired by a collection of Australian verse which Lighthall discovered in a local bookshop. Subtitled "Voices from the Forests and Waters, the Settlements and Cities of Canada", the anthology brought together many new writers just establishing their names, as well as a number already familiar to their audience. Although Lighthall in the introduction estimates the existence in Canada of as many as three hundred male poets and "lady singers", he confines his choice to 59 writers. The anthology was very popular and Lighthall brought out a shorter edition with the same publisher in 1891 and another edition for the Canterbury Poets Series under the title *Canadian Poems and Lays.* His introduction is important for its comments on the state of Canadian literature and criticism in its day.

TEXT:

Songs of the Great Dominion. London: Walter Scott, 1889.

See also:

John Murray Gibbon in *Leading Canadian Poets*, ed. W. P. Percival. Toronto: Ryerson, 1948.

Introduction to *Songs of the Great Dominion*

The poets whose songs fill this book are voices cheerful with the consciousness of young might, public wealth, and heroism. Through them, taken all together, you may catch something of great Niagara falling, of brown rivers rushing with foam, of the crack of the rifle in the haunts of the moose and caribou, the lament of vanishing races singing their death-song as they are swept on to the cataract of oblivion, the rural sounds of Arcadias just rescued from surrounding wildernesses by the axe, shrill war-whoops of Iroquois battle, proud traditions of contests with the French and the Americans, stern and sorrowful cries of valour rising to curb rebellion. The tone of them is *courage*; – for to hunt, to fight, to hew out a farm, one must be a man! Through their new hopes, doubts, exultations, questionings, the virility of fighting races is the undertone. Canadians are, for the most part, the descendants of armies, officers and men, and every generation of them has stood up to battle.

The delight of a clear atmosphere runs through it too, and the rejoicings of that Winter Carnival which is only possible in the most athletic country in the world; with the glint of that heavenly Palace of illumined pearl, which is the February pilgrimage of North America.

Canada, Eldest Daughter of the Empire, is the Empire's completest type! She is the full-grown of the family, – the one first come of age and gone out into life as a nation; and she has in her young hands the solution of all those questions which must so interest every true Briton, proud and careful of the acquisitions of British discovery and conquest. She is Imperial in herself, we sons of her think, as the number, the extent, and the lavish natural wealth of her Provinces, each not less than some empire of Europe, rises in our minds; as we picture her coasts and gulfs and kingdoms and islands, on the Atlantic on one side, and the Pacific on the other; her four-thousand-mile panorama of noble rivers, wild forests, ocean-like prairies; her towering snow-capped Rockies waking to the tints of sunrise in the West; in the East her hoary Laurentians, oldest of hills. She has by far the richest extent of fisheries, forests, wheat lands, and fur regions in the world; some of the greatest public works; some of the loftiest mountain-ranges, the vastest rivers, the healthiest and most beautifully varied seasons. She has the best ten-elevenths of Niagara Falls, and the best half of the Inland Seas. She stands fifth among the nations in the tonnage of her commercial marine. Her population is about five million souls. Her Valley of the Saskatchewan alone, it has been scientifically computed, will support eight hundred millions. In losing the United States, Britain lost the *smaller* half of her American possessions: – the Colony of the Maple Leaf is about as large as Europe.

But what would material resources be without a corresponding greatness in man? Canada is also Imperial in her traditions. Her French race are still conscious that they are the remnants of a power which once ruled North America from Hudson Bay to the Gulf of Mexico. Existing English Canada is the result of simply the noblest epic migration the world has ever seen: – more loftily epic than the retirement of Pius Aeneas from Ilion, – the withdrawal, namely, out of the rebel Colonies, of the thirty-five thousand United Empire Loyalists after the War of the Revolution. "Why did you come here?" was asked of one of the first settlers of Saint John, New Brunswick, a man whose life was without a stain; – "Why did you come here, when you and your associates were almost certain to endure the sufferings and absolute want of shelter and food which you have narrated?" "*Why did we come here?"* replied he, with emotion which brought tears: – *"For our loyalty."*

Canada has, of historic right, a voice also in the Empire of to-day, and busies herself not a little in studying its problems. For example, the question whether that Empire will last is being asked. Her history has a reply to that: – IT WILL, IF IT SETS CLEARLY BEFORE IT A DEFINITE IDEAL THAT MEN WILL SUFFER AND DIE FOR; and such an Ideal – worthy of long and patient endeavour – may be found in broad-minded advance towards the voluntary Federation of Mankind. She has a special history, too, which even under the overshadowing greatness of that of the Empire – in which she also owns her part – is one of interest. First explored in 1535, by Jacques-Cartier, of St Malo, by command of Francis I., and its settlement established in 1608 through the foundation of Quebec by the devoted and energetic Maker of French Canada, Samuel de Champlain, its story down to the Conquest in 1759-63 is full of romance, – Jesuit missionaries, explorers, chevaliers, painted Indian war-parties, the rich fur trade, and finally the great struggle under Montcalm, closing with his expiry and Wolfe's at the hour of the fall of Quebec, passing like a panorama. Then came the entry of the Loyalists, and from that to the present there has been a steady unfolding to power and culture, broken only by the brave war of 1812, and a French, and two half-breed, rebellions. She is, to-day, next to the United States, the strongest factor in American affairs.

The Literature of this daughter-nation in the West, as distilled by its poets, ought to be interesting to Englishmen. That other Colonial poetic literature, presented in the Australian volume of this series, has shown that there can be a signal attractiveness in such a picture of a fresh world. On the part of Canada the semi-tropical Australian surroundings are matched in beauty by a Northern atmosphere of objects which make vivid contrasts with them; her native races were the noblest of savage tribes; while the Imperial and National feelings, developing in two such different hemispheres, are instructive in their divergences and similarities. The romantic life of each Colony also has a special flavour, – Australian rhyme is a poetry of the *horse*; Canadian, of the *canoe*.

Now, who are those who are drinking these inspirations and breathing them into song? In communing with them, we shall try to transport you to the Canadian clime itself. You shall come out with us as a guest of its skies and air, paddling over bright lakes and down savage rivers; singing French *chansons* to the swing of our paddles, till we come into the settlements; and shall be swept along on great rafts of timber by the majestic St. Lawrence, to moor at historic cities whose streets and harbours are thronged with the commerce of all Europe and the world. You shall hear there the chants of a new nationality, weaving in with songs of the Empire, of its heroes, of its Queen.

A word first about the personnel of our conductors. The foremost name in Canadian song at the present day is that of Charles George Douglas Roberts, poet, canoeist, and Professor of Literature, who has struck the supreme note of Canadian nationality in his "Canada" and "Ode for the Canadian Confederacy." His claim to supremacy lies, for the rest, chiefly in the quality of the two volumes, "Orion and other Poems," which he published in 1880 at the age of twenty-one, and "In Divers Tones," which appeared in 1887. The style and taste of Roberts at its best – and he is frequently very good – are characterised by two different elements – a striking predilection for the pictorial ideals and nature-poetry of classical Greece; and a noble passion, whose fire and music resemble and approach Tennyson's. "Orion," "Actaeon," "Off Pelorus," and "The Pipes of Pan" are purely Greek, drawn direct from "ancient founts of inspiration." On the other hand, his "O Child of Nations, giant-limbed!" which stirs every true Canadian like a trumpet, is, though of different subject and metre, of the stamp and calibre of "Locksley Hall." His pure Hellenic poems must be dismissed from consideration here, but an account of the man himself makes it proper to say of them that they have obtained for him a growing recognition in the ranks of general English literature; and that his feeling for beauty of colour and form is so really artistically correct as well as rich, that he deserves a permanent place in the Gallery of *Word-painters.*

Roberts loves his country fervently, as is apparent in all his Canadian themes. His heart dwells with fondness on the scenes of his Maritime Provinces, "the long dikes of Tantramar," and the ebb-tide sighing out, "reluctant for the reed-beds"; and he was one of the first to sing Confederation. His sympathy is also Britain's:

> "Let a great wrong cry to heaven,
>   Let a giant necessity come;
> And now as of old she can strike,
>   She will strike, and strike home!"

The personal quality in his poetry is distinguished, next to richness of colour and artistic freedom of emotional expression, by manliness. Roberts is a high-thinking, generous man. He speaks with a voice of power and leadership, and never with a mean note or one of heedless recklessness. This manliness and dignity render him particularly fitted for the great work which Canada at present offers her sons, and as he is only twenty-nine we hope to see his future a great one.

In point of time, however, the first important national poet was not Roberts, but nature-loving Charles Sangster, a born son of the Muses, and who was long the people's favourite. Sangster is a kind of Wordsworth, with rather more fire, and of course a great deal less metaphysical and technical skill. He has the unevenness and frequent flatness of Wordsworth, but is as close a personal friend of the mountains, lakes, and woods.

"I have laid my cheek to Nature's, put my puny hands in hers."

Glowingly he takes us, in "St Lawrence and the Saguenay," down the grandeurs of that unrivalled tour – the great River, its rapids, cities, mountains, and "Isles of the Blest." Defective education in youth deprived him of the resources of modern art, which Roberts uses so freely, making a good deal of his poetry the curious spectacle of inborn strivings after perfect ideals driven to expression in abstractions rather than in concrete clothing of colours and forms; for instance:

"All my mind has sat in state
   Pondering on the deathless soul:
   What must be the *Perfect Whole*
When the atom is so great!

God! I fall in spirit down,
   Low as Persian to the sun;
   All my senses, one by one,
In the stream of *Thought* must drown."

Sangster's nervous system was broken down by the grind of newspaper toil and civil service tread-milling, and he has not written or published for twenty years; yet, though poetry has still lately been given a particularly small share of attention in Canada, his "Brock," "Song for Canada," his lines on Quebec, and many striking passages from his poems, are treasured in the popular memory.

But the most striking volume next to those of Roberts—indeed more boldly new than his—is that of the late brilliant Isabella Valancy Crawford. This wonderful girl, living in the "Empire" Province of Ontario, early saw the possibilities of the new field around her, and had she lived longer might have made a really matchless name. It was only in 1884 that her modest blue card-covered volume of two hundred and twenty-four pages came out. The sad story of unrecognised genius and death was re-enacted. "Old Spooks's Pass; Malcolm's Katie, and other Poems," as it was doubly entitled (the names at least were against it!), almost dropped from the press. Scarcely anybody noticed it in Canada. It made no stir, and in little more than two years the authoress died. She was a high-spirited, passionate girl, and there is very little doubt that the neglect her book received was the cause of her death. Afterwards, as usual, a good many people began to find they had overlooked work of merit. Miss Crawford's verse was, in fact, seen to be phenomenal. Setting aside her dialect poems, like "Old Spooks's Pass" (which, though the dialect is a trifle artificial, resulted in hitting off some good pictures of imaginary rustic characters), the style peculiarly her own has seldom been equalled for strength, colour, and originality: –

> "Low the sun beat on the land,
>   Purple slope and olive wood;
> With the wine cup in his hand,
>   Vast the Helot herdsman stood."
>
>   *   *   *
>
> "Day was at her high unrest;
>   Fevered with the wine of light,
> Loosing all her golden vest,
>   Reeled she towards the coming Night."

Miss Crawford's poetry is packed with able stuff. It is worth a share of attention from the whole Anglo-Saxon world. The splendour of Canadian colour, the wonderful blue skies of that clear climate, the Heaven's-forests of its autumn, the matchless American sunsets and sunrises, imbued her like Roberts. A poetess of such original nature could not but strike boldly into Canadian subjects. "Malcolm's Katie; a Love Story," is an idyl of a true man who goes forth and cuts him a home with his axe, and of a maiden who remains true to him, until he returns for their union. Few finer bits were ever written by any one or anywhere than the passage which we give, from "Shanties grew," down to its glorious climax in the song, "O Love will build his lily walls." It seems to us that this is the most effective known use of a lyric introduced into a long poem. Her works, including a good deal never yet published, were to be brought before the English public in a new volume. A letter of hers, concerning the unpublished material, stated that it contained some of her best work.

The poets best known and most favourite next to Roberts and Sangster, are – besides Isabella Crawford – M'Lachlan, Kirby, and tender-hearted John Reade. Reade is one the charms of whose style are sweetness and culture. He is best known by his "Merlin, and Other Poems" (1870), composed of short lyrics, led off by "The Prophecy of Merlin," which is a Tennysonian Idyll of the King, foreshadowing the greatness of the British Empire. His style turns everything it touches into grace, but it appeals to the inner circle rather than the folk, and seems to shrink away from touching organ-keys. For examples of this grace of his, I should like to quote his "The Inexpressible," or "Good Night," but cannot do so here.

The claim of first place is awarded by the feelings of no small number to Alexander M'Lachlan, the human-hearted vigorous Scottish Radical, whose stanzas have such a singing rhythm and direct sympathy. They were a few years ago made a special feature of the great comic paper *Grip*, the *Punch* of Canada, and his popularity is shown by the presentation by his admirers a short time since of a homestead farm, upon which he now lives. His "Idylls of the Dominion," from which the poems quoted in this book are principally drawn, are so characteristic both of himself and of pioneerdom, that he is called "The Burns of Canada." He has lived the whole life of them, as a settler and a lover of the soil, – chopped his first tree, penetrated the mysterious "Hall of Shadows," listened to the cheerful bobolink's little aria, communed with "October" in her splendour and her sadness, and experienced the appalling sensations created by fire in the forest as he describes it.

William Kirby deserves a high position for his beautiful "Canadian Idylls" (based on history, while M'Lachlan's are upon life), from which the "Spina Christi," quoted here, is drawn. There are also some able descriptions in his long-known "U. E." (Loyalist) poem, from which is taken his passage on Niagara. Steeped in the romance of Canadian history, he wrote many years ago a magnificent novel founded upon the Quebec legend of the Chien d'Or, which has remained the most popular of Canadian stories. Kirby's strong point is his graphic descriptions.

One name I have not yet pronounced, though every Canadian no doubt has looked for it. A sombre shadow towers in the background of the group, – a man apart from the rest, – Charles Heavysege, author of the drama "Saul." When "Saul" came out in 1857, and a copy fell into the hands of Nathaniel Hawthorne, Heavysege became famous. He was pronounced the greatest dramatist since Shakespeare. The *North British Review* for August 1858 spoke of the book as follows: –

"Of 'Saul, a Drama, in three parts,' published anonymously at Montreal, we have before us perhaps the only copy which has crossed the Atlantic. At all events we have heard of no other, as it is probable we should have done, through some public or private notice, seeing that the work is indubitably one of the most remarkable English poems ever written out of Great Britain."

The *North British* reviewer was later, by no means alone, in its praise, and it became the fashion among tourists to Montreal to buy a copy of "Saul."

Heavysege had a very strange and original cast of mind. The following brief poem may be read as being characteristic of him: –

"Open, my heart, thy ruddy valves;
   It is thy master calls;
Let me go down, and, curious trace
   Thy labyrinthine halls.
Open, O heart, and let me view
   The secrets of thy den;
Myself unto myself now show
   With introspective ken.
Expose thyself, thou covered nest
   Of passions, and be seen;
Stir up thy brood, that in unrest
   Are ever piping keen,
Ah! what a motley multitude,
   Magnanimous and mean!"

He was originally a drama-composing carpenter, then a journalist in Montreal, and wore out his soul at the drudgery of the latter occupation and in poverty. To get out the third edition of "Saul" he was forced to borrow the money, which he was never able to repay. In person he was a small, very reticent man, who walked along the streets altogether locked up in himself, so that a literary acquaintance of his says Heavysege's appearance always reminded him exactly of "The Yellow Dwarf," –

> "He walked our streets, and no one knew
> That something of celestial hue
> Had passed along; a toil-worn man
> Was seen, – no more; the fire that ran
> Electric through his veins, and wrought
> Sublimity of soul and thought,
> And kindled into song, no eye
> Beheld."

He died in 1869. A man apart he has remained. His work is in no sense distinctively Canadian. Canadians do not read him; but they claim him as perhaps their greatest, most original writer, if they could weigh him aright and appreciate him; and he will probably always command their awe, and refuse to be forgotten.

Sympathy with the prairie and the Indian has produced the best verse of Charles Mair, who has dramatised the story of the immortal British ally Tecumseh, and lately from his North-West home gives us "The Last Bison;" and who has lived a life (some details of which you will find in the Biographical Notes) almost as Indian and North-West as his poems. "The Last Bison," he says, was suggested to him by what happened before his own eyes near the elbow of the North Saskatchewan some eight years ago. "Not a buffalo," so far as he knows, "has been seen on that river since. There are some animals in private collections; a small band perhaps exist in the fastnesses of Montana, and a few wood buffaloes still roam the Mackenzie River region; but the wild bison of the plains may now be looked upon as extinct." We may add, that it was lately reported by an Indian that he had tracked a herd of seven in the northerly region of the Peace River. He shot four bulls and a calf out of the seven! The North-West has also given happy inspirations to "Barry Dane" as a bird of passage.

John Hunter-Duvar, the author of "De Roberval" and Squire of "Hernewood," in Prince Edward Island, described in "The Emigration of the Fairies," derives his verse largely from the life and legends of the surrounding regions, shaped by his library.

George Martin, of Montreal, has digged in the gold mine of old

French legend, with the result of "Marguerite; or, The Isle of Demons," a weird and sad story of De Roberval's desertion of his niece, in one of the early expeditions.

Arthur Wentworth Eaton and George Murray have explored the same mine with signal success, – the latter, who is very well known as a *litterateur*, producing the fine ballad "How Canada was Saved." (The same story has been well put in Martin's "Heroes of Ville-Marie.")

Bliss Carman has earned special honour for the originality and finish of his lyrics. Arthur John Lockhart, in his "Masque of Minstrels," – particularly in "Gaspereau," – sings as a bird of exile warbling towards home, for he lives just over the frontier. William Wilfred Campbell is the poet of the Great Lakes, which he has studied with a perfect love, resulting in those beautiful "Lake Lyrics" of his, which the reader will stop to admire. A bit of work of particular attractiveness has been done by William M'Lennan in his well-known translations of the old French *chansons*. Archibald Lampman has written perfectly exquisite pre-Raphaelite descriptions, with the finish and sparkle of jewellers' work.

I should have liked to quote more fully than has been possible from the "Lyrics on Freedom, Love, and Death" of the late George Frederick Cameron; but his fire and generosity of spirit belong rather to the world than to Canadian inspiration, and we are therefore confined here to a few lesser pieces of his. He died early, like so many other sons of genius.

Among names of special grace or promise are to be added those of "Laclède," John Talon-Lespérance, the well-known *litterateur*, and Fellow of the Royal Society of Canada; Barry Straton, Duncan Campbell Scott, Frederick George Scott, John Henry Brown, Dr. Aeneas M'Donald Dawson, F. R. S. C.; Arthur Weir (the author of "Fleurs de Lys"); Dr. Charles Edwin Jakeway; the late Honourables d'Arcy M'Gee and Joseph Howe; Ernest J. Chapman, E. W. Thomson, Carroll Ryan, William Wye Smith, Phillips Stewart, J. J. Proctor, J. A. Richey; the aged but bright G. W. Wicksteed, Q.C.; H. L. Spencer; Evan M'Coll, the Gaelic-English "Bard of Lochfyne"; Messrs. Dunn, Shanly, Haliburton, M'Donell, James M'Carroll, J. H. Bowes, K. L. Jones, S. J. Watson, T. G. Marquis, M'Alpine Taylor, the late Francis Rye, the late John Lowry Stuart, the late Charles Pelham Mulvaney, H. R. A. Pocock (author of spirited North-West pieces), Alexander Rae Garvie, and M'Pherson, the early Nova Scotia singer, whose "I Long for Spring, enchanting Spring," has a bell-like silveriness. Some of these I have been unable to get at. A bright and erratic name, which I am sorry I cannot represent, is that of the journalist George T. Lanigan ("Allid"), – "the most brilliant journalist who ever lived," says Mr. George Murray. Lanigan wrote with equal felicity in French and English, and his humour was inexhaustible. I regret that space forbids me to add in the body of the book two good things by D. B. Kerr and Emily M'Manus. The latter's subject is the crescent province of the West: –

"MANITOBA.

"Softly the shadows of prairie-land wheat
Ripple and riot adown to her feet;
Murmurs all Nature with joyous acclaim,
Fragrance of summer and shimmer of flame;
Heedless she hears while the centuries slip: –
Chalice of poppy is laid on her lip.

"Hark! From the East comes a ravishing note, –
Sweeter was never in nightingale's throat, –
Silence of centuries thrills to the song,
Singing their silence awaited so long;
Low, yet it swells to the heaven's blue dome,
Child-lips have called the wild meadow-land 'Home!'

"Deep, as she listens, a dewy surprise
Dawns in the languor that darkens her eyes;
Swift the red blood through her veins, in its flow,
Kindles to rapture her bosom aglow;
Voices are calling, where silence had been, –
'Look to thy future, thou Mother of Men!'

"Onward and onward! Her fertile expanse
Shakes as the tide of her children advance;
Onward and onward! Her blossoming floor
Yields her an opium potion no more;
Onward! and soon on her welcoming soil
Cities shall palpitate, myriads toil."

One peculiar feature of this literature, indeed, is its strength in lady singers. The number who have produced true poetry seems to indicate something special in the conditions of a new country. Verily one has not to read far in that noble, patriotic book, "Laura Secord," to acknowledge that Mrs. Sarah Anne Curzon writes with the power and spirit of masculinity. How these women sympathise with the pluck of the heroes! The best war-songs of the late half-breed rebellion were written by Annie Rothwell, of Kingston, who had only a name for prose novels until the spirit of militarism was thus lit in her. "Fidelis" (Agnes Maude Machar), who is frequently given the credit of being the first of our poetesses, shows some of it, but excels in a graceful subjectivity which unfortunately is unfitted for representative quotation here; a remark which applies with still more hapless effect to the philosophic thought of Mary Morgan ("Gowan Lea"). Kate Seymour Maclean, authoress of "The Coming of the Princess," is mistress of a style of singular richness; and some of the brightest writing, both prose and verse, is done by "Seranus," of Toronto (Mrs. S. Frances Harrison), who is working good service to our literature in a number of ways. Her "Old Régime," and "Rose Latulippe," express what has been called her "half-French heart," and breathe the air of the fertile, scarcely-wrought field of French Canadian life. Then there are "Fleurange," who wrote the best Carnival Poem, "The Italian Boy's Dream;" E. Pauline Johnson, daughter of Head-Chief Johnson, of the Mohawks of Brantford, who gives us poetry of a high stamp, and of great interest on account of her descent; "Esperance" (Alice Maud Ardagh); Mrs. Leprohon; Mary Barry Smith; Helen Fairbairn; M. J. Katzmann Lawson; the late Miss E. M. Nash; Pamelia Vining Yule, "Clare Everest"; Janet Carnochan; Mrs. Edgar Jarvis, "Jeanie Gray"; Isabel Macpherson; Louisa Murray, a well-known authoress, who, besides much fine prose, has written "Merlin's Cave," one of the best of Canadian undistinctive poems, and Ethelwyn Wetherald, authoress of many exquisite sonnets. Even from the beginning – fifty years ago, for there was no native poetry to speak of before that – we had Susanna Moodie, one of the famous Strickland sisters, authoress of "Roughing it in the Bush" (which book, by the way, did the country's progress a good deal of harm), who gave us the best verses we had during many years, and some of the most patriotic.

Some of those lines of "Fidelis" to which I referred, express so well the spirit of this preface, that I return to her name to quote them: –

CANADA TO THE LAUREATE

" 'And that true north, whereof we lately heard
A strain to shame us! Keep you to yourselves,
So loyal is too costly! Friends, your love
Is but a burden: loose the bond and go,
Is this the tone of Empire?
                  – *Tennyson's Ode to the Queen.*

"We thank thee, Laureate, for thy kindly words
Spoken for us to her to whom we look
With loyal love, across the misty sea;
Thy noble words, whose generous tone may shame
The cold and heartless strain that said "Begone,
We want your love no longer; all our aim
Is riches – *that* your love can *not* increase!'
Fain would we tell them that we do not seek
To hang dependent, like a helpless brood
That, selfish, drag a weary mother down;
For we have British hearts and British blood
That leaps up, eager, when the danger calls!
Once and again, our sons have sprung to arms
To fight in Britain's quarrel, – *not our own,* –
And drive the covetous invader back,
Who would have let us, peaceful, keep our.own.
So we had cast the British name away.

> Canadian blood has dyed Canadian soil,
> For Britain's honour, that we deemed our own,
> Nor do we ask but for the right to keep
> Unbroken, still, the cherished filial tie
> That binds us to the distant sea-girt isle
> Our fathers loved, and taught their sons to love,
> As the dear home of freemen, brave and true,
> And loving *honour* more than ease or gold!"

Many more writers than those above named, in all to a number which might be roughly placed at three hundred, have at various times produced really good verse.

A curious Indian song, representing a small but unique song-literature which has sprung up among the tribe at Caughnawaga Reservation, near Montreal, since barbaric times, "from the sheer necessity of singing when together," was translated specially for me by Mr. John Waniente Jocks, the son of a Six-nation chief of that Reservation. Mr Jocks, who is a law student, is of pure Mohawk origin.

A few general remarks are now in order. The present is an imperfect presentation of Canadian poetry from a purely literary point of view, on account of the limitation of treatment; for it is obvious that if only what illustrates the country and its life *in a distinctive way* be chosen, the subjective and unlocal literature must be necessarily passed over, entraining the omission of most of the poems whose merit lies in perfection of finish. It is therefore greatly to be desired that a purely literary anthology may soon be brought together by someone. Such a collection was made in 1867, in the Rev. Edward Hartley Dewart's "Selections," which have ever since remained the standard book of reference for that period; but it has become antiquated, no longer represents what is being done, and most of the best authors, such as Roberts, Miss Crawford, Hunter-Duvar, Talon-Lespérance, and "Fidelis" have come into the field since its publication. Two or three other partial collections have been made, the best being Seranus's "Canadian Birthday Book," which affords a miniature survey of the chief verse-writers, both French and English. The most remarkable point of difference between the selections of Dewart and the poetry which has followed, is the tone of exultation and confidence which the singers have assumed since Confederation, for up to that epoch the verse was apologetic and depressed. Everything now points hopefully. Not only is the poetry more confident, but far better. A good deal of the best verse in American magazines is written in Canada.

The arrangement of the present collection has been devised in order to give a sketch of Canadian things in something like related order. I have introduced such broad principles of order as the contributions permitted, grouping them into sections, which respectively treat of the Imperial Spirit, the New Nationality, the Indian, the *Voyageur* and

Habitant, Settlement Life, Historical Incidents, Places, and Seasons. They give merely, it should be understood, a sketch of the range of the subjects. Canadian history, for example, as anyone acquainted with Parkman will know, perfectly teems with noble deeds and great events, of which only a small share have been sung, whereof there is only space here for a much smaller share. The North-West and British Columbia, that Pacific clime of charm, – the gold-diggings Province, land of salmon rivers, and of the Douglas firs which hide daylight at noonday, – have been scarcely sung at all, owing to their newness. Pieces which take origin from them ought to be remarked as rare. The poetry of the Winter Carnival, splendid scenic spectacle of gay Northern arts and delights, is only rudimentary also. Those who have been present at the thrilling spectacle of the nocturnal storming of the Ice Palace in Montreal, when the whole city, dressing itself in the picturesque snow-shoe costume and arraying its streets in lights and colours, rises as one man in a tumultuous enthusiasm; must feel that something of a future lies before the poetry of these strange and wonderful elements. Here a word suggests itself concerning the climate of Canada. Winter is not perpetual, but merely, in most parts, somewhat long. It does not strike the inhabitants as intolerably severe. It is the season of most of their enjoyments; gives them their best roads; is indispensable to some industries, such as lumbering; and the clear nights and diamond days are sparklingly beautiful. Furthermore, the climate is not one but several. In British Columbia, it is so equable the whole year that roses sometimes bloom out of doors in January, and cactus is a native plant. In the Niagara peninsula, grapes and peaches are crops raised yearly in immense quantities, and the sycamore and acacia are so frequent as to have called out more than one poem. On the plains, temperature grows milder in proportion as you approach to the Rocky Mountains.

To omit a bow to the French would be ungracious. Forming about a fourth of the population, they have a literature which was within the last generation much more fecund than the English, and contains remarkable writing. We have devoted a special appendix to *ipsis verbis* specimens of Chauveau, Sulte, Fréchette, and Le May, leaders who have been very highly honoured in France. The charming old Chanson literature, in which numbers of medieval ballads brought over in past days from the *mère-patrie* are embalmed, is treated in another appendix, while in our text, the renderings of William M'Lennan are given for some of the best of them. "Entre Paris and St Denis," it is to be noted, preserves a remarkable machinery of sorcery; the quaintness and beauty of the others will speak for themselves.

In concluding, I desire to express my sense of shortcoming in the work, but believe it will be generally admitted that I have spared no necessary trouble.

The editor regrets to say that through an accidental cause unnecessary to explain, more MSS. were sent to the publishers than the volume required. As no time could be lost the general editor had no recourse except to undertake the difficult task of cutting down the matter, which he did in accordance with his best judgment, but guided by the sole criterion of the symmetry of the work. Some good poetry originally included has not found a place owing to the necessary reduction, and apology is tendered where unintentional injustice has resulted.

Acknowledgments are due to many kind persons, of whom the principal are duly mentioned in a note of thanks at the close of the volume.

And now, the canoes are packed, our *voyageurs* are waiting for us, the paddles are ready, let us start!

Charles G. D. Roberts (1860-1943)

Referred to as the "Father of Canadian Literature," Charles G. D. Roberts was both a noted poet and short story writer and the leader of the first real literary movement in Canada. His poetry was a catalyst for the talents of Bliss Carman, Archibald Lampman, Duncan Campbell Scott, and William Wilfred Campbell and he influenced many other young poets and prose-writers of the period.

Born in 1860 near Fredericton, Charles G. D. Roberts was the eldest son of a remarkable family. His grandfather was headmaster of Fredericton Collegiate; his father was an amateur painter, musician and poet, and his mother was related to the family of Ralph Waldo Emerson. Both Charles' sister Elizabeth and his brother George (Theoodore Goodridge Roberts) were writers, as well as his cousin Bliss Carman, and George's son was the noted Canadian painter Goodridge Roberts. In 1861 the family moved to Westcock near Sackville, the country of the Tantramar marshes, and this area is the setting for several poems, stories and novels. In 1874, Roberts attended Fredericton Collegiate with Bliss Carman under the tutelage of George C. Parkin who stimulated their interest in literature and in particular, in Tennyson. Roberts graduated from the University of New Brunswick in 1879 and taught for several years, first near Chatham and then in Fredericton. In November 1883 he became the editor of a new periodical *The Week* managed by Goldwyn Smith in Toronto, and in this position he encouraged many young writers and poets. But quarreling with Smith over his policy of annexation to the United States, Roberts left Toronto several months later and settled in Windsor, Nova Scotia as Professor at King's College, remaining here until 1895.

Roberts' first publication was a series of three articles in an agricultural journal at the age of eleven, and *Orion and Other Poems* appeared in 1880 just after his graduation from university; its avid reception has been described vividly by Archibald Lampman (See Lampman "Two Canadian Poets"). He wrote vigorously at Windsor, but in 1895 he resigned, and for eighteen months worked in Fredericton as a freelance journalist. In 1897, after separating from his wife, he moved to New York and over the next twenty years, he travelled extensively from his base first in New York, then in Paris after 1907 and London after 1912. He served in the first world war as a Lieutenant training recruits and officers and after 1917, as a Canadian Press Correspondent in France. In 1925, he returned to Canada and began a series of lecture tours from Charlottetown to Vancouver.

He had already been honoured in Canada by election to the Royal Society in 1890 and was awarded a Doctor of Laws degree by the University of New Brunswick in 1906. In 1926 he became the president of the Toronto branch of the Canadian Authors' Association and in 1927, the National President. Also in 1926, he was the first recipient of the Lorne Pierce Gold Medal for literature, and in 1935 he was knighted by King George V. He received a Doctor of Literature degree in 1942 from Mount Allison, in the Tantramar area of which he had written so vividly. In Toronto, where he lived for the remainder of his life, he helped to edit *The Standard Dictionary of Canadian Biography* (1934-8) and *The Canadian Who's Who* (1936-9) and three anthologies, *Poems of Wild Life* (1885), *Northland Lyrics* (1899) and *Flying Colours* (1942). He remarried in 1943 but died in November of the same year.

Charles G. D. Roberts' literary output was extensive. He published ten books of poetry: *Orion and Other Poems* (1880), *In Divers Tones* (1886), *Songs of the Common Day* (1893), *The Book of the Native* (1896), *New York Nocturnes and Other Poems* (1898), *The Book of the Rose* (1903), *Poems* (1907), *New Poems* (1919), *The Sweet o' the Year and Other Poems* (1925), *The Iceberg and Other Poems* (1934), and *Selected Poems* (1936). In addition he wrote six historical romances: *The Forge in the Forest* (1896), *A Sister to Evangeline* (1898), *The Heart of the Ancient Wood* (1900), *Barbara Ladd* (1902), *The Heart That Knows* (1906) and *In the Morning of Time* (1919) and eighteen collections of short stories, including *Earth's Enigmas* (1896), *The Kindred of the Wild* (1902), *The Watchers of the Trails* (1904), *The Haunters of the Silences* (1907) and *Kings in Exile* (1909). He also published two travelguides: *The Canadian Guide-Book* (1891), and *The Land of Evangeline* (1895), and two histories: *A History of Canada* (1897), and *Discoveries and Exploration in the* [*Nineteenth*] *Century*.

Although Roberts' poetry ranges over a period of some fifty years and a variety of styles and techniques, he remains in the poetic tradition of the nineteenth century rather than that of the world which produced Yeats and Eliot. Most critics agree that his earlier works are among his best, in particular the descriptive poems and sonnets of *In Divers Tones* and *Songs of the Common Day*. The short stories reveal a rather different facet of nature, "red in tooth and claw". Like those of his contemporary Ernest Thompson Seton, their predominant theme is the Darwinian struggle for survival. Roberts adapted the animal story from its classical and mediaeval origins as allegory, and employed it in a manner which is distinctively Canadian to convey his message that nature is indifferent and ruthless, preying upon one species to maintain another. Ironically in "When Twilight Falls on the Stump Lots", none win the battle for survival.

TEXT

Selected Poems of Sir Charles G. D. Roberts. Toronto: Ryerson, 1936.
The Kindred of The Wild. Boston: L. C. Page, 1902.

See also

James Cappon. *Roberts and the Influences of His Times*. Toronto: Briggs, 1905; and *Charles G. D. Roberts*. Toronto: Ryerson, 1925.
William Keith. *Charles G. D. Roberts*. Toronto: Copp Clark, 1969.
Desmond Pacey. *Ten Canadian Poets*. Toronto: Ryerson, 1958.
Elsie M. Pomeroy. *Sir Charles G. D. Roberts: A Biography*. Toronto: Ryerson, 1943.

An Ode for the Canadian Confederacy

Awake, my country, the hour is great with change!
   Under this gloom which yet obscures the land,
From ice-blue strait and stern Laurentian range
   To where giant peaks our western bounds command,
A deep voice stirs, vibrating in men's ears
   As if their own hearts throbbed that thunder forth,
A sound wherein who hearkens wisely hears
   The voice of the desire of this strong North, –
      This North whose heart of fire
      Yet knows not its desire
Clearly, but dreams, and murmurs in the dream.
The hour of dreams is done. Lo, on the hills the gleam!

Awake, my country, the hour of dreams is done!
   Doubt not, nor dread the greatness of thy fate.
Tho' faint souls fear the keen confronting sun,
   And fain would bid the morn of splendour wait;
Tho' dreamers, rapt in starry visions, cry
   "Lo, yon thy future, yon thy faith, thy fame!"
And stretch vain hands to stars, thy fame is nigh,
   Here in Canadian hearth, and home, and name, –
      This name which yet shall grow
      Till all the nations know
Us for a patriot people, heart and hand
Loyal to our native earth, our own Canadian land!

O strong hearts, guarding the birthright of our glory,
 Worth your best blood this heritage that ye guard!
These mighty streams resplendent with our story,
 These iron coasts by rage of seas unjarred, –
What fields of peace these bulwarks well secure!
 What vales of plenty those calm floods supply!
Shall not our love this rough, sweet land make sure,
 Her bounds preserve inviolate, though we die?
  O strong hearts of the North,
  Let flame your loyalty forth,
And put the craven and base to an open shame,
Till earth shall know the Child of Nations by her
  name!

(1887)

Prologue

Across the fog the moon lies fair,
 Transfused with ghostly amethyst,
O white Night, charm to wonderment
 The cattle in the mist!

Thy touch, O grave Mysteriarch,
 Makes dull, familiar things divine.
O grant of thy revealing gift
 Be some small portion mine!

Make thou my vision sane and clear,
 That I may see what beauty clings
In common forms, and find the soul
 Of unregarded things!

(1936)

The Deserted Wharf

The long tides sweep
  Around its sleep,
The long red tides of Tantramar.
  Around its dream
  They hiss and stream,
Sad for the ships that have sailed afar.

How many lips
  Have lost their bloom,
How many ships
  Gone down to gloom,
Since keel and sail
  Have fled out from me
Over the thunder and strain of the sea!

Its kale-dark sides
  Throb in the tides;
The long winds over it spin and hum;
  Its timbers ache
  For memory's sake,
And the throngs that never again will come.

How many lips
  Have lost their bloom,
How many ships
  Gone down to gloom,
Since keel and sail
  Have fled out from me
Over the thunder and strain of the sea!

(1936)

Tantramar Revisited

Summers and summers have come, and gone with the flight of the
   swallow;
Sunshine and thunder have been, storm, and winter, and frost;
Many and many a sorrow has all but died from remembrance,
Many a dream of joy fall'n in the shadow of pain.
Hands of chance and change have marred, or moulded, or broken,
Busy with spirit or flesh, all I most have adored;
Even the bosom of Earth is strewn with heavier shadows, –
Only in these green hills, aslant to the sea, no change!
Here where the road that has climbed from the inland valleys and
   woodlands,
Dips from the hill-tops down, straight to the base of the hills, –
Here, from my vantage-ground, I can see the scattering houses,
Stained with time, set warm in orchards, meadows, and wheat,
Dotting the broad bright slopes outspread to southward and eastward.
Wind-swept all day long, blown by the south-east wind.

Skirting the sunbright uplands stretches a riband of meadow,
Shorn of the labouring grass, bulwarked well from the sea,
Fenced on its seaward border with long clay dykes from the turbid
Surge and flow of the tides vexing the Westmoreland shores.
Yonder, toward the left, lie broad the Westmoreland marshes, –
Miles on miles they extend, level, and grassy, and dim,
Clear from the long red sweep of flats to the sky in the distance,
Save for the outlying heights, green-rampired Cumberland Point;
Miles on miles outrolled, and the river-channels divide them, –
Miles on miles of green, barred by the hurtling gusts.

Miles on miles beyond the tawny bay is Minudie.
There are the low blue hills; villages gleam at their feet.
Nearer a white sail shines across the water, and nearer
Still are the slim, grey masts of fishing boats dry on the flats.
Ah, how well I remember those wide red flats, above tide-mark
Pale with scurf of the salt, seamed and baked in the sun!
Well I remember the piles of blocks and ropes, and the net-reels
Wound with the beaded nets, dripping and dark from the sea!
Now at this season the nets are unwound; they hang from the rafters
Over the fresh-stowed hay in upland barns, and the wind
Blows all day through the chinks, with the streaks of sunlight, and
   sways them
Softly at will; or they lie heaped in the gloom of a loft.

Now at this season the reels are empty and idle; I see them
Over the lines of the dykes, over the gossiping grass.
Now at this season they swing in the long strong wind, thro' the
   lonesome
Golden afternoon, shunned by the foraging gulls.
Near about sunset the crane will journey homeward above them;
Round them, under the moon, all the calm night long,
Winnowing soft grey wings of marsh-owls wander and wander,
Now to the broad, lit marsh, now to the dusk of the dike.
Soon, thro' their dew-wet frames, in the live keen freshness of
   morning,
Out of the teeth of the dawn blows back the awakening wind.
Then, as the blue day mounts, and the low-shot shafts of the sunlight
Glance from the tide to the shore, gossamers jewelled with dew
Sparkle and wave, where late sea-spoiling fathoms of drift-net
Myriad-meshed, uploomed sombrely over the land.
Well I remember it all. The salt, raw scent of the margin;
While, with men at the windlass, groaned each reel, and the net,
Surging in ponderous lengths, uprose and coiled in its station;
Then each man to his home, – well I remember it all!

Yet, as I sit and watch, this present peace of the landscape, –
Stranded boats, these reels empty and idle, the hush,
One grey hawk slow-wheeling above yon cluster of haystacks, –
More than the old-time stir this stillness welcomes me home.
Ah, the old-time stir, how once it stung me with rapture, –
Old-time sweetness, the winds freighted with honey and salt!
Yet will I stay my steps and not go down to the marshland, –
Muse and recall far off, rather remember than see, –
Lest on too close sight I miss the darling illusion,
Spy at their task even here the hands of chance and change.

(1887)

The Herring Weir

Back to the green deeps of the outer bay
   The red and amber currents glide and cringe,
   Diminishing behind a luminous fringe
Of cream-white surf and wandering wraiths of spray.
Stealthily, in the old reluctant way,
   The red flats are uncovered, mile on mile,
   To glitter in the sun a golden while.
Far down the flats, a phantom sharply grey.

The herring weir emerges, quick with spoil.
   Slowly the tide forsakes it. Then draws near,
   Descending from the farm-house on the height,
A cart, with gaping tubs. The oxen toil
   Sombrely o'er the level to the weir,
   And drag a long black trail across the light.

(1893)

The Flight of the Geese

I hear the low wind wash the softening snow,
   The low tide loiter down the shore. The night,
   Full filled with April forecast, hath no light.
The salt wave on the sedge-flat pulses slow.
Through the hid furrows lisp in murmurous flow
   The thaw's shy ministers; and hark! The height
   Of heaven grows weird and loud with unseen flight
Of strong hosts prophesying as they go!

High through the drenched and hollow night their
     wings
   Beat northward hard on Winter's trail. The sound
Of their confused and solemn voices, borne
Athwart the dark to their long Arctic morn,
   Comes with a sanction and an awe profound,
A boding of unknown, foreshadowed things.

(1893)

Frogs

Here, in the red heart of the sunset lying,
    My rest an islet of brown weeds blown dry,
    I watch the wide bright heavens hovering nigh,
My plain and pools in lucent splendours dyeing!
My view dreams over the rosy wastes, descrying
    The reed-tops fret the solitary sky;
    And all the air is tremulous to the cry
Of myriad frogs on mellow pipes replying.

For the unrest of passion, here is peace;
    And eve's cool drench for midday soil and taint!
To tirèd ears, how sweetly brings release
    This limpid babble from life's unstilled complaint;
    While under tirèd eye-lids, lapse and faint
The noon's derisive visions, – fade and cease!

(1893)

In an Old Barn

Tons upon tons the brown-green fragrant hay
    O'erbrims the mows beyond the time-warped eaves,
    Up to the rafters where the spider weaves,
Though few flies wander his secluded way.
Through a high chink one lonely golden ray,
    Wherein the dust is dancing, slants unstirred.
    In the dry hush some rustlings light are heard,
Of winter-hidden mice at furtive play.

Far down, the cattle in their shadowed stalls,
    Nose-deep in clover fodder's meadowy scent,
    Forget the snows that whelm their pasture streams,
The frost that bites the world beyond their walls.
    Warm housed, they dream of summer, well content
    In day-long contemplation of their dreams.

(1893)

The Potato Harvest

A high bare field, brown from the plough, and borne
   Aslant from sunset; amber wastes of sky
   Washing the ridge; a clamour of crows that fly
In from the wide flats where the spent tides mourn
To yon their rocking roosts in pines wind-torn;
   A line of grey snake-fence, that zigzags by
   A pond and cattle; from the homestead nigh
The long deep summonings of the supper horn.

Black on the ridge, against that lonely flush,
   A cart, and stoop-necked oxen; ranged beside
      Some barrels; and the day-worn harvest-folk,
Here emptying their baskets, jar the hush
   With hollow thunders. Down the dusk hillside
      Lumbers the wain; and day fades out like smoke.

(1887)

The Pea-Fields

These are the fields of light, and laughing air,
   And yellow butterflies, and foraging bees,
   And whitish, wayward blossoms winged as these,
And pale green tangles like a seamaid's hair.
Pale, pale the blue, but pure beyond compare,
   And pale the sparkle of the far-off seas
   A-shimmer like these fluttering slopes of peas,
And pale the open landscape everywhere.

From fence to fence a perfumed breath exhales
   O'er the bright pallor of the well-loved fields, –
My fields of Tantramar in summer-time;
   And, scorning the poor feed their pasture yields,
Up from the bushy lots the cattle climb
   To gaze with longing through the grey, mossed rails.

(1893)

The Frosted Pane

One night came Winter noiselessly, and leaned
  Against my window-pane.
In the deep stillness of his heart convened
  The ghosts of all his slain.

Leaves, and ephemera, and stars of earth,
  And fugitives of grass, –
White spirits loosed from bonds of mortal birth,
  He drew them on the glass.

(1896)

Life and Art

Said Life to Art – "I love thee best
  Not when I find in thee
My very face and form, expressed
  With dull fidelity,

"But when in thee my craving eyes
  Behold continually
The mystery of my memories
  And all I long to be."

(1896)

Philander's Song

I sat and read Anacreon.
   Moved by the gay, delicious measure
I mused that lips were made for love,
   And love to charm a poet's leisure.

And as I mused a maid came by
   With something in her look that caught me.
Forgotten was Anacreon's line,
   But not the lesson he had taught me.

(1927)

Autochthon

I

I am the spirit astir
   To swell the grain
When fruitful suns confer
   With labouring rain;
I am the life that thrills
   In branch and bloom;
I am the patience of abiding hills,
   The promise masked in doom.

II

When the sombre lands are wrung
   And storms are out,
And giant woods give tongue,
   I am the shout;
And when the earth would sleep,
   Wrapped in her snows,
I am the infinite gleam of eyes that keep
   The post of her repose.

III

I am the hush of calm,
    I am the speed,
  The flood-tide's triumphing psalm,
    The marsh-pool's heed;
  I work in the rocking roar
    Where cataracts fall;
I flash in the prismy fire that dances o'er
    The dew's ephemeral ball.

IV

I am the voice of wind
    And wave and tree,
  Of stern desires and blind,
    Of strength to be;
  I am the cry by night
    At point of dawn,
The summoning bugle from the unseen height,
    In cloud and doubt withdrawn.

V

I am the strife that shapes
    The stature of man,
  The pang no hero escapes,
    The blessing, the ban;
  I am the hammer that moulds
    The iron of our race,
The omen of God in our blood that a people beholds,
    The foreknowledge veiled in our face.

(1896)

The Place of His Rest

The green marsh-mallows
    Are over him.
  Along the shallows
    The pale lights swim.

Wide air, washed grasses,
   And waveless stream;
And over him passes
   The drift of dream; –

The pearl-hue down
   Of the poplar seed;
The elm-flower brown;
   And the sway of the reed;

The blue moth, winged
   With a flake of sky;
The bee, gold ringed;
   And the dragon-fly.

Lightly the rushes
   Lean to his breast;
A bird's wing brushes
   The place of his rest.

The far-flown swallow,
   The gold-finch flame, –
They come, they follow
   The paths he came.

'Tis the land of No Care
   Where now he lies,
Fulfilled the prayer
   Of his weary eyes,

And while around him
   The kind grass creeps,
Where peace hath found him
   How sound he sleeps.

Well to his slumber
   Attends the year:
Soft rains without number
   Soft noons, blue clear,

With nights of balm,
   And the dark, sweet hours
Brooding with calm,
   Pregnant with flowers.

See how she speeds them,
  Each childlike bloom,
And softly leads them
  To tend his tomb! –

The white-thorn nears
  As the cowslip goes;
Then the iris appears;
  And then, the rose.

(1919)

Grey Rocks and the Greyer Sea

Grey rocks, and greyer sea,
  And surf along the shore –
And in my heart a name
  My lips shall speak no more.

The high and lonely hills
  Endure the darkening year –
And in my heart endure
  A memory and a tear.

Across the tide a sail
  That tosses, and is gone –
And in my heart the kiss
  That longing dreams upon.

Grey rocks, and greyer sea,
  And surf along the shore –
And in my heart the face
  That I shall see no more.

(1893)

Severance

The tide falls, and the night falls,
   And the wind blows in from the sea,
And the bell on the bar it calls and calls,
   And the wild hawk cries from his tree.

The late crane calls to his fellows gone
   In long flight over the sea,
And my heart with the crane flies on and on,
   Seeking its rest and thee.

O Love, the tide returns to the strand,
   And the crane flies back oversea,
But he brings not my heart from his far-off land
   For he brings not thee to me.

(1936)

When Twilight Falls on the Stump Lots

THE wet, chill first of the spring, its blackness made tender by the lilac wash of the afterglow, lay upon the high, open stretches of the stump lots. The winter-whitened stumps, the sparse patches of juniper and bay just budding, the rough-mossed hillocks, the harsh boulders here and there up-thrusting from the soil, the swampy hollows wherein a coarse grass began to show green, all seemed anointed, as it were, to an ecstasy of peace by the chrism of that paradisal colour. Against the lucid immensity of the April sky the thin tops of five or six soaring ram-pikes aspired like violet flames. Along the skirts of the stump lots a fir wood reared a ragged-crested wall of black against the red amber of the horizon.

Late that afternoon, beside a juniper thicket not far from the centre of the stump lots, a young black and white cow had given birth to her first calf. The little animal had been licked assiduously by the mother's caressing tongue till its colour began to show of a rich dark red. Now it had struggled to its feet, and, with its disproportionately long, thick legs braced wide apart, was beginning to nurse. Its blunt wet muzzle and thick lips tugged eagerly, but somewhat blunderingly as yet, at the unaccustomed teats; and its tail lifted, twitching with delight, as the first warm streams of mother milk went down its throat. It was a pathetically awkward, unlovely little figure, not yet advanced to that youngling winsomeness which is the heritage, to some degree and at some period, of the infancy of all the kindreds that breathe upon the earth. But to the young mother's eyes it was the most beautiful of things. With her head twisted far around, she nosed and licked its heaving flanks as it nursed; and between deep, ecstatic breathings she uttered in her throat low murmurs, unspeakably tender, of encourage- ment and caress. The delicate but pervading flood of sunset colour had the effect of blending the ruddy-hued calf into the tones of the landscape; but the cow's insistent blotches of black and white stood out sharply, refusing to harmonise. The drench of violet light was of no avail to soften their staring contrasts. They made her vividly conspicuous across the whole breadth of the stump lots, to eyes that watched her from the forest coverts.

The eyes that watched her – long, fixedly, hungrily – were small and red. They belonged to a lank she-bear, whose gaunt flanks and rusty coat proclaimed a season of famine in the wilderness. She could not see the calf, which was hidden by a hillock and some juniper scrub; but its presence was very legibly conveyed to her by the mother's solicitous watchfulness. After a motionless scrutiny from behind the screen of fir branches, the lean bear stole noiselessly forth from the shadows into the great wash of violet light. Step by step, and very slowly, with the patience that endures because confident of its object, she crept toward that oasis of mothering joy in the vast emptiness of the stump lots. Now crouching, now crawling, turning to this side and to that, taking advantage of every hollow, every thicket, every hillock, every aggressive stump, her craft succeeded in eluding even the wild and menacing watchfulness of the young mother's eyes.

The spring had been a trying one for the lank she-bear. Her den, in a dry tract of hemlock wood some furlongs back from the stump lots, was a snug little cave under the uprooted base of a lone pine, which had somehow grown up among the alien hemlocks only to draw down upon itself at last, by its superior height, the fury of a passing hurricane. The winter had contributed but scanty snowfall to cover the bear in her sleep; and the March thaws, unseasonably early and ardent, had called her forth to activity weeks too soon. Then frosts had come with belated severity, sealing away the budding tubers, which are the bear's chief dependence for spring diet; and worst of all, a long stretch of intervale meadow by the neighbouring river, which had once been rich in ground-nuts, had been ploughed up the previous spring and subjected to the producing of oats and corn. When she was feeling the pinch of meagre rations, and when the fat which a liberal autumn of blueberries had laid up about her ribs was getting as shrunken as the last snow in the thickets, she gave birth to two hairless and hungry little cubs. They were very blind, and ridiculously small to be born of so big a mother; and having so much growth to make during the next few months, their appetites were immeasurable. They tumbled, and squealed, and tugged at their mother's teats, and grew astonishingly, and made huge haste to cover their bodies with fur of a soft and silken black; and all this vitality of theirs made a strenuous demand upon their mother's milk. There were no more bee trees left in the neighbourhood. The long wanderings which she was forced to take in her search for roots and tubers were in themselves a drain upon her nursing powers. At last, reluctant though she was to attract the hostile notice of the settlement, she found herself forced to hunt on the borders of the sheep pastures. Before all else in life was it important to her that these two tumbling little ones in the den should not go hungry. Their eyes were open now – small and dark and whimsical, their ears quaintly large and inquiring for their roguish little faces. Had she not been driven by the unkind season to so much hunting and foraging, she would have passed near all her time rapturously in the den under the pine root, fondling those two soft miracles of her world.

With the killing of three lambs – at widely scattered points, so as to mislead retaliation – things grew a little easier for the harassed bear; and presently she grew bolder in tampering with the creatures under man's protection. With one swift, secret blow of her mighty paw she struck down a young ewe which had strayed within reach of her hiding-place. Dragging her prey deep into the wood, she fared well upon it for some days, and was happy with her growing cubs. It was just when she had begun to feel the fasting which came upon the exhaustion of this store that, in a hungry hour, she sighted the conspicuous markings of the black and white cow.

It is altogether unusual for the black bear of the eastern woods to attack any quarry so large as a cow, unless under the spur of fierce hunger or fierce rage. The she-bear was powerful beyond her fellows. She had the strongest possible incentive to bold hunting, and she had lately grown confident beyond her wont. Nevertheless, when she began her careful stalking of this big game which she coveted, she had no definite intention of forcing a battle with the cow. She had observed that cows, accustomed to the protection of man, would at times leave their calves asleep and stray off some distance in their pasturing. She had even seen calves left all by themselves in a field, from morning till night, and had wondered at such negligence in their mothers. Now she had a confident idea that sooner or later the calf would lie down to sleep, and the young mother roam a little wide in search of the scant young grass. Very softly, very self-effacingly, she crept nearer step by step, following up the wind, till at last, undiscovered, she was crouching behind a thick patch of juniper, on the slope of a little hollow not ten paces distant from the cow and the calf.

By this time the tender violet light was fading to a grayness over hillock and hollow; and with the deepening of the twilight the faint breeze, which had been breathing from the northward, shifted suddenly and came in slow, warm pulsations out of the south. At the same time the calf, having nursed sufficiently, and feeling his baby legs tired of the weight they had not yet learned to carry, laid himself down. On this the cow shifted her position. She turned half round, and lifted her head high. As she did so a scent of peril was borne in upon her fine nostrils. She recognised it instantly. With a snort of anger she sniffed again; then stamped a challenge with her fore hoofs, and levelled the lance-points of her horns toward the menace. The next moment her eyes, made keen by the fear of love, detected the black outline of the bear's head through the coarse screen of the juniper. Without a second's hesitation, she flung up her tail, gave a short bellow, and charged.

The moment she saw herself detected, the bear rose upon her hindquarters; nevertheless she was in a measure surprised by the sudden blind fury of the attack. Nimbly she swerved to avoid it, aiming at the same time a stroke with her mighty forearm, which, if it had found its mark, would have smashed her adversary's neck. But as she struck out, in the act of shifting her position, a depression of the ground threw her off her balance. The next instant one sharp horn caught her slantingly in the flank, ripping its way upward and inward, while the mad impact threw her upon her back.

Grappling, she had her assailant's head and shoulders in a trap, and her gigantic claws cut through the flesh and sinew like knives; but at the desperate disadvantage of her position she could inflict no disabling blow. The cow, on the other hand, though mutilated and streaming with blood, kept pounding with her whole massive weight, and with short tremendous shocks crushing the breath from her foe's ribs.

Presently, wrenching herself free, the cow drew off for another battering charge; and as she did so the bear hurled herself violently down the slope, and gained her feet behind a dense thicket of bay shrub. The cow, with one eye blinded and the other obscured by blood, glared around for her in vain, then, in a panic of mother terror, plunged back to her calf.

Snatching at the respite, the bear crouched down, craving that invisibility which is the most faithful shield of the furtive kindred. Painfully, and leaving a drenched red trail behind her, she crept off from the disastrous neighbourhood. Soon the deepening twilight sheltered her. But she could not make haste; and she knew that death was close upon her.

Once within the woods, she struggled straight toward the den that held her young. She hungered to die licking them. But destiny is as implacable as iron to the wilderness people, and even this was denied her. Just a half score of paces from the lair in the pine root, her hour descended upon her. There was a sudden redder and fuller gush upon the trail; the last light of longing faded out of her eyes; and she lay down upon her side.

The merry little cubs within the den were beginning to expect her, and getting restless. As the night wore on, and no mother came, they ceased to be merry. By morning they were shivering with hunger and desolate fear. But the doom of the ancient wood was less harsh than its wont, and spared them some days of starving anguish; for about noon a pair of foxes discovered the dead mother, astutely estimated the situation, and then, with the boldness of good appetite, made their way into the unguarded den.

As for the red calf, its fortune was ordinary. Its mother, for all her wounds, was able to nurse and cherish it through the night; and with morning came a searcher from the farm and took it, with the bleeding mother, safely back to the settlement. There it was tended and fattened, and within a few weeks found its way to the cool marble slabs of a city market.

Bliss Carman (1861-1929)

A first cousin of Charles G. D. Roberts, Bliss Carman was the most prolific poet of the Confederation Group, with twenty individual volumes of poetry, two books of masques and four books of essays. At one time, Carman was considered the greatest poet in Canada and he had the highest reputation of any Canadian poet abroad; indeed three full studies of his life were published during his lifetime. To-day Carman is less popular than his contemporaries Roberts, Lampman and D. C. Scott.

Born on April 15, 1861 at Fredericton, Bliss Carman was the son of a barrister and of Sophia Bliss, Roberts' aunt and related to Ralph Waldo Emerson. At Fredericton Collegiate Carman came under the influence of the great teacher George R. Parkin who "gave me all my enthusiasm for learning and all my love for poetry."; in 1878 he received the Douglas Gold Medal in Latin and Greek and graduated at the head of his class. He attended the University of New Brunswick, then a small college with four professors and forty students, but did not maintain his standards and graduated in 1881 with only Second Class Honours. After a year at home, he went abroad, and studied in Edinburgh for the University of London External Examinations, but failing mathematics, he returned to Canada in August of 1881. In Fredericton again, he tried teaching and the law, and gave tutorials to eke out the family finances, and wrote a paper for the University of New Brunswick for which he received an M.A. degree in 1884. The deaths of his father in 1885 and his mother in early 1896 cut him off from his roots, and he left Fredericton and Canada.

At Harvard Carman attempted further graduate work in 1886-7 but did not complete his courses. Here however he came under the influence of the philosophy scholar Josiah Royce and of Richard Hovey, a young American poet. After two or three years spent in reading and writing, Carman turned to journalism and was employed intermittently over a period of years on the staffs of the New York *Independent*, a small religious weekly *Current Literature*, *The Cosmopolitan*, *The Literary World*, *The Atlantic Monthly* and *The Gentleman's Journal*. Between these periods he visited friends, the Hoveys, the Roberts family, and his sister and her husband. In 1897, he met Mary Perry King, wife of a doctor, and she became the predominant influence on his life and poetry. Carman lived near the Kings for the remainder of his life, in the summers at Haines Falls and in the winters at New Canaan, Connecticut. After 1906, his life became easier. Yet he was always plagued by a shortage of money, and in 1921 began lecture tours in Canada and the States to raise funds, continuing for the next eight years of his life despite failing health. He died in 1929 in New Canaan.

Carman received much recognition during his lifetime. In 1906, he was awarded an honourary degree from the University of New Brunswick and later from McGill and Trinity College, Hartford. In 1925 he was elected corresponding member of the Royal Society of Canada and in 1929 received the Lorne Pierce Gold Medal; the medal of the Poetry Society of America was awarded after his death.

Carman's first poems appeared in the University of New Brunswick *Monthly* to which he also contributed a column after 1883; from 1886 to 1889, his poetry was published in the Harvard *Monthly*, the *Atlantic Monthly* and *The Century*. His first volume *Low Tide on Grand Pré* was published in 1893 and followed by *Songs from Vagabondia* (1894), written in collaboration with Richard Hovey. This vein was so successful that he mined it in *More Songs from Vagabondia* (1896), *Last Songs from Vagabondia* (1901) and *Echoes from Vagabondia* (1912). Another series, *The Pipes of Pan*, reveals his interest in ballads and mythology: *From the Book of Myths, The Green Book of the Bards* (1898), *Songs from a Northern Garden* (1904), *Songs of the Sea Children* (1904) and *From the Book of Valentines* (1905). In addition he published *Behind the Arras (1895), Ballads of Lost Haven: A Book of the Sea* (1897), *By the Aurelian Wall and other Elegies* (1898), *April Airs* (1916), *Later Poems* (1921), *Ballads and Lyrics* (1923), *Far Horizons* (1925), *Wild Garden* (1929) and *Sanctuary* (1929). He also translated from the Greek poet Sappho in *Sappho: One Hundred Lyrics* (1904) and collaborated with Mrs. King on two masques, *Daughters of the Dawn* (1913) and *Earth's Deities and Other Masques* (1914). During this time he published several books of essays: *The Kinship of Nature* (1904), *The Friendship of Art* (1904), *The Poetry of Life* (1905) and *The Making of Personality* (1908), the last with Mrs. King. He also edited several anthologies: *The World's Best Literature* in ten volumes (1904), *The Oxford Book of American Verse* (1907), and with Lorne Pierce *Our Canadian Literature* (1922; enlarged in 1923).

Although much of his poetry is of little concern today, Carman has written a number of poems of enduring interest and relevance. Indeed Desmond Pacey has called "Low Tide on Grand Pré" "the most nearly perfect poem to come out of Canada in the nineteenth century", and Irving Layton in his anthology of love poetry *Love Where the Nights are Long* includes three selections by Carman. Carman's descriptions of nature are general and vague rather than concrete and specific like those of Roberts and Lampman, and evoke a mood or atmosphere in line with his theory that the best poetry "moves us pleasurably", the metre and rhythm exerting a mesmeric effect on the mind ("Subconscious Art"). His aesthetic essay "Realism in Letters" develops his belief in art as ideal, as "the embodiment of perfection"

which represents life both as it is and as it may be ("Sanity and Art");
it thus becomes a prophecy of the progress of mankind. The essay is
an interesting statement of Carman's poetic beliefs and those of this
generation of poets in Canada.

TEXT:

Bliss Carman's Poems. Toronto: McClelland and Stewart, 1931.
Sappho: One Hundred Lyrics. Boston: Page, 1904.

See also:

James Cappon. *Bliss Carman and the Literary Currents and Influ-
ences of his Time*. Toronto: Ryerson, 1930.
Desmond Pacey. "Bliss Carman" in *Ten Canadian Poets*. Toronto:
Ryerson, 1958.
Donald Stephens. *Bliss Carman*. New York: Twayne, 1967.

A Vagabond Song

There is something in the autumn that is native to my blood –
Touch of manner, hint of mood;
And my heart is like a rhyme,
With the yellow and the purple and the crimson keeping time.

The scarlet of the maples can shake me like a cry
Of bugles going by.
And my lonely spirit thrills
To see the frosty asters like a smoke upon the hills.

There is something in October sets the gypsy blood astir;
We must rise and follow her,
When from every hill of flame
She calls and calls each vagabond by name.

(1896)

The Vagabonds

"Such as wake on the night and sleep on the day, and haunt customable taverns and alehouses and routs about, and no man wot from whence they came, nor whither they go." – *Old English Statute.*

We are the vagabonds of time,
  And rove the yellow autumn days,
When all the roads are gray with rime
  And all the valleys blue with haze.

We came unlooked for as the wind
  Trooping across the April hills,
When the brown waking earth had dreams
  Of summer in the Wander Kills.

How far afield we joyed to fare,
  With June in every blade and tree!
Now with the sea-wind in our hair
  We turn our faces to the sea.

We go unheeded as the stream
  That wanders by the hill-wood side,
Till the great marshes take his hand
  And lead him to the roving tide.

The roving tide, the sleeping hills,
  These are the borders of that zone
Where they may fare as fancy wills
  Whom wisdom smiles and calls her own.

It is a country of the sun,
  Full of forgotten yesterdays,
When Time takes Summer in his care,
  And fills the distance of her gaze.

It stretches from the open sea
  To the blue mountain and beyond;
The world is Vagabondia
  To him who is a vagabond.

In the beginning God made man
  Out of the wandering dust, men say;
And in the end his life shall be
  A wandering wind and blown away.

We are the vagabonds of time,
   Willing to let the world go by,
With joy supreme, with heart sublime,
   And valor in the kindling eye.

We have forgotten where we slept,
   And guess not where we sleep to-night,
Whether among the lonely hills
   In the pale streamers' ghostly light

We shall lie down and hear the frost
   Walk in the dead leaves restlessly,
Or somewhere on the iron coast
   Learn the oblivion of the sea.

It matters not. And yet I dream
   Of dreams fulfilled and rest somewhere
Before this restless heart is stilled
   And all its fancies blown to air.

Had I my will! . . . The sun burns down
   And something plucks my garment's hem:
The robins in their faded brown
   Would lure me to the south with them.

'Tis time for vagabonds to make
   The nearest inn. Far on I hear
The voices of the Northern hills
   Gather the vagrants of the year.

Brave heart, my soul! Let longings be!
   We have another day to wend.
For dark or waylay what care we
   Who have the lords of time to friend?

And if we tarry or make haste,
   The wayside sleep can hold no fear.
Shall fate unpoise, or whim perturb,
   The calm-begirt in dawn austere?

There is a tavern, I have heard,
   Not far, and frugal, kept by One
Who knows the children of the Word,
   And welcomes each when day is done.

Some say the house is lonely set
   In Northern night, and snowdrifts keep
The silent door; the hearth is cold,
   And all my fellows gone to sleep . . . .

Had I my will! I hear the sea
   Thunder a welcome on the shore;
I know where lies the hostelry
   And who should open me the door.

(1893)

Daisies

Over the shoulders and slopes of the dune
I saw the white daisies go down to the sea,
A host in the sunshine, an army in June,
The people God sends us to set our heart free.

The bobolinks rallied them up from the dell,
The orioles whistled them out of the wood;
And all of their singing was, "Earth, it is well!"
And all of their dancing was, "Life, thou art good!"

(1896)

Low Tide on Grand Pré

The sun goes down, and over all
   These barren reaches by the tide
Such unelusive glories fall,
   I almost dream they yet will bide
   Until the coming of the tide.

And yet I know that not for us,
　　By any ecstasy of dream,
He lingers to keep luminous
　　A little while the grievous stream,
　　Which frets, uncomforted of dream —

A grievous stream, that to and fro
　　Athrough the fields of Acadie
Goes wandering, as if to know
　　Why one beloved face should be
　　So long from home and Acadie.

Was it a year or lives ago
　　We took the grasses in our hands,
And caught the summer flying low
　　Over the waving meadow lands,
　　And held it there between our hands?

The while the river at our feet —
　　A drowsy inland meadow stream —
At set of sun the after-heat
　　Made running gold, and in the gleam
　　We freed our birch upon the stream.

There down along the elms at dusk
　　We lifted dripping blade to drift,
Through twilight scented fine like musk,
　　Where night and gloom awhile uplift,
　　Nor sunder soul and soul adrift.

And that we took into our hands
　　Spirit of life or subtler thing —
Breathed on us there, and loosed the bands
　　Of death, and taught us, whispering,
　　The secret of some wonder-thing.

Then all your face grew light, and seemed
　　To hold the shadow of the sun;
The evening faltered, and I deemed
　　That time was ripe, and years had done
　　Their wheeling underneath the sun.

So all desire and all regret,
　　And fear and memory, were naught;
One to remember or forget
　　The keen delight our hands had caught;
　　Morrow and yesterday were naught.

The night has fallen, and the tide . . .
   Now and again comes drifting home,
Across these aching barrens wide,
   A sigh like driven wind or foam:
   In grief the flood is bursting home.

(1893)

A Windflower

Between the roadside and the wood,
   Between the dawning and the dew,
A tiny flower before the sun,
   Ephemeral in time, I grew.

And there upon the trail of spring,
   Not death nor love nor any name
Known among men in all their lands
   Could blur the wild desire with shame.

But down my dayspan of the year
   The feet of straying winds came by;
And all my trembling soul was thrilled
   To follow one lost mountain cry.

And then my heart beat once and broke
   To hear the sweeping rain forebode
Some ruin in the April world,
   Between the woodside and the road.

To-night can bring no healing now;
   The calm of yesternight is gone;
Surely the wind is but the wind,
   And I a broken waif thereon.

(1893)

Marian Drury

Marian Drury, Marian Drury,
  How are the marshes full of the sea!
Acadie dreams of your coming home
  All year through, and her heart gets free, –

Free on the trail of the wind to travel,
  Search and course with the roving tide,
All year long where his hands unravel
  Blossom and berry the marshes hide.

Marian Drury, Marian Drury,
  How are the marshes full of the surge!
April over the Norland now
  Walks in the quiet from verge to verge.

Burying, brimming, the building billows
  Fret the long dikes with uneasy foam.
Drenched with gold weather, the idling willows
  Kiss you a hand from the Norland home.

Marian Drury, Marian Drury,
  How are the marshes full of the sun!
Blomidon waits for your coming home,
  All day long where the white winds run.

All spring through they falter and follow,
  Wander, and beckon the roving tide,
Wheel and float with the veering swallow,
  Lift you a voice from the blue hillside.

Marian Drury, Marian Drury,
  How are the marshes full of the rain!
April over the Norland now
  Bugles for rapture, and rouses pain, –

Halts before the forsaken dwelling,
  Where in the twilight, too spent to roam,
Love, whom the fingers of death are quelling,
  Cries you a cheer from the Norland home.

Marian Drury, Marian Drury,
   How are the marshes filled with you!
Grand Pré dreams of your coming home, –
   Dreams while the rainbirds all night through,

Far in the uplands calling to win you,
   Tease the brown dusk on the marshes wide;
And never the burning heart within you
   Stirs in your sleep by the roving tide.

(1893)

The Eavesdropper

In a still room at hush of dawn,
   My Love and I lay side by side
And heard the roaming forest wind
   Stir in the paling autumn-tide.

I watched her earth-brown eyes grow glad
   Because the round day was so fair;
While memories of reluctant night
   Lurked in the blue dusk of her hair.

Outside, a yellow maple tree,
   Shifting upon the silvery blue
With tiny multitudinous sound,
   Rustled to let the sunlight through.

The livelong day the elvish leaves
   Danced with their shadows on the floor;
And the lost children of the wind
   Went straying homeward by our door.

And all the swarthy afternoon
   We watched the great deliberate sun
Walk through the crimsoned hazy world,
   Counting his hilltops one by one.

Then as the purple twilight came
   And touched the vines along our eaves,
Another Shadow stood without
   And gloomed the dancing of the leaves.

The silence fell on my Love's lips;
   Her great brown eyes were veiled and sad
With pondering some maze of dream,
   Though all the splendid year was glad.

Restless and vague as a gray wind
   Her heart had grown, she knew not why.
But hurrying to the open door,
   Against the verge of western sky

I saw retreating on the hills,
   Looming and sinister and black,
The stealthy figure swift and huge
   Of One who strode and looked not back.

(1893)

A Remembrance

Here in lovely New England
When summer is come, a sea-turn
Flutters a page of remembrance
In the volume of long ago.

Soft is the wind over Grand Pré,
Stirring the heads of the grasses,
Sweet is the breath of the orchards
White with their apple-blow.

There at their infinite business
Of measuring time forever,
Murmuring songs of the sea,
The great tides come and go.

Over the dikes and the uplands
Wander the great cloud shadows,
Strange as the passing of sorrow,
Beautiful, solemn, and slow.

For, spreading her old enchantment
Of tender ineffable wonder,
Summer is there in the Northland!
How should my heart not know?

(1916)

The Garden of Dreams

My heart is a garden of dreams
Where you walk when day is done,
Fair as the royal flowers,
Calm as the lingering sun.

Never a drouth comes there,
Nor any frost that mars,
Only the wind of love
Under the early stars, –

The living breath that moves
Whispering to and fro,
Like the voice of God in the dusk
Of the garden long ago.

(1916)

From *Sappho*

XXIII

I loved thee, Atthis, in the long ago,
When the great oleanders were in flower
In the broad herded meadows full of sun.
And we would often at the fall of dusk
Wander together by the silver stream,
When the soft grass-heads were all wet with dew
And purple-misted in the fading light.
And joy I knew and sorrow at thy voice,
And the superb magnificence of love, –
The loneliness that saddens solitude,
And the sweet speech that makes it durable, –
The bitter longing and the keen desire,
The sweet companionship through quiet days
In the slow ample beauty of the world,
And the unutterable glad release
Within the temple of the holy night.
O Atthis, how I loved thee long ago
In that fair perished summer by the sea!

LIV

How soon will all my lovely days be over,
And I no more be found beneath the sun, –
Neither beside the many-murmuring sea,
Nor where the plain-winds whisper to the reeds,
Nor in the tall beech-woods among the hills
Where roam the bright-lipped Oreads, nor along
The pasture-sides where berry-pickers stray
And harmless shepherds pipe their sheep to fold!

For I am eager, and the flame of life
Burns quickly in the fragile lamp of clay.
Passion and love and longing and hot tears
Consume this mortal Sappho, and too soon
A great wind from the dark will blow upon me,
And I be no more found in the fair world,
For all the search of the revolving moon
And patient shine of everlasting stars.

LXXVIII

Once in the shining street,
In the heart of a seaboard town,
As I waited, behold, there came
The woman I loved.

As when, in the early spring,
A daffodil blooms in the grass,
Golden and gracious and glad,
The solitude smiled.

(1904)

Vestigia

I took a day to search for God,
And found Him not. But as I trod
By rocky ledge, through woods untamed,
Just where one scarlet lily flamed,
I saw His footprint in the sod.

Then suddenly, all unaware,
Far off in the deep shadows, where
A solitary hermit thrush
Sang through the holy twilight hush –
I heard His voice upon the air.

And even as I marvelled how
God gives us Heaven here and now,
In a stir of wind that hardly shook
The poplar leaves beside the brook –
His hand was light upon my brow.

At last with evening as I turned
Homeward, and thought what I had learned
And all that there was still to probe –
I caught the glory of His robe
Where the last fires of sunset burned.

Back to the world with quickening start
I looked and longed for any part
In making saving Beauty be . . .
And from that kindling ecstasy
I knew God dwelt within my heart.

(1921)

The Ships of St. John

Smile, you inland hills and rivers!
Flush, you mountains in the dawn!
But my roving heart is seaward
With the ships of gray St. John.

Fair the land lies, full of August,
Meadow island, shingly bar,
Open barns and breezy twilight,
Peace and the mild evening star.

Gently now this gentlest country
The old habitude takes on,
But my wintry heart is outbound
With the great ships of St. John.

Once in your wide arms you held me,
Till the man-child was a man,
Canada, great nurse and mother
Of the young sea-roving clan.

Always your bright face above me
Through the dreams of boyhood shone;
Now far alien countries call me
With the ships of gray St. John.

Swing, you tides, up out of Fundy!
Blow, you white fogs, in from sea!
I was born to be your fellow;
You were bred to pilot me.

At the touch of your strong fingers,
Doubt, the derelict, is gone;
Sane and glad I clear the headland
With the white ships of St. John.

Loyalists, my father, builded
This gray port of the gray sea,
When the duty to ideals
Could not let well-being be.

When the breadth of scarlet bunting
Puts the wreath of maple on,
I must cheer too, – slip my moorings
With the ships of gray St. John.

Peerless-hearted port of heroes,
Be a word to lift the world,
Till the many see the signal
Of the few once more unfurled.

Past the lighthouse, past the nunbuoy,
Past the crimson rising sun,
There are dreams go down the harbor
With the tall ships of St. John.

In the morning I am with them
As they clear the island bar, –
Fade, till speck by speck the midday
Has forgotten where they are.

But I sight a vaster sea-line,
Wider lee-way, longer run,
Whose discoverers return not
With the ships of gray St. John.

(1897)

The Ghost-Yard of the Goldenrod

When the first silent frost has trod
The ghost-yard of the goldenrod,

And laid the blight of his cold hand
Upon the warm autumnal land,

And all things wait the subtle change
That men call death, is it not strange

That I – without a care or need,
Who only am an idle weed –

Should wait unmoved, so frail, so bold,
The coming of the final cold!

(1916)

Threnody for a Poet

Not in the ancient abbey,
Nor in the city ground,
Not in the lonely mountains,
Nor in the blue profound,
Lay him to rest when his time is come
And the smiling mortal lips are dumb;

Here in the decent quiet
Under the whispering pines,
Where the dogwood breaks in blossom
And the peaceful sunlight shines,
Where wild birds sing and ferns unfold,
When spring comes back in her green and gold.

And when that mortal likeness
Has been dissolved by fire,
Say not above the ashes,
"Here ends a man's desire."
For every year when the blue-birds sing,
He shall be part of the lyric spring.

Then dreamful-hearted lovers
Shall hear in wind and rain
The cadence of his music,
The rhythm of his refrain,
For he was a blade of the April sod
That bowed and blew with the whisper of God.

(1916)

From *The Friendship of Art*

REALISM IN LETTERS

THE question of realism in art after all must surely be one of quantity and proportion. Every one must agree that a certain amount of realism is needed; the difficulty is only to know how much. That art must be an image of nature goes without saying. It is the business of art to create a mimic world in which we may take delight. The features of that world must in the main resemble those of our own old and well-loved universe, else we should be set to wander through a country so strange that we should soon be lost.

Perhaps our first pleasure in art is a childish delight at its verisimilitude. "How true to life," we exclaim, as the eye recognizes in the human creation a likeness to something in the outward world. Unmitigated realism would in truth give us nothing else. And the pleasure which a great many people get from current fiction and contemporary art depends on having this very simple and childish sense gratified. They like stories about places that are familiar to them, and concerning types of character entirely within their range of comprehension. Anything exceptional and unusual demands an effort of the imagination before it can be appreciated; and this effort the average mind is unwilling to make, – so lethargic and timid are we for the most part in facing the unknown.

But the best art and literature are always exceptional. There is always a quality of adventure in them. They represent the courageous daring of the artist in creating new forms, in propounding new truths, in establishing newer and nobler standards of conduct and enjoyment. They reflect the progress of humanity. Not only that; they foretell and direct progress. All the ideals which humanity has put in practice with so much pains and toil were first enunciated by the artist, and by him presented to us in alluring and intelligible shape. It is never enough, and it never has been enough, that the arts should give us only images of things we know, and proclaim accepted truths. They have always had another trend as well; they have always been employed in expressing novel truths, no less important than the old, and in clothing those truths in new forms no less beautiful than the older forms to which we have been accustomed.

Art and literature, therefore, have never been mere copies of nature; they have always contained the element of novelty, – a novelty more radical and profound than the fortuitous variations of nature. The forms of nature are, indeed, beautiful, varied, and satisfying; and the forms of art must have these qualities, too. At the same time they must have much greater flexibility and power of adaptation than the forms of nature. Nature, so far as we can observe, proceeds by a law so stable as to seem unchanging. The growth of man proceeds in the guidance of a questing and illimitable imagination. So that the settled and infinitely deliberate procedure of nature will not serve his restless purposes at all. Unless he can add thought to nature, – unless he can introduce imagination and forethought and invention and hope and aspiration into life, – how much better is he than the creatures?

Now whatever comes under the head of art, whether literature or painting, music or sculpture or acting or architecture, being the expression of man, must reflect his inward life, – his words and thoughts, his instant desires and his far-off hopes or fears. If art were no more than an imitation of nature in faithful guise, it would surely never have been born. Certainly it could never have attained any exalted place in our esteem such as we have accorded it; nor could it have wielded that incalculable influence which we know it has always possessed. It is only because art and literature are supernatural that they pull at our hearts for ever. It is only because they partake at times of the superhuman, deriving an inspiration we know not whence, that they offer us an unfailing source of refreshment and power. They embody for us average men and women suggestions for a life more fair and perfect than ever occurred to us. They not only indicate an existence more worthy and beautiful than our own, they actually portray it. That is why we enjoy them; and that is the only reason that we enjoy them without satiety. Once given the perilous gift of self-consciousness, the large slow contentment of nature is no longer possible. We must have ideals, however faulty, and beliefs and opinions, however erroneous. These beliefs and ideals it has always been the destiny of art to embody. That is the one great business of art. And as our beliefs and ideals grow with our growth, they find new housing for themselves first of all in the arts.

Realism, then, is essential, but it is not everything. The Palace of Art is built to house a more admirable company than any of our present acquaintance. The members of that company may even seem at times almost more than human. And yet they must remain like ourselves, and the Palace must remain a possible palace, else we lose interest. The soul can only be touched with emulation by what comes within range of its own power. Art must be realistic, or it will have no hold on our interest; it must be more than realistic, or it will not be able to make that hold permanent. It must present the ideal at least as vividly as it does the real, for the one is as important as the other.

As we go about this lovely world, scenes and incidents attract us and enchant us for a moment or for longer. And these scenes we delight to recall. We travel, and we bring home photographs of the places we have visited, reminders of our happy hours. It would seem that nothing could be more faithful than these mechanically accurate reproductions of the face of nature. And yet they are not wholly satisfying; a fleeting glimpse preserved in a sketch in pencil or water-colour may be far more satisfactory. The photograph reproduces a hundred details which the eye missed when it first came upon the scene; and at the same time misses the charm and the atmosphere with which we ourselves may have endowed the place as we gazed upon it. The sketch, on the other hand, omits these details, just as our eye omitted them originally, and yet preserves the atmosphere of our first delighted vision. Can it be said then that the photograph is more true than the painting? More true to the object, yes; but not more true to our experience of the object. And that is the important thing; that is what art must always aim at.

Archibald Lampman (1861-1899)

One of the key poets of the Confederation Group or "maple leaf school," Archibald Lampman is the favourite of many students and critics to-day for his detailed and sensitive descriptions of the Canadian landscape. Northrop Frye in *The Bush Garden* refers to the supremacy of Lampman over his contemporaries and E. K. Brown in his *On Canadian Poetry* pays tribute to him: as "the nearest approach to a Canadian classic in verse. . . . His poetry deserves to be read everywhere that people care for what is authentic in literature."

Archibald Lampman was born in November, 1861, in the little town of Morpeth, Upper Canada, on the shores of Lake Erie. As the son of a Church of England clergyman, himself a poet, and his wife who was a skilled musician, Lampman received an appropriate heritage. In 1867 the Lampmans moved to Gore's Landing, Rice Lake and here he came into contact with Susannah Moodie and her sister Catharine Parr Traill. He attended Cobourg Collegiate Institute, and in 1876 entered Trinity College School, Port Hope, proceeding on to Trinity College, Toronto in 1879. After graduation he taught high school at Orangeville for four months only, and in January 1883 went to Ottawa as a third-class clerk in the Post Office Department where he was to remain for the rest of his life, being promoted to second-class clerk in October of 1893. In Ottawa, Lampman, despite many critics' contention, was part of a stimulating intellectual circle which included Duncan Campbell Scott, William Wilfred Campbell, W. D. Le Seur, the socialist Macoun and A. C. Campbell; he also was acquainted with the pioneer poet Charles Sangster who worked with him in the post office. Yet Lampman was not happy here. At seven he had suffered from rheumatic fever which left his heart permanently weak. In the 1890's ill health, failure to achieve promotion in the post office, and the deaths of his first son in 1894 and his father in March of 1897 contributed to his melancholy and he remarked that he was becoming "morbid, subject to dreadful moods and hypochondria." After a spell of influenza in January 1898, he was absent from work until October, and fell ill again in January 1899 with influenza followed by penumonia. He died in February.

Lampman had begun to write poetry in Trinity College School, and he continued in university, publishing essays and poems in the college magazine *Rouge et Noir*. His excitement as an undergraduate on first seeing Charles G. D. Roberts' *Orion and Other Poems* has become a classic of Canadian criticism: "I sat up all night reading and re-reading *Orion* in a state of the wildest excitement. . . . It seemed to me a wonderful thing that such work could be done by a Canadian, by a young man, one of ourselves." In Ottawa, Lampman was successful in placing his poems in Canada in such magazines as *The Week, The Canadian Monthly, The Canadian Illustrated News* and in the United States in *Scribner's, Harper's, The Atlantic Monthly, The Cosmopolitan*, and *The Independent*. He was also elected to the Royal Society of Canada in 1895. Yet he published his first volume *Among the Millet* (1888) at his own expense, and his second volume *Lyrics of Earth* (1893) was in search of a publisher for three years. A third book *Alcyone* was in process of printing at his death. In the following year, his friend Duncan Campbell Scott published an edition of Lampman's poems with a memoir and in 1925, another edition *Lyrics of Earth: Poems and Ballads. At the Long Sault and Other Poems* was published by Scott in collaboration with E. K. Brown in 1943, after their joint discovery of the narrative title poem in manuscript.

Lampman believed that the poet should become "a sensitive recorder of nature", and many of his best poems are descriptions which, as in his best-known poem "Heat", recreate in language, the visual detail, the precise atmosphere and mood of the landscape. Other works contrast the turmoil of the city, its restlessness and discord, with the peace of nature, comment on social problems, and delineate the artistic process. The lecture "Two Canadian Poets", delivered in Ottawa on February 19, 1891, queries the existence of a Canadian literature and analyzes the reasons for a delay in developing a native culture. Like his column "At the Mermaid Inn" which appeared in the Toronto *Globe* in 1892 and 1893, it indicates his considerable ability as a critic as well as a poet.

TEXT:

Archibald Lampman's Poems. D. C. Scott, ed. Toronto: Morang, 1900.
"Two Canadian Poets: A Lecture, 1891." *University of Toronto Quarterly*, XIII, July 1944. (Abridged; for full text see above or *Masks of Poetry*. Toronto: McClelland and Stewart, 1962).
At the Mermaid Inn. Arthur S. Bourinot, ed. Ottawa: Bourinot, 1956.

See also:

Arthur S. Bourinot. *Five Canadian Poets*. Montreal: Quality Press, 1956.
E. K. Brown. *On Canadian Poetry*. Toronto: Ryerson, 1947.
C. Y. Connor. *Archibald Lampman: Canadian Poet of Nature*. New York: Carrier (1929).
Michael Gnarowski, ed. *Critical Views of Archibald Lampman*. Toronto: Ryerson, 1970.
Norman Gregor Guthrie. *The Poetry of Archibald Lampman*. Toronto: Musson, 1927.
Desmond Pacey. *Ten Canadian Poets*. Toronto: Ryerson, 1958.

Voices of Earth

We have not heard the music of the spheres,
The song of star to star, but there are sounds
More deep than human joy and human tears,
That Nature uses in her common rounds;
The fall of streams, the cry of winds that strain
The oak, the roaring of the sea's surge, might
Of thunder breaking afar off, or rain
That falls by minutes in the summer night.
These are the voices of earth's secret soul,
Uttering the mystery from which she came.
To him who hears them grief beyond control,
Or joy inscrutable without a name,
Wakes in his heart thoughts bedded there,
   impearled,
Before the birth and making of the world.

(1899)

Hepaticas

The trees to their innermost marrow
   Are touched by the sun;
The robin is here and the sparrow:
   Spring is begun!

The sleep and the silence are over:
   These petals that rise
Are the eyelids of earth that uncover
   Her numberless eyes.

(1900)

A Sunset at Les Eboulements

Broad shadows fall. On all the mountain side
The scythe-swept fields are silent. Slowly home
By the long beach the high-piled hay-carts come,
Splashing the pale salt shallows. Over wide
Fawn-coloured wastes of mud the slipping tide,
Round the dun rocks and wattled fisheries,
Creeps murmuring in. And now by twos and
   threes,
O'er the slow spreading pools with clamorous
   chide,
Belated crows from strip to strip take flight.
Soon will the first star shine; yet ere the night
Reach onward to the pale-green distances,
The sun's last shaft beyond the gray sea-floor
Still dreams upon the Kamouraska shore,
And the long line of golden villages.

(1900)

Heat

From plains that reel to southward, dim,
   The road runs by me white and bare;
Up the steep hill it seems to swim
   Beyond, and melt into the glare.
Upward half-way, or it may be
   Nearer the summit, slowly steals
A hay-cart, moving dustily
   With idly clacking wheels.

By his cart's side the wagoner
  Is slouching slowly at his ease,
Half-hidden in the windless blur
  Of white dust puffing to his knees.
This wagon on the height above,
  From sky to sky on either hand,
Is the sole thing that seems to move
  In all the heat-held land.

Beyond me in the fields the sun
  Soaks in the grass and hath his will;
I count the marguerites one by one;
  Even the buttercups are still.
On the brook yonder not a breath
  Disturbs the spider or the midge.
The water-bugs draw close beneath
  The cool gloom of the bridge.

Where the far elm-tree shadows flood
  Dark patches in the burning grass,
The cows, each with her peaceful cud,
  Lie waiting for the heat to pass.
From somewhere on the slope near by
  Into the pale depth of the noon
A wandering thrush slides leisurely
  His thin revolving tune.

In intervals of dreams I hear
  The cricket from the droughty ground;
The grasshoppers spin into mine ear
  A small innumerable sound.
I lift mine eyes sometimes to gaze:
  The burning sky-line blinds my sight:
The woods far off are blue with haze:
  The hills are drenched in light.

And yet to me not this or that
  Is always sharp or always sweet;
In the sloped shadow of my hat
  I lean at rest, and drain the heat;
Nay more, I think some blessed power
  Hath brought me wandering idly here:
In the full furnace of this hour
  My thoughts grow keen and clear.

(1888)

Morning on the Lievre

Far above us where a jay
Screams his matins to the day,
Capped with gold and amethyst,
Like a vapour from the forge
Of a giant somewhere hid,
Out of hearing of the clang
Of his hammer, skirts of mist
Slowly up the woody gorge
Lift and hang.

Softly as a cloud we go,
Sky above and sky below,
Down the river; and the dip
Of the paddles scarcely breaks,
With the little silvery drip
Of the water as it shakes
From the blades, the crystal deep
Of the silence of the morn,
Of the forest yet asleep;
And the river reaches borne
In a mirror, purple gray,
Sheer away
To the misty line of light,
Where the forest and the stream
In the shadow meet and plight,
Like a dream.

From amid a stretch of reeds,
Where the lazy river sucks
All the water as it bleeds
From a little curling creek,
And the muskrats peer and sneak
In around the sunken wrecks
Of a tree that swept the skies
Long ago,
On a sudden seven ducks
With a splashy rustle rise,
Stretching out their seven necks,
One before, and two behind,
And the others all arow,
And as steady as the wind
With a swivelling whistle go,
Through the purple shadow led,
Till we only hear their whir
In behind a rocky spur,
Just ahead.

(1888)

In May

Grief was my master yesternight;
   To-morrow I may grieve again;
   But now along the windy plain
     The clouds have taken flight.

The sowers in the furrows go;
   The lusty river brimmeth on;
   The curtains from the hills are gone;
     The leaves are out; and lo,

The silvery distance of the day,
   The light horizons, and between
   The glory of the perfect green,
     The tumult of the May.

The bob-o-links at noonday sing
  More softly than the softest flute,
  And lightlier than the lightest lute
    Their fairy tambours ring.

The roads far off are towered with dust;
  The cherry-blooms are swept and thinned;
  In yonder swaying elms the wind
    Is charging gust on gust.

But here there is no stir at all;
  The ministers of sun and shadow
  Hoard all the perfumes of the meadow
    Behind a grassy wall.

An infant rivulet wind-free
  Adown the guarded hollow sets,
  Over whose brink the violets
    Are nodding peacefully.

From pool to pool it prattles by;
  The flashing swallows dip and pass,
  Above the tufted marish grass,
    And here at rest am I.

I care not for the old distress,
  Nor if to-morrow bid me moan;
  To-day is mine, and I have known
    An hour of blessedness.

(1895)

By an Autumn Stream

Now overhead,
Where the rivulet loiters and stops,
The bittersweet hangs from the tops
Of the alders and cherries
Its bunches of beautiful berries,
Orange and red.

And the snowbirds flee,
Tossing up on the far brown field,
Now flashing and now concealed,
Like fringes of spray
That vanish and gleam on the gray
Field of the sea.

Flickering light,
Come the last of the leaves down borne,
And patches of pale white corn
In the wind complain,
Like the slow rustle of rain
Noticed by night.

Withered and thinned,
The sentinel mullein looms,
With the pale gray shadowy plumes
Of the goldenrod;
And the milkweed opens its pod,
Tempting the wind.

Aloft on the hill,
A cloudrift opens and shines
Through a break in its gorget of pines,
And it dreams at my feet
In a sad, silvery sheet,
Utterly still.

All things that be
Seem plunged into silence, distraught,
By some stern, some necessitous thought:
It wraps and enthralls
Marsh, meadow, and forest; and falls
Also on me.

(1895)

In November

The hills and leafless forests slowly yield
    To the thick-driving snow. A little while
    And night shall darken down. In shouting file
The woodmen's carts go by me homeward-wheeled,
Past the thin fading stubbles, half concealed,
    Now golden-gray, sowed softly through with snow,
    Where the last ploughman follows still his row,
Turning black furrows through the whitening field.
Far off the village lamps begin to gleam.
    Fast drives the snow, and no man comes this way;
        The hills grow wintry white, and bleak winds
            moan
        About the naked uplands. I alone
    Am neither sad, nor shelterless, nor gray,
Wrapped round with thought, content to watch and
        dream.

(1888)

Winter Evening

To-night the very horses springing by
Toss gold from whitened nostrils. In a dream
The streets that narrow to the westward gleam
Like rows of golden palaces; and high
From all the crowded chimneys tower and die
A thousand aureoles. Down in the west
The brimming plains beneath the sunset rest,
One burning sea of gold. Soon, soon shall fly
The glorious vision, and the hours shall feel
A mightier master; soon from height to height,
With silence and the sharp unpitying stars,
Stern creeping frosts, and winds that touch like
    steel,
Out of the depth beyond the eastern bars,
Glittering and still shall come the awful night.

(1900)

The Coming of Winter

Out of the Northland sombre weirds are calling;
A shadow falleth southward day by day;
Sad summer's arms grow cold; his fire is falling;
    His feet draw back to give the stern one way.

It is the voice and shadow of the slayer,
    Slayer of loves, sweet world, slayer of dreams;
Make sad thy voice with sober plaint and prayer;
    Make gray the woods, and darken all thy streams.

Black grows the river, blacker drifts the eddy;
    The sky is gray; the woods are cold below:
O make thy bosom and thy sad lips ready
    For the cold kisses of the folding snow.

(1888)

An Impression

I heard the city time-bells call
    Far off in hollow towers,
And one by one with measured fall
    Count out the old dead hours;

I felt the march, the silent press
    Of time, and held my breath;
I saw the haggard dreadfulness
    Of dim old age and death.

(1888)

Reality

I stand at noon upon the heated flags
  At the bleached crossing of two streets, and dream,
  With brain scarce conscious, how the hurrying stream
Of noonday passengers is done. Two hags
Stand at an open doorway piled with bags
  And jabber hideously. Just at their feet
  A small, half-naked child screams in the street.
A blind man yonder, a mere hunch of rags,
Keeps the scant shadow of the eaves, and scowls,
  Counting his coppers. Through the open glare
  Thunders an empty wagon, from whose trail
A lean dog shoots into the startled square,
  Wildly revolves and soothes his hapless tail,
Piercing the noon with intermittent howls.

(1892, 1925)

The City

Canst thou not rest, O city,
  That liest so wide and fair;
Shall never an hour bring pity,
  Nor end be found for care?

Thy walls are high in heaven,
  Thy streets are gay and wide,
Beneath thy towers at even
  The dreamy waters glide.

Thou art fair as the hills at morning,
  And the sunshine loveth thee,
But its light is a gloom of warning
  On a soul no longer free.

The curses of gold are about thee,
   And thy sorrow deepeneth still;
One madness within and without thee,
   One battle blind and shrill.

I see the crowds for ever
   Go by with hurrying feet;
Through doors that darken never
   I hear the engines beat.

Through days and nights that follow
   The hidden mill-wheel strains;
In the midnight's windy hollow
   I hear the roar of trains.

And still the day fulfilleth,
   And still the night goes round,
And the guest-hall boometh and shrilleth,
   With the dance's mocking sound.

In chambers of gold elysian,
   The cymbals clash and clang,
But the days are gone like a vision
   When the people wrought and sang.

And toil hath fear for neighbour,
   Where singing lips are dumb,
And life is one long labour,
   Till death or freedom come.

Ah! the crowds that for ever are flowing –
   They neither laugh nor weep –
I see them coming and going,
   Like things that move in sleep:

Gray sires and burdened brothers,
   The old, the young, the fair,
Wan cheeks of pallid mothers,
   And the girls with golden hair.

Care sits in many a fashion,
   Grown gray on many a head,
And lips are turned to ashen
   Whose years have right to red.

Canst thou not rest, O city,
    That liest so wide, so fair;
Shall never an hour bring pity,
    Nor end be found for care?

(1888)

The City of the End of Things

Beside the pounding cataracts
Of midnight streams unknown to us
'Tis builded in the leafless tracts
And valleys huge of Tartarus.
Lurid and lofty and vast it seems;
It hath no rounded name that rings,
But I have heard it called in dreams
The City of the End of Things.

Its roofs and iron towers have grown
None knoweth how high within the night,
But in its murky streets far down
A flaming terrible and bright
Shakes all the stalking shadows there,
Across the walls, across the floors,
And shifts upon the upper air
From out a thousand furnace doors;
And all the while an awful sound
Keeps roaring on continually,
And crashes in the ceaseless round
Of a gigantic harmony.
Through its grim depths re-echoing
And all its weary height of walls,
With measured roar and iron ring,
The inhuman music lifts and falls.
Where no thing rests and no man is,
And only fire and night hold sway;
The beat, the thunder and the hiss
Cease not, and change not, night nor day.

And moving at unheard commands,
The abysses and vast fires between,
Flit figures that with clanking hands
Obey a hideous routine;
They are not flesh, they are not bone,
They see not with the human eye,
And from their iron lips is blown
A dreadful and monotonous cry;
And whoso of our mortal race
Should find that city unaware,
Lean Death would smite him face to face,
And blanch him with its venomed air:
Or caught by the terrific spell,
Each thread of memory snapt and cut,
His soul would shrivel and its shell
Go rattling like an empty nut.

It was not always so, but once,
In days that no man thinks upon,
Fair voices echoed from its stones,
The light above it leaped and shone:
Once there were multitudes of men,
That built that city in their pride,
Until its might was made, and then
They withered age by age and died.
But now of that prodigious race,
Three only in an iron tower,
Set like carved idols face to face,
Remain the masters of its power;
And at the city gate a fourth,
Gigantic and with dreadful eyes,
Sits looking toward the lightless north,
Beyond the reach of memories;
Fast rooted to the lurid floor,
A bulk that never moves a jot,
In his pale body dwells no more,
Or mind or soul, – an idiot!
But sometime in the end those three
Shall perish and their hands be still,
And with the master's touch shall flee
Their incommunicable skill.
A stillness absolute as death
Along the slacking wheels shall lie,
And, flagging at a single breath,
The fires that moulder out and die.
The roar shall vanish at its height,

And over that tremendous town
The silence of eternal night
Shall gather close and settle down.
All its grim grandeur, tower and hall,
Shall be abandoned utterly,
And into rust and dust shall fall
From century to century;
Nor ever living thing shall grow,
Nor trunk of tree, nor blade of grass;
No drop shall fall, no wind shall blow,
Nor sound of any foot shall pass:
Alone of its accursèd state,
One thing the hand of Time shall spare,
For the grim Idiot at the gate
Is deathless and eternal there.

(1900)

The Piano

Low brooding cadences that dream and cry
Life's stress and passion echoing straight and clear;
Wild flights of notes that clamour and beat high
Into the storm and battle, or drop sheer;
Strange majesties of sound beyond all words
Ringing on clouds and thunderous heights
    sublime;
Sad detonance of golden tones and chords
That tremble with the secret of all time;
O wrap me round; for one exulting hour
Possess my soul, and I indeed shall know
The wealth of living, the desire, the power,
The tragic sweep, the Apollonian glow;
All life shall stream before me; I shall see,
With eyes unblanched, Time and Eternity.

(1900)

Music

O, take the lute this brooding hour for me –
The golden lute, the hollow crying lute –
Nor call me even with thine eyes; be mute,
And touch the strings; yea, touch them tenderly;
Touch them and dream, till all thine heart in thee
Grow great and passionate and sad and wild.
Then on me, too, as on thine heart, O child,
The marvellous light, the stress divine shall be,
And I shall see, as with enchanted eyes,
The unveiled vision of this world flame by,
Battles and griefs, and storms and phantasies,
The gleaming joy, the ever-seething fire,
The hero's triumph and the martyr's cry,
The pain, the madness, the unsearched desire.

(1888)

The Violinist

In Dresden in the square one day,
    His face of parchment, seamed and gray,
With wheezy bow and proffered hat,
    An old blind violinist sat.

Like one from whose worn heart the heat
    Of life had long ago retired,
He played to the unheeding street
    Until the thin old hands were tired.

Few marked the player how he played,
    Or how the child beside his knee
Besought the passers-by for aid
    So softly and so wistfully.

A stranger passed. The little hand
   Went forth, so often checked and spurned.
The stranger wavered, came to stand,
   Looked round with absent eyes and turned.

He saw the sightless withered face,
   The tired old hands, the whitened hair,
The child with such a mournful grace,
   The little features pinched and spare.

"I have no money, but," said he,
   "Give me the violin and bow.
I'll play a little, we shall see,
   Whether the gold will come or no."

With lifted brow and flashing eyes
   He faced the noisy street and played.
The people turned in quick surprise,
   And every foot drew near and stayed.

First from the shouting bow he sent
   A summons, an impetuous call;
Then some old store of grief long pent
   Broke from his heart and mastered all.

The tumult sank at his command,
   The passing wheels were hushed and stilled;
The burning soul, the sweeping hand
   A sacred ecstasy fulfilled.

The darkness of the outer strife,
   The weariness and want within,
The giant wrongfulness of life,
   Leaped storming from the violin.

The jingling round of pleasure broke,
   Gay carriages were drawn anear,
And all the proud and haughty folk
   Leaned from their cushioned seats to hear.

And then the player changed his tone,
   And wrought another miracle
Of music, half a prayer, half moan,
   A cry exceeding sorrowful.

A strain of pity for the weak,
  The poor that fall without a cry,
The common hearts that never speak,
  But break beneath the press and die.

Throughout the great and silent crowd
  The music fell on human ears,
And many kindly heads were bowed,
  And many eyes were warm with tears.

"And now your gold," the player cried,
  "While love is master of your mood;"
He bowed, and turned, and slipped aside,
  And vanished in the multitude.

And all the people flocked at that,
  The money like a torrent rolled,
Until the gray old battered hat
  Was bursting to the brim with gold.

And loudly as the giving grew,
  The question rose on every part,
If any named or any knew
  The stranger with so great a heart,

Or what the moving wonder meant,
  Such playing never heard before;
A lady from her carriage leant,
  And murmured softly, "It was Spohr."

(1900)

To Death

Methought in dreams I saw my little son –
My little son that in his cradle died;
No more a babe, but all his childhood done,
A full-grown man. Deep-browed and tender-eyed,
I knew him by the subtle touch of me,
And by his mother's look, and by the eyes
We hold in such remembrance piteously,
And the bright smile so quick for sweet replies.
O Death, I would that from thy front of stone
My grief could wring one word, or my tears draw
On the strange night of life, one single gleam!
Was he whom by the gift of sleep I saw
The living shape of my belovèd gone,
My very son, or but a fleeting dream.

(1900)

White Pansies

Day and night pass over, rounding,
    Star and cloud and sun,
Things of drift and shadow, empty
    Of my dearest one.

Soft as slumber was my baby,
    Beaming bright and sweet;
Daintier than bloom or jewel
    Were his hands and feet.

He was mine, mine all, mine only,
    Mine and his the debt;
Earth and Life and Time are changers;
    I shall not forget.

Pansies for my dear one – heartsease –
  Set them gently so;
For his stainless lips and forehead,
  Pansies white as snow.

Would that in the flower-grown little
  Grave they dug so deep,
I might rest beside him, dreamless,
  Smile no more, nor weep.

(1899)

We Too Shall Sleep

Not, not for thee,
Belovèd child, the burning grasp of life
Shall bruise the tender soul. The noise, and strife,
And clamour of midday thou shalt not see;
But wrapped for ever in thy quiet grave,
Too little to have known the earthly lot,
Time's clashing hosts above thine innocent head,
Wave upon wave,
Shall break, or pass as with an army's tread,
And harm thee not.

A few short years
We of the living flesh and restless brain
Shall plumb the deeps of life and know the strain,
The fleeting gleams of joy, the fruitless tears;
And then at last when all is touched and tried,
Our own immutable night shall fall, and deep
In the same silent plot, O little friend,
Side by thy side,
In peace that changeth not, nor knoweth end,
We too shall sleep.

  (1899)

Two Canadian Poets: A Lecture

In the last twenty years great advances have been made in this country, and many things have been accomplished which are a source of hope and comfort to those who are beginning to feel for Canada the enthusiasm of Fatherland. Already there are many among us whose fathers and grandfathers have lived and died upon this soil, who are neither British, French nor German, but simply Canadians. For them everything connected with the honour and wellbeing of their country has come to be a matter of daily interest. The enthusiasm of Fatherland, the attachment to native soil, the love of the name of our country, is one of those generous impulses which have always been a moral necessity and an encouraging help to people who do not live by bread alone. It is getting rather customary in our time to underrate patriotism as one of the virtues, and to substitute in its place cosmopolitanism or the enthusiasm for the advancement of all mankind, making no distinction in favour of any country. Nothing could be finer than that; but unfortunately our energies, if made to cover too wide a ground, are apt to lose themselves in mere speculation, and to fall short of practical effect. Perhaps it is safer therefore to be interested chiefly in the welfare of our own country, provided that we do nothing to hinder the just advancement of that of others. At any rate the true spirit of patriotism has always been a considerable factor in the best upward movements of the human race. Let us however discountenance blatant patriotism, as we would discountenance everything that is suspicious and ridiculous. Dr. Johnson's old saying about patriotism holds true in a new country like ours more markedly than in any other, and there are a greater number of those who find that it pays to be extremely zealous about their Fatherland. Already there is a good deal of talk in the public press which reminds one a little of Elijah Pogram and Jefferson Brick. At this time when our country's destiny, its very independent existence perhaps, is a matter of doubt and anxiety, it behooves us to be silent and do no boasting, but look seriously about us for the wisest thing to be said and done at each crisis.

A good deal is being said about Canadian literature, and most of it takes the form of question and answer as to whether a Canadian literature exists. Of course it does not. It will probably be a full generation or two before we can present a body of work of sufficient excellence as measured by the severest standards, and sufficiently marked with local colour, to enable us to call it a Canadian literature. It is only within the last quarter of a century that the United States have produced anything like a distinctive American literature. There was scarcely any peculiar literary quality in the work of the age of Longfellow and Hawthorne to mark it decidedly as American. But within the last twenty-five or thirty years, along with the evolution of a marked American race, certain noticeable American peculiarities of mind and character have been developed, which have strongly affected literary expression. Our country is still in the house-building, land-breaking stage, and all its energies must go to the laying of a foundation of material prosperity upon which a future culture may be built. Those capable minds, which in old and long-civilized countries might be drawn into literature, in Canada are forced into the more practical paths. They are engaged in making fortunes and founding families. Their descendants, the people who shall inherit the fortune, leisure, station, secured by them, will be the writers or the readers of the age when a Canadian literature comes to be. At present our people are too busy to read, too busy at least to read with discernment, and where there are no discerning readers there will be no writers. Also our educational institutions – even our best universities – are yet too raw to develop a literary spirit. All they can now be expected to do is to furnish the country with smart lawyers, competent physicians, able business men. As we advance in age and the settled conditions of life, these things will be gradually changed. There will arise a leisured class, a large body of educated people, who will create a market for literature and a literary atmosphere. And when that happens a literature will be produced for them. If our country becomes an independent, compacted, self-supporting nation, which is, or ought to be, the dream of all of us, its social and climatic conditions will in the course of time evolve a race of people having a peculiar national temperament and bent of mind, and when that is done, we shall have a *Canadian* literature.

It is no doubt futile to speculate on the character of a thing as yet so remote as a Canadian literature; yet one might hazard a thought or two on that subject. We know that climatic and scenic conditions have much to do with the moulding of national character. In the climate of this country we have the pitiless severity of the climate of Sweden, with the sunshine and the sky of the north of Italy, a combination not found in the same degree anywhere else in the world. The northern winters of Europe are seasons of terror and gloom; our winters are seasons of glittering splendour and incomparable richness of colour. At the same time we have the utmost diversity of scenery, a country exhibiting every variety of beauty and grandeur. A Canadian race, we imagine, might combine the energy, the seriousness, the perseverance of the Scandinavians with something of the gayety, the elasticity, the quickness of spirit of the south. If these qualities could be united in a literature, the result would indeed be something novel and wonderful.

But if we have not yet anything that we can call a full Canadian literature, we are not without our writers. Every Canadian who has read no further than the newspapers has heard of Judge Haliburton, Charles Heavysege, Dr. Kingsford, Dr. Bourinot, W. D. Lesueur, the

Abbé Casgrain, Sir William Dawson, Octave Crémazie, Louis Fréchette, Professor Alexander, Professor Roberts, Miss Machar, Hunter Duvar. These are names of which we have reason to be proud. In the last decade or two a small quantity of work of very decided excellence has been produced by Canadians. If we confine our view to pure literature, a great deal of this small quantity of excellent work has been done in verse. It is natural that the poet should be the most conspicuous product of the awakening literary impulse in a new country like ours. The philosopher, the historian, the critic, the novelist are more likely to represent a long-established civilization. In a new and sparsely settled land the urgent problems of life do not force themselves on the attention of men as they do in the midst of dense populations. Consequently, though they may interest themselves in the study of philosophy as a matter of culture, they are not likely to produce much original work of that sort. The field for the historian is also not very extensive. The critic has no place because he has nothing to examine. Even the novelist is likely to be a later product, for it is in the press of the older civilizations, where life in all its variety throngs about him, that he finds birth, food and stimulus. But for the poet the beauty of external nature and the aspects of the most primitive life are always a sufficient inspiration. On the borders of civilization, the poet is pretty sure to be the literary pioneer. For the poet of external nature no country is richer in inspiration than ours. For the balladist or the narrative writer we have at least as good a field as our neighbours of the United States. For the dramatic poet, if a dramatic poet could be produced in our age, there are, I should think, several excellent subjects in [the] history of old French Canada.

In searching for a subject for this paper I could not think of any upon which I could have greater pleasure in writing than the one I have chosen, viz., the writings in verse of two Canadians, Professor Charles G. D. Roberts and the late George Frederick Cameron. The first is a writer whose marked quality of imagination and powerful gift of style have gained him attention both in England and the United States; but what specially prompted me to choose this subject was a desire to say something of the late Mr. Cameron, a writer of a higher order of excellence as judged from the purest standpoint, of some very remarkable qualities of feeling and expression, who has not, as far as I can learn, attracted the attention he deserves.

As regards Mr. Roberts' work, I have always had a personal feeling which perhaps induces me to place a higher estimate upon it in some respects than my hearers will care to accept. To most younger Canadians who are interested in literature, especially those who have written themselves, Mr. Roberts occupies a peculiar position. They are accustomed to look up to him as in some sort the founder of a school, the originator of a new era in our poetic activity. I hope my hearers will pardon me, if I go out of my way to illustrate this fact by describing the effect Mr. Roberts' poems produced upon me when I first met with them.

It was almost ten years ago, and I was very young, an undergraduate at college. One May evening somebody lent me *Orion and Other Poems,* then recently published. Like most of the young fellows about me I had been under the depressing conviction that we were situated hopelessly on the outskirts of civilization, where no art and no literature could be, and that it was useless to expect that anything great could be done by any of our companions, still more useless to expect that we could do it ourselves. I sat up all night reading and re-reading *Orion* in a state of the wildest excitement and when I went to bed I could not sleep. It seemed to me a wonderful thing that such work could be done by a Canadian, by a young man, one of ourselves. It was like a voice from some new paradise of art calling to us to be up and doing. A little after sunrise I got up and went out into the college grounds. The air, I remember, was full of the odour and cool sunshine of the spring morning. The dew was thick upon the grass. All the birds of our Maytime seemed to be singing in the oaks, and there were even a few adder-tongues and trilliums still blossoming on the slope of the little ravine. But everything was transfigured for me beyond description, bathed in an old-world radiance of beauty [by] the magic of the lines that were sounding in my ears, those divine verses, as they seemed to me, with their Tennyson-like richness and strange, earth-loving, Greekish flavour. I have never forgotten that morning, and its influence has always remained with me.

I am now able to discuss Mr. Roberts' deficiencies. I know that he lacks tenderness, variety, elasticity, and that he never approaches the nobler attitudes of feeling; yet that early work of his has a special and mysterious charm for me – and it is indeed excellent, of an astonishing gift in workmanship, with passages here and there which in their way are almost unsurpassable.

Almost all the verse-writing published in Canada before the appearance of *Orion* was of a more or less barbarous character. The drama of *Saul* by Charles Heavysege and some of Heavysege's sonnets are about the only exceptions which can be made to this statement. Mr. Roberts was the first Canadian writer in verse who united a strong original genius with a high degree of culture and an acute literary judgment. He was the first to produce a style strongly individual in tone, and founded on the study of the best writers. Mr. Cameron, although a poet of greater spontaneity, a more passionate force and a much higher range of feeling than Mr. Roberts, does not equal him in perfection of style. He neither aimed at nor attained the same artistic excellence of workmanship.

Mr. Roberts' work, so far as it is available for purposes of criticism, is contained in two small volumes: the first, *Orion and Other Poems* published in 1880, when he was still an undergraduate of the University of New Brunswick, and not yet twenty years of age; the second, *In Divers Tones*, published in 1887, when he was in his twenty-seventh year. The first volume was of course immature, but it was an immaturity full of promise, and full of exhilaration for the poet's younger contemporaries. Some of the work in it is astonishing indeed for a Canadian schoolboy of eighteen or nineteen. Two of the poems included in this volume, "Memnon" and the "Ode to Drowsihood," had already attracted the admiration of Dr. Holland, the late editor of the *Century*, and had been published in that magazine. The second volume, that of 1887, may be considered the work of Mr. Roberts' maturity, for he has published nothing as good since. In this the promise of the first was strengthened and in part fulfilled. A few of the poems were remarkable accomplishments, and the workmanship of them all excellent enough to secure Mr. Roberts a high place among the writers of the continent.

All Mr. Roberts' writing is of a very scholarly character; it is the work of an artist and a student, possessed of a decided original tone of feeling. In each of his volumes, the longest and most important work is a poem in blank verse, the subject chosen from Greek classic legend, "Orion" in the first and "Actaeon" in the second. In these poems Mr. Roberts has won the rare distinction of having succeeded admirably in blank verse – a severe test. The blank verse of "Orion" and "Actaeon" is an interesting study. It has a highly original quality, and at the same time shows a curious mingling of many influences. It is the workmanship of a student of Homer, influenced largely by Milton and Tennyson, somewhat also by Keats and Matthew Arnold. I do not know of any writer, with the exception of Matthew Arnold in his "Balder Dead," who has given to blank verse a more charming touch of Homer than Mr. Roberts. His verse is not quite so Homeric in its lightness and swift movement as that of "Balder Dead" but it has more weight and a greater fulness of music. It is touched somewhat with the halt and restraint of Milton, corrected with a spice of the rich impulsiveness of Tennyson's "Oenone." On the whole it is very fine; probably no better has been done on this side of the Atlantic.

The style, which in its immaturity showed so much imagination and intellectual force in "Orion," is developed, pruned and compacted in "Actaeon." Here the verse is full of strength and melody, cleanly wrought and excellently balanced. While reminding one of the Greek, of Tennyson, and of Matthew Arnold, it is so penetrated and coloured by Mr. Roberts' own peculiar picturesque quality as to form an altogether original style. The "Actaeon" is certainly the best poem of that kind that has been written in America, and as regards workmanship I think it will stand comparison favourably with Tennyson's "Oenone."

*   *   *

It is always difficult to form an estimate of any contemporary writer; but I think that any one who has read through Mr. Roberts' two volumes, particularly the second, will conclude that he has been in contact with a very clever man, a scholar, a man of wide culture, variously appreciative, evincing especially a sort of deep physical satisfaction in the contemplation of nature, united to a strenuous and original gift of expression. He will find in him passion, strong, though not of the finest ring, a rich and masterful imagination, the genuine faculty of verse, an ear intolerant of any failure, and a cool and subtle literary judgment, but I think he will also find him wanting in spontaneity, in elasticity, in genuine tenderness, and in delicacy of feeling. His want of tenderness and genuine delicacy appear most strongly in two love poems, included in his second volume, "Tout ou rien" and "In Notre Dame," the first a declaration which could only proceed from the most boundless and pitiless egotism; the other, to me a still more disagreeable poem, an expression of brawny passion, pitched in an exaggerated and over-sensuous key.

In Mr. Roberts' work, notwithstanding the great ability that has gone to the making of it, there is often a certain weightiness and deliberateness of phrase, which suggests too strongly the hand of the careful workman, and robs it of the fullest effect of spontaneity. Although his poems are written upon many various subjects and either of his books might appear upon a cursory glance to be somewhat remarkable for variety, only three or four really different notes are struck, and all the poems are found to be attuned to these. Mr. Roberts is purely an emotional and artistic poet like Poe or Rossetti, and never attempts to lead us to any of the grander levels of thought and feeling. He has nothing to teach us beyond some new phases of the beauty of nature, which he has interpreted admirably; and altogether his work impresses us as the product of a strong artistic talent, rather than of a soul accustomed to the atmosphere of the nobler and severer beauty.

Mr. Roberts is a living poet. It is an easier and in a certain sense a more satisfactory task to speak of one of our writers who is no longer living. I refer to the late Mr. Cameron of Kingston. Of him above all other of our poets Canadians have reason to think with pride. He was a writer of rare spontaneity, whose genuine poetic impulse rings in every line. He had all the fervour, the breadth and energy of thought, the sensitive humanity, that Professor Roberts lacks. He was unequal and careless: there are not many of his poems which do not show frequent weaknesses and blemishes: but he goes straight to his thought, and the thought, even if it be at times a trifle dark, is always sharp from the battle of life. In Mr. Cameron's work we reach a larger and fresher atmosphere; we come into contact with a soul serious, sensitive, passionate, a man who dwells among genuine thoughts and genuine feelings, and speaks a language full of spontaneity, force, and dignity.

There is a strong Byronic quality in Cameron's genius, and his utterance has the Byronic nerve and imperious directness. It is penetrating, elastic, and full of high sound. Cameron's gift was purely a lyric one. He was a poet of life, and his work rings with the truth of experience. The joy, the grief, the passion, the aspiration, the weariness of life, are there, uttered with rapt sincerity and careless self-revelation. Cameron was young when he died – only thirty-three – and that short life appears from the evidence of his verse and what little I can learn of him, to have been very full, very varied, and on the whole not happy. His verse is in the main sad, bitter, and pessimistic, though this dark hue is relieved now and then by tender and genial touches, and some brave thoughts. But in Cameron there is no attitudinizing; his gloom is a darkness and bitterness bred of experience; and when he speaks the language of purpose and hope, his utterance is simple, manly and bracing. There are some of Cameron's poems that one cannot read without the profoundest thrill of admiration and reverence. They have a largeness of outlook, a passionate keenness of love or anger or pity, of praise or denunciation, and are spoken with a proud greatness of tongue, that make one doubt whether any praise is too high to be awarded to the memory of their author. Some day Cameron's name will stand high upon the list of the poets of this age; and there are one or two short poems of his that will be found in the collections of the English masterpieces of all time. There is one little poem, written in 1885, the last year of his life, that for grace and dignity of expression you can rank with anything in the language.

> Ah me! the mighty love that I have borne
>   To thee, sweet Song! A perilous gift was it
> My mother gave me that September morn
>   When sorrow, song, and life were at one altar lit.

* * *

... It will perhaps be said that Mr. Cameron like Professor Roberts has not actually taught us many things in a certain sense. Yet he has left us in his own degree the same sort of gift that Heine left to the world, the picture of a brilliant, passionate, imperfect human soul, and the record of its eager contact with the world. Such a life-work may not be of much use to us for guidance, but it will always be intensely interesting and intensely stimulating to the students of literature and life. Mr. Cameron's work, as I have said, is often faulty, and incomplete, often much too facile, but it has the authority and impressiveness of strong feeling, based upon an independent judgment of life in a nature genuinely poetic.

With George Frederick Cameron and Professor Roberts Canada has, so to speak, taken a place in the poetic literature of the world, and I believe that the work of these two writers is well worthy of our attention, not only as Canadians but as students of literature generally. It is our duty also, not only as Canadians, but as lovers of all literature, to see that a man like the late Mr. Cameron, whose life work lies finished before us, is not forgotten. That a body of writing, instinct with so true a poetic energy, should have been produced by a native of our own country, the product of our own soil, is a matter for national pride and encouragement.

From *At the Mermaid Inn*

(SATURDAY, JUNE 18, 1892)

The happiest man is he who has cultivated to the utmost the sense of beauty. The man who is able at all times to find perfect and prolonged satisfaction in the contemplation of a tree, a field, a flower or a "spear of grass," can never be bored save by his fellow-creatures. For him life is full of variety; every moment comes to him laden with some unique enjoyment, every hour is crowded with a multitude of fleeting but exquisite impressions. If health and a reasonable destiny attend him he cannot be otherwise than happy; pessimism for him is impossible. The beautiful is everywhere about us. As a matter of fact there is nothing fashioned by nature herself that is not beautiful, either in itself or in its relation to its surroundings. You do not need to go to the Rocky Mountains or the Yosemite Valley in order to find the beautiful; it is in the next field; it is at your feet. Wherever there is earth and any live or growing thing not perverted by the hand of man, there is a study in beauty that one cannot exhaust. The capacity for the enjoyment of natural beauty is rare in its perfection. He whose first impulse on projecting an excursion into the country is to carry with him a gun or fishing rod has certainly not attained it. To the real lover of nature the gun and the fishing rod are an encumbrance. Even the scientist – great as is the enjoyment to be derived from the mere acquisition of knowledge – does not experience the illimitable delight that falls to the lot of the pure loafer who has accustomed his eye to the perception of every beauty. To such a man as John Burroughs or Bradford Torrey life cannot offer any greater good than they have; and this serene source of satisfaction is in a greater or less degree within the reach of every man, if he will but accustom himself to the intelligent use of his senses.

(SATURDAY, AUGUST 27, 1892)

Those who do accomplish anything in literature in this country have, at any-rate, the grim satisfaction of knowing that if it is not what they might have done under more favorable circumstances, it is at least the product of sheer natural talent. The Canadian litterateur must depend solely upon himself and nature. He is almost without the exhilaration of lively and frequent literary intercourse – that force and variety of stimulus which counts for so much in the fructification of ideas. The human mind is like a plant, it blossoms in order to be fertilised, and to bear seed must come into actual contact with the mental dispersion of others. Of this natural assistance, the Canadian writer gets the least possible, and, if out of the poverty of his opportunities he accomplishes something, let him not be blamed for being perhaps, a little boastful and inclined to rate himself at a little more than his actual worth.

Our only remedies for this want is an occasional visit to the American literary centres, or to London if we are fortunate enough to have the means of getting there, and the friendly help of books, especially those memoirs which distinguished people in the older countries have left behind them for the entertainment and encouragement of those that come after. For the rest we shall have to do our best to create by degrees what we so much feel the need of now, by drawing toward one another as much as possible and bridging the long distances that separate us by friendly and helpful correspondence.

(SATURDAY, OCTOBER 1, 1892)

Some little discussion having arisen in regard to one of Mr. Bliss Carman's poems, it is not inopportune to say something in regard to Mr. Carman in general. The number of people who have the time or inclination to interest themselves in young contemporary writers is always very limited, and of the few who care to do so in this country, still fewer, I fancy, have any notion of the immense promise – nay, more than promise, the immense accomplishment – there is in Mr. Carman's work. Mr. Carman has published very little of his work, probably because he is confronted by the same obstacle that stands in the way of every new writer of obstinate originality – the impenetrable stupidity that [is the] invariable shortsightedness of publishers. Those few personal friends of Mr. Carman, however, who have been specially favored with an opportunity to judge his work, know that there is hardly any limit to the expectation that may be had of their friend's future. With great imaginative power and a most uncommon gift of musical versification, he has discovered and taken up a quite new poetic standpoint. His poems are suffused with a new and peculiar and most beautiful imaginative spirit, a spirit which is that of our own northern land, developed in the atmosphere of the Norse, with tinges of Indian legend. Many people will complain of his obscurity, and he is often – very often – obscure, because he does not aim at conveying clearly-cut images and ideas, but prefers, in obedience to a powerful impulse of his own mind, to steep his reader's imagination in splendid moods through the agency of magnificent metrical effects and a vast and mysterious imagery. Whether obscure or not, for the true lover of poetry there is one presence that covers a multitude of faults – the presence of beauty. We cavil in vain at a man's work if it is beautiful, and Mr. Carman's work is exquisitely beautiful.

Note: The poem referred to is Majory Darrow which was first discussed in *The Week,* Sept. 16, '92 – A leading editorial appeared in the issue of Sept. 30, '92 – The poem originally appeared in *The Independent.*

Duncan Campbell Scott (1862-1947)

In his own time, Duncan Campbell Scott was the least known of the four major Confederation poets: Scott, Charles G. D. Roberts, Bliss Carman and Archibald Lampman. Yet in many ways, it is Scott who seems most contemporary to-day and whose poems appeal to the younger generation. As well as writing, Scott managed a busy career in the Civil Service which led him to the top of his department, and spent considerable time editing the works of his friend Lampman after the latter's early death.

Duncan Campbell Scott was born in Ottawa, on August 2, 1862, son of a Methodist preacher who had emigrated from England to America in 1834, and to Canada in 1837. Scott grew up in various small towns of Ontario and Quebec, where he came into contact with the habitants and lumbermen who appear in his stories and narrative poems; he also acquired knowledge of Indian life from his father who had been a missionary for some years. In 1874 he attended school in Smiths Falls, and in 1877 and 1878 he completed two years of university preparation at Wesleyan College, Stanstead, Quebec. His hopes for a medical career were not fulfilled as the family had little money, and in 1879 he was employed, at the request of John A. Macdonald, as copying clerk in the Department of Indian Affairs at $1.50 per day. He remained here for fifty-two years; in 1893 he became Chief Clerk, in 1896 Secretary, in 1909 Superintendent of Indian Education and in 1923 Deputy Superintendent General of Indian Affairs, the highest permanent office in the department. He retired in 1931, a year after his second marriage, and he and his wife travelled in America and abroad. He died in 1947.

Scott did not begin writing poetry in earnest until after 1883 when he met Archibald Lampman, a fellow civil servant; Lampman provided the initial encouragement and soon Scott began to publish poems and stories. In collaboration with Lampman and William Wilfred Campbell, who left the ministry for the civil service in 1891, Scott wrote a column, "At the Mermaid Inn," for the Toronto *Globe*; it ran in 1892 and 1893 and discussed contemporary life and literature, both in Canada and abroad. In 1893 Scott published his first volume of verse *The Magic House and Other Poems*, followed by *Labour and the Angel* (1898), *New World Lyrics and Ballads* (1905), and *Via Borealis*, seven poems on north-western Ontario (1906). In 1907, the sudden death of Scott's only child Elizabeth affected him deeply and there is a long period before *Lundy's Lane and Other Poems* (1916), *Beauty and Life* (1921), and *The Green Cloister* (1935). His *Collected*

Poems appeared in 1916. Scott also wrote two volumes of short stories: *In the Village of Viger* (1896) and *The Witching of Elspie* (1923). A late volume, *The Circle of Affection*, published a few months before his death, contains late short stories and poems, a number of early unpublished works and several essays. A one-act play *Pierre* was produced in 1923 by the Ottawa Little Theatre and a light satire, *Byron on Wordsworth, being discovered stanzas of Don Juan*, came out in 1924. In the midst of this busy life as civil servant and creative writer, Scott found time to edit the poems of his friend Lampman: the *Memorial Edition of Archibald Lampman* with a memoir by Scott (1900), *Lyrics of Earth* (1925), and *The Selected Poems of Archibald Lampman* (1947); he also collaborated with E. K. Brown in *At the Long Sault and Other New Poems*, a collection discovered among Lampman's manuscripts. Scott was joint editor of the Makers of Canada series with Pelham Edgar, and contributed *John Graves Simcoe* (1905); he also wrote a biography and critical sketch of the painter Walter J. Phillips (1947).

Despite his own diffidence concerning his poetry, Scott was given critical acclaim in his day. He was elected to the Royal Society of Canada in 1899 to replace Lampman, and became honorary secretary in 1911 and President in 1921, when he delivered his inaugural address "Poetry and Progress" (1922) on the nature of the imagination and the state of poetry in contemporary Canada.

Although Scott has written a number of landscape poems in the manner of his contemporaries Roberts, Carman, Lampman and Campbell, it is his narratives which mark a new departure in Canadian poetry with their vivid action and their sharp contrasts in line length, sound and rhythm to convey a specific mood. These narratives treat such subject areas as the often tragic lives of the lumberjacks along the Ottawa River or the predicament of the artist, as in "The Piper of Arll," which has been interpreted as a comment on the fate of the Canadian imagination. But his most distinctive works are the Indian and Eskimo poems which, drawn from a lifetime of experience with the Indian Department, reveal a strong sympathy with the conquered races and a recognition of the tensions which pull them apart both as a group and individually. His short stories too are vivid. *In the Village of Viger*, like Leacock's *Sunshine Sketches*, consists of separate stories interrelated by a common setting and common characters. The detached tone and restrained narrative style underline the irony of life in a little town which has its share of ambition, unscrupulousness, insanity and blindness both physical and mental, as well as the more idyllic elements of love, compassion, dedication and faith.

TEXT:

The Poems of Duncan Campbell Scott. Toronto: McClelland and Stewart, 1926.

The Green Cloister. Toronto: McClelland, 1935.
The Circle of Affection. Toronto: McClelland and Stewart, 1947.
In the Village of Viger, Boston: Copeland and Day, 1896.

See also:
E. K. Brown. *On Canadian Poetry*. Toronto: Ryerson, 1944.
Desmond Pacey. *Ten Canadian Poets*. Toronto: Ryerson, 1958.
In the Village of Viger and Other Stories, introd. S. L. Dragland.
   Toronto: New Canadian Library, 1973.

At Murray Bay

Curling off the points and shallows
   Tides turn out and stream away,
Winning all the willing water
   From the shoals of Murray Bay.

Flushed with pink and meshed with silver
   Wide the beaches lie unfurled,
Where the Murray strives to sweeten
   All the oceans of the world.

Far and faintly far to southward
   Like a hamlet dim of dreams,
White the line of Kamouraska
   In the mirage floats and gleams

Where the orient waters wander
   Ebbing slowly with the light,
Burning deep with purple shadows
   Cap à l'Aigle fronts the night.

Night that calmly moving onward
   Fresh with breezes from the sea,
Pacing up the river floorways
   Kindles lights at St. Denis.

Fills the land with slumber shadows,
 While for her imperial rest
Venus sinks in languid splendour
 Down her caverns in the west.

(early-1947)

At Les Eboulements

The bay is set with ashy sails,
 With purple shades that fade and flee,
And curling by in silver wales,
 The tide is straining from the sea.

The grassy points are slowly drowned,
 The water laps and over-rolls,
The wicker pêche; with shallow sound
 A light wave labours on the shoals.

The crows are feeding in the foam,
 They rise in crowds tumultuously,
'Come home,' they cry, 'come home, come home,
 And leave the marshes to the sea.'

(1893)

Memory

I see a schooner in the bay
 Cutting the current into foam;
One day she flies and then one day
 Comes like a swallow veering home.

I hear a water miles away
    Go sobbing down the wooded glen;
One day it lulls and then one day
    Comes sobbing on the wind again.

Remembrance goes but will not stay;
    That cry of unpermitted pain
One day departs and then one day
    Comes sobbing to my heart again.

(1893)

At Delos

An iris-flower with topaz leaves,
    With a dark heart of deeper gold,
Died over Delos when light failed
    And the night grew cold.

No wave fell mourning in the sea
    Where age on age beauty had died;
For that frail colour withering away
    No sea-bird cried.

There is no grieving in the world
    As beauty fades throughout the years:
The pilgrim with the weary heart
    Brings to the grave his tears.

(1947)

Ecstasy

The shore-lark soars to his topmost flight,
　　Sings at the height where morning springs,
What though his voice be lost in the light,
　　The light comes dropping from his wings.

MOUNT, my soul, and sing at the height
　　Of thy clear flight in the light and the air,
Heard or unheard in the night in the light
　　Sing there! Sing there!

(1916)

The Leaf

This silver-edged geranium leaf
Is one sign of a bitter grief
Whose symbols are a myriad more;
They cluster round a carven stone
Where she who sleeps is never alone
For two hearts at the core,

Bound with her heart make one of three,
A trinity in unity,
One sentient heart that grieves;
And myriad dark-leaved memories keep
Vigil above the triune sleep, –
Edged all with silver are the leaves.

(1916)

Thirteen Songs

IV

Sorrow is come like a swallow to nest,
Winging him up from the wind and the foam;
Mine is the heart that he loves the best,
He dreams of it when he dreams of home.

Strange! in the daylight off he flies,
Swift to the south away to the sea;
But when in the west the ruby dies,
With the growing stars he comes back to me.

With the salt, cool wind in his wing,
And the rush of tears that tingle and start,
With a throb at the throat so he cannot sing,
He nestles him into my lonely heart.

And he tells me of something I cannot name,
Something the sea with the sea-wind sings,
That somehow he and love are the same,
That they float and fly with the same swift wings.

I cherish and cherish my timid guest,
For O, he has grown so dear to me
That my heart would break if he left his nest,
And dwelt in the strange land down by the sea.

(1893)

XIII

Lay thy cheek to mine, love,
    Once before I go;
Memories throng and quiver, love,
    In the afterglow.

All the rippling springtimes
    Full of crocus lights;
When the dawns came too soon
    And tardy were the nights.

All the dusky summers
  By the fruitful hill;
Thinking both the one thought
  When the heart was still.

Deep, untroubled autumns,
  Fallen leaves and rime;
Musing on the treasure
  Of the old time.

Where my journey leads, love,
  There is cold and snow;
Lay thy cheek to mine, love,
  Once before I go.

(1898)

The Closed Door

The dew falls and the stars fall,
The sun falls in the west,
But never more
Through the closed door,
Shall the one that I loved best
Return to me:
A salt tear is the sea,
All earth's air is a sigh,
But they never can mourn for me
With my heart's cry,
For the one that I loved best
Who caressed me with her eyes,
And every morning came to me,
With the beauty of sunrise,
Who was health and wealth and all,
Who never shall answer my call,
While the sun falls in the west,
The dew falls and the stars fall.

(1916)

The Piper of Arll

There was in Arll a little cove
Where the salt wind came cool and free:
A foamy beach that one would love,
If he were longing for the sea.

A brook hung sparkling on the hill,
The hill swept far to ring the bay;
The bay was faithful, wild or still,
To the heart of the ocean far away.

There were three pines above the comb
That, when the sun flared and went down,
Grew like three warriors reaving home
The plunder of a burning town.

A piper lived within the grove,
Tending the pasture of his sheep;
His heart was swayed with faithful love,
From the springs of God's ocean clear and deep.

And there a ship one evening stood,
Where ship had never stood before;
A pennon bickered red as blood,
An angel glimmered at the prore.

About the coming on of dew,
The sails burned rosy, and the spars
Were gold, and all the tackle grew
Alive with ruby-hearted stars.

The piper heard an outland tongue,
With music in the cadenced fall;
And when the fairy lights were hung,
The sailors gathered one and all,

And leaning on the gunwales dark,
Crusted with shells and dashed with foam,
With all the dreaming hills to hark,
They sang their longing songs of home.

When the sweet airs had fled away,
The piper, with a gentle breath,
Moulded a tranquil melody
Of lonely love and longed-for death.

When the fair sound began to lull,
From out the fireflies and the dew,
A silence held the shadowy hull,
Until the eerie tune was through.

Then from the dark and dreamy deck
An alien song began to thrill;
It mingled with the drumming beck,
And stirred the braird upon the hill.

Beneath the stars each sent to each
A message tender, till at last
The piper slept upon the beach,
The sailors slumbered round the mast.

Still as a dream till nearly dawn,
The ship was bosomed on the tide;
The streamlet, murmuring on and on,
Bore the sweet water to her side.

Then shaking out her lawny sails,
Forth on the misty sea she crept;
She left the dawning of the dales,
Yet in his cloak the piper slept.

And when he woke he saw the ship,
Limned black against the crimson sun;
Then from the disc he saw her slip,
A wraith of shadow – she was gone.

He threw his mantle on the beach,
He went apart like one distraught,
His lips were moved – his desperate speech
Stormed his inviolable thought.

He broke his human-throated reed,
And threw it in the idle rill;
But when his passion had its mead,
He found it in the eddy still.

He mended well the patient flue,
Again he tried its varied stops;
The closures answered right and true,
And starting out in piercing drops,

A melody began to drip
That mingled with a ghostly thrill
The vision-spirit of the ship,
The secret of his broken will.

Beneath the pines he piped and swayed,
Master of passion and of power;
He was his soul and what he played,
Immortal for a happy hour.

He, singing into nature's heart,
Guiding his will by the world's will,
With deep, unconscious, childlike art
Had sung his soul out and was still.

And then at evening came the bark
That stirred his dreaming heart's desire;
It burned slow lights along the dark
That died in glooms of crimson fire.

The sailors launched a sombre boat,
And bent with music at the oars;
The rhythm throbbing every throat,
And lapsing round the liquid shores,

Was that true tune the piper sent,
Unto the wave-worn mariners,
When with the beck and ripple blent
He heard that outland song of theirs.

Silent they rowed him, dip and drip,
The oars beat out an exequy,
They laid him down within the ship,
They loosed a rocket to the sky.

It broke in many a crimson sphere
That grew to gold and floated far,
And left the sudden shore-line clear,
With one slow-changing, drifting star.

Then out they shook the magic sails,
That charmed the wind in other seas,
From where the west line pearls and pales,
They waited for a ruffling breeze.

But in the world there was no stir,
The cordage slacked with never a creak,
They heard the flame begin to purr
Within the lantern at the peak.

They could not cry, they could not move,
They felt the lure from the charmed sea;
They could not think of home or love
Or any pleasant land to be.

They felt the vessel dip and trim,
And settle down from list to list;
They saw the sea-plain heave and swim
As gently as a rising mist.

And down so slowly, down and down,
Rivet by rivet, plank by plank;
A little flood of ocean flown
Across the deck, she sank and sank.

From knee to breast the water wore,
It crept and crept; ere they were ware
Gone was the angel at the prore,
They felt the water float their hair.

They saw the salt plain spark and shine,
They threw their faces to the sky;
Beneath a deepening film of brine
They saw the star-flash blur and die.

She sank and sank by yard and mast,
Sank down the shimmering gradual dark;
A little drooping pennon last
Showed like the black fin of a shark.

And down she sank till, keeled in sand,
She rested safely balanced true,
With all her upward gazing band,
The piper and the dreaming crew.

And there, unmarked of any chart,
In unrecorded deeps they lie,
Empearled within the purple heart
Of the great sea for aye and aye.

Their eyes are ruby in the green
Long shaft of sun that spreads and rays,
And upward with a wizard sheen
A fan of sea-light leaps and plays.

Tendrils of or and azure creep,
And globes of amber light are rolled,
And in the gloaming of the deep
Their eyes are starry pits of gold.

And sometimes in the liquid night
The hull is changed, a solid gem,
That glows with a soft stony light,
The lost prince of a diadem.

And at the keel a vine is quick,
That spreads its bines and works and weaves
O'er all the timbers veining thick
A plenitude of silver leaves.

(1898)

At the Cedars

You had two girls – Baptiste –
One is Virginie –
Hold hard – Baptiste!
Listen to me.

The whole drive was jammed
In that bend at the Cedars,
The rapids were dammed
With the logs tight rammed
And crammed; you might know
The Devil had clinched them below.

We worked three days – not a budge,
'She's as tight as a wedge, on the ledge,'
Says our foreman;
'Mon Dieu! boys, look here,
We must get this thing clear.'
He cursed at the men
And we went for it then;
With our cant-dogs arow,
We just gave he-yo-ho;
When she gave a big shove
From above.

The gang yelled and tore
For the shore,
The logs gave a grind
Like a wolf's jaws behind,
And as quick as a flash,
With a shove and a crash,
They were down in a mash,
But I and ten more,
All but Isaàc Dufour,
Were ashore.

He leaped on a log in the front of the rush,
And shot out from the bind
While the jam roared behind;
As he floated along
He balanced his pole
And tossed us a song.
But just as we cheered,
Up darted a log from the bottom
Leaped thirty feet square and fair,
And came down on his own.

He went up like a block
With the shock,
And when he was there
In the air,
Kissed his hand
To the land;
When he dropped
My heart stopped,
For the first logs had caught him
And crushed him;
When he rose in his place
There was blood on his face.

There were some girls, Baptiste,
Picking berries on the hillside,
Where the river curls, Baptiste,
You know – on the still side
One was down by the water,
She saw Isaàc
Fall back.

She did not scream, Baptiste,
She launched her canoe;
It did seem, Baptiste,
That she wanted to die too,
For before you could think
The birch cracked like a shell
In that rush of hell,
And I saw them both sink –

Baptiste! –
He had two girls,
One is Virginie,
What God calls the other
Is not known to me.

(1893)

The Onondaga Madonna

She stands full-throated and with careless pose,
This woman of a weird and waning race,
The tragic savage lurking in her face,
Where all her pagan passion burns and glows;
Her blood is mingled with her ancient foes,
And thrills with war and wildness in her veins;
Her rebel lips are dabbled with the stains
Of feuds and forays and her father's woes.

And closer in the shawl about her breast,
The latest promise of her nation's doom,
Paler than she her baby clings and lies,
The primal warrior gleaming from his eyes;
He sulks, and burdened with his infant gloom,
He draws his heavy brows and will not rest.

(1898)

The Half-breed Girl

She is free of the trap and the paddle,
    The portage and the trail,
But something behind her savage life
    Shines like a fragile veil.

Her dreams are undiscovered,
    Shadows trouble her breast,
When the time for resting cometh
    Then least is she at rest.

Oft in the morns of winter,
    When she visits the rabbit snares,
An appearance floats in the crystal air
    Beyond the balsam firs.

Oft in the summer mornings
    When she strips the nets of fish,
The smell of the dripping net-twine
    Gives to her heart a wish.

But she cannot learn the meaning
    Of the shadows in her soul,
The lights that break and gather,
    The clouds that part and roll,

The reek of rock-built cities,
    Where her fathers dwelt of yore,
The gleam of loch and shealing,
    The mist on the moor,

Frail traces of kindred kindness,
   Of feud by hill and strand,
The heritage of an age-long life
   In a legendary land.

She wakes in the stifling wigwam,
   Where the air is heavy and wild,
She fears for something or nothing
   With the heart of a frightened child.

She sees the stars turn slowly
   Past the tangle of the poles,
Through the smoke of the dying embers,
   Like the eyes of dead souls.

Her heart is shaken with longing
   For the strange, still years,
For what she knows and knows not,
   For the wells of ancient tears.

A voice calls from the rapids,
   Deep, careless and free,
A voice that is larger than her life
   Or than her death shall be.

She covers her face with her blanket,
   Her fierce soul hates her breath,
As it cries with a sudden passion
   For life or death.

(1906)

The Forsaken

I

Once in the winter,
Out on a lake
In the heart of the north-land,
Far from the Fort
And far from the hunters,
A Chippewa woman
With her sick baby,
Crouched in the last hours
Of a great storm.
Frozen and hungry,
She fished through the ice
With a line of the twisted
Bark of the cedar,
And a rabbit-bone hook
Polished and barbed;
Fished with the bare hook
All through the wild day,
Fished and caught nothing;
While the young chieftain
Tugged at her breasts,
Or slept in the lacings
Of the warm *tikanagan*.
All the lake-surface
Streamed with the hissing
Of millions of iceflakes,
Hurled by the wind;
Behind her the round
Of a lonely island
Roared like a fire
With the voice of the storm
In the deeps of the cedars.
Valiant, unshaken,
She took of her own flesh,
Baited the fish-hook,

Drew in a gray-trout,
Drew in his fellow,
Heaped them beside her,
Dead in the snow.
Valiant, unshaken,
She faced the long distance,
Wolf-haunted and lonely,
Sure of her goal
And the life of her dear one;
Tramped for two days,
On the third in the morning,
Saw the strong bulk
Of the Fort by the river,
Saw the wood-smoke
Hang soft in the spruces,
Heard the keen yelp
Of the ravenous huskies
Fighting for whitefish:
Then she had rest.

II

Years and years after,
When she was old and withered,
When her son was an old man
And his children filled with vigour,
They came in their northern tour on the verge of winter,
To an island in a lonely lake.
There one night they camped, and on the morrow
Gathered their kettles and birch-bark
Their rabbit-skin robes and their mink-traps,
Launched their canoes and slunk away through the islands,
Left her alone forever,
Without a word of farewell,
Because she was old and useless,
Like a paddle broken and warped,
Or a pole that was splintered.
Then, without a sigh,
Valiant, unshaken,
She smoothed her dark locks under her kerchief,
Composed her shawl in state,
Then folded her hands ridged with sinews and corded
    with veins,
Folded them across her breasts spent with the nourishing
    of children,

Gazed at the sky past the tops of the cedars,
Saw two spangled nights arise out of the twilight,
Saw two days go by filled with the tranquil sunshine,
Saw, without pain, or dread, or even a moment of longing:
Then on the third great night there came thronging and
   thronging
Millions of snowflakes out of a windless cloud;
They covered her close with a beautiful crystal shroud,
Covered her deep and silent.
But in the frost of the dawn,
Up from the life below,
Rose a column of breath
Through a tiny cleft in the snow,
Fragile, delicately drawn,
Wavering with its own weakness,
In the wilderness a sign of the spirit,
Persisting still in the sight of the sun
Till day was done.
Then all light was gathered up by the hand of God and
   hid in His breast,
Then there was born a silence deeper than silence,
Then she had rest.

(1905)

On the Way to the Mission

They dogged him all one afternoon,
Through the bright snow,
Two whitemen servants of greed;
He knew that they were there,
But he turned not his head;
He was an Indian trapper;
He planted his snow-shoes firmly,
He dragged the long toboggan
Without rest.

The three figures drifted
Like shadows in the mind of a seer;
The snow-shoes were whispers
On the threshold of awe;
The toboggan made the sound of wings,
A wood-pigeon sloping to her nest.

The Indian's face was calm.
He strode with the sorrow of fore-knowledge,
But his eyes were jewels of content
Set in circles of peace.

They would have shot him;
But momently in the deep forest,
They saw something flit by his side:
Their hearts stopped with fear.
Then the moon rose.
They would have left him to the spirit,

But they saw the long toboggan
Rounded well with furs,
With many a silver fox-skin,
With the pelts of mink and of otter.
They were the servants of greed;
When the moon grew brighter
And the spruces were dark with sleep,

They shot him.
When he fell on a shield of moonlight
One of his arms clung to his burden;
The snow was not melted:
The spirit passed away.

Then the servants of greed
Tore off the cover to count their gains;
They shuddered away into the shadows,
Hearing each the loud heart of the other.
Silence was born.

There in the tender moonlight,
  As sweet as they were in life,
Glimmered the ivory features,
  Of the Indian's wife.

In the manner of Montagnais women
  Her hair was rolled with braid;
Under her waxen fingers
  A crucifix was laid.

He was drawing her down to the Mission,
  To bury her there in spring,
When the bloodroot comes and the windflower
  To silver everything.

But as a gift of plunder
  Side by side were they laid,
The moon went on to her setting
  And covered them with shade.

(1905)

The Desjardins

Just at the foot of the hill, where the bridge crossed the Blanche, stood one of the oldest houses in Viger. It was built of massive timbers. The roof curved and projected beyond the eaves, forming the top of a narrow veranda. The whole house was painted a dazzling white except the window-frames, which were green. There was a low stone fence between the road and the garden, where a few simple flowers grew. Beyond the fence was a row of Lombardy poplars, some of which had commenced to die out. On the opposite side of the road was a marshy field, where by day the marsh marigolds shone, and by night, the fire-flies. There were places in this field where you could thrust down a long pole and not touch bottom. In the fall a few musk-rats built a house there, in remembrance of the time when it was a favourite wintering-ground. In the spring the Blanche came up and flowed over it. Beyond that again the hill curved round, with a scarped, yellowish slope.

In this house lived Adèle Desjardin with her two brothers, Charles and Philippe. Their father was dead, and when he died there was hardly a person in the whole parish who was sorry. They could remember him as a tall, dark, forbidding-looking man, with long arms out of all proportion to his body. He had inherited his fine farm from his father, and had added to and improved it. He had always been prosperous, and was considered the wealthiest man in the parish. He was inhospitable, and became more taciturn and morose after his wife died. His pride was excessive and kept him from associating with his neighbours, although he was in no way above them. Very little was known about his manner of life, and there was a mystery about his father's death. For some time the old man had not been seen about the place, when one day he came from the city, dead, and in his cofin, which was thought strange. This gave rise to all sorts of rumour and gossip; but the generally accredited story was, that there was insanity in the family and that he had died crazy.

However cold Isidore Desjardin was to his neighbours, no one could have charged him with being unkind or harsh with his children, and as they grew up he gave them all the advantages which it was possible for them to have. Adèle went for a year to the Convent of the Sacré Coeur in the city, and could play tunes on the piano when she came back; so that she had to have a piano of her own, which was the first one ever heard in Viger. She was a slight, angular girl, with a dark, thin face and black hair and eyes. She looked like her father, and took after him in many ways. Charles, the elder son, was like his grandfather, tall and muscular, with a fine head and a handsome face. He was studious and read a great deal, and was always talking to the curé about studying the law. Philippe did not care about books; his father could never keep him at school. He was short and thick-set and had merry eyes, set deep in his head. "Someone must learn to look after things," he said, and when his father died he took sole charge of everything.

If the Desardins were unsociable with others, they were happy among themselves. Almost every evening during the winter, when the work was done, they would light up the front room with candles, and Adèle would play on the piano and sing. Charles would pace to and fro behind her, and Philippe would thrust his feet far under the stove, that projected from the next room through the partition, and fall fast asleep. Her songs were mostly old French songs, and she could sing "Partant pour la Syrie" and "La Marseillaise." This last was a favourite with Charles; he could not sing himself, but he accompanied the music by making wild movements with his arms, tramping heavily up and down before the piano, and shouting out so loudly as to wake Philippe, "Aux armes, citoyens!" On fine summer evenings Philippe and Adèle would walk up and down the road, watching the marsh fire-flies, and pausing on the bridge to hear the fish jump in the pool, and the deep, vibrant croak of the distant frogs. It was not always Philippe who walked there with Adèle; he sometimes sat on the veranda and watched her walk with someone else. He would have waking dreams, as he smoked, that the two figures moving before him were himself and someone into whose eyes he was looking.

At last it came to be reality for him, and then he could not sit quietly and watch the lovers; he would let his pipe go out, and stride impatiently up and down the veranda. And on Sunday afternoons he would harness his horse, dress himself carefully, and drive off with short laughs, and twinklings of the eyes, and wavings of the hands. They were evidently planning the future, and it seemed a distance of vague happiness.

Charles kept on his wonted way; if they talked in the parlour, they could hear him stirring upstairs; if they strolled in the road, they could see his light in the window. Philippe humoured his studious habits; he only worked in the mornings; in the afternoons he read, history principally. His favourite study was the "Life of Napoleon Buonaparte," which seemed to absorb him completely. He was growing more retired and preoccupied every day – lost in deep reveries, swallowed of ambitious dreams.

It had been a somewhat longer day than usual in the harvest-field, and it was late when the last meal was ready. Philippe, as he called Charles, from the foot of the stair, could hear him walking up and down, seemingly reading out loud, and when he received no response to his demand he went up the stairs. Pushing open the door, he saw his brother striding up and down the room, with his hands clasped behind him and his head bent, muttering to himself.

"Charles!" He seemed to collect himself, and looked up. "Come down to supper!" They went downstairs together. Adèle and Philippe kept up a conversation throughout the meal, but Charles hardly spoke. Suddenly he pushed his plate away and stood upright, to his full height; a look of calm, severe dignity came over his face.

"I!" said he; "I am the Great Napoleon!"

"Charles!" cried Adèle, "what is the matter?"

"The prosperity of the nation depends upon the execution of my plans. Go!" said he, dismissing some imaginary person with an imperious gesture.

They sat as if stunned, and between them stood this majestic figure with outstretched hand. Then Chalres turned away and commenced to pace the room.

"It has come!" sobbed Adèle, as she sank on her knees beside the table.

"There is only one thing to do," said Philippe, after some hours of silence. "It is hard; but there is only one thing to do." The room was perfectly dark; he stood in the window, where he had seen the light die out of the sky, and now in the marshy field he saw the fire-flies gleam. He knew that Adèle was in the dark somewhere beside him, for he could hear her breathe. "We must cut ourselves off; we must be the last of our race." In those words, which in after years were often on his lips, he seemed to find some comfort, and he continued to repeat them to himself.

Charles lay in bed in a sort of stupor for three days. On Sunday morning he rose. The church bells were ringing. He met Philippe in the hall.

"Is this Sunday?" he asked.

"Yes."

"Come here!" They went into the front room.

"This is Sunday, you say. The last thing I remember was you telling me to go in – that was Wednesday. What has happened?" Philippe dropped his head in his hands.

"Tell me, Philippe, what has happened?"

"I cannot."

"I must know, Philippe; where have I been?"

"On Wednesday night," said he, as if the words were choking him, "you said, 'I am the Great Napoleon!' Then you said something about the nation, and you have not spoken since."

Charles dropped on his knees beside the table against which Philippe was leaning. He hid his face in his arms. Philippe, reaching across, thrust his fingers into his brother's brown hair. The warm grasp came as an answer to all Charles's unasked questions; he knew that, whatever might happen, his brother would guard him.

For a month or two he lay wavering between two worlds; but when he saw the first snow, and lost sight of the brown earth, he at once commenced to order supplies, to write despatches, and to make preparations for the gigantic expedition which was to end in the overthrow of the Emperor of all the Russias. And the snow continues to bring him this activity; during the summer he is engaged, with no very definite operations, in the field, but when winter comes he always prepares for the invasion of Russia. With the exception of certain days of dejection and trouble, which Adèle calls the Waterloo days, in the summer he is triumphant with perpetual victory. On a little bare hill, about a mile from the house, from which you can get an extensive view of the sloping country, he watches the movements of the enemy. The blasts at the distant quarries sound in his ears like the roar of guns. Beside him the old grey horse, that Philippe has set apart for his service, crops the grass or stands for hours patiently. Down in the shallow valley the Blanche runs, glistening; the mowers sway and bend; on the horizon shafts of smoke rise, little clouds break away from the masses and drop their quiet shadows on the fields. And through his glass Charles watches the moving shadows, the shafts of smoke, and the swaying mowers, watches the distant hills fringed with beech-groves. He despatches his aides-de-camp with important orders, or rides down the slope to oversee the fording of the Blanche. Half-frightened village boys hide in the long grass to hear him go muttering by. In the autumn he comes sadly up out of the valley, leading his horse, the rein through his arm and his hands in his coat-sleeves. The sleet dashes against him, and the wind rushes and screams around him, as he ascends the little knoll. But whatever the weather, Philippe waits in the road for him and helps him dismount. There is something heroic in his short figure.

"Sire, my brother!" he says; – "Sire, let us go in!"

"Is the King of Rome better?"

"Yes."

"And the Empress?"

"She is well."

Only once has a gleam of light pierced these mists. It was in the year when, as Adèle said, he had had two Waterloos and had taken to his bed in consequence. One evening Adèle brought him a bowl of gruel. He stared like a child awakened from sleep when she carried in the lamp. She approached the bed, and he started up.

"Adèle!" he said, hoarsely, and pulling her face down, kissed her lips. For a moment she had hope, but with the next week came winter; and he commenced his annual preparations for the invasion of Russia.

Isabella Valancy Crawford (1850-1887)

Almost unknown during her lifetime, Isabella Valancy Crawford attempted to live by her writing in a period when few authors could support themselves, and died of heart disease at thirty-seven just at the time when she was beginning to gain recognition for her efforts. In an article in the *Canadian Magazine* of 1895, E. J. Hathaway observed: "Had she lived, she undoubtedly would have occupied a place in the world of letters with the very best of her time", and Northrop Frye in *The Bush Garden* comments on her "remarkable mythopoeic imagination" and identifies her as "one of the subtlest poets that Canada has produced".

Isabella Valancy Crawford was born in Dublin on December 25, 1850 to parents of Scots descent. In search of the New World of affluence, her parents moved to Canada with their twelve children about 1858 and settled in Paisley on the Saugeen River, where Dr. Crawford set up a local practice. Here Isabella and her sister were taught English, Latin and French at home, and Isabella read extensively in her father's library. The town was just emerging from the bush and here Isabella came into contact with nature and the drama of the woodsmen which is reflected in many of her writings. Some eight years later, after the death of nine of the children, the Crawfords moved to Lakefield on the Kawartha Lakes, home of Catharine Parr Traill and her sister Susannah Moodie and described in its early days in their books *The Backwoods of Canada* and *Roughing It in the Bush*. The Crawfords lived in Lakefield about six years and then moved to Peterborough. In 1875 Isabella's father died, her brother went to Algoma, and Isabella was left with the support of her mother and a younger sister. When Emma Naomi died shortly after, Isabella and Mrs. Crawford moved to Toronto, the centre of culture in Canada at that time, and lived first in lodgings on Adelaide Street and later over a grocery shop on the corner of King and John Streets. She died suddenly in Toronto on February 12, 1887.

Isabella began writing for money after 1875; she penned poems and short stories in profusion for all available markets, although it was rare to receive very much for poetry. About this time she was awarded a prize of six hundred dollars in a short story competition, a considerable sum at that time, but she received only $100 of it as the corporation which provided the prize had failed. In Toronto, Isabella was closer to the literary scene and sold poems in *The Globe* and *The Telegram*, but she received little encouragement from the literary editor of *The Week* who told her they "didn't pay for poetry". In

1884 she published at her own expense *Old Spookses' Pass, Malcolm's Katie and Other Poems*. Her *Collected Poems* appeared in 1905, edited by John Garvin.

Old Spookses' Pass, Malcolm's Katie and Other Poems received considerable attention in England with favourable reviews in the London *Atheneum*, the *Spectator,* the *Illustrated London News* and the *National Graphic,* but it sold only fifty copies before Crawford's death; a cheaply-bound book with a paper cover, it was rebound in cloth in 1898 and the remaining copies sold well. In his eulogy in the introduction of the *Collected Poems,* John Garvin remarked: "A great poet dwelt among us and we scarce knew her. Hers was a master mind which illumined with imagination, emotion and originality the noblest and profoundest thoughts of her time". Certainly the range of her material is exceptionally broad for her time and embraces classical, biblical, mediaeval and Norse subjects, as well as local myths and legends in "Malcolm's Katie" and the cowboy ballad in "Spookses' Pass". In both the lyrics and the narratives, the theme of love is central, but is balanced by a preoccupation with struggle and death. Much of the poetry possesses vigour, spontaneity and a richness of imagery rare in Canadian writing of the period. Crawford also experiments with a range of forms from the short lyric through the more sustained longer poem to the dramatic monologue and the narrative, and employs a style varying from classic restraint to Swinburnian lushness and the picturesqueness of the dialect poems. Such works as "The Deacon and his Daughter" reveal a strong wit and a sense of the ludicrous in life which is also rare in Canadian poetry.

TEXT:

The Collected Poems of Isabella Valancy Crawford. John Garvin, ed., introduction by Ethelwyn Wetherald. Toronto: William Briggs, 1905.

See also:

Roy Daniells in *The Literary History of Canada.* Toronto: University of Toronto Press, 1965.

Katharine Hale (Mrs. John Garvin). *Isabella Valancy Crawford.* Toronto: Ryerson, 1923.

Introduction by James Reaney to *Collected Poems.* Toronto: University of Toronto Press, 1972.

March

Shall Thor with his hammer
   Beat on the mountain,
As on an anvil,
   A shackle and fetter?

Shall the lame Vulcan
   Shout as he swingeth
God-like his hammer,
   And forge thee a fetter?

Shall Jove, the Thunderer,
   Twine his swift lightnings
With his loud thunders,
   And forge thee a shackle?

"No," shouts the Titan,
   The young lion-throated;
"Thor, Vulcan, nor Jove
   Cannot shackle and bind me."

Tell what will bind thee,
   Thou young world-shaker,
Up vault our oceans,
   Down fall our forests.

Ship masts and pillars
   Stagger and tremble,
Like reeds by the margins
   Of swift running waters.

Men's hearts at thy roaring
   Quiver like harebells
Smitten by hailstones,
   Smitten and shaken.

"O sages and wise men!
   O bird-hearted tremblers!
Come, I will show ye
   A shackle to bind me.

I, the lion-throated,
   The shaker of mountains!
I, the invincible,
   Lasher of oceans!

Past the horizon,
   Its ring of pale azure
Past the horizon,
   Where scurry the white clouds,

There are buds and small flowers –
   Flowers like snowflakes,
Blossoms like rain-drops,
   So small and tremulous.

These in a fetter
   Shall shackle and bind me,
Shall weigh down my shouting
   With their delicate perfume!"

But who this frail fetter
   Shall forge on an anvil,
With hammer of feather
   And anvil of velvet?

"Past the horizon
   In the palm of a valley,
Her feet in the grasses,
   There is a maiden.

She smiles on the flowers,
   They widen and redden;
She weeps on the flowers,
   They grow up and kiss her.

She breathes in their bosoms,
   They breathe back in odours;
Inarticulate homage,
   Dumb adoration.

She shall wreathe them in shackles,
   Shall weave them in fetters;
In chains shall she braid them,
   And me shall she fetter.

I, the invincible;
    March, the earth-shaker;
March, the sea-lifter;
    March, the sky-render;

March, the lion-throated.
    April, the weaver
Of delicate blossoms,
    And moulder of red buds –

Shall, at the horizon,
    Its ring of pale azure,
Its scurry of white clouds,
    Meet in the sunlight."

(1905)

The Camp of Souls

My white canoe, like the silvery air
    O'er the River of Death that darkly rolls
When the moons of the world are round and fair,
    I paddle back from the "Camp of Souls."
When the wishton-wish in the low swamp grieves
Come the dark plumes of red "Singing Leaves."

Two hundred times have the moons of spring
    Rolled over the bright bay's azure breath
Since they decked me with plumes of an eagle's wing,
    And painted my face with the "paint of death,"
And from their pipes o'er my corpse there broke
The solemn rings of the blue "last smoke."

Two hundred times have the wintry moons
    Wrapped the dead earth in a blanket white;
Two hundred times have the wild sky loons
    Shrieked in the flush of the golden light
Of the first sweet dawn, when the summer weaves
Her dusky wigwam of perfect leaves.

Two hundred moons of the falling leaf
   Since they laid my bow in my dead right hand
And chanted above me the "song of grief"
   As I took my way to the spirit land;
Yet when the swallow the blue air cleaves
Come the dark plumes of red "Singing Leaves."

White are the wigwams in that far camp,
   And the star-eyed deer on the plains are found;
No bitter marshes or tangled swamp
   In the Manitou's happy hunting-ground!
And the moon of summer forever rolls
Above the red men in their "Camp of Souls."

Blue are its lakes as the wild dove's breast,
   And their murmurs soft as her gentle note;
As the calm, large stars in the deep sky rest,
   The yellow lilies upon them float;
And canoes, like flakes of the silvery snow,
Thro' the tall, rustling rice-beds come and go.

Green are its forests; no warrior wind
   Rushes on war trail the dusk grove through,
With leaf-scalps of tall trees mourning behind;
   But South Wind, heart friend of Great Manitou,
When ferns and leaves with cool dews are wet,
Blows flowery breaths from his red calumet.

Never upon them the white frosts lie,
   Nor glow their green boughs with the "paint of
      death";
Manitou smiles in the crystal sky,
   Close breathing above them His life-strong breath
And He speaks no more in fierce thunder sound,
So near is His happy hunting-ground.

Yet often I love, in my white canoe,
   To come to the forests and camps of earth:
'Twas there death's black arrow pierced me through;
   'Twas there my red-browed mother gave me birth:
There I, in the light of a young man's dawn,
Won the lily heart of dusk "Springing Fawn."

And love is a cord woven out of life,
　And dyed in the red of the living heart;
And time is the hunter's rusty knife,
　That cannot cut the red strands apart:
And I sail from the spirit shore to scan
Where the weaving of that strong cord began.

But I may not come with a giftless hand,
　So richly I pile, in my white canoe,
Flowers that bloom in the spirit land,
　Immortal smiles of Great Manitou.
When I paddle back to the shores of earth
I scatter them over the white man's hearth.

For love is the breath of the soul set free;
　So I cross the river that darkly rolls,
That my spirit may whisper soft to thee
　Of *thine* who wait in the "Camp of Souls."
When the bright day laughs, or the wan night grieves,
Come the dusky plumes of red "Singing Leaves."

(1905)

A Harvest Song

The noon was as a crystal bowl
　The red wine mantled through;
Around it like a Viking's beard
　The red-gold hazes blew,
As tho' he quaffed the ruddy draught
　While swift his galley flew.

This mighty Viking was the Night;
　He sailed about the earth,
And called the merry harvest-time
　To sing him songs of mirth;
And all on earth or in the sea
　To melody gave birth.

The valleys of the earth were full
   To rocky lip and brim
With golden grain that shone and sang
   When woods were still and dim,
A little song from sheaf to sheaf –
   Sweet Plenty's cradle-hymn.

O gallant were the high tree-tops,
   And gay the strain they sang!
And cheerfully the moon-lit hills
   Their echo-music rang!
And what so proud and what so loud
   As was the ocean's clang!

But O the little humming song
   That sang among the sheaves!
'Twas grander than the airy march
   That rattled thro' the leaves,
And prouder, louder, than the deep,
   Bold clanging of the waves:

"The lives of men, the lives of men
   With every sheaf are bound!
We are the blessing which annuls
   The curse upon the ground!
And he who reaps the Golden Grain
   The Golden Love hath found."

(1905)

Said the West Wind

I love old earth! Why should I lift my wings,
My misty wings, so high above her breast
That flowers would shake no perfumes from their
   hearts,
And waters breathe no whispers to the shores?
I love deep places builded high with woods,
Deep, dusk, fern-closed, and starred with nodding
   blooms,
Close watched by hills, green, garlanded and tall.

On hazy wings, all shot with mellow gold,
I float, I float thro' shadows clear as glass;
With perfumed feet I wander o'er the seas,
And touch white sails with gentle finger-tips;
I blow the faithless butterfly against
The rose-red thorn, and thus avenge the rose;
I whisper low amid the solemn boughs,
And stir a leaf where not my loudest sigh
Could move the emerald branches from their calm, –
Leaves, leaves, I love ye much, for ye and I
Do make sweet music over all the earth!

I dream by glassy ponds, and, lingering, kiss
The gold crowns of their lilies one by one,
As mothers kiss their babes who be asleep
On the clear gilding of their infant heads,
Lest if they kissed the dimple on the chin,
The rose flecks on the cheek or dewy lips,
The calm of sleep might feel the touch of love,
And so be lost. I steal before the rain,
The longed-for guest of summer; as his fringe
Of mist drifts slowly from the mountain peaks,
The flowers dance to my fairy pipe and fling
Rich odours on my wings, and voices cry,
"The dear West Wind is damp, and rich with scent;
We shall have fruits and yellow sheaves for this."

At night I play amid the silver mists,
And chase them on soft feet until they climb
And dance their gilded plumes against the stars;
At dawn the last round primrose star I hide
By wafting o'er her some small fleck of cloud,
And ere it passes comes the broad, bold Sun
And blots her from the azure of the sky,
As later, toward his noon, he blots a drop
Of pollen-gilded dew from violet cup
Set bluely in the mosses of the wood.

(1905)

Laughter

Laughter wears a lilied gown –
` She is but a simple thing;
Laughter's eyes are water-brown,
Ever glancing up and down
    Like a woodbird's restless wing.

Laughter slender is and round –
    She is but a simple thing;
And her tresses fly unbound,
And about her brow are found
    Buds that blossom by Mirth's spring.

Laughter loves to praise and play –
    She is but a simple thing –
With the children small who stray
Under hedges, where the May
    Scents and blossoms richly fling.

Laughter coyly peeps and flits –
    She is but a simple thing –
Round the flower-clad door, where sits
Maid who dimples as she knits,
    Dreaming in the rosy spring.

Laughter hath light-tripping feet –
    She is but a simple thing;
Ye may often Laughter meet
In the hayfield, gilt and sweet,
    Where the mowers jest and sing.

Laughter shakes the bounteous leaves –
    She is but a simple thing –
On the village ale-house eaves,
While the angered swallow grieves
    And the rustic revellers sing.

Laughter never comes a-nigh –
    She's a wise though simple thing –
Where men lay them down to die;
Nor will under stormy sky
    Laughter's airy music ring.

(1905)

Where, Love, Art Hid?

"Love like a shadow flies."
>   – *Merry Wives of Windsor.*

"At brightest dawn I'll rise and take
   Long, ruddy lances from the sun,
And search with them each shady brake
   To see where Love hath gone.
      Love, Love, where liest thou?
      "Thou shalt not find me so."

I'll filch the brightest star on high
   And tie it to my pilgrim's staff;
And by its rays I'll onward hie
   To see where Love doth laugh.
      Love, Love, where dost thou lie?
      "Oh, not in shadows by!"

I'll climb the rainbow's rosy bridge,
   And peep the pearlèd clouds above;
I'll cling to Luna's diamond edge,
   Or I will find thee, Love!
      Love, Love, beware my net!
      "Thou shalt not find me yet."

I'll take the dandelion's crown
   And blow its silver plumes to rout;
And wheresoe'er they flutter down
   I'll seek for Love about.
      Love, shall I find thee, say?
      "Not thro' a summer's day."

I'll shake the oxlip's freckled bell,
   And toss thee from it like a bee;
The small white daisy in the dell,
   Love, shall not shelter thee.
      Love, wilt thou to me yield?
      "Nay, thou art far a-field."

I'll search the hearts of pearls down deep,
   A hundred fathoms, in the south;
Beneath a monarch's lashes peep,
    Kiss wide the rose's mouth.
      Ho! Gossip Love, I'll capture thee!
      "Nay, nay, that cannot be;
      Seek Love, and Love will flee!"

(1905)

Love's Forget-me-not

When Spring in sunny woodland lay,
   And gilded buds were sparely set
On oak tree and the thorny may,
   I gave my love a violet.
"O Love," she said, and kissed my mouth
   With one light, tender maiden kiss,
"There are no rich blooms in the south
   So fair to me as this!"

When Summer reared her haughty crest,
   We paused beneath the ruddy stars;
I placed a rose upon her breast,
   Plucked from the modest casement bars.
"O Love," she said, and kissed my mouth –
   Heart, heart, rememb'rest thou the bliss? –
"In east or west, in north or south,
   I know no rose but this!"

When Autumn raised the purple fruit
   In clusters to his bearded lips,
I laid a heartsease on the lute
   That sang beneath her finger-tips.
"O Love," she said – and fair her eyes
   Smiled thro' the dusk upon the lea –
"No heartsease glows beneath the skies
   But this thou givest me!"

When Winter wept at shaking doors,
   And holly trimmed his ermine vest,
And wild winds maddened on the moors,
   I laid a flower upon her breast.
"Dear Heart," I whispered to the clay,
   Which stilly smiled yet answered not,
"Bear thou to Heaven itself away
   True love's Forget-me-not!"

(1905)

From "Malcolm's Katie"

O Love builds on the azure sea,
   And Love builds on the golden sand,
And Love builds on the rose-winged cloud,
   And sometimes Love builds on the land!

O if Love build on sparkling sea,
   And if Love build on golden strand,
And if Love build on rosy cloud,
   To Love these are the solid land!

O Love will build his lily walls,
   And Love his pearly roof will rear
On cloud, or land, or mist, or sea —
   Love's solid land is everywhere!

(1905)

I'll Lauch to See the Year In

Gin I should live to seventeen,
   Gin Jock should live to twenty,
Gin I be lucky wi' my wheel,
   Gin mackerel be plenty,
Gin Jock's auld kizzen gies a boat,
   Gin Auntie Jean gies gearin',
Gin Uncle Dauvit gies a goat,
   I'll lauch to see the year in.

Gin Minnie gies her braw white hen,
   Gin Daddie says, "God bless her!"
Gin plenishin' be spun by then,
   Gin Grannie gies the dresser,
Gin Dugald gies the oaken kist
   (He'll no' do that, I'm fearin'),
Gin rise the sun wi'out a mist,
   I'll lauch to see the year in.

Gin kindly win's the boaties blaw,
   Gin saft the auld waves wimple,
Gin ilka net a fu' draucht draw,
   Gin plenty shews a dimple,
Gin neebors canty are an' weel,
   Gin ilka thing looks cheerin',
Gin no ane hae an empty crool,
   I'll lauch to see the year in.

Gin loups the sea on New Year's Day,
   Gin shines the red sun rarely,
Gin ilka thing comes as I say,
   Gin nature smiles sae fairly,
Gin I get Jock an' Jock gets me,
   Gin baith get plenty gearin',
Gin no' a strae should fa' our way,
   We'll lauch to see the year in.

(1905)

The Deacon and His Daughter

He saved his soul an' saved his pork
   With old time presarvation;
He didn't hold with creosote
   Or new plans uv salvation
He sed thet "works would show the man,
The smokehouse tell upon the ham."

He didn't, when he sunk a well,
   Inspect the stuns and gravel
Tew prove thet Moses wus a dunce
   Unfit fur furrin travel:
He marvelled at them works uv God –
An' broke 'em up tew mend the road.

An' when the circus cum around,
   He hitched his sleek old horses,
An' in his rattlin' waggon took
   His dimpled household forces –
The boys tew wonder at the clown
An' think his lot life's highest crown.

He wondered at the zebras wild,
   Nor knew 'em painted donkeys;
An' when he gev the boys a dime
   Fur cakes tew feed the monkeys,
He never thought, in enny shape,
He hed descended frum an ape.

An' when he saw sum shaller-pate,
   With smallest brain possession,
He uttered no filosofy
   On Natur's retrogression
Tew ancient types, by Darwin's rule;
He simply sed, "Wal, durn a fool!"

He never hed an enemy
   But once a year, tew meetin',
When he and Deacon Maybee fought
   On questions uv free seatin',
Or which should be the one t' rebuke
Pastor fur kissin' sister Luke.

His farm wus well enough, but stones
   Kind uv stern, ruthless facts is;
An' he jest made out tew save a mite
   An' pay his righteous taxes,
An' mebbe tote sum flour an' pork
Tew poor old critters past their work.

But on the neatest thing he hed
   Around the place or dwellin'
I guess he never paid a red
   Uv taxes. No mushmelon
Wus rounder, pinker, sweeter than
The old man's daughter, Minta Ann.

I've been a Philadelfy's show
   An' other sim'lar fusses,
An' seen a mighty sight uv stone
   Minarveys and Venusses,
An' Sikeys clad in flowers an' wings,
But not much show uv factory things.

I've seen the hull entire crowd
   Uv Jove's female relations,
An' I feel tew make a solemn swar
   On them thar "Lamentations,"
Thet as a sort uv gen'ral plan
I'd ruther spark with Minta Ann.

You'd ought tew see her dimpled chin,
   With one red freckle on it,
Her brown eyes glancing underneath
   Her tilted shaker bonnet:
I vow, I often did desire
They'd set the plaguey thing a-fire.

You'd ought tew hear thet thar gal sing
   On Sabbath, up tew meetin',
You'd kind uv feel high lifted up,
   Yer soul fur Heaven fleetin',
An' then, came supper, down she'd tie
Ye tew this earth with punkin pie!

I tell ye, stranger, 'twus a sight
   Fur poetry and speeches
Tew see her sittin' on the stoop
   A-peelin' scarlet peaches
Inter the kettle at her feet, –
I tell ye, 'twus a show complete.

Drip-droppin' thru the rustlin' vine
   The sunbeams cum a-flittin',
An' sort uv danced upon the floor,
   Chased by the tabby kitten;
Losh! tew see the critter's big surprise
When them beams slipped inter Minta's eyes!

An' down her brow her pretty har
   Cum curlin', crinklin', creepin'
In leetle yaller mites uv rings,
   Inter them bright eyes peepin',
Es run the tendrils uv the vine
Tew whar the merry sunbeams shine.

But losh! her smile wus drefful shy
   An' kept her white lids under;
Jest as when darkens up the sky
   An' growls away the thunder,
Them skeery speckled trout will hide
Beneath them white pond-lilies' pride.

An' then her heart, 'twas made clar thru
   Uv Californy metal,
Chock full uv things es sugar sweet
   Es a presarvin' kettle.
The beaux went crazed fur menny a mile
When I got the kettle on the bile.

The good old deacon's gone tew whar
   Thar ain't no wild contentions
On Buildin' Funds' Committees an'
   No taxes nor exemptions;
Yet still I sorter feel he preaches,
An' Minta Ann presarves my peaches.

(1905)

George Frederick Cameron (1854-1885)

George Frederick Cameron died just before his thirty-first birthday, and his poetry was published posthumously by his brother in 1887. Despite his premature death, however, Cameron did attract some attention on the Canadian poetic scene. In a letter to J. E. Wetherell, Archibald Lampman hails Cameron as "most certainly the poet of most genuine poetic energy this country has yet produced. There are half a dozen things of his that I would not give for all that the rest of us have written . . . . The poem without a title ["Ah Me! The Mighty Love"] . . . I would include in any selection of English masterpieces however restricted, and the second one, 'Standing on Tiptoe', is almost as fine."

George Frederick Cameron was born at New Glasgow, Nova Scotia on September 24, 1854, eldest son of James Cameron and his wife Jessie. He attended the local high school where he read Virgil and Cicero in the original and applied himself to the study of poetry. The family moved to Boston in 1869 and here Cameron studied law at the University of Boston, articling in a law office after 1872. However he found time for extensive literary work and contributed to a number of journals. In 1882 he returned to Canada; he entered Queen's University, and here won first prize in 1883 for the best original poem. In March of the same year he became editor of the Kingston *News*, a position he held till shortly before his death from heart failure on September 17, 1885.

In 1887 his brother Charles J. Cameron edited a collection of his poetry *Lyrics on Freedom, Love and Death*; although it was three hundred pages in length, Charles Cameron remarked in the preface that it "represents about one fourth of his life work". He promised a later collection if public response was good but this was never undertaken. George Cameron also wrote an opera *Leo, the Royal Cadet* which was set to music by Oscar F. Telgman and was performed on June 27 1889 in the Kingston Opera House and later in Ottawa, Utica, Guelph, Stratford, Woodstock and Toronto. Although the title *Lyrics on Freedom, Love and Death* suggests Cameron's central themes: politics, love, and a preoccupation with death which runs throughout his work, he is also concerned with the problem of the artist, his search for meaning and truth, as are his contemporaries Lampman and D. C. Scott in "The Piper of Arll". In his lecture "Two Canadian Poets", Lampman praises Cameron highly as "a writer of rare spontaneity" and "a poet of life . . . [whose] works ring with the truth of experience".

TEXT:

Lyrics on Freedom, Love and Death. ed. Charles J. Cameron. Kingston: Shannon, 1887.

See also:

Archibald Lampman's "Two Canadian Poets" in this text and in full in *Masks of Poetry.* Toronto: McClelland and Stewart, 1962.

A. S. Bourinot. *Five Canadian Poets*, Montreal: Quality Press, 1956.

M. J. in *Canadian Bookman* 13, 170-80 (September, 1931).

To the West Wind

West wind, come from the west land
   Fair and far!
Come from the fields of the best land
   Upon our star!

Come, and go to my sister
   Over the sea:
Tell her how much I have missed her,
   Tell her for me!

Odors of lilies and roses –
   Set them astir;
Cull them from gardens and closes, –
   Give them to her!

Say I have loved her, and love her:
   Say that I prize
Few on the earth here above her,
   Few in the skies!

Bring her, if worth the bringing,
   A brother's kiss.
Should she ask for a song of his singing,
   Give her this!

(1887)

Amoris Finis

And now I go with the departing sun:
   My day is dead and all my work is done.
No more for me the pleasant moon shall rise
   To show the splendor in my dear one's eyes;
No more the stars shall see us meet; we part
   Without a hope, or hope of hope, at heart;
For Love lies dead, and at his altar, lo,
Stands in his room, self-crowned and crested, – *Woe!*

(1887)

Passion

As when the wildfire sweeps o'er prairie wide,
   Devours the nettle choking up the way,
Breathes on the lily nodding there in pride
   And turns its plume to darkness and decay:

So o'er the soul the flame of passion goes,
   Destroys the hideous and alike the fair, –
Alike the rankest weed, the rarest rose, –
   And leaves alone a waste of ashes there.

(1887)

My Life.

All for a luckless love –
　A boyish blunder –
The heaven keeps black above,
　As Earth is under!

Tost like a leaf by the wind
　In the winter weather;
Tost by a Power unkind
　Hither and thither!

Tost as a weed on the tide
　Of a shoreless ocean!
No haven wherein to hide –
　Eternal motion!

No knowledge of whither bound –
　My courage failing:
Darkness and mist around –
　Eternal sailing!

(1879, 1887)

[Ah, Me! The Mighty Love]

Ah, me! the mighty love that I have borne
　To thee, sweet Song! A perilous gift was it
My mother gave me that September morn
　When sorrow, song, and life were at one altar lit.

A gift more perilous than the priest's: his lore
　Is all of books and to his books extends;
And what they see and know he knows – no more,
　And with their knowing all his knowing ends.

A gift more perilous than the painter's: he
   In his divinest moments only sees
The inhumanities of color, we
   Feel each and all the inhumanities.

(1885, 1887)

With All My Singing

With all my singing, I can never sing
   A gay, glad song – an honest song of mirth:
In vain my fingers seek some tender string
   Whose voice would catch the dainty ear of earth.
Why is it so? Because the fount and spring
   Of all my song was sorrow; it had birth
In gloom, and desolation, and dark hours, –
'Twas not the offspring of the happy flowers.

(1887)

Standing On Tiptoe

Standing on tiptoe ever since my youth
   Striving to grasp the future just above,
I hold at length the only future – Truth,
   And Truth is Love.

I feel as one who being awhile confined
   Sees drop to dust about him all his bars: –
The clay grows less, and, leaving it, the mind
   Dwells with the stars.

(September, 1885, 1887)

My Spring Is Over

My spring is over, all my summer past:
The autumn closes, – winter now appears:
And I, a helpless leaf before its blast,
Am whirled along amid the eternal years
To realize my hopes, – or end my fears.

(September, 1885, 1887)

Frederick George Scott (1861-1944)

Father of the contemporary Canadian poet F. R. Scott, Frederick Geoge Scott was also recognized in his day as a poet, a secondary member of the Confederation Group which included Roberts, Carman, Lampman and Scott and which came to maturity after 1867. Called "the poet of the Laurentians", Scott has written much of his best work in this region of Quebec, but his themes range from lyrics on religion, love and death to patriotic and imperial poems written during the First World War. In the Toronto *Globe* in 1916, M. O. Hammond remarked of Scott: "His work in any one field would attract attention; taken in mass it marks him as a sturdy, developing interpreter of his country and his times".

Frederick George Scott was born in Montreal in 1861 and grew up in this city where his father held the chair of anatomy at McGill University for forty years. He attended high school in Montreal, and continued on to Bishop's University in Lennoxville where he was awarded a B.A. in 1881 and an M.A. in 1884. His interest in theology led to advanced studies in King's College, London, and he was ordained deacon in the Anglican Church in 1884 and priest in 1886. His advancement in the church was steady. He served first as a curate at Coggleshall, Essex from 1886-7, then as rector in Drummondville, Quebec from 1887-96. In 1896 he became curate of St. Matthews Church, Montreal and in 1899 rector. He was made Canon of Holy Trinity Cathedral, Quebec in 1906, and Archdeacon of the Diocese of Quebec in 1925. He also served during this time as Army chaplain attached to the 8th Royal Rifles, Quebec in 1906, becoming Senior Chaplain of the first Canadian Division overseas during the First World War. He was wounded in service and was awarded a CMG in 1916 and a DSO in 1918; after the war he became the Dominion Chaplain of the army and navy veterans.

In the midst of this busy theological and military career, Scott published a number of volumes over a period of some fifty years, including fourteen books of poetry: *The Soul's Quest and Other Poems* (1888), *My Lattice and Other Poems* (1894). *The Unnamed Lake and Other Poems* (1897), *Poems Old and New* (1900), *Hymns of Empire and Other Poems* (1906), *Poems* (1910), *In the Battle Silences* (1916, *Poems* (1918), *In Sun and Shade* (1928), *New Poems* (1929), *Selected Poems* (1933), *Collected Poems* (1934), *Poems* (1936) and *Collected Poems* (1937). *Lift Up Your Hearts* (1941), a collection of poems of the Second World War, was sponsored by the Canadian Legion and royalties from the 250,000 copies were devoted to the benefit of veterans. Scott also wrote a didactic novel *Elton Hazlewood* (1891), a mystery play *Key of Life* (1907), and his reminiscences *The Great War as I Saw It* (1922), and edited a church hymnal in 1906. He received a number of honours and awards; he was elected to the Royal Society of Canada in 1900, and received a D.C.L. from his alma mater, Bishop's University in 1902, an LL.D. from McGill in 1926 and a D.D. from King's University in 1927.

In F. G. Scott's best work, Desmond Pacey notes "some of the quiet dignity of Matthew Arnold". Among these works are the simple descriptions of the Laurentian region with their sensitive record of the sights and sounds of the natural world and their impingement on the life of man; elsewhere nature is employed as setting and to evoke the mood of the poet. Scott also treats effectively the themes of love, death and religion. The most ambitious work, "Wahonomin", recalls the message of such poems as Sangster's "Lament of Shingwa-konce", Mair's "The Last Bison", or Pauline Johnson's "Silhouette", foreboding the complete destruction of a way of life by the encroachment of "civilization".

TEXT.

Poems. London: Constable, 1910.
Collected Poems. Vancouver: Clarke & Stewart, 1934.

See also:

W. P. Percival in *Leading Canadian Poets*. Toronto: Ryerson, 1948.
O. J. Stevenson in *A People's Best*. Toronto: Musson, 1927.

The Unnamed Lake

It sleeps among the thousand hills
   Where no man ever trod,
And only nature's music fills
   The silences of God.

Great mountains tower above its shore,
   Green rushes fringe its brim,
And o'er its breast for evermore
   The wanton breezes skim.

Dark clouds that intercept the sun
   Go there in Spring to weep,
And there, when Autumn days are done,
   White mists lie down to sleep.

Sunrise and sunset crown with gold
   The peaks of ageless stone,
Where winds have thundered from of old
   And storms have set their throne.

No echoes of the world afar
   Disturb it night or day,
But sun and shadow, moon and star
   Pass and repass for aye.

'Twas in the grey of early dawn
   When first the lake we spied,
And fragments of a cloud were drawn
   Half down the mountain side.

Along the shore a heron flew,
   And from a speck on high
That hovered in the deepening blue,
   We heard the fish-hawk's cry.

Among the cloud-capt solitudes,
   No sound the silence broke,
Save when, in whispers down the woods,
   The guardian mountains spoke.

Through tangled brush and dewy brake,
   Returning whence we came,
We passed in silence, and the lake
   We left without a name.

(1897)

The Mill-stream

Clear down the mountain, 'neath the arching
    green,
  And o'er mossed boulders dappled by the sun,
  With many a leap the laughing waters run.
They tumble fearless down each dark ravine,
And roam through caves where day has never
    been:
  Until, at last, the open pool is won,
  Where, by their prisoned strength, man's work
    is done
In that old mill which branching cedars screen.

Here, all day long, the massy logs, updrawn
  Against the biting saw, are loud with shrieks.
    Here, too, at night, are stars and mystery,
And nature sleeping; and, all round at dawn,
  The rugged utterance of mountain peaks
    Against the infinite silence of the sky.

(1906)

Song

(From the Italian of Guarini)

When the leaves are falling, Dearest,
  And you seek the quiet mound
Where I slumber, you will find it
  With a wealth of blossoms crowned.

Gather, then, for thy bright tresses
  Those that from my heart have sprung;
They're the love-thoughts that I spoke not,
  And the songs I left unsung.

(1906)

Moonlight

When my lady goes in beauty
   Down the moonlit ways,
All the little stars in heaven
   Sing her praise.

All the twinkling leaves together
   Whisper softly in amaze,
When my lady goes by moonlight
   Down the woodland ways.

(1929)

Estrangement

Do you remember how, one autumn night,
   We sat upon the rocks and watched the sea
In dreamlike silence while the moonlight fell
    On you and me?

How, as we lingered musing, side by side,
   A cold, white mist crept down and hid the sea
And dimmed the moon, and how the air grew chill
    Round you and me?

The mist and chill of that drear autumn night,
   When we sat silent looking on the sea,
I often think has never passed away
    From you and me.

(1882, 1888)

Love's Footprints

Love once wandered on the shore
  Where these lonely mountains stand,
And the surf for evermore
  Whitens down the waste of sand.

Here are footprints! see, he went
  By the sea's edge in his play;
Here perchance his bow was bent,
  And his target was the spray.

There he stooped and wrote his name –
  Straggling letters by the tide –
And when sunset bursts in flame
  Over shore and mountain-side,

Brightly will the letters glow,
  Golden will those footprints be,
Made by young Love long ago
  As he wandered by the sea.

(1900)

Death and the Child

Death met a little child beside the sea;
  The child was ruddy and his face was fair,
  His heart was gladdened with the keen salt
    air,
Full of the young waves' laughter and their glee.
Then Death stooped down and kissed him,
    saying: 'To thee,
  My child, will I give summers rare and bright,
  And flowers, and morns with never noon or
    night,
Or clouds to darken, if thou'lt come with me.'

Then the child gladly gave his little hand,
And walked with Death along the shining sand,
  And prattled gaily, full of hope, and smiled
As a white mist curled round him on the shore
And hid the land and sea for evermore –
  Death hath no terrors for a little child.

(1900)

By the Sea

I hear a ghostly passing bell
  In the thunder of the sea,
By day and night it tolls the knell
  Of all that is to be;
No hands have set it in its place
  Nor compassed it with bars,
It hangs beneath the dome of space
  And swings among the stars.

The silent ages come and go,
  They perish in the gloom,
But still the bell swings to and fro
  And sounds the note of doom.
The deep reverberations roll
  Far off from sea and shore,
But somewhere in my secret soul
  They sound for evermore.

(1906)

The Divinity

I peered through spaces of the air
　　At mountain peaks and glittering seas,
But though His handiwork was there,
　　I did not find my God in these.

I scoured the caverns of the skies
　　Beyond the stars which crown the pole,
Then gave up searching and my eyes
　　Beheld Him centred in my soul.

(1910)

Crucifixion

Lord, must I bear the whole of it, or none?
'Even as I was crucified, My son.'

Will it suffice if I the thorn-crown wear?
'To take the scourge My shoulders were made
　　bare.'

My hands, O Lord, must I be pierced in both?
'Twain gave I to the hammer, nothing loth,'

But surely, Lord, my feet need not be nailed?
'Had Mine not been, then love had not prevailed.'

What need I more, O Lord, to fill my part?
'Only the spear-point in thy broken heart.'

(1910)

The Wayside Cross

A wayside cross at set of day
Unto my spirit thus did say –

'O soul, my branching arms you see
Point four ways to infinity.

'One points to infinite above,
To show the height of heavenly love.

'Two point to infinite width, which shows
That heavenly love no limit knows.

'One points to infinite beneath,
To show God's love is under death.

'The four arms join, an emblem sweet
That in God's heart all loves will meet.'

I thanked the cross as I turned away
For such sweet thoughts in the twilight grey.

(1888)

Wahonomin

THE INDIANS' JUBILLEE HYMN TO THE QUEEN

Great mother! from the depths of forest wilds,
From mountain pass and burning sunset plain,
We, thine unlettered children of the woods,
Upraise to thee the everlasting hymn
Of nature, language of the skies and seas,
Voice of the birds and sighings of the pine
In wintry wastes. We know none other tongue,
Nor the smooth speech that, like the shining leaves,
Hides the rough stems beneath. We bring our song,

Wood-fragrant, rough, yet autumn-streaked with love,
And lay it as a tribute at thy feet.
But should it vex thee thus to hear us sing,
Sad in the universal joy that crowns
This year of years, and shouldst thou deem our voice
But death-cry of the ages that are past,
Bear with us – say, 'My children of the woods,
In language learnt from bird and wood and stream,
From changing moons and stars and misty lakes,
Pour forth their love, and lay it at my feet;
The voice is wild and strange, untuned to ear
Of majesty, ill-timed to fevered pulse
Of this young age, and meteor-souls that flash
New paths upon night's dome; yet will I hear
This singing of my children ere they die.'

Great mother! thou art wise, they say, and good,
And reignest like the moon in autumn skies,
The world about thy feet. We have not seen
Thy face, nor the wild seas of life that surge
Around thy throne; but we have stood by falls,
Deep-shadowed in the silence of the woods,
And heard the water-thunders, and have said,
'Thus is the voice of men about our Queen.
What is the red man but the forest stream,
The cry of screech-owl in the desert wilds?
This flood that overflows the hills and plains
Is not for us. Back, Westward, Northward, ay,
Up to eternal winter 'neath the stars,
Our path must be in silence, till the snows
And sun and wind have bleached our children's
    bones.
The red must go; the axe and plough and plane
Are not for him. We perish with the pine,
We vanish in the silence of the woods;
Our footsteps, like the war-trail in the snow,
Grow fainter while the new spring buds with life.'

Great mother! the white faces came with words
Of love and hope, and pointed to the skies,
And in the sunrise splendour set the throne
Of the Great Spirit, and upon the cross
Showed us His Son, and asked a throne for Him.
Their speech was music; but in camp at night
We brooded o'er the matter round the fire,
The shadowy pines about us, and the stars,
Set in the silent heavens, looking down.
We brooded o'er the matter days and years,
For thus each thought and thus each spake in words:
'We children of the woods have lived and died
In these our forests, since the first moon tipped
Their thousand lakes and rivers with her beams,
Pale silver in the fading sky of even.
Our fathers' faces kindled in the glow
Of setting suns; they read the starlit sky;
They heard the Spirit's breathing on the storm,
And on the quaking earth they felt His tread;
But never yet the story of His Son
Was wafted to them from the sighing woods,
Or bird or stream. Our fathers' God is ours;
And as for these new words, we watch and wait.'

Great mother! we have waited days and years,
Through spring and summer – summer, autumn, spring;
Brooding in silence, for anon we dreamed
A bird's voice in our hearts half sung, ''Tis true.'
We listened and we watched the pale-face come,
When, lo! new gods came with them – gods of iron
And fire, that shook the forests as they rushed,
Filling with thunder and loud screeching, plains,
Mountains, and woods, and dimming with their
   breath
The shining skies. These new gods, who were they,
That came devouring all, and blackening earth
And sky with smoke and thunder? We knew not,
But fled in terror further from the face
Of these white children and their gods of iron;
We heard no more their story of the Son,
And words of love. Their own lives were not love,
But war concealed and fire beneath the ash.
Thus ever now the burden of our speech –
We perish with the pine tree and the bird,
We vanish in the silence of the woods,
The white man's hunting-ground, it is not ours;

We care not for his gods of iron and fire;
Our home is in the trackless wilds, the depths
Of mountain solitudes, by starlit lakes,
By noise of waters in the unchanging woods.
Great mother! we have wondered that thy sons,
Thy pale sons, should have left thy side and come
To these wild plains, and sought the haunts of bears
And red men. Why their battle with the woods?
Whither they go upon their gods of iron,
Out of the golden sunrise to the mists
Of purple evening in the setting west?
Their lives have scarce as many moons as ours,
Nor happier are. We know not what they seek;
For death's cold finger chills their fevered life,
As in the wilds he stills the meanest worm,
And death flies with them over all their paths,
And waits them in the heart of wildest waste;
They cannot break his power. Forgive these thoughts
If, as they rise like mists, they dim the gold
That zones thy brow. They came to us at night,
As we have sat in council round the fire;
They seemed the echo of the sighing pines
Far in our soul. One evening rose a chief,
White-headed, bowed with years, one hand on
     staff,
One on death's arm, preparing for the way.
'My sons,' he said, 'these people are not wise.
We bide our time, and they will pass away;
Then shall the red man come like bird in spring,
And build the broken camp, and hunt and fish
In his old woods. These people pass away;
For I have thought through many nights and days,
And wondered what they seek; and now I know,
And knowing, say these people are not wise.
They found these plains beneath the burning west,
And westward, ever westward, still they press,
Seeking the shining meadows of the land
Where the sun sleeps, and, folded 'neath his wings,
The happy spirits breathe eternal day.
But I have lived through five score changing years,
And I have talked with wintry-headed chiefs,
And I have heard that kingdom is not reached
Through woods and plains, but by the bridge of death.
This people is not wise: we bide our time.'

Great mother! they have told us that the snows
Of fifty winters sleep about thy throne,
And buds of spring now blossom with sweet breath
Beneath thy tread. They tell us of the sea,
And other lands, where other children dwell;
Of mighty cities and the gleam of gold,
Of empires wider than the shining plains
Viewed from giant hill, that lift thy throne above
The clouded mountain-tops. They tell us, too,
Of wonders in the home of man; of gods
Of iron and fire made servants, and of fire
Snatched from the clouds to flash man's swiftest
     thought;
But these are not for us. The forest flower
Droops in the haunts of man; it needs the sky,
And smokeless air, and glances of the sun
Through rustling leaves. We perish with the woods;
The plains are all before thee. Send thy sons
To plant and build, and drive their flashing gods,
Startling the forests, till, like ocean's bounds,
Thine empire rolls in splendour from wide east
To widest west, broad fields of gold for thee
And thy white children; but our spirits wait
Amid the silent ages, and we pass
To where our fathers dwell, by silent streams,
And hunt in trackless wilds through cloudless days.
The wheels of thy great empire, as it moves
From east to west, from south to icy north,
Crush us to earth. We perish with the woods.
Great mother, if the changing moons have brought
Thee nearer to the darksome bridge that spans
The gulf between this and the eternal day,
If thy path and thy children's be the same,
And thy feet follow where thy fathers went,
Perchance thy soul upon earth's utmost verge,
The eternal sky about thee, and the deeps
Unfathomable beyond – perchance thy soul,
Grown weary with the fever of thy life,
May yearn for song of bird, and sighing pine,
And silent meditation of the woods;
Perchance, when, looking back from infinite skies
To restless man, thy soul, too, echoes, 'Why?'
'Where?' and 'Whither?' and thy heart may love
This death-song of thy children, ere they pass
With bird and forest to the silent land.
Perchance the white face told us what was true,

And love and hope wait by the throne of God.
The ruffled lake gives out but broken gleams
Of the clear stars above; so, restless life
May be the troubled reflex of the skies.
The world rolls onward, ever on and on,
Through clouded vast and moans of dying years,
Into the depths of sunset; but the light
Blinds our dim eyes, we cannot see the goal.
The spirit of the world is not for us;
We perish with the pine tree and the bird;
We bow our heads in silence. We must die.

(1888)

William Wilfred Campbell (1858-1918)*

Among the first generation of poets to grow up in Canada after Confederation, William Wilfred Campbell was born two or three years before the major "Confederation Poets" Roberts, Carman, Lampman and D. C. Scott. Campbell is less known than these contemporaries (indeed friends, for he worked in the Civil Service with Lampman and Scott); yet he has a wider range than any of them except Roberts, as a dramatist, poet, novelist, short-story writer and critic.

William Wilfred Campbell was born in June 1858 in Berlin, Ontario (now Kitchener) where his father was a clergyman of the Church of England. He grew up in Farmersville north of the St. Lawrence, and in Stafford and Meaford; finally in 1872 the family settled in Wiarton on the Bruce Peninsula. Here Campbell attended the Owen Sound High School and subsequently taught at Zion and later at Purple Valley. Intending to follow his grandfather and father into the ministry, he entered Wycliffe College at the University of Toronto, and then the Episcopal Divinity School in Cambridge, Massachusetts. Upon ordination in 1886, he served first in West Claremont, Massachusetts, then in 1888 in St. Stephen, New Brunswick, and in 1890 in Southhampton on Lake Huron.

In May of 1891, however, he left the church, moved to Ottawa and joined the Civil Service, first in the Department of Railways and Canals, and in 1893 in the Department of Militia and Defence, and here he met Lampman and Duncan Campbell Scott. In 1908 Campbell was transferred to the Dominion Archives and in 1917 was commissioned to write the history of the Imperial Munitions Board in Canada, but a cold contracted in December developed into pneumonia and he died on New Year's Day, 1918:

Campbell's literary career began early. During university he contributed both prose and poetry to *The Varsity* and later in Massachusetts he published in *Harper's Monthly* and the *Atlantic*; here he met Oliver Wendell Holmes who encouraged him in his literary work. He published five books of poetry: *Snowflakes and Sunbeams* (1888), *Lake Lyrics and Other Poems* (1889), *The Dread Voyage and Other Poems* (1893), *Beyond the Hills of Dream* (1899) and *Sagas of Vaster Britain* (1914), as well as his *Collected Poems* (1905). A second *Collected Poems* appeared posthumously in 1923 and included poems planned for a sixth volume. He also wrote a series of dramas: "Mordred"

---

* These dates are not the traditional ones ascribed to Campbell's life but are derived from the evidence of Professor Klinck in his study, *Wilfred Campbell, op. cit.*

and "Hildebrand" (1895) and "Daulac" and "Morning", published with the first two works in *Poetic Tragedies* (1908), as well as several unpublished plays, "Brockenfield", Robespierre", "Sanio" and "The Admiral's Daughter", and three novels *Richard Frizell* (in *The Christian Guardian* 1901), *Ian of the Oracdes or The Armourer of Girnigoe* (1906), and *A Beautiful Rebel: A Romance of the War of 1812* (1909). Campbell also wrote several prose works: *The Beauty, History, Romance and Mystery of the Canadian Lake Region* (1910), *The Scotsman in Canada* (1911) and the text for Mower Martin's colour illustrations in *Canada* (1907). He edited *The Oxford Book of Canadian Verse* in 1914 and *Poems of Loyalty by British and Canadian Authors* in the same year. In 1894 Campbell was elected to the Royal Society of Canada and became Vice-President in 1900, President in 1901, and Secretary from 1903 to 1911. He received a Doctor of Laws in 1906 from Aberdeen University.

Known as "the Canadian Wordsworth", Campbell wrote his best poems on his own native Lake District, in the area of the Bruce Peninsula which lies between Georgian Bay and Lake Huron. These poems illustrate his claim in the introduction to the *Collected Poems* that "simplicity and directness are essential to the highest class of verse" and anticipate the treatment of landscape by his successors, A. J. M. Smith and F. R. Scott. His poetry touches on many other themes as well, on politics and patriotism, on nature and art, on society, love and death. The literary comments in "At the Mermaid Inn" indicate his keen critical mind. These columns, which appeared in the Toronto *Globe* from 1892 to 1893 under the initials of Campbell, Lampman and D. C. Scott, represent, with Lampman's lecture "Two Canadian Poets", the best of Canadian criticism in this period.

TEXT:

The Poems of Wilfred Campbell. Toronto: Briggs, 1905.
At the Mermaid Inn. ed. Arthur S. Bourinot. Ottawa: Bourinot, 1957.

See also:
C. F. Klinck. *Wilfred Campbell; A Study in Late Provincial Victorianism.* Toronto: Ryerson, 1942.

To the Lakes

Blue, limpid, mighty, restless lakes,
   God's mirrors underneath the sky;
Low rimmed in woods and mists, where wakes,
   Through murk and moon, the marsh-bird's cry.

Where ever on, through drive and drift,
   'Neath blue and grey, through hush and moan,
Your ceaseless waters ebb and lift,
   Past shores of century-crumbling stone.

And under ever-changing skies,
   Swell, throb, and break on kindling beach;
Where fires of dawn responsive rise,
   In answer to your mystic speech.

Past lonely haunts of gull and loon,
   Past solitude of land-locked bays,
Whose bosoms rise to meet the moon
   Beneath their silvered film of haze.

Where mists and fogs – in ghostly bands,
   Vague, dim, moon-clothed in spectral white –
Drift in from far-off haunted lands,
   Across the silences of night.

(1889)

Lake Huron

(OCTOBER.)

Miles and miles of lake and forest,
Miles and miles of sky and mist,
Marsh and shoreland where the rushes
Rustle, wind and water kissed;
Where the lake's great face is driving,
Driving, drifting into mist.

Miles and miles of crimson glories,
Autumn's wondrous fires ablaze;
Miles of shoreland, red and golden,
Drifting into dream and haze;
Dreaming where the woods and vapours
Melt in myriad misty ways.

Miles and miles of lake and forest,
Miles and miles of sky and mist;
Wild birds calling, where the rushes
Rustle, wind and water kissed;
Where the lake's great face is driving,
Driving, drifting into mist.

(1889)

To the Ottawa

Out of the northern wastes, lands of winter and death,
    Regions of ruin and age, spaces of solitude lost;
        You wash and thunder and sweep,
            And dream and sparkle and creep,
                Turbulent, luminous, large,
                Scion of thunder and frost.

Down past woodland and waste, lone as the haunting of
            even,
    Of shriveled and wind-moaning night when Winter
            hath wizened the world;
        Down past hamlet and town,
            By marshes, by forests that frown,
                Brimming their desolate banks,
                Your tides to the ocean are hurled.

(1899)

An October Evening

The woods are haggard and lonely,
  The skies are hooded for snow,
The moon is cold in heaven,
  And the grasses are sere below.

The bearded swamps are breathing
  A mist from meres afar,
And grimly the Great Bear circles
  Under the pale Pole Star.

There is never a voice in heaven,
  Nor ever a sound on earth,
Where the spectres of winter are rising
  Over the night's wan girth.

There is slumber and death in the silence,
  There is hate in the winds so keen;
And the flash of the north's great sword-blade
  Circles its cruel sheen.

The world grows agèd and wintry,
  Love's face peakèd and white;
And death is kind to the tired ones
  Who sleep in the north to-night.

(1893)

The Flight of the Gulls

Out over the spaces,
The sunny, blue places,
  Of water and sky;
Where day on day merges
  In nights that reel by;
Through calms and through surges,
Through stormings and lulls,
O, follow,
      Follow,
The flight of the gulls.

With wheeling and reeling,
With skimming and stealing,
  We wing with the wind,
Out over the heaving
Of grey waters, leaving
  The lands far behind,
And dipping ships' hulls.
O, follow,
      Follow,
The flight of the gulls.

Up over the thunder
Of reefs that lie under,
  And dead sailors' graves;
Like snowflakes in summer,
Like blossoms in winter,
  We float on the waves,
And the shore-tide that pulls.
O, follow,
      Follow,
The flight of the gulls.

Would you know the wild vastness
Of the lakes in their fastness,
   Their heaven's blue span;
Then come to this region,
   From the dwellings of man.
Leave the life-care behind you,
That nature annuls,
And follow,
       Follow,
The flight of the gulls.

(1889)

Wind

I am Wind, the deathless dreamer
   Of the summer world;
Tranced in snows of shade and shimmer,
   On a cloud scarp curled.

Fluting through the argent shadow
   And the molten shine
Of the golden, lonesome summer
   And its dreams divine.

All unseen, I walk the meadows,
   Or I wake the wheat,
Speeding o'er the tawny billows
   With my phantom feet.

All the world's face, hushed and sober,
   Wrinkles where I run;
Turning sunshine into shadow,
   Shadow into sun.

Stirring soft the breast of waters
   With my winnowing wings,
Waking the grey ancient wood
   From hushed imaginings.

Where the blossoms drowse in languors,
   Or a vagrant sips,
Lifting nodding blade or petal
   To my cooling lips;

Far from gloom of shadowed mountain,
   Surge of sounding sea,
Bud and blossom, leaf and tendril,
   All are glad of me.

Loosed in sunny deeps of heaven,
   Like a dream, I go,
Guiding light my genie-driven
   Flocks, in herds of snow; –

Ere I moor them o'er the thirsting
   Woods and fields beneath,
Dumbly yearning, from their burning
   Dream of parchèd death.

Not a sorrow do I borrow
   From the golden day,
Not a shadow holds the meadow
   Where my footsteps stray;

Light and cool, my kiss is welcome
   Under sun and moon,
To the weary vagrant wending
   Under parchèd noon;

To the languid, nodding blossom
   In its moonlit dell,
All earth's children sad and yearning
   Know and love me well.

Without passion, without sorrow,
   Driven in my dream,
Through the season's trance of sleeping
   Cloud and field and stream; –

Haunting woodlands, lakes and forests,
   Seas and clouds impearled,
I am Wind, the deathless dreamer
   Of the summer world.

(1905)

Return No More!

Return no more, O splendid sun,
    Sweet days come back no more:
Bring back no more the budding hours,
    The springtime to my door.

The calling bird, the wakening brook
    Make mock upon mine ear:
For she who loved them with me then
    Went out with yesteryear.

Fold, fold the year for aye in snows,
    Howl, Winter, by my door:
For she, my rose, my bloom of life,
    Is snow for evermore.

(1905)

From *At The Mermaid Inn*

(SATURDAY, MARCH 12, 1892)

In another place I have referred to the lack of interest in the national
literature in our universities and colleges. Now, all intellectual men
will admit that this is a grave condition of things, to say the least. We
all know that the ideal university ought to be the centre of the best
culture and aspirations of the growing national life, and it is to them
that we look for the coming thought and inspiration that is to make or
mar the future. It is true of all great foreign seats of learning. How
about Canada? I would like to ask some of our most ardent patriots –
some of those who are so sure of our "certain glorious future" – do
they know how many professors of literature and history there are in
our many colleges who are deeply imbued with the national spirit;
who are truly Canadians in birth, hope, sympathy and education? If
we have not been merely playing at nation-building this is a grave and
all-important question, and will go far towards solving the much-
bemoaned question – the Canadian contempt and lack of feeling for a
Canadian literature and nationality. The younger Canadians who have

been born on Canadian soil will be put off no longer with indifference or contempt. Even the most ardent believer in the unity of the empire must admit that we are no longer mere colonists. Canada for the Canadian must be the first thing now, or else we must reluctantly admit that we have no country at all; and God help the young Canadian who has to bitterly admit that without any fault of his own he is "a man without a country."

(SATURDAY, JUNE 11, 1892)

There are two kinds of poetry that may develop in a country, one born of the soil, and yet dependent on universal sympathy for its audience; the other largely of local growth, and the result of the various vicissitudes of national development. They may both be great in their way, but the latter is the most certain to acquire a quick sympathy. It is patriotic, cast in a large and heroic mould, and a necessary part of the pulse-beat of the day. Such a school was the great New England one of the era prior to and following the civil war. It was human and popular, and the writers were necessarily strong men, with large human instincts and enthusiasms. But it might be said that the time made them as much as they helped to make the time, and that much of their largeness of mould and high ethical vision was due to the high pitch of the national spirit at the time they wrote. Then again, their work contained much sentiment that was merely local and passing, but of no effect now when the community is not pitched to appreciate it. They had a note that was impossible in a less heroic day, but it carried them beyond the natural which endures, and so rendered their work necessarily ephemeral. Much of the work of Whittier, Longfellow and Lowell is of this class, and, as literature of immediate interest, perished with the passing of the time and events that gave it being. When we go back to the works of these poets to find poems of enduring beauty on subjects that might be treated about, and have been treated about, in all ages of our literature, we find that what they have left is small indeed. If we look for complete poems that will rank with the old English masterpieces we have to be chary in our choice. Longfellow has many tender and heroic tales in verse, and his Hiawatha, while not original in construction, is almost an epic, but it has not that haunting beauty of expression to be found in the best work of many of the greater poets. It is diffuse and full of mannerisms, and grows tiresome after much repeating. The opening and closing lines of Evangeline are fine, but the poem as a whole also is diffuse, and lacks solidity even in the nature descriptions, for which there was great scope given. It is a decided failure as a great poem, if not as a story, and much of the charm lies in the pathos of the incident embodied. Many of his shorter pieces are by far his best. A noted reader for a famous New England publishing house told me that he always considered Longfellow did his best work in "Voices of the Night," his first small published volume, and I think he was right, though for pure beauty and simplicity, in my opinion, "The Wreck of the Hesperus" is his finest bit of work. This poem, while not by any means his most ambitious attempt, is such as a poet might accomplish in any age, even of less heroic pitch than that in which he wrote. To Whittier and Lowell this test is even more applicable than to Longfellow. Freedom was the great inspiration that gave the key-note to both, and yet poems like "Snowbound", "In School Days" and "Maud Muller" are the gems that one leaves to posterity, while the other will endure in such poems of deep insight as "Extreme Unction," and nature descriptions as found in "The Dandelion," and in "Indian Summer." The former class of verse, which I mentioned at the beginning of this article, is that produced in an unheroic age, such as ours is to-day in Canada, when the ethical pulse is even below the normal, certainly not above it, and when to be a true poet one must be a born singer, without the aid of any unusually strenuous environment to inspire the song. This class of singers run no great chance of being overrated in their generation. They may leave no lofty epics or funeral paeons to mark the historical eras, but their note, if true, is liable to be deep and lasting. They are interpreters rather than chroniclers, and their message from humanity or nature, or from both, if they are great enough, is sincere and direct. There is a shallow idea that the length of a poem is the test of a poet's greatness. But, on the contrary, most of the greater poets have written at the most half a dozen poems, and most of them less than a hundred lines, that have given them their claims to immortality. The greatest epics in all languages are but, as some one said of Milton's "Paradise Lost," rare cases of beauty in a desert of verbiage. Like in all other cults, there is no end of writing and of the making of books, and happy is the man who has produced one poem that can be classed with those of even a century's endurance.

(SATURDAY, DECEMBER 3RD, 1892)

Now and then, when I meet in any of our literary journals that hysterical shriek, "Have we a literature?" I turn in my despair to that elaborate compendium, "The Songs of the Great Dominion," which is regarded by many as containing the canon of the Canadian Parnassus. And if I do not emerge therefrom quite as comforted and refreshed as I ought to be, I do not need to be asked why, save by those who have not perused the volume. So far as heroic labor is concerned, Mr. Lighthall deserves the place he has made for himself as the latest patron of all persons living in the Dominion who at any time or other have been ambitious to express themselves in rhyme, the most important of which, at least judged from his patriotic standpoint, he has collected into a volume. No one knows now better than Mr. Lighthall does, that not more than a dozen of the sixty names mentioned in his anthology have ever laid serious claim to real poetical achievement, and that certainly not more than half that number have any title to lengthy remembrance even in Canada. The serious objections to be taken to this work, and they are grave objections, aside from the utter lack of literary standard observed in the volume, are that true Canadian literature as it now exists is neither represented nor even foreshadowed in its pages and that Canada is represented as a crude colony, whose literature, if it could be called by such a name, is merely associated with superficial canoe and carnival songs, backwoods and Indian tales told in poor rhyme, and all tied together by pseudo-patriotic hurrahs, which are about as representative of our true nationality as they are of literature. Now, it is far from my purpose to cast any slur on a Canadian literary undertaking, and Mr. Lighthall, as a sincere and high-minded patriot, as a literary man of lofty ideals, commands our respect and serious consideration, and it is not in any carping spirit that I approach his work at this date. But, at the same time, we have a serious question to consider, if Mr. Lighthall's anthology is to be considered of any importance at all, and that question is the fair representation of our best literature both abroad and in our own country. As far as Canada is concerned, Mr. Lighthall's anthology might even at this day be regarded as obsolete, in the light of the remarkable strides our literature has taken. But when we *remember that this work is being sold in England* and goes into the hands of cultured English men and women as representative of our best work and our claim for rank in the literature of the day, we cannot help but feel that we are being imposed upon, if such a term is not too hard under the circumstances. No wonder that *Sir Charles Dilke, on reading the book,* set Canadian literature down as even inferior to that of Australia, while the truth is that as far as culture is concerned alone we rank with the best young writers to-day in the language. If editors of anthologies only knew that it is no compliment to an author, and often a serious injury to his prospects, to be represented by his poorest work, they would be more serious and unbiassed in their selections. It is very unfair to a number of authors to judge them all by the subject matter, as Mr. Lighthall has done. The writer who has no mere local interest has no prominence in this book. The result is a false basic for judgment and a general foreign misunderstanding as to our literature. To give one instance of the peculiar misrepresentation, the one writer who is sufficiently accentuated to raise him from the promiscuous heap is spoken of as "poet and canoeist," while the fact that he is a professor in a college is cast altogether into the shade.*

Note: *He refers to C. G. D. Roberts.—Sir C. W. Dilke was proprietor of *The Athenaeum.* See *Songs of the Great Dominion* selected and edited by W. D. Lighthall, Montreal 1889.

Pauline Johnson (1861-1913)

"The sole poetic voice of the Indian people of Canada", as she has been called by Marcus Van Steen, Pauline Johnson was hailed in her day both nationally and internationally as a poet of dual race and of outstanding talent. In 1913 the English critic Theodore Watts-Dunton remarked "Her death is not only a great loss to those who knew and loved her; it is a great loss to Canadian literature and to the Canadian nation. I must think that she will hold a memorable place among poets in virtue of her descent and also in virtue of the work she has left behind."

Born on March 10, 1861 in Brantford, Ontario, Pauline Johnson was the fourth child of Chief George Johnson and of Emily Howells, sister-in-law of the Anglican missionary on the Brantford Reserve and related to the novelist W. D. Howells. Although she declared a love for native customs, Pauline grew up in very different circumstances to those of most Indian girls. The elegant house "Chiefswood", which her father built on the banks of the Grand River as a present for his bride, boasted a library filled with the best books. Pauline's mother, it is claimed, read Byron and Keats to her children instead of Mother Goose, and before she was twelve, Pauline had read all of Scott and Longfellow, and much of Shakespeare, Byron and Emerson. She was educated largely at home but also attended the day school on the reserve for three years and Brantford Collegiate Institute from 1877-9, at the same time as Sara Jeannette Duncan. The years from 1879 to 1884 she spent quietly at home, reading, writing and visiting. Then on the death of her father in 1884, she moved with her mother and sister to Brantford where Evelyn took a job with the Indian office and Pauline attempted to make a living by her pen. In 1892 she began a series of public performances of her poetry which would last until 1909 and take her across Canada and the United States and into the concert halls and drawing-rooms of London. In 1897 she was joined by Walter McRaye who recited the poetry of W. H. Drummond just then coming into vogue. It was Miss Johnson's practice to appear during the first half of the performance in native dress and in the second half, in evening gown, to signify her dual inheritance.

Pauline hoped to leave the stage after several years, but the death of her mother in 1898 and a broken engagement in the same year left her unsettled, and for the next decade she spent a large part of her time on tour. In 1909 she finally retired and settled in Vancouver. Here she made many friends, in particular Chief Joe of the Capilano Tribe who related to her various tales of Squamish custom and tradition. In May of 1912,

Pauline Johnson entered a private hospital in Vancouver and died the following year.

Pauline's first poems were published in New York magazines but she received encouragement from Charles G. D. Roberts, at that time literary editor of *The Week*, and he brought out her first poems to appear in Canada. W. D. Lighthall included two poems in his *Songs of the Great Dominion* and these received high praise by the English critic Theodore Watts-Dunton. Her first collection of poetry, *The White Wampum,* appeared in 1895 and her second *Canadian-Born* in 1903. *Flint and Feather,* her collected poems (1912), was a selection by the ladies of the I.O.D.E. of her poems already in print. It is believed that a number of love poems were destroyed on her death by her sister and her literary executor, Walter McRaye. Pauline also published a collection of the tales recounted to her by Chief Joe, *Legends of Vancouver* (1911), and a collection of boys' stories, *The Shagganappi* (1912). *The Moccasin Maker*, a biography of her mother's childhood and her early life, appeared after her death, in 1913.

Despite her Indian inheritance, Johnson shares with the Canadian poets of her generation the strong influence of Wordsworth, Keats and Shelley and of their successors Tennyson and Swinburne. Many of the poems are descriptions of landscape which, like those of Carman, evoke a general emotion or mood rather than a precise picture and here, as in Carman's poems, the rhythm is often predominant. Even the Indian poems are not without evidence of her British education, although much of the material and tone is derived from the Indian tales and legends narrated to her by her grandfather Smoke Johnson, himself a noted orator. A number of these poems recall earlier narratives such as Sangster's "The Lament of Shingwakonce" or his "Taapookaa: A Huron Legend", or the works of her contemporary Duncan Campbell Scott and of Frederick George Scott in his "Wahonomin".

TEXT:

Flint and Feather. Toronto: Musson, 1912.

See also:

Walter McRaye. *Pauline Johnson and Her Friends.* Toronto: Ryerson, 1967.

Marcus Van Steen. *Pauline Johnson: Her Life and Work.* Toronto: Musson, 1965.

The Song My Paddle Sings

West wind blow from your prairie nest?
Blow from the mountains, blow from the west.
The sail is idle, the sailor too;
O! wind of the west, we wait for you.
Blow, blow!
I have wooed you so,
But never a favour you bestow.
You rock your cradle the hills between,
But scorn to notice my white lateen.

I stow the sail, unship the mast:
I wooed you long but my wooing's past;
My paddle will lull you into rest.
O! drowsy wind of the drowsy west,
Sleep, sleep,
By your mountain steep,
Or down where the prairie grasses sweep!
Now fold in slumber your laggard wings,
For soft is the song my paddle sings.

August is laughing across the sky,
Laughing while paddle, canoe and I,
Drift, drift,
Where the hills uplift
On either side of the current swift.

The river rolls in its rocky bed;
My paddle is plying its way ahead;
Dip, dip,
While the waters flip
In foam as over their breast we slip.

And oh, the river runs swifter now;
The eddies circle about my bow.
Swirl, swirl!
How the ripples curl
In many a dangerous pool awhirl!

And forward far the rapids roar,
Fretting their margin for evermore.
Dash, dash,
With a mighty crash,
They seethe, and boil, and bound, and splash.

Be strong, O paddle! be brave, canoe!
The reckless waves you must plunge into.
Reel, reel.
On your trembling keel,
But never a fear my craft will feel.

We've raced the rapid, we're far ahead!
The river slips through its silent bed.
Sway, sway,
As the bubbles spray
And fall in tinkling tunes away.

And up on the hills against the sky,
A fir tree rocking its lullaby,
Swings, swings,
Its emerald wings,
Swelling the song that my paddle sings.

(1895)

Marshlands

A thin wet sky, that yellows at the rim,
And meets with sun-lost lip the marsh's brim.

The pools low lying, dank with moss and mould,
Glint through their mildews like large cups of gold.

Among the wild rice in the still lagoon,
In monotone the lizard shrills his tune.

The wild goose, homing, seeks a sheltering,
Where rushes grow, and oozing lichens cling.

Late cranes with heavy wing, and lazy flight,
Sail up the silence with the nearing night.

And like a spirit, swathed in some soft veil,
Steals twilight and its shadows o'er the swale.

Hushed lie the sedges, and the vapours creep,
Thick, grey and humid, while the marshes sleep.

(1895)

Harvest Time

Pillowed and hushed on the silent plain,
Wrapped in her mantle of golden grain,

Wearied of pleasuring weeks away,
Summer is lying asleep to-day, –

Where winds come sweet from the wild-rose briers
And the smoke of the far-off prairie fires;

Yellow her hair as the golden rod,
And brown her cheeks as the prairie sod;

Purple her eyes as the mists that dream
At the edge of some laggard sun-drowned stream;

But over their depths the lashes sweep,
For Summer is lying to-day asleep.

The north wind kisses her rosy mouth,
His rival frowns in the far-off south,

And comes caressing her sunburnt cheek,
And Summer awakes for one short week, –

Awakes and gathers her wealth of grain,
Then sleeps and dreams for a year again.

(1903)

Fire-Flowers

And only where the forest fires have sped,
   Scorching relentlessly the cool north lands,
A sweet wild flower lifts its purple head,
And, like some gentle spirit sorrow-fed,
   It hides the scars with almost human hands.

And only to the heart that knows of grief,
   Of desolating fire, of human pain,
There comes some purifying sweet belief,
Some fellow-feeling beautiful, if brief.
   And life revives, and blossoms once again.

(1903)

Where Leaps the Ste. Marie

I

WHAT dream you in the night-time
   When you whisper to the moon?
What say you in the morning?
   What do you sing at noon?
When I hear your voice uplifting,
Like a breeze through branches sifting,
And your ripples softly drifting
   To the August airs a-tune.

II

Lend me your happy laughter,
   Ste. Marie, as you leap;
Your peace that follows after
   Where through the isles you creep.
Give to me your splendid dashing,
Give your sparkles and your splashing,
Your uphurling waves down crashing,
   Then, your aftermath of sleep.

(1903)

Low Tide at St. Andrews

(NEW BRUNSWICK)

The long red flats stretch open to the sky,
Breathing their moisture on the August air.
The seaweeds cling with flesh-like fingers where
The rocks give shelter that the sands deny;
And wrapped in all her summer harmonies
St. Andrews sleeps beside her sleeping seas.

The far-off shores swim blue and indistinct,
Like half-lost memories of some old dream.
The listless waves that catch each sunny gleam
Are idling up the waterways land-linked,
And, yellowing along the harbour's breast,
The light is leaping shoreward from the west.

And naked-footed children, tripping down,
Light with young laughter, daily come at eve
To gather dulse and sea clams and then heave
Their loads, returning laden to the town,
Leaving a strange grey silence when they go, –
The silence of the sands when tides are low.

(1903)

The Birds' Lullaby

I

Sing to us, cedars; the twilight is creeping
  With shadowy garments, the wilderness through;
All day we have carolled, and now would be
        sleeping,
  So echo the anthems we warbled to you;
    While we swing, swing,
    And your branches sing,
And we drowse to your dreamy whispering.

II

Sing to us, cedars; the night-wind is sighing,
  Is wooing, is pleading, to hear you reply;
And here in your arms we are restfully lying,
  And longing to dream to your soft lullaby;
    While we swing, swing,
    And your branches sing,
  And we drowse to your dreamy whispering.

III

Sing to us, cedars; your voice is so lowly,
  Your breathing so fragrant, your branches so
        strong;
Our little nest-cradles are swaying so slowly,
  While zephyrs are breathing their slumberous
        song.
    And we swing, swing,
    While your branches sing,
  And we drowse to your dreamy whispering.

(1895)

Lullaby of the Iroquois

Little brown baby-bird, lapped in your nest,
    Wrapped in your nest,
    Strapped in your nest,
Your straight little cradle-board rocks you to rest;
    Its hands are your nest;
    Its bands are your nest;
It swings from the down-bending branch of the oak;
You watch the camp flame, and the curling grey
        smoke;
But, oh, for your pretty black eyes sleep is best, –
Little brown baby of mine, go to rest.

Little brown baby-bird swinging to sleep,
    Winging to sleep,
    Singing to sleep,
Your wonder-black eyes that so wide open keep,
    Shielding their sleep,
    Unyielding to sleep,
The heron is homing, the plover is still,
The night-owl calls from his haunt on the hill,
Afar the fox barks, afar the stars peep, –
Little brown baby of mine, go to sleep.

(1903)

The Corn Husker

Hard by the Indian lodges, where the bush
    Breaks in a clearing, through ill-fashioned fields,
She comes to labour, when the first still hush
    Of autumn follows large and recent yields.

Age in her fingers, hunger in her face,
    Her shoulders stooped with weight of work and
        years,
But rich in tawny colouring of her race,
    She comes a-field to strip the purple ears.

And all her thoughts are with the days gone by,
    Ere might's injustice banished from their lands
Her people, that to-day unheeded lie,
    Like the dead husks that rustle through her
      hands.

(1903)

Silhouette

The sky-line melts from russet into blue,
Unbroken the horizon, saving where
A wreath of smoke curls up the far, thin air,
And points the distant lodges of the Sioux.

Etched where the lands and cloudlands touch and
    die
A solitary Indian tepee stands,
The only habitation of these lands,
That roll their magnitude from sky to sky.

The tent poles lift and loom in thin relief,
The upward floating smoke ascends between,
And near the open doorway, gaunt and lean,
And shadow-like, there stands an Indian Chief.

With eyes that lost their lustre long ago,
With visage fixed and stern as fate's decree,
He looks towards the empty west, to see
The never-coming herd of buffalo.

Only the bones that bleach upon the plains,
Only the fleshless skeletons that lie
In ghastly nakedness and silence, cry
Out mutely that naught else to him remains.

(1903)

Christmastide

I may not go to-night to Bethlehem,
Nor follow star-directed ways, nor tread
The paths wherein the shepherds walked, that led
To Christ, and peace, and God's good will to men.

I may not hear the Herald Angel's song
Peal through the Oriental skies, nor see
The wonder of that Heavenly company
Announce the King the world had waited long.

The manger throne I may not kneel before,
Or see how man to God is reconciled,
Through pure St. Mary's purer, holier child;
The human Christ these eyes may not adore.

I may not carry frankincense and myrrh
With adoration to the Holy One;
Nor gold have I to give the Perfect Son,
To be with those wise kings a worshipper.

Not mine the joy that Heaven sent to them,
For ages since Time swung and locked his gates,
But I may kneel without – the star still waits
To guide me on to holy Bethlehem.

(1895)

Through Time and Bitter Distance

Unknown to you, I walk the cheerless shore,
  The cutting blast, the hurl of biting brine
May freeze, and still, and bind the waves at war,
  Ere you will ever know, O! Heart of mine,
That I have sought, reflected in the blue
  Of those sea depths, some shadow of your eyes;
Have hoped the laughing waves would sing of you,
  But this is all my starving sight descries –

I

Far out at sea a sail
   Bends to the freshening breeze,
Yields to the rising gale
   That sweeps the seas;

II

Yields, as a bird wind-tossed,
   To saltish waves that fling
Their spray, whose rime and frost
   Like crystals cling

III

To canvas, mast and spar,
   Till, gleaming like a gem,
She sinks beyond the far
   Horizon's hem.

IV

Lost to my longing sight,
   And nothing left to me
Save an oncoming night, –
   An empty sea.

(1903)

In Grey Days

Measures of oil for others,
   Oil and red wine,
Lips laugh and drink, but never
   Are the lips mine.

Worlds at the feet of others,
   Power gods have known,
Hearts for the favoured round me
   Mine beats, alone.

Fame offering to others
   Chaplets of bays,
I with no crown of laurels,
   Only grey days.

Sweet human love for others,
   Deep as the sea,
God-sent unto my neighbour –
   But not to me.

Sometime I'll wrest from others
   More than all this,
I shall demand from Heaven
   Far sweeter bliss.

What profit then to others,
   Laughter and wine?
I'll have what most they covet –
   Death, will be mine.

(1912)

Good-bye

Sounds of the seas grow fainter,
   Sounds of the sands have sped;
The sweep of gales,
The far white sails,
   Are silent, spent and dead.

Sounds of the days of summer
   Murmur and die away,
And distance hides
The long, low tides,
   As night shuts out the day.

(1903)

William Henry Drummond (1854-1907)

One of the most popular poets of the late nineteenth and early twentieth century, William Henry Drummond was hailed by Louis Fréchette, Canada's "poet laureate", as "the pathfinder of a new land of song", a title given to Fréchette by Longfellow. Drummond's portraits of French Canadians, Fréchette remarks, are sympathetic and authentic: "[he is] true to the life and character of the French-Canadian *habitant* in his every relation, civic, social and religious". In his day Drummond was in vogue everywhere in English Canada and indeed Pauline Johnson was accompanied on her readings tours across Canada, the United States and England by Walter McRaye, who recited the poems of Drummond to enthusiastic local audiences.

William Henry Drummond was born on April 13, 1854 in County Leitrim, Ireland. Two years later, the family moved to Tawley, a small village on the Bay of Donegal and here he attended school. In 1864 the family emigrated to Montreal. Following the death of his father several months later, William attended private school for a few terms and then sought work to help his mother and three younger brothers. His first position, as a telegrapher in the little lumbering village of Bord-à-Plouffe brought him into contact with the *habitants, voyageurs* and lumbermen who inhabit his best work. After several years of work, William was able to resume his high school studies in Montreal and continued on to McGill and Bishop's Medical College where he was known more for his athletic proficiency in snow-shoeing and hammer-throwing than for his scholastic record. In 1884 he graduated in medicine. For several months he was House Surgeon of Western Hospital in Montreal and then practised medicine in Stornaway and Knowlton, little villages on Lake Megantic. In 1898 he returned to Montreal and for several years taught medical jurisprudence at McGill. He was elected to the Royal Society of Canada in 1899 and granted a D.C.L. at Bishop's College. In 1905 he left his practice to join his brothers at the Drummond Mines in Cobalt, and here he died of a cerebral hemorrhage on April 6, 1907.

Drummond's first volume of poems, *The Habitant*, appeared in 1897 and was followed by *Johnny Courteau and Other Poems* (1901) and *The Voyageur and Other Poems* (1905). After his death, his wife edited *The Great Fight*, a collection of poems and prose written largely after 1905. *The Poetical Works* of William Henry Drummond appeared in 1912 and *The Complete Poems* in 1926.

The Habitant was composed in the family home on Mountain Street, Montreal and read aloud to his mother and brothers. It was illustrated by Drummond's friend Frederick Simpson Coburn, and the manuscript was carried to New York by one of his brothers and accepted by Putnam's. The first edition of 1897 sold out rapidly, and many subsequent editions followed of this and his succeeding works. Like his contemporaries Ralph Connor and Robert Service, Drummond made effective use of local and picturesque elements of the Canadian scene. His best-known work, "The Wreck of the Julie Plante", was also his first; the story was told to him by Gideon Plouffe and the refrain continued to haunt him afterwards: "An' de win' she blow, blow, blow". Drummond himself apparently did not like this poem, and his wife remarks that he never recited it, but it was well-known across America even before *The Habitant* appeared in print.

TEXT:

The Habitant and Other French Canadian Poems. New York: Putnam, 1897.

See also:

The Great Fight. edited and with a biographical sketch by May Harvey Drummond. New York: Putnam (Toronto: Musson), 1908.
Habitant Poems. ed. Arthur L. Phelps., Toronto: New Canadian Library, 1961.

De Habitant

De place I get born, me, is up on de reever
    Near foot of de rapide dat 's call Cheval
      Blanc
Beeg mountain behin' it, so high you can't
      climb it
    An' whole place she 's mebbe two honder
      arpent.

De fader of me, he was habitant farmer,
    Ma gran' fader too, an' hees fader also,
Dey don't mak' no monee, but dat is n't fonny
    For it's not easy get ev'ryt'ing, you mus'
      know –

All de sam' dere is somet'ing dey got ev'ry-
    boddy,
  Dat's plaintee good healt', wat de monee
    can't geev,
So I'm workin' away dere, an' happy for stay
    dere
  On farm by de reever, so long I was leev.

O! dat was de place w'en de spring tam she 's
    comin',
  W'en snow go away, an' de sky is all blue –
W'en ice lef' de water, an' sun is get hotter
  An' back on de medder is sing de gou-glou –

W'en small sheep is firs' comin' out on de
    pasture,
  Deir nice leetle tail stickin' up on deir back,
Dey ronne wit' deir moder, an' play wit' each
    oder
  An' jomp all de tam jus' de sam' dey was
    crack –

An' ole cow also, she 's glad winter is over,
  So she kick herse'f up, an' start off on de
    race
Wit' de two-year-ole heifer, dat's purty soon
    lef' her,
  W'y ev'ryt'ing's crazee all over de place!

An' down on de reever de wil' duck is quackin'
  Along by de shore leetle san' piper ronne –
De bullfrog he 's gr-rompin' an doré is jompin'
  Dey all got deir own way for mak' it de
    fonne.

But spring 's in beeg hurry, an' don't stay long
    wit' us
  An' firs' t'ing we know, she go off till nex'
    year,
Den bee commence hummin', for summer is
    comin'
  An' purty soon corn 's gettin' ripe on de ear.

Dat's very nice tam for wake up on de morning
  An' lissen de rossignol sing ev'ry place,
Feel sout' win' a-blowin' see clover a-growin'
  An' all de worl' laughin' itself on de face.

Mos' ev'ry day raf' it is pass on de rapide
   De voyageurs singin' some ole chanson
'Bout girl down de reever – too bad dey mus'
    leave her,
But comin' back soon' wit' beaucoup d'argent.

An' den w'en de fall an' de winter come roun'
    us
   An' bird of de summer is all fly away,
W'en mebbe she 's snowin' and' nort' win' is
    blowin'
An' night is mos' t'ree tam so long as de day.

You t'ink it was bodder de habitant farmer?
   Not at all – he is happy an' feel satisfy,
An' cole may las' good w'ile, so long as de
    wood-pile
   Is ready for burn on de stove by an' bye.

W'en I got plaintee hay put away on de stable
   So de sheep an' de cow, dey got no chance
    to freeze,
An' de hen all togedder – I don't min' de
    wedder –
   De nort' win' may blow jus' so moche as she
    please.

An' some cole winter night how I wish you can
    see us,
   W'en I smoke on de pipe, an' de ole woman
    sew
By de stove of T'ree Reever – ma wife's fader
    geev her
   On day we get marry, dat 's long tam ago –

De boy an' de girl, dey was readin' it's lesson,
   De cat on de corner she 's bite heem de pup,
Ole "Carleau" he 's snorin' an' beeg stove is
    roarin'
   So loud dat I 'm scare purty soon she bus'
    up.

Philomene – dat 's de oldes' – is sit on de
    winder
  An' kip jus' so quiet lak wan leetle mouse,
She say de more finer moon never was shiner –
   Very fonny, for moon is n't dat side de
    house.

But purty soon den, we hear foot on de outside,
   An' some wan is place it hees han' on de
    latch,
Dat 's Isidore Goulay, las' fall on de Brulé
   He 's tak' it firs' prize on de grand plough-
    in' match.

Ha! ha! Philomene! – dat was smart trick you
    play us
   Come help de young feller tak' snow from
    hees neck,
Dere 's not'ing for hinder you come off de
    winder
   W'en moon you was look for is come, I ex-
    pec' –

Isidore, he is tole us de news on de parish
   'Bout hees Lajeunesse Colt—travel two forty,
    sure,
'Bout Jeremie Choquette, come back from
     Woonsocket
   An' t'ree new leetle twin on Madame Vail-
    lancour'.

But nine o'clock strike, an' de chil'ren is
    sleepy,
   Mese'f an' ole woman can't stay up no more
So alone by de fire – 'cos dey say dey ain't   tire –
   We lef' Philomene an' de young Isidore.

I s'pose dey be talkin' beeg lot on de kitchen
   'Bout all de nice moon dey was see on de
    sky,
For Philomene 's takin' long tam get awaken
   Nex' day, she 's so sleepy on bote of de eye.

We leev very quiet 'way back on de contree
  Don't put on sam style lak de big village,
W'en we don't get de monee you t'ink dat is
  fonny
    An' mak' plaintee sport on de Bottes Sau-
    vages.

But I tole you – dat 's true – I don't go on de
  city
    If you geev de fine house an' beaucoup
    d'argent –
I rader be stay me, an' spen' de las' day me
    On farm by de rapide dat 's call Cheval
    Blanc.

Dat 's wan of dem ting's, ev'ry tam on de
  fashion,
    An' 'bout nices' t'ing dat was never be seen.
Got not'ing for say me – I spark it sam' way
  me
    W'en I go see de moder ma girl Philomene.

(1897)

The Wreck of the "Julie Plante"

A LEGEND OF LAC-ST. PIERRE.

On wan dark night on Lac St. Pierre,
  De win' she blow, blow, blow,
An' de crew of de wood scow "Julie Plante"
  Got scar't an' run below –
For de win' she blow lak hurricane
  Bimeby she blow some more,
An' de scow bus' up on Lac St. Pierre
  Wan arpent from de shore.

De captinne walk on de fronte deck,
   An' walk de hin' deck too –
He call de crew from up de hole
   He call de cook also.
De cook she 's name was Rosie,
   She come from Montreal,
Was chambre maid on lumber barge,
   On de Grande Lachine Canal.

De win' she blow from nor'-eas'-wes,' –
   De sout' win' she blow too,
W'en Rosie cry "Mon cher captinne,
   Mon cher, w'at I shall do?"
Den de Captinne t'row de big ankerre,
   But still the scow she dreef,
De crew he can't pass on de shore,
   Becos' he los' hees skeef.

De night was dark lak' wan black cat,
   De wave run high an' fas',
W'en de captinne tak' de Rosie girl
   An' tie her to de mas'.
Den he also tak' de life preserve,
   An' jomp off on de lak',
An' say, "Good-bye, ma Rosie dear,
   I go drown for your sak'."

Nex' morning very early
   'Bout ha'f-pas' two – t'ree – four
De captinne – scow – and' de poor Rosie
   Was corpses on de shore,
For de win' she blow lak' hurricane
   Bimeby she blow some more,
An' de scow bus' up on Lac St. Pierre,
   Wan arpent from de shore.

MORAL

Now all good wood scow sailor man
   Tak' warning by dat storm
An' go an' marry some nice French girl
   An' leev on wan beeg farm.
De win' can blow lak' hurricane
   An' s'pose she blow some more,
You can't get drown on Lac St. Pierre
   So long you stay on shore.

(1897)

Robert Service (1874-1958)

The unrivalled "poet of the Yukon", Robert Service was a prolific writer who vowed to compose one thousand poems before he died "if the Lord of Scribes will spare me to finish the task". A bank clerk who came to the Yukon, Service was a white collar worker but his name became synonymous with the rough-and-ready life of miners and prospectors in the Canadian North-West. He achieved his goal; his Collected Works total two volumes and 1700 pages, and it has been claimed that, before his death, he sold more copies of his works than any other living English writer.

Born in Preston, England in 1874, Service moved with his family to Glasgow at the age of six and here he was educated. He left school at fourteen and worked for a short period in an office; he then was employed for the next seven years by the Commercial Bank of Scotland. During this period, he experimented with sports, poetry and the stage, and for a year attended evening classes at the University of Glasgow. In 1894 he emigrated to British Columbia. For the next several years he worked at itinerant jobs along the North American coast, unloading crates, picking oranges, and acting as cowhand; for another four years he clerked in a store. In 1902, he returned to banking and joined the Bank of Commerce at Victoria who transferred him to Vancouver, then in 1904 to Whitehorse and in 1906 to Dawson. In 1908, he was receiving enough royalties to retire and write his popular novel *The Trail of '98*. Following its publication in 1911, he moved to France where he married a French girl and kept houses in Paris, Brittany and the Riviera. During the First World War, he served in the first Ambulance Corps. Except for extensive travels and two periods in Hollywood, he lived in France until his death in Brittany in 1958.

His first volume of poems *Songs of a Sourdough* (1907) was followed rapidly over the years by *The Spell of the Yukon* (1907), *Ballads of a Cheechako* (1909), *Rhymes of a Rolling Stone* (1912), *Rhymes of a Red-Cross Man* (1916), *Ballads of a Bohemian* (1921), *Twenty Bath-tub Ballads* (1939), *Bar-Room Ballads* (1940), *Songs of a Sun-Lover* (1949), *Rhymes of a Roughneck* (1950), *Lyrics of a Low brow* (1951), *Rhymes of a Rebel* (1952), *Songs for my Supper* (1953), *Carols of an Old Codger* (1954), *Rhymes for My Rags* (1956) and *Songs of the High North* (1958). He also published his *Complete Poetical Works* (1921), *Collected Verse* (1930), *Complete Poems* (1933, 1940, 1942) and *More Collected Verse* (1956) as well as six novels: *The Trail of '98* filmed by M.G.M., *The Pretender* (1914),

The Poisoned Paradise (1922), *The Roughneck* (1923), *The Master of the Microbe* (1926) and *The House of Fear* (1927). His autobiography appeared in two volumes: *Ploughman of the Moon* (1945) and *Harper of Heaven* (1948).

In his autobiography Service remarked of his Yukon verse: "I wrote of human nature, of the life of the mining camp, of the rough miners and the dance-hall girls. Vice seemed to me a more vital subject for poetry than virtue, more colourful, more dramatic . . . ." He took the names for his characters from the bank ledgers, and the story is told that a certain Sam McGee withdrew his account from the bank but never succeeded in living down his reputation. *Songs of a Sourdough*, Service claimed, began as a series of poems which he kept in a drawer under his shirts. When he had collected thirty pieces, he sent them to a publisher with $100 to cover the expenses of printing; the cheque was returned and, he adds, thousands of copies were sold even before the book appeared in print. Copies of this book alone in British and North American editions have numbered in the millions, and it is for this and the works immediately following (*The Spell of the Yukon, Ballads of a Cheechako* and *Rhymes of a Rolling Stone*) that Service earned his reputation.

TEXT:

Songs of a Sourdough. Toronto, Briggs, 1907.

See also:

The Ploughman of the Moon. New York: Dodd Mead, 1945.
Harper of Heaven. New York: Dodd Mead, 1948.

The Spell of the Yukon

I wanted the gold, and I sought it;
   I scrabbled and mucked like a slave.
Was it famine or scurvy – I fought it;
   I hurled my youth into a grave.
I wanted the gold and I got it –
   Came out with a fortune last fall, –
Yet somehow life's not what I thought it,
   And somehow the gold isn't all.

No! There's the land. (Have you seen it?)
   It's the cussedest land that I know,
From the big, dizzy mountains that screen it
   To the deep, deathlike valleys below.
Some say God was tired when He made it:
   Some say it's a fine land to shun;
Maybe: but there's some as would trade it
   For no land on earth – and I'm one.

You come to get rich (damned good reason),
   You feel like an exile at first;
You hate it like hell for a season.
   And then you are worse than the worst.
It grips you like some kinds of sinning;
   It twists you from foe to a friend;
It seems it's been since the beginning;
   It seems it will be to the end.

I've stood in some mighty-mouthed hollow
   That's plumb-full of hush to the brim;
I've watched the big, husky sun wallow
   In crimson and gold, and grow dim,
Till the moon set the pearly peaks gleaming,
   And the stars tumbled out, neck and crop;
And I've thought that I surely was dreaming,
   With the peace o' the world piled on top.

The summer – no sweeter was ever;
   The sunshiny woods all athrill;
The greyling aleap in the river,
   The bighorn asleep on the hill.
The strong life that never knows harness;
   The wilds where the caribou call;
The freshness, the freedom, the farness –
   O God! how I'm stuck on it all.

The winter! the brightness that blinds you,
   The white land locked tight as a drum,
The cold fear that follows and finds you,
   The silence that bludgeons you dumb.
The snows that are older than history,
   The woods where the weird shadows slant;
The stillness, the moonlight, the mystery,
   I've bade 'em good-bye – but I can't.

There's a land where the mountains are
    nameless,
  And the rivers all run God knows where;
There are lives that are erring and aimless,
  And deaths that just hang by a hair;
There are hardships that nobody reckons;
  There are valleys unpeopled and still;
There's a land – oh, it beckons and beckons,
  And I want to go back – and I will.

They're making my money diminish;
  I'm sick of the taste of champagne.
Thank God! when I'm skinned to a finish
  I'll pike to the Yukon again.
I'll fight – and you bet it's no sham-fight;
  It's hell! – but I've been there before;
And it's better than this by a damsite –
  So me for the Yukon once more.

There's gold, and it's haunting and haunting;
  It's luring me on as of old;
Yet it isn't the gold that I'm wanting,
  So much as just finding the gold.
It's the great, big, broad land 'way up yonder,
  It's the forests where silence has lease;
It's the beauty that thrills me with wonder,
  It's the stillness that fills me with peace.

(1907)

The Shooting of Dan McGrew

A bunch of the boys were whooping it up in the Malamute saloon;
The kid that handles the music-box was hitting a jag-time tune;
Back of the bar, in a solo game, sat Dangerous Dan McGrew,
And watching his luck was his light-o'-love, the lady that's known as
  Lou.

When out of the night, which was fifty below, and into the din and
the glare,
There stumbled a miner fresh from the creeks, dog-dirty, and loaded
for bear.
He looked like a man with a foot in the grave, and scarcely the
strength of a louse,
Yet he tilted a poke of dust on the bar, and he called for drinks for
the house.
There was none could place the stranger's face, though we searched
ourselves for a clue;
But we drank his health, and the last to drink was Dangerous Dan
McGrew.

There's men that somehow just grip your eyes, and hold them hard
like a spell;
And such was he, and he looked to me like a man who had lived in
hell;
With a face most hair, and the dreary stare of a dog whose day is
done,
As he watered the green stuff in his glass, and the drops fell one by
one.
Then I got to figgering who he was, and wondering what he'd do,
And I turned my head – and there watching him was the lady that's
known as Lou.

His eyes went rubbering round the room, and he seemed in a kind of
daze,
Till at last that old piano fell in the way of his wandering gaze.
The rag-time kid was having a drink; there was no one else on the
stool,
So the stranger stumbles across the room, and flops down there like a
fool.
In a buckskin shirt that was glazed with dirt he sat, and I saw him
sway;
Then he clutched the keys with his talon hands – my God! but that
man could play!

Were you ever out in the Great Alone, when the moon was awful
  clear,
And the icy mountains hemmed you in with a silence you most could
  hear;
With only the howl of a timber wolf, and you camped there in the
  cold,
A half-dead thing in a stark, dead world, clean mad for the muck
  called gold;
While high overhead, green, yellow and red, the North Lights swept
  in bars –
Then you've a haunch what the music meant . . . hunger and night and
  the stars.

And hunger not of the belly kind, that's banished with bacon and
  beans;
But the gnawing hunger of lonely men for a home and all that it
  means;
For a fireside far from the cares that are, four walls and a roof above;
But oh! so cramful of cosy joy, and crowned with a woman's love;
A woman dearer than all the world, and true as Heaven is true –
(God! how ghastly she looks through her rouge, – the lady that's
  known as Lou).

Then on a sudden the music changed, so soft that you scarce could
  hear;
But you felt that your life had been looted clean of all that it once
  held dear;
That someone had stolen the woman you loved; that her love was a
  devil's lie;
That your guts were gone, and the best for you was to crawl away and
  die.
'Twas the crowning cry of a heart's despair, and it thrilled you
  through and through –
"I guess I'll make it a spread misere," said Dangerous Dan McGrew.

The music almost died away . . . then it burst like a pent-up flood;
And it seemed to say, "Repay, repay," and my eyes were blind with
  blood.
The thought came back of an ancient wrong, and it stung like a frozen
  lash,
And the lust awoke to kill, to kill . . . then the music stopped with a
  crash.

And the stranger turned, and his eyes they burned in a most peculiar
    way;
In a buckskin shirt that was glazed with dirt he sat, and I saw him
    sway;
Then his lips went in in a kind of grin, and he spoke, and his voice
    was calm;
And, "Boys," says he, "you don't know me, and none of you care a
    damn;
But I want to state, and my words are straight, and I'll bet my poke
    they're true,
That one of you is a hound of hell . . . and that one is Dan McGrew."

Then I ducked my head, and the lights went out, and two guns blazed
    in the dark;
And a woman screamed, and the lights went up, and two men lay stiff
    and stark;
Pitched on his head, and pumped full of lead, was Dangerous Dan
    McGrew,
While the man from the creeks lay clutched to the breast of the lady
    that's known as Lou.

These are the simple facts of the case, and I guess I ought to know;
They say that the stranger was crazed with "hooch," and I'm not
    denying it's so.
I'm not so wise as the lawyer guys, but strictly between us two –
The woman that kissed him and – pinched his poke – was the lady
    that's known as Lou.

(1907)

The Cremation of Sam McGee

There are strange things done in the midnight
    sun
  By the men who moil for gold;
The Arctic trails have their secret tales
  That would make your blood run cold;
The Northern Lights have seen queer sights;
  But the queerest they ever did see
Was that night on the marge of Lake Lebarge
  I cremated Sam McGee.

Now Sam McGee was from Tennessee, where the cotton blooms and
   blows.
Why he left his home in the South to roam round the Pole God only
   knows.
He was always cold, but the land of gold seemed to hold him like a
   spell;
Though he'd often say in his homely way that he'd "sooner live in
   hell."

On a Christmas Day we were mushing our way over the Dawson trail.
Talk of your cold! through the parka's fold it stabbed like a driven
   nail.
If our eyes we'd close, then the lashes froze, till sometimes we couldn't
   see;
It wasn't much fun, but the only one to whimper was Sam McGee.

And that very night as we lay packed tight in our robes beneath the
   snow,
And the dogs were fed, and the stars o'erhead were dancing heel and
   toe,
He turned to me, and, "Cap," says he, "I'll cash in this trip, I guess;
And if I do, I'm asking that you won't refuse my last request."

Well, he seemed so low that I couldn't say no; then he says with a sort
   of moan:
"It's the cursèd cold, and it's got right hold till I'm chilled clean
   through to the bone.
Yet 'taint being dead, it's my awful dread of the icy grave that pains;
So I want you to swear that, foul or fair, you'll cremate my last
   remains."

A pal's last need is a thing to heed, so I swore I would not fail;
And we started on at the streak of dawn, but God! he looked ghastly
   pale.
He crouched on the sleigh, and he raved all day of his home in
   Tennessee;
And before nightfall a corpse was all that was left of Sam McGee.

There wasn't a breath in that land of death, and I hurried, horror
   driven,
With a corpse half-hid that I couldn't get rid because of a promise
   given;
It was lashed to the sleigh, and it seemed to say: "You may tax your
   brawn and brains,
But you promised true, and it's up to you to cremate those last
   remains."

Now a promise made is a debt unpaid, and the trail has its own stern
  code.
In the days to come, though my lips were dumb, in my heart how I
  cursed that load.
In the long, long night, by the lone firelight, while the huskies, round
  in a ring,
Howled out their woes to the homeless snows – O God! how I loathed
  the thing.

And every day that quiet clay seemed to heavy and heavier grow;
And on I went, though the dogs were spent and the grub was getting
  low;
The trail was bad, and I felt half mad, but I swore I would not give
  in;
And I'd often sing to the hateful thing, and it hearkened with a grin.

Till I came to the marge of Lake Lebarge, and a derelict there lay;
It was jammed in the ice, but I saw in a trice it was called the "Alice
  May."
And I looked at it, and I thought a bit, and I looked at my frozen
  chum:
Then, "Here," said I, with a sudden cry, "is my cre-ma-tor-eum!"

Some planks I tore from the cabin floor, and I lit the boiler fire;
Some coal I found that was lying around, and I heaped the fuel
  higher;
The flames just soared, and the furnace roared – such a blaze you
  seldom see;
And I burrowed a hole in the glowing coal, and I stuffed in Sam
  McGee.

Then I made a hike, for I didn't like to hear him sizzle so;
And the heavens scowled, and the huskies howled, and the wind
  began to blow.
It was icy cold, but the hot sweat rolled down my cheeks, and I don't
  know why;
And the greasy smoke in an inky cloak went streaking down the sky.

I do not know how long in the snow I wrestled with grisly fear;
But the stars came out and they danced about ere again I ventured
  near;
I was sick with dread, but I bravely said: "I'll just take a peep inside.
I guess he's cooked, and it's time I looked," . . . then the door I opened
  wide –

And there sat Sam, looking cool and calm, in the heart of the furnace
   roar;
And he wore a smile you could see a mile, and he said: "Please close
   that door.
It's fine in here, but I greatly fear you'll let in the cold and storm –
Since I left Plumtree, down in Tennessee, it's the first time I've been
   warm."

There are strange things done in the midnight sun
   By the men who moil for gold;
The Arctic trails have their secret tales
   That would make your blood run cold;
The Northern Lights have seen queer sights,
   But the queerest they ever did see
Was that night on the marge of Lake Lebarge
   I cremated Sam McGee.

(1907)

William Kirby (1817-1906)

A devoted Tory and defender of the King, the Dominion, and the Church of England, William Kirby is noted chiefly to-day for his novel *The Golden Dog*, an authentic recreation of the Canada of the French regime. Although he received little financial reward for nearly twelve years of research, he did receive recognition through election as a charter member of the Royal Society of Canada. His happiest moment occurred at Government House in May, 1883 when Princess Louise remarked to him how she, her brother Prince Leopold and her mother Queen Victoria had enjoyed the novel.

Born in 1817 in Kingston-Upon-Hull, Yorkshire, England, William Kirby was descended from an English family of Danish origins; in 1832 at the age of fifteen he emigrated with his family to the United States, first to New York and then to Cincinnatti. Apprenticed to his father as a journeyman tanner, he studied in the evenings and on Sundays and learned to read Latin, Greek, French, German, Italian, Swedish and some Indian dialects. In 1839, after the suppression of Mackenzie and Papineau in Upper and Lower Canada, Kirby crossed the border as "the last of the Loyalists" to aid in "the defence of the Provinces". He visited Toronto, Montreal and Quebec, and eventually settled in Niagara-on-the-Lake after flipping a coin to see where he should live. He obtained employment as a tanner and several months later leased a business of his own, but lost possession when a partner absconded with the funds. In 1846 he taught school in Hamilton, and in 1850 took a position as editor of the *Niagara Mail*, to which he had already contributed under the pseudonym of "Britannicus". He retained this position until 1863. In 1861 he became Reeve of Niagara-on-the-Lake, in 1863 Curator of the Military Reserve, in 1865 magistrate of Lincoln County, and in 1871 collector of customs at Niagara, appointed by Sir John A. Macdonald. He was one of the original Fellows of the Royal Society of Canada, founded in 1882, and joined the Council in 1887, proposing Charles Mair and Charles G. D. Roberts as Fellows. He died at Niagara on June 23, 1906.

Kirby's most significant literary work, *The Golden Dog*, was first published in 1887. In addition he wrote several dramas: *Joseph in Egypt*, performed in the Niagara Court House in August and September of 1876, *Queen Esther* performed at the Court House in December 1880, *The Queen's Own*, a poetic farce, and *Beaumanoir*, a dramatization of *The Golden Dog*. His attack on the British American League and his "Counter-Manifesto to the Abolitionists of Montreal" were published in *The Niagara Mail* in 1849 and in pamphlet form in the same year under the name of Britannicus. In 1859 also appeared *The U.E.: A Tale of Upper Canada,* an epic of twelve cantos which was published anonymously but with the symbol of *The Niagara Mail*; in 1884 he brought out *The Canadian Idylls*, a series of long and uneven poems reprinted in 1894. Kirby's *Annals of Niagara* (1896) is still an authoritative work on the area.

Inspired by James MacPherson Le Moine's *Maple Leaves, The Golden Dog* is a historic romance concerning the last years of the French regime and the corruption of the French court which led to Wolfe's victory in 1759, the same period as Gilbert Parker's *The Seats of the Mighty.* Kirby spent nearly twelve years after 1865 researching his subject in local histories, and guide books. Sixteen hundred pages in the original, it was published abridged by Lovell Adams of New York in 1877 and again in a second edition in the same year by Worthington. It was not until 1896 that L. C. Page brought out an "authorized edition", still abridged, from which Kirby received about $100 before his death.

The plot of the novel is complex, an integration of several tales: "The Golden Dog", Chateau Bigot, La Corriveau, and the story of Carolyne de Castin published by Amédée Papineau in 1837. The central plot concerns the Intendant Bigot's design to encourage a romance between his mistress, the scheming Angélique des Meloises, and Le Gardeur de Repentigny so as to manipulate the young man into slaying the Bourgeois Philibert, owner of the store the Golden Dog, wealthy trader, and rival of the corrupt Grand Company. The temptation of Le Gardeur in the Great Hall of the Chateau Beaumanoir is a key scene in the novel.

TEXT:

The Golden Dog. Boston: L. C. Page, 1896.

See also:

Lorne Pierce. *The Portrait of a Tory Loyalist*. Toronto: Macmillan, 1929.
William Renwick Riddell. *William Kirby*. Toronto: Ryerson, n.d.

From *The Golden Dog*

CHAPTER VII.

THE INTENDANT BIGOT.

The Chateau of Beaumanoir had, since the advent of the Intendant Bigot, been the scene of many a festive revelry that matched, in bacchanalian frenzy, the wild orgies of the Regency and the present debaucheries of Croisy and the *petits appartements* of Versailles. Its splendor, its luxury, its riotous feasts lasting without intermission sometimes for days, were the themes of wonder and disgust to the unsophisticated people of New France, and of endless comparison between the extravagance of the Royal Intendant and the simple manners and inflexible morals of the Governor-General.

The great hall of the Château, the scene of the gorgeous feasts of the Intendant, was brilliantly illuminated with silver lamps, glowing like globes of sunlight as they hung from the lofty ceiling, upon which was painted a fresco of the apotheosis of Louis XIV., where the Grand Monarque was surrounded by a cloud of Condés, Orléanois, and Bourbons, of near and more remote consanguinity. At the head of the room hung a full-length portrait of Marquise de Pompadour, the mistress of Louis XV., and the friend and patroness of the Intendant Bigot; her bold, voluptuous beauty seemed well fitted to be the presiding genius of his house. The walls bore many other paintings of artistic and historic value. The King and Queen; the dark-eyed Montespan; the crafty Maintenon; and the pensive beauty of Louise de la Vallière, the only mistress of Louis XIV. who loved him for his own sake, and whose portrait, copied from this picture, may still be seen in the chapel of the Ursulines of Quebec, where the fair Louise is represented as St. Thaïs kneeling at prayer among the nuns.

The table in the great hall, a masterpiece of workmanship, was made of a dark Canadian wood then newly introduced, and stretched the length of the hall. A massive gold epergne of choicest Italian art, the gift of La Pompadour, stood on the centre of the table. It represented Bacchus enthroned on a tun of wine, presenting flowing cups to a dance of fauns and satyrs.

Silver cups of Venetian sculpture and goblets of Bohemian manufacture sparkled like stars upon the brilliant table, brimming over with the gold and ruby vintages of France and Spain; or lay overturned amid pools of wine that ran down upon the velvet carpet. Dishes of Parmesan cheese, caviare, and other provocatives to thirst stood upon the table, amid vases of flowers and baskets of the choicest fruits of the Antilles.

Round this magnificent table sat a score or more of revellers – in the garb of gentlemen, but all in disorder and soiled with wine; their countenances were inflamed, their eyes red and fiery, their tongues loose and loquacious. Here and there a vacant or overturned chair showed where a guest had fallen in the debauch and been carried off by the valets, who in gorgeous liveries waited on the table. A band of musicians sat up in a gallery at the end of the hall, and filled the pauses of the riotous feast with the ravishing strains of Lulli and Destouches.

At the head of the table, first in place as in rank, sat François Bigot, Intendant of New France. His low, well-set figure, dark hair, small, keen black eyes, and swarthy features full of fire and animation, bespoke his Gascon blood. His countenance was far from comely, – nay, when in repose, even ugly and repulsive, – but his eyes were magnets that drew men's looks towards him, for in them lay the force of a powerful will and a depth and subtlety of intellect that made men fear, if they could not love him. Yet when he chose – and it was his usual mood – to exercise his blandishments on men, he rarely failed to captivate them, while his pleasant wit, courtly ways, and natural gallantry towards women, exercised with the polished seductiveness he had learned in the Court of Louis xv., made François Bigot the most plausible and dangerous man in New France.

He was fond of wine and music, passionately addicted to gambling, and devoted to the pleasant vices that were rampant in the Court of France, finely educated, able in the conduct of affairs, and fertile in expedients to accomplish his ends. François Bigot might have saved New France, had he been honest as he was clever; but he was unprincipled and corrupt: no conscience checked his ambition or his love of pleasure. He ruined New France for the sake of himself and his patroness and the crowd of courtiers and frail beauties who surrounded the King, whose arts and influence kept him in his high office despite all the efforts of the *Honnêtes Gens*, the good and true men of the Colony, to remove him.

He had already ruined and lost the ancient Colony of Acadia, through his defrauds and malversations as Chief Commissary of the Army, and instead of trial and punishment, had lately been exalted to the higher and still more important office of Royal Intendant of New France.

On the right of the Intendant sat his bosom friend, the Sieur Cadet, a large, sensual man, with twinkling gray eyes, thick nose, and full red lips. His broad face, flushed with wine, glowed like the harvest moon rising above the horizon. Cadet had, it was said, been a butcher in Quebec. He was now, for the misfortune of his country, Chief Commissary of the Army and a close confederate of the Intendant.

On the left of the Intendant sat his Secretary, De Pean, crafty and unscrupulous, a parasite, too, who flattered his master and ministered to his pleasures. De Pean was a military man, and not a bad soldier in the field; but he loved gain better than glory, and amassed an enormous fortune out of the impoverishment of his country.

Le Mercier, too, was there, Commandant of Artillery, a brave officer, but a bad man; Varin, a proud, arrogant libertine, Commissary of Montreal, who outdid Bigot in rapine and Cadet in coarseness; De Breard, Comptroller of the Marine, a worthy associate of Penisault, whose pinched features and cunning leer were in keeping with his important office of chief manager of the Friponne. Perrault, D'Estebe, Morin, and Vergor, all creatures of the Intendant, swelled the roll of infamy, as partners of the Grand Company of Associates trading in New France, as their charter named them – the "Grand Company of Thieves," as the people in their plain Norman called them who robbed them in the King's name and, under pretence of maintaining the war, passed the most arbitrary decrees, the only object of which was to enrich themselves and their higher patrons at the Court of Versailles.

The rest of the company seated round the table comprised a number of dissolute seigneurs and gallants of fashion about town – men of great wants and great extravagance, just the class so quaintly described by Charlevoix, a quarter of a century previous, as "gentlemen thoroughly versed in the most elegant and agreeable modes of spending money, but greatly at a loss how to obtain it."

Among the gay young seigneurs who had been drawn into the vortex of Bigot's splendid dissipation, was the brave, handsome Le Gardeur de Repentigny – a captain of the Royal Marine, a Colonial corps recently embodied at Quebec. In general form and feature Le Gardeur was a manly reflex of his beautiful sister Amélie, but his countenance was marred with traces of debauchery. His face was inflamed, and his dark eyes, so like his sister's, by nature tender and true, were now glittering with the adder tongues of the cursed wine-serpent.

Taking the cue from Bigot, Le Gardeur responded madly to the challenges to drink from all around him. Wine was now flooding every brain, and the table was one scene of riotous debauch.

"Fill up again, Le Gardeur!" exclaimed the Intendant, with a loud and still clear voice; "the lying clock says it is day – broad day, but neither cock crows nor day dawns in the Château of Beaumanoir, save at the will of its master and his merry guests! Fill up, companions all! The lamp-light in the wine-cup is brighter than the clearest sun that ever shone!"

"Bravo Bigot! name your toast, and we will pledge it till the seven stars count fourteen!" replied Le Gardeur, looking hazily at the great clock in the hall. "I see four clocks in the room, and every one of them lies if it says it is day!"

"You are mending, Le Gardeur de Repentigny! You are worthy to belong to the Grand Company! But you shall have my toast. We have drank it twenty times already, but it will stand drinking twenty times more. It is the best prologue to wine ever devised by wit of man – a woman – ''

"And the best epilogue too, Bigot!" interjected Varin, visibly drunk; "but let us have the toast, my cup is waiting."

"Well, fill up all, then; and we will drink the health, wealth, and love by stealth, of the jolliest dame in sunny France – The Marquise de Pompadour!"

"La Pompadour! La Pompadour!" Every tongue repeated the name, the goblets were drained to the bottoms, and a thunder of applause and clattering of glasses followed the toast of the mistress of Louis xv., who was the special protectress of the Grand Company, – a goodly share of whose profits in the monopoly of trade in New France was thrown into the lap of the powerful favorite.

"Come, Varin! your turn now!" cried Bigot, turning to the Commissary; "a toast for Ville Marie! Merry Montreal! where they eat like rats of Poitou, and drink till they ring the fire-bells, as the Bordelais did to welcome the collectors of the gabelle. The Montrealers have not rung the fire-bells yet against you, Varin, but they will by and by!"

Varin filled his cup with an unsteady hand until it ran over, and propping his body against the table as he stood up, replied, "A toast for Ville Marie! and our friends in need! – The blue caps of the Richelieu!" This was in allusion to a recent ordinance of the Intendant, authorizing him to seize all the corn in store at Montreal and in the surrounding country – under pretence of supplying the army, and really to secure the monopoly of it for the Grand Company.

The toast was drunk, amid rapturous applause. "Well said, Varin!" exclaimed Bigot; "that toast implied both business and pleasure: the business was to sweep out the granges of the farmers; the pleasure is to drink in honor of your success."

"My foragers sweep clean!" said Varin, resuming his seat, and looking under his hand to steady his gaze. "Better brooms were never made in Besançon. The country is swept as clean as a ball-room. Your Excellency and the Marquise might lead the dance over it, and not a straw lie in your way!"

"And did you manage it without a fight, Varin?" asked the Sieur d'Estebe, with a half sneer.

"Fight! Why fight? The habitans will never resist the King's name. We conjure the devil down with that. When we skin our eels we don't begin at the tail! If we did, the habitans would be like the eels of Mélun – cry out before they were hurt. No! no! D'Estebe! We are more polite in Ville Marie. We tell them the King's troops need the corn. They doff their caps, and with tears in their eyes, say, 'Monsieur le Commissaire, the King can have all we possess, and ourselves too, if he will only save Canada from the Bostonnais.' This is better than stealing the honey and killing the bees that made it, D'Estebe!"

"But what became of the families of the habitans after this swoop of your foragers?" asked the Seigneur de Beauce, a country gentleman who retained a few honorable ideas floating on top of the wine he had swallowed.

"Oh! the families – that is, the women and children, for we took the men for the army. You see, De Beauce," replied Varin, with a mocking air, as he crossed his thumbs like a peasant of Languedoc when he wishes to inspire belief in his words, "the families have to do what the gentlemen of Beauce practise in times of scarcity – breakfast by gaping! or they can eat wind, like the people of Poitou: it will make them spit clean!"

De Beauce was irritated at the mocking sign and the proverbial allusion to the gaping of the people of Beauce. He started up in wrath, and striking his fist on the table, "Monsieur Varin!" cried he, "do not cross your thumbs at me, or I will cut them off! Let me tell you the gentlemen of Beauce do not breakfast on gaping, but have plenty of corn to stuff even a Commissary of Montreal!"

The Sieur Le Mercier, at a sign from Bigot, interposed to stop the rising quarrel. "Don't mind Varin," said he, whispering to De Beauce; "he is drunk, and a row will anger the Intendant. Wait, and by and by you shall toast Varin as the chief baker of Pharoah, who got hanged because he stole the King's corn."

"As he deserves to be, for his insult to the gentlemen of Beauce," insinuated Bigot, leaning over to his angry guest, at the same time winking good-humoredly to Varin. "Come, now, De Beauce, friends all, *amantium irae*, you know – which is Latin for love – and I will sing you a stave in praise of this good wine, which is better than Bacchus ever drank." The Intendant rose up, and holding a brimming glass in his hand, chanted in full, musical voice a favorite ditty of the day, as a ready mode of restoring harmony among the company:

"'Amis! dans ma bouteille,
Voilà le vin de France!
C'est le bon vin qui danse ici,
C'est le bon vin qui danse.
    Gai lon la!
    Vive la lirette!
    Des Filettes
    Il y en aura!'

Vivent les Filettes! The girls of Quebec – first in beauty, last in love, and nowhere in scorn of a gallant worthy of them!" continued Bigot. "What say you, De Pean? Are you not prepared to toast the belles of Quebec?"

"That I am, your Excellency!" De Pean was unsteady upon his feet, as he rose to respond to the Intendant's challenge. He pot-valiantly drew his sword, and laid it on the table. "I will call on the honorable company to drink this toast on their knees, and there is my sword to cut the legs off any gentleman who will not kneel down and drink a full cup to the bright eyes of the belle of Quebec – The incomparable Angélique des Meloises!"

The toast suited their mood. Every one filled up his cup in honor of a beauty so universally admired.

"Kneel down, all," cried the Intendant, "or De Pean will hamstring us!" All knelt down with a clash – some of them unable to rise again. "We will drink to the Angélique charms of the fair Des Meloises. Come now, all together! – as the jolly Dutchmen of Albany say, '*Upp seys over*!'"

Such of the company as were able resumed their seats amid great laughter and confusion, when the Sieur Deschenaux, a reckless young gallant, ablaze with wine and excitement, stood up, leaning against the table. His fingers dabbled in his wine-cup as he addressed them, but he did not notice it.

"We have drunk with all the honors," said he, "to the bright eyes of the belle of Quebec. I call on every gentleman now, to drink to the still brighter eyes of the belle of New France!"

"Who is she? Name! name!" shouted a dozen voices; "who is the belle of New France!"

"Who is she? Why, who can she be but the fair Angélique, whom we have just honored?" replied De Pean, hotly, jealous of any precedence in that quarter.

"Tut!" cried Deschenaux, "you compare glowworms with evening stars, when you pretend to match Angélique des Meloises with the lady I propose to honor! I call for full brimmers – cardinal's hats – in honor of the belle of New France – the fair Amélie de Repentigny!"

Le Gardeur de Repentigny was sitting leaning on his elbow, his face beaming with jollity, as he waited, with a full cup, for Deschenaux's toast. But no sooner did he hear the name of his sister from those lips than he sprang up as though a serpent had bit him. He hurled his goblet at the head of Deschenaux with a fierce imprecation, and drew his sword as he rushed towards him.

"A thousand lightnings strike you! How dare you pollute that holy name, Deschenaux? Retract that toast instantly, or you shall drink it in blood – retract, I say!"

The guests rose to their feet in terrible uproar. Le Gardeur struggled violently to break through a number of those who interposed between him and Deschenaux, who, roused to frenzy by the insult from Le Gardeur, had also drawn his sword, and stood ready to receive the assault of his antagonist.

The Intendant, whose courage and presence of mind never forsook him, pulled Deschenaux down upon his seat and held fast his sword arm, shouting in his ear, –

"Are you mad, Deschenaux? You knew she was his sister, and how he worships her! Retract the toast – it was inopportune! Besides, recollect we want to win over De Repentigny to the Grand Company!"

Deschenaux struggled for a minute, but the influence of the Intendant was all-powerful over him. He gave way. "Damn De Repentigny," said he, "I only meant to do honor to the pretty witch. Who would have expected him to take it up in that manner?"

"Any one who knows him; besides," continued the Intendant, "if you must toast his sister, wait till we get him body and soul made over to the Grand Company, and then he will care no more for his sister's fame than you do for yours."

"But the insult! He has drawn blood with the goblet," said Deschenaux, wiping his forehead with his fingers; "I cannot pardon that!"

"Tut, tut; fight him another day. But you shall not fight here! Cadet and Le Mercier have pinned the young Bayard, I see; so you have a chance to do the honorable, Deschenaux; go to him, retract the toast, and say you had forgotten the fair lady was his sister."

Deschenaux swallowed his wrath, rose up, and sheathed his sword. Taking the Intendant by the arm, he went up to Le Gardeur, who was still trying to advance. Deschenaux held up his hand deprecatingly. "Le Gardeur," said he, with an air of apparent contrition, "I was wrong to offer that toast. I had forgotten the fair lady was your sister. I retract the toast, since it is disagreeable to you, although all would have been proud to drink it."

Le Gardeur was as hard to appease as he was easy to excite to anger. He still held his drawn sword in his hand.

"Come!" cried Bigot, "you are as hard to please as Villiers Vendôme, whom the King himself could not satisfy. Deschenaux says he is sorry. A gentleman cannot say more; so shake hands and be friends, De Repentigny.'

Impervious to threats, and often to reason, Le Gardeur could not resist an appeal to his generosity.

He sheathed his sword, and held out his hand with frank forgiveness. "Your apology is ample, Sieur Deschenaux. I am satisfied you meant no affront to my sister! It is my weak point, messieurs," continued he, looking firmly at the company, ready to break out had he detected the shadow of a sneer upon any one's countenance. "I honor her as I do the queen of heaven. Neither of their names ought to be spoken here."

"Well said! Le Gardeur," exclaimed the Intendant. "That's right, shake hands, and be friends again. Blessed are quarrels that lead to reconciliation and the washing out of feuds in wine. Take your seats, gentlemen."

There was a general scramble back to the table. Bigot stood up in renewed force.

"Valets!" cried he, "bring in now the largest cups! We will drink a toast five fathoms deep, in water of life strong enough to melt Cleopatra's pearls, and to a jollier dame than Egypt's queen. But first we will make Le Gardeur de Repentigny free of the guild of noble partners of the company of adventurers trading in New France."

The valets flew in and out. In a few moments the table was replenished with huge drinking-cups, silver flagons, and all the heavy impedimenta of the army of Bacchus.

"You are willing to become one of us, and enter the jolly guild of the Grand Company?" exclaimed the Intendant, taking Le Gardeur by the hand.

"Yes, I am a stranger, and you may take me in. I claim admission," replied Le Gardeur with drunken gravity, "and by St. Pigot! I will be true to the guild!"

Bigot kissed him on both cheeks. "By the boot of St. Benoit! you speak like the King of Yvetot. Le Gardeur de Repentigny, you are fit to wear fur in the Court of Burgundy."

"You can measure my foot, Bigot," replied Le Gardeur, "and satisfy the company that I am able to wear the boot of St. Benoit."

"By jolly St. Chinon! and you shall wear it, Le Gardeur," exclaimed Bigot, handing him a quart flagon of wine, which Le Gardeur drank without drawing breath. "That boot fits," shouted the Intendant exultingly; "now for the chant! I will lead. Stop the breath of any one who will not join in the chorus."

The Intendant in great voice led off a macaronic verse of Molière, that had often made merry the orgies of Versailles:

"'Bene, bene, bene, respondere!
Dignus, dignus es, entrare
In nostro laeto corpore!'"

A tintamarre of voices and a jingle of glasses accompanied the violins and tambours de Basque as the company stood up and sang the song, winding up with a grand burst at the chorus:

"'Vivat! vivat! vivat! cent fois vivat!
Novus socius qui tam bene parlat!
Mille mille annis et manget et bibat,
Fripet et friponnat!'"

Hands were shaken all round, congratulations, embracings, and filthy kisses showered upon Le Gardeur to honor his admission as a partner of the Grand Company.

"And now," continued Bigot, "we will drink a draught long as the bell rope of Notre Dame. Fill up brimmers of the quintessence of the grape, and drain them dry in honor of the Friponne!"

The name was electric. It was, in the country, a word of opprobrium, but at Beaumanoir it was laughed at with true Gallic nonchalance. Indeed, to show their scorn of public opinion, the Grand Company had lately launched a new ship upon the Great Lakes to carry on the fur trade, and had appropriately and mockingly named her, "*La Friponne*."

The toast of *La Friponne* was drunk with applause, followed by a wild bacchanalian song.

The Sieur Morin had been a merchant in Bordeaux whose bond was held in as little value as his word. He had lately removed to New France, transferred the bulk of his merchandise to the Friponne, and become an active agent of the Grand Company.

"*La Friponne!*" cried he; "I have drunk success to her with all my heart and throat; but I say she will never wear a night-cap and sleep quietly in our arms until we muzzle the Golden Dog that barks by night and by day in the Rue Buade."

"That is true, Morin!" interrupted Varin. "The Grand Company will never know peace until we send the Bourgeois, his master, back to the Bastille. The Golden Dog is – "

"Damn the Golden Dog!" exclaimed Bigot, passionately. "Why do you utter his name, Varin, to sour our wine? I hope one day to pull down the Dog, as well as the whole kennel of the insolent Bourgeois." Then, as was his wont, concealing his feelings under a mocking gibe, "Varin," said he, "they say that it is your marrow bone the Golden Dog is gnawing – ha! ha! ha!"

"More people beleive it is your Excellency's!" Varin knew he was right, but aware of Bigot's touchiness on that point, added, as is the wont of panders to great men, "It is either yours or the Cardinal's."

"Let it be the Cardinal's, then! He is still in purgatory, and there will wait the arrival of the Bourgeois, to balance accounts with him."

Bigot hated the Bourgeois Philibert as one hates the man he has injured. Bigot had been instrumental in his banishment years ago from France, when the bold Norman count defended the persecuted Jansenists in the Parliament of Rouen. The Intendant hated him now for his wealth and prosperity in New France. But his wrath turned to fury when he saw the tablet of the Golden Dog, with its taunting inscription, glaring upon the front of the magazine in the Rue Buade. Bigot felt the full meaning and significance of the words that burned into his soul, and for which he hoped one day to be revenged.

"Confusion to the whole litter of the Golden Dog, and that is the party of the *Honnêtes Gens!*" cried he. "But for that canting savant who plays the Governor here, I would pull down the sign and hang its master up in its stead to-morrow!"

The company now grew still more hilarious and noisy in their cups. Few paid attention to what the Intendant was saying. But De Repentigny heard him utter the words, "Oh, for men who dare do men's deeds!" He caught the eye of De Repentigny, and added, "But we are all cowards in the Grand Company, and are afraid of the Bourgeois."

The wine was bubbling in the brain of Le Gardeur. He scarcely knew what the Intendant said, but he caught the last words.

"Whom do you call cowards, Chevalier? I have joined the Grand Company. If the rest are cowards, I am not: I stand ready to pluck the peruke off the head of any man in New France, and carry it on my sword to the Place d'Armes, where I will challenge all the world to come and take it!"

"Pish! that is nothing! give me man's work. I want to see the partner in the Grand Company who dare pull down the Golden Dog."

"I dare! and I dare!" exclaimed a dozen voices at once in response to the appeal of the Intendant, who craftily meant his challenge to ensnare only Le Gardeur.

"And I dare; and I will, too, if you wish it, Chevalier!" shouted Le Gardeur, mad with wine, and quite oblivious of the thousand claims of the father of his friend, Pierre Philibert, upon him.

"I take you at your word, Le Gardeur! and bind your honor to it in the presence of all these gentlemen," said Bigot with a look of intense satisfaction.

"When shall it be done – to-day?" Le Gardeur seemed ready to pluck the moon from the sky in his present state of ecstasy.

"Why, no, not to-day; not before the pear is ripe will we pluck it! Your word of honor will keep till then?"

Bigot was in great glee over the success of his stratagem to entrap De Repentigny.

"It will keep a thousand years!" replied Le Gardeur, amid a fresh outburst of merriment round the board which culminated in a shameless song, fit only for a revel of satyrs . . . .

Ernest Thompson Seton (1860-1946)

An author, artist and naturalist, Ernest Thompson Seton was the author of a wide range of books including tales of animal life based on factual observation, studies of woodcraft and histories of animal and bird-life which still remain definitive to-day. With Charles G. D. Roberts he is the originator and the main exponent of the animal story, a genre which is native to Canada, and his works have been read avidly by many generations of young people over the past seventy years. In his stories Seton combines the practical knowledge of the woodsman with the eye of an artist and the scientific knowledge of a naturalist.

Ernest Thompson Seton was born Ernest Thompson in Durham, England on August 14, 1860. He was descended from the Scottish Setons who sided with the Stuarts in 1745 and hid in England after the Battle of Culloden under the name of Thompson. This name Ernest's father inherited through his mother's line after the death of a first cousin. Ernest changed Thompson to Thompson Seton but to please his mother he used Seton Thompson during her lifetime. Ernest's father was a ship-owner in the Merchant Marine but after the loss of three ships he emigrated to Canada in 1866 with his wife and ten sons, settling in Lindsay, Ontario and then, after 1870, in Toronto. Here Seton was educated at the Toronto Grammar School, now the Collegiate Institute on Jarvis Street, and then at the Ontario College of Art, graduating in 1879 as Gold Medalist. The same year he returned to England to study art; he won a scholarship to study at the Royal Academy for seven years but ill health forced him to return to Canada in 1881, and in 1882 he joined his brother on a homestead near Carberry, Manitoba. At this time he was appointed Official Naturalist for the Province of Manitoba. In 1883 he went to New York City where he was commissioned by Century Publications to do 1,000 animal illustrations for their new twelve-volume dictionary. He travelled to Paris in 1890 and for most of the next six years was engaged in studying art under several French masters. In 1896 he returned to the United States where he remained for the rest of his life. He was engaged in the organization of a boys' group, the Woodcraft Indians which became the Woodcraft League in 1902, and in 1910 he chaired the committee to establish the Boy Scouts of America. He wrote the first Scout handbook and held the post of Chief Scout until 1915. He then moved with his wife to Sante Fé, New Mexico where he founded Seton Village, and lived there until his death on October 12, 1946.

Seton's first best-seller was also his first book of stories *Wild Animals I Have Known* (1898). He published over a dozen similar books, as well as differing combinations of the same tales: *Trail of a Sand-Hill Stag*

(1899), *The Biography of a Grizzly* (1900), *Lives of the Hunted* (1901), *Two Little Savages* (1903), *Monarch the Big Bear of Tallac* (1904), *Animal Heroes* (1905), *Woodmyth and Fable* (1905), *The Biography of a Silver Fox* (1909), *Wild Animals at Home* (1913), *Wild Animal Ways* (1916), *The Preacher of Cedar Mountain* (1917), *Woodland Tales* (1921), *Bannertail, the Story of a Grey Squirrel* (1923), and *The Biography of an Arctic Fox* (1937). Seton also wrote a drama, "The Wild Animal Play for Children" (1900), and his autobiography *Trail of an Artist-Naturalist* (1940). In 1891 he published *The Birds of Manitoba*, a study for the Smithsonian Institute and in 1909 *Life-Histories of Northern Animals, An Account of the Mammals of Manitoba* in two volumes. His *Lives of Game Animals*, an eight-volume account of all the game animals from Mexico to the Arctic, appeared from 1925 to 1928 and was awarded the John Burroughs Medal and the Elliott Gold Medal, the highest award a naturalist can receive. He also wrote *Mainly about Wolves* (1927), *Animal Tracks and Hunter Signs* (1958), a travelogue *The Arctic Prairies: A Canoe Journey of 2,000 miles in Search of the Caribou* (1911), and two books of illustrations, *Pictures of Wild Animals* (1901) and *Bird Portraits* (1901).

Between 1891 and 1893, Seton wrote a series of scientific papers on the nature of birds and animals, based on field records and scientific observation. The first of his animal biographies, "Lobo, King of the Currumpaw" combines factual detail with swift-paced narrative centred on the life of a "hero" which Seton defines as "an individual of unusual gifts and achievements. Whether . . . man or animal" (*Animal Heroes*). Seton comments in the introduction to a collection of his stories, *The Best of Ernest Thompson Seton:*

> These stories are true. Although I have left the line of historical truth in many places, the animals in this book were all real characters. They lived the lives I have depicted, and showed the stamp of heroism and personality more strongly by far than it has been the power of my pen to tell. . . . The real personality of the individual, and his view of life are my theme, rather than the ways of the race in general.

Like most of his stories, "Lobo" ends tragically for "there is only one way to make an animal's history un-tragic, and that is to stop before the last chapter" (*Lives of the Hunted*). The story was first published in *Scribner's Magazine* in November of 1894.

TEXT:

Wild Animals I Have Known. New York: Scribner, 1898.

See also:

Trail of an Artist-Naturalist. New York: Scribner, 1940.
Julia M. Seton. *By a Thousand Fires.* New York: Doubleday, 1967.

Lobo, The King of Currumpaw

I

Currumpaw is a vast cattle range in northern New Mexico. It is a land of rich pastures and teeming flocks and herds, a land of rolling mesas and precious running waters that at length unite in the Currumpaw River, from which the whole region is named. And the king whose despotic power was felt over its entire extent was an old gray wolf.

Old Lobo, or the king, as the Mexicans called him, was the gigantic leader of a remarkable pack of gray wolves, that had ravaged the Currumpaw Valley for a number of years. All the shepherds and ranchmen knew him well, and, wherever he appeared with his trusty band, terror reigned supreme among the cattle, and wrath and despair among their owners. Old Lobo was a giant among wolves, and was cunning and strong in proportion to his size. His voice at night was well-known and easily distinguished from that of any of his fellows. An ordinary wolf might howl half the night about the herdsman's bivouac without attracting more than a passing notice, but when the deep roar of the old king came booming down the cañon, the watcher bestirred himself and prepared to learn in the morning that fresh and serious inroads had been made among the herds.

Old Lobo's band was but a small one. This I never quite understood, for usually, when a wolf rises to the position and power that he had, he attracts a numerous following. It may be that he had as many as he desired, or perhaps his ferocious temper prevented the increase of his pack. Certain is it that Lobo had only five followers during the latter part of his reign. Each of these, however, was a wolf of renown, most of them were above the ordinary size, one in particular, the second in command, was a veritable giant, but even he was far below the leader in size and prowess. Several of the band, besides the two leaders, were especially noted. One of those was a beautiful white wolf, that the Mexicans called Blanca; this was supposed to be a female, possibly Lobo's mate. Another was a yellow wolf of remarkable swiftness, which, according to current stories, had, on several occasions, captured an antelope for the pack.

It will be seen, then, that these wolves were thoroughly well-known to the cowboys and shepherds. They were frequently seen and oftener heard, and their lives were intimately associated with those of the cattlemen, who would so gladly have destroyed them. There was not a stockman on the Currumpaw who would not readily have given the value of many steers for the scalp of any one of Lobo's band, but they seemed to possess charmed lives, and defied all manner of devices to kill them. They scorned all hunters, derided all poisons, and continued, for at least five years, to exact their tribute from the Currumpaw ranchers to the extent, many said, of a cow each day. According to this estimate, therefore, the band had killed more than two thousand of the finest stock, for, as was only too well-known, they selected the best in every instance.

The old idea that a wolf was constantly in a starving state, and therefore ready to eat anything, was as far as possible from the truth in this case, for these freebooters were always sleek and well-conditioned, and were in fact most fastidious about what they ate. Any animal that had died from natural causes, or that was diseased or tainted, they would not touch, and they even rejected anything that had been killed by the stockmen. Their choice and daily food was the tenderer part of a freshly killed yearling heifer. An old bull or cow they disdained, and though they occasionally took a young calf or colt, it was quite clear that veal or horseflesh was not their favorite diet. It was also known that they were not fond of mutton, although they often amused themselves by killing sheep. One night in November, 1893, Blanca and the yellow wolf killed two hundred and fifty sheep, apparently for the fun of it, and did not eat an ounce of their flesh.

These are examples of many stories which I might repeat, to show the ravages of this destructive band. Many new devices for their extinction were tried each year, but still they lived and throve in spite of all the efforts of their foes. A great price was set on Lobo's head, and in consequence poison in a score of subtle forms was put out for him, but he never failed to detect and avoid it. One thing only he feared – that was firearms, and knowing full well that all men in this region carried them, he never was known to attack or face a human being. Indeed, the set policy of his band was to take refuge in flight whenever, in the daytime, a man was descried, no matter at what distance. Lobo's habit of permitting the pack to eat only that which they themselves had killed, was in numerous cases their salvation, and the keenness of his scent to detect the taint of human hands or the poison itself, completed their immunity.

On one occasion, one of the cowboys heard the too familiar rallying-cry of Old Lobo, and stealthily approaching, he found the Currumpaw pack in a hollow, where they had 'rounded up' a small herd of cattle. Lobo sat apart on a knoll, while Blanca with the rest was endeavoring to 'cut out' a young cow, which they had selected; but the cattle were standing in a compact mass with their heads outward, and presented to the foe a line of horns, unbroken save when some cow, frightened by a fresh onset of the wolves, tried to retreat into the middle of the herd. It was only by taking advantage of these breaks that the wolves had succeeded at all in wounding the selected cow, but she was far from being disabled, and it seemed that Lobo at length lost patience with his followers, for he left his position on the hill, and, uttering a deep roar, dashed toward the herd. The terrified rank broke at his charge, and he sprang in among them. Then the cattle scattered like the pieces of a bursting bomb. Away went the chosen victim, but ere she had gone twenty-five yards Lobo was upon her. Seizing her by the neck he suddenly held back with all his force and so threw her heavily to the ground. The shock must have been tremendous, for the heifer was thrown heels over head. Lobo also turned a somersault, but immediately recovered himself, and his followers falling on the poor cow, killed her in a few seconds. Lobo took no part in the killing – after having thrown the victim, he seemed to say, "Now, why could not some of you have done that at once without wasting so much time?"

The man now rode up shouting, the wolves as usual retired, and he, having a bottle of strychnine, quickly poisoned the carcass in three places, then went away, knowing they would return to feed, as they had killed the animals themselves. But next morning, on going to look for his expected victims, he found that, although the wolves had eaten the heifer, they had carefully cut out and thrown aside all those parts that had been poisoned.

The dread of this great wolf spread yearly among the ranchmen, and each year a larger price was set on his head, until at last it reached $1,000, an unparalleled wolf-bounty, surely; many a good man has been hunted down for less. Tempted by the promised reward, a Texan ranger named Tannerey came one day galloping up the cañon of the Currumpaw. He had a superb outfit for wolf-hunting – the best of guns and horses, and a pack of enormous wolf-hounds. Far out on the plains of the Panhandle, he and his dogs had killed many a wolf, and now he never doubted that, within a few days, old Lobo's scalp would dangle at his saddle-bow.

Away they went bravely on their hunt in the gray dawn of a summer morning, and soon the great dogs gave joyous tongue to say that they were already on the track of their quarry. Within two miles, the grizzly band of Currumpaw leaped into view, and the chase grew fast and furious. The part of the wolf-hounds was merely to hold the wolves at bay till the hunter could ride up and shoot them, and this usually was easy on the open plains of Texas; but here a new feature of the country came into play, and showed how well Lobo had chosen his range; for the rocky cañons of the Currumpaw and its tributaries intersect the prairies in every direction. The old wolf at once made for the nearest of these and by crossing it got rid of the horsemen. His band then scattered and thereby scattered the dogs, and when they reunited at a distant point of course all of the dogs did not turn up, and the wolves, no longer outnumbered, turned on their pursuers and killed or desperately wounded them all. That night when Tannerey mustered his dogs, only six of them returned, and of these, two were terribly lacerated. This hunter made two other attempts to capture the royal scalp, but neither of them was more successful than the first, and on the last occasion his best horse met its death by a fall; so he gave up the chase in disgust and went back to Texas, leaving Lobo more than ever the despot of the region.

Next year, two other hunters appeared, determined to win the promised bounty. Each believed he could destroy this noted wolf, the first by means of a newly devised poison, which was to be laid out in an entirely new manner; the other a French Canadian, by poison assisted with certain spells and charms, for he firmly believed that Lobo was a veritable 'loup-garou,' and could not be killed by ordinary means. But cunningly compounded poisons, charms, and incantations were all of no avail against this grizzly devastator. He made his weekly rounds and daily banquets as aforetime, and before many weeks had passed, Calone and Laloche gave up in despair and went elsewhere to hunt.

In the spring of 1893, after his unsuccessful attempt to capture Lobo, Joe Calone had a humiliating experience, which seems to show that the big wolf simply scorned his enemies, and had absolute confidence in himself. Calone's farm was on a small tributary of Currumpaw, in a picturesque cañon, and among the rocks of this very cañon, within a thousand yards of the house, old Lobo and his mate selected their den and raised their family that season. There they lived all summer, and killed Joe's cattle, sheep, and dogs, but laughed at all his poisons and traps, and rested securely among the recesses of the cavernous cliffs, while Joe vainly racked his brain for some method of smoking them out, or of reaching them with dynamite. But they escaped entirely unscathed, and continued their ravages as before. "There's where he lived all last summer," said Joe, pointing to the face of the cliff, "and I couldn't do a thing with him. I was like a fool to him."

II

This history, gathered so far from the cowboys, I found hard to believe until in the fall of 1893, I made the acquaintance of the wily marauder, and at length came to know him more thoroughly than anyone else. Some years before, in the Bingo days, I had been a wolf-hunter, but my occupations since then had been of another sort, chaining me to stool and desk. I was much in need of a change, and when a friend, who was also a ranch-owner on the Currumpaw, asked me to come to New Mexico and try if I could do anything with this predatory pack, I accepted the invitation and, eager to make the acquaintance of its king, was as soon as possible among the mesas of that region. I spent some time riding about to learn the country, and at intervals, my guide would point to the skeleton of a cow to which the hide still adhered, and remark, "That's some of his work."

It became quite clear to me that, in this rough country, it was useless to think of pursuing Lobo with hounds and horses, so that poison or traps were the only available expedients. At present we had no traps large enough, so I set to work with poison.

I need not enter into the details of a hundred devices that I employed to circumvent this 'loup-garou'; there was no combination of strychnine, arsenic, cyanide, or prussic acid, that I did not essay; there was no manner of flesh that I did not try as bait; but morning after morning, as I rode forth to learn the result, I found that all my efforts had been useless. The old king was too cunning for me. A single instance will show his wonderful sagacity. Acting on the hint of an old trapper, I melted some cheese together with the kidney fat of a freshly killed heifer, stewing it in a china dish, and cutting it with a bone knife to avoid the taint of metal. When the mixture was cool, I cut it into lumps, and making a hole in one side of each lump, I inserted a large dose of strychnine and cyanide, contained in a capsule that was impermeable by any odor; finally I sealed the holes up with pieces of the cheese itself. During the whole process, I wore a pair of gloves steeped in the hot blood of the heifer, and even avoided breathing on the baits. When all was ready, I put them in a raw-hide bag rubbed all over with blood, and rode forth dragging the liver and kidneys of the beef at the end of a rope. With this I made a ten-mile circuit, dropping a bait at each quarter of a mile, and taking the utmost care, always, not to touch any with my hands.

Lobo, generally, came into this part of the range in the early part of each week, and passed the latter part, it was supposed, around the base of Sierra Grande. This was Monday, and that same evening, as we were about to retire, I heard the deep bass howl of his majesty. On hearing it one of the boys briefly remarked, "There he is, we'll see."

The next morning I went forth, eager to know the result. I soon came on the fresh trail of the robbers, with Lobo in the lead – his track was always easily distinguished. An ordinary wolf's forefoot is 4½ inches long, that of a large wolf 4¾ inches, but Lobo's, as measured a number of times, was 5½ inches from claw to heel; I afterward found that his other proportions were commensurate, for he stood three feet high at the shoulder, and weighed 150 pounds. His trail, therefore, though obscured by those of his followers, was never difficult to trace. The pack had soon found the track of my drag, and as usual followed it. I could see that Lobo had come to the first bait, sniffed about it, and had finally picked it up.

Then I could not conceal my delight. "I've got him at last," I exclaimed; "I shall find him stark within a mile," and I galloped on with eager eyes fixed on the great broad track in the dust. It led me to the second bait and that also was gone. How I exulted – I surely have him now and perhaps several of his band. But there was the broad paw-mark still on the drag; and though I stood in the stirrup and scanned the plain I saw nothing that looked like a dead wolf. Again I followed – to find now that the third bait was gone – and the king-wolf's track led on to the fourth, there to learn that he had not really taken a bait at all, but had merely carried them in his mouth. Then having piled the three on the fourth, he scattered filth over them to express his utter contempt for my devices. After this he left my drag and went about his business with the pack he guarded so effectively.

This is only one of many similar experiences which convinced me that poison would never avail to destroy this robber, and though I continued to use it while awaiting the arrival of the traps, it was only because it was meanwhile a sure means of killing many prairie wolves and other destructive vermin.

About this time there came under my observation an incident that will illustrate Lobo's diabolic cunning. These wolves had at least one pursuit which was merely an amusement, it was stampeding and killing sheep, though they rarely ate them. The sheep are usually kept in flocks of from one thousand to three thousand under one or more shepherds. At night they are gathered in the most sheltered place available, and a herdsman sleeps on each side of the flock to give additional protection. Sheep are such senseless creatures that they are liable to be stampeded by the veriest trifle, but they have deeply ingrained in their nature one, and perhaps only one, strong weakness, namely, to follow their leader. And this the shepherds turn to good account by putting half a dozen goats in the flock of sheep. The latter recognize the superior intelligence of their bearded cousins, and when a night alarm occurs they crowd around them, and usually are thus saved from a stampede and are easily protected. But it was not always so. One night late in last November, two Perico shepherds were aroused by an onset of wolves. Their flocks huddled around the goats, which being neither fools nor cowards, stood their ground and were bravely defiant; but alas for them, no common wolf was heading this attack. Old Lobo, the weir-wolf, knew as well as the shepherds that the goats were the moral force of the flock, so hastily running over the backs of the densely packed sheep, he fell on these leaders, slew them all in a few minutes, and soon had the luckless sheep stampeding in a thousand different directions. For weeks afterward I was almost daily accosted by some anxious shepherd, who asked, "Have you seen any stray OTO sheep lately?" and usually I was obliged to say I had; one day it was, "Yes, I came on some five or six carcasses by Diamond Springs;" or another, it was to the effect that I had seen a small 'bunch' running on the Malpai Mesa; or again, "No, but Juan Meira saw about twenty, freshly killed, on the Cedra Monte two days ago."

At length the wolf traps arrived, and with two men I worked a whole week to get them properly set out. We spared no labor or pains, I adopted every device I could think of that might help to insure success. The second day after the traps arrived, I rode around to inspect, and soon came upon Lobo's trail running from trap to trap. In the dust I could read the whole story of his doings that night. He had trotted along in the darkness, and although the traps were so carefully concealed, he had instantly detected the first one. Stopping the onward march of the pack, he had cautiously scratched around it until he had disclosed the trap, the chain, and the log, then left them wholly exposed to view with the trap still unsprung, and passing on he treated over a dozen traps in the same fashion. Very soon I noticed that he stopped and turned aside as soon as he detected suspicious signs on the trail, and a new plan to outwit him at once suggested itself. I set the traps in the form of an H; that is, with a row of traps on each side of the trail, and one on the trail for the cross-bar of the H. Before long, I had an opportunity to count another failure. Lobo came trotting along the trail, and was fairly between the parallel lines before he detected the single trap in the trail, but he stopped in time, and why and how he knew enough I cannot tell; the Angel of the wild things must have been with him, but without turning an inch to the right or left, he slowly and cautiously backed on his own tracks, putting each paw exactly in its old track until he was off the dangerous ground. Then returning at one side he scratched clods and stones with his hind feet till he had sprung every trap. This he did on many other occasions, and although I varied my methods and redoubled my precautions, he was never deceived, his sagacity seemed never at fault, and he might have been pursuing his career of rapine to-day, but for an unfortunate alliance that proved his ruin and added his name to the long list of heroes who, unassailable when alone, have fallen through the indiscretion of a trusted ally.

III

Once or twice, I had found indications that everything was not quite right in the Currumpaw pack. There were signs of irregularity, I thought; for instance there was clearly the trail of a smaller wolf running ahead of the leader, at times, and this I could not understand until a cowboy made a remark which explained the matter.

"I saw them to-day," he said, "and the wild one that breaks away is Blanca." Then the truth dawned upon me, and I added, "Now I know that Blanca is a she-wolf, because were a he-wolf to act thus, Lobo would kill him at once."

This suggested a new plan. I killed a heifer, and set one or two rather obvious traps about the carcass. Then cutting off the head, which is considered useless offal, and quite beneath the notice of a wolf, I set it a little apart and around it placed six powerful steel traps properly deodorized and concealed with the utmost care. During my operations I kept my hands, boots, and implements smeared with fresh blood, and afterward sprinkled the ground with the same, as though it had flowed from the head; and when the traps were buried in the dust

I brushed the place over with the skin of a coyote, and with a foot of the same animal made a number of tracks over the traps. The head was so placed that there was a narrow passage between it and some tussocks, and in this passage I buried two of my best traps, fastening them to the head itself.

Wolves have a habit of approaching every carcass they get the wind of, in order to examine it, even when they have no intention of eating of it, and I hoped that this habit would bring the Currumpaw pack within reach of my latest stratagem. I did not doubt that Lobo would detect my handiwork about the meat, and prevent the pack approaching it, but I did build some hopes on the head, for it looked as though it had been thrown aside as useless.

Next morning, I sallied forth to inspect the traps, and there, oh, joy! were the tracks of the pack, and the place where the beef-head and its traps had been was empty. A hasty study of the trail showed that Lobo had kept the pack from approaching the meat, but one, a small wolf, had evidently gone on to examine the head as it lay apart and had walked right into one of the traps.

We set out on the trail, and within a mile discovered that the hapless wolf was Blanca. Away she went, however, at a gallop, and although encumbered by the beef-head, which weighed over fifty pounds, she speedily distanced my companion who was on foot. But we overtook her when she reached the rocks, for the horns of the cow's head became caught and held her fast. She was the handsomest wolf I had ever seen. Her coat was in perfect condition and nearly white.

She turned to fight, and raising her voice in the rallying cry of her race, sent a long howl rolling over the cañon. From far away upon the mesa came a deep response, the cry of Old Lobo. That was her last call, for now we had closed in on her, and all her energy and breath were devoted to combat.

Then followed the inevitable tragedy, the idea of which I shrank from afterward more than at the time. We each threw a lasso over the neck of the doomed wolf, and strained our horses in opposite directions until the blood burst from her mouth, her eyes glazed, her limbs stiffened and then fell limp. Homeward then we rode, carrying the dead wolf, and exulting over this, the first death-blow we had been able to inflict on the Currumpaw pack.

At intervals during the tragedy, and afterward as we rode homeward, we heard the roar of Lobo as he wandered about on the distant mesas, where he seemed to be searching for Blanca. He had never really deserted her, but knowing that he could not save her, his deep-rooted dread of firearms had been too much for him when he saw us approaching. All that day we heard him wailing as he roamed in his quest, and I remarked at length to one of the boys, "Now, indeed, I truly know that Blanca was his mate."

As evening fell he seemed to be coming toward the home cañon, for his voice sounded continually nearer. There was an unmistakable note of sorrow in it now. It was no longer the loud, defiant howl, but a long, plaintive wail; "Blanca! Blanca!" he seemed to call. And as night came down, I noticed that he was not far from the place where we had overtaken her. At length he seemed to find the trail, and when he came to the spot where we had killed her, his heart-broken wailing was piteous to hear. It was sadder than I could possibly have believed. Even the stolid cowboys noticed it, and said they had "never heard a wolf carry on like that before." He seemed to know exactly what had taken place, for her blood had stained the place of her death.

Then he took up the trail of the horses and followed it to the ranch-house. Whether in hopes of finding her there, or in quest of revenge, I know not, but the latter was what he found, for he surprised our unfortunate watchdog outside and tore him to little bits within fifty yards of the door. He evidently came alone this time, for I found but one trail next morning, and he had galloped about in a reckless manner that was very unusual with him. I had half expected this, and had set a number of additional traps about the pasture. Afterward I found that he had indeed fallen into one of these, but such was his strength, he had torn himself loose and cast it aside.

I believed that he would continue in the neighborhood until he found her body at least, so I concentrated all my energies on this one enterprise of catching him before he left the region, and while yet in this reckless mood. Then I realized what a mistake I had made in killing Blanca, for by using her as a decoy I might have secured him the next night.

I gathered in all the traps I could command, one hundred and thirty strong steel wolf-traps, and set them in fours in every trail that led into the cañon; each trap was separately fastened to a log, and each log was separately buried. In burying them, I carefully removed the sod and every particle of earth that was lifted we put in blankets, so that after the sod was replaced and all was finished the eye could detect no trace of human handiwork. When the traps were concealed I trailed the body of poor Blanca over each place, and made of it a drag that circled all about the ranch, and finally I took off one of her paws and made with it a line of tracks over each trap. Every precaution and device known to me I used, and retired at a late hour to await the result.

Once during the night I thought I heard Old Lobo, but was not sure of it. Next day I rode around, but darkness came on before I completed the circuit of the north cañon, and I had nothing to report. At supper one of the cowboys said, "There was a great row among the cattle in the north cañon this morning, maybe there is something in the traps there." It was afternoon of the next day before I got to the place referred to, and as I drew near a great grizzly form arose from the ground, vainly endeavoring to escape, and there revealed before me stood Lobo, King of the Currumpaw, firmly held in the traps. Poor old hero, he had never ceased to search for his darling, and when he found the trail her body had made he followed it recklessly, and so fell into the snare prepared for him. There he lay in the iron grasp of all four traps, perfectly helpless, and all around him were numerous tracks showing how the cattle had gathered about him to insult the fallen despot, without daring to approach within his reach. For two days and two nights he had lain there, and now was worn out with struggling. Yet, when I went near him, he rose up with bristling mane and raised his voice, and for the last time made the cañon reverberate with his deep bass roar, a call for help, the muster call of his band. But there was none to answer him, and, left alone in his extremity, he whirled about with all his strength and made a desperate effort to get at me. All in vain, each trap was a dead drag of over three hundred pounds, and in their relentless fourfold grasp, with great steel jaws on every foot, and the heavy logs and chains all entangled together, he was absolutely powerless. How his huge ivory tusks did grind on those cruel chains, and when I ventured to touch him with my rifle-barrel he left grooves on it which are there to this day. His eyes glared green with hate and fury, and his jaws snapped with a hollow 'chop,' as he vainly endeavored to reach me and my trembling horse. But he was worn out with hunger and struggling and loss of blood, and he soon sank exhausted to the ground.

Something like compunction came over me, as I prepared to deal out to him that which so many had suffered at his hands.

"Grand old outlaw, hero of a thousand lawless raids, in a few minutes you will be but a great load of carrion. It cannot be otherwise." Then I swung my lasso and sent it whistling over his head. But not so fast; he was yet far from being subdued, and, before the supple coils had fallen on his neck he seized the noose, and, with one fierce chop, cut through its hard thick strands, and dropped it in two pieces at his feet.

Of course I had my rifle as a last resource, but I did not wish to spoil his royal hide, so I galloped back to the camp and returned with a cowboy and a fresh lasso. We threw to our victim a stick of wood which he seized in his teeth, and before he could relinquish it our lassoes whistled through the air and tightened on his neck.

Yet before the light had died from his fierce eyes, I cried, "Stay, we will not kill him; let us take him alive to the camp." He was so completely powerless now that it was easy to put a stout stick through his mouth, behind his tusks, and then lash his jaws with a heavy cord which was also fastened to the stick. The stick kept the cord in, and the cord kept the stick in, so he was harmless. As soon as he felt his jaws were tied he made no further resistance, and uttered no sound, but looked calmly at us and seemed to say, "Well, you have got me at last, do as you please with me." And from that time he took no more notice of us.

We tied his feet securely, but he never groaned, nor growled, nor turned his head. Then with our united strength [we] were just able to put him on my horse. His breath came evenly as though sleeping, and his eyes were bright and clear again, but did not rest on us. Afar on the great rolling mesas they were fixed, his passing kingdom, where his famous band was now scattered. And he gazed till the pony descended the pathway into the cañon, and the rocks cut off the view.

By travelling slowly we reached the ranch in safety, and after securing him with a collar and a strong chain, we staked him out in the pasture and removed the cords. Then for the first time I could examine him closely, and proved how unreliable is vulgar report where a living hero or tyrant is concerned. He had *not* a collar of gold about his neck, nor was there on his shoulders an inverted cross to denote that he had leagued himself with Satan. But I did find on one haunch a great broad scar, that tradition says was the fang-mark of Juno, the leader of Tannerey's wolf-hounds – a mark which she gave him the moment before he stretched her lifeless on the sand of the cañon.

I set meat and water beside him, but he paid no heed. He lay calmly on his breast, and gazed with those steadfast yellow eyes away past me down through the gateway of the cañon, over the open plains – his plains – nor moved a muscle when I touched him. When the sun went down he was still gazing fixedly across the prairie. I expected he would call up his band when night came, and prepared for them, but he had called once in his extremity, and none had come; he would never call again.

A lion shorn of his strength, an eagle robbed of his freedom, or a dove bereft of his mate, all die, it is said, of a broken heart; and who will aver that this grim bandit could bear the three-fold brunt, heart-whole? This only I know, that when the morning dawned, he was lying there still in his position of calm repose, but his spirit was gone – the old king-wolf was dead.

I took the chain from his neck, a cowboy helped me to carry him to the shed where lay the remains of Blanca, and as we laid him beside her, the cattle-man exclaimed: "There, you *would* come to her, now you are together again."

James de Mille (1833-1880)

Until the publication in 1969 of *A Strange Manuscript Found in a Copper Cylinder* in the New Canadian Library Series, James de Mille was almost an unknown figure in Canadian literature. Yet Archibald MacMechan writing in the *Canadian Magazine* in 1906 remarked: "He was in his time the widest read and the most productive of Canadian writers. He is still in many ways the most remarkable". Certainly in output, de Mille is in the top rank of Canadian writers, among Gilbert Parker, Charles G. D. Roberts, Bliss Carman, and Ralph Connor; he published over 30 books in little over twenty years and was still writing at forty-six, the year of his sudden death.

On August 23, 1833, James de Mille was born to the Demills, a family of probable Loyalist descent who emigrated from New York State. James' father was a well-to-do merchant and shipowner in Saint John and later, the Governor of Acadia College; his mother was descended from a surgeon in the Revolutionary War. At fifteen de Mille was sent to Horton Academy for a year and in 1849-50 he attended Acadia College, matriculating in 1850. For the next eighteen months he toured Europe with his older brother, an experience which aroused his interest in Italian literature and which he made use of in later novels. He then entered Brown University, Rhode Island, as a sophomore and bypassing the B.A. degree, received his M.A. in 1854. For a year he visited friends in Cincinatti, and in 1855 returned to Saint John where he opened a bookshop in partnership with a Mr. Fillimore, an enterprise which failed and left him in debt. From 1861 to 1864 he held a Chair of Classics at Acadia and in 1864 he became Professor of History and Rhetoric at Dalhousie College, where he remained until his death in 1880.

De Mille had written from an early age; while in Europe he kept a journal of his travels, profusely illustrated, like his university lecture notes and his copy-book, with pen-and-ink sketches and caricatures. At an early age he contributed stories to papers such as the *Waverly Magazine* of Boston and to his brother Budd's paper, *The Watchman* of Saint John, as well as an article to *Putnam's*, "Acadia, the Home of Evangeline". His first published novels, *The Martyrs of the Catacombs: A Tale of Ancient Rome* (1865) and *Helen's Household* (1867), drew extensively on his knowledge of Italy and his Italian studies at Brown but his first real success was *The Dodge Club* written about 1860 but not appearing until 1868 in *Harper's Monthly Magazine*. Many of his stories were in the manner of Wilkie Collins, Charles Reade and Jules Verne, novels of adventure and sensation.

But he also wrote historical fiction, humorous and satiric novels and two boys' series, *The Young Dodge Club: The Winged Lion* and *Among the Brigands* (1871) and The Boys of Wolfville College series: *The Boys of Grand Pré School* (1870), *Lost in the Fog* (1871), *Fire in the Woods* (1872), *Picked Up Adrift* (1872) and *The Treasure of the Seas* (1873). Other novels are *Cord and Crease* (1869), *The Lady of the Ice* (1870), *The Cryptogram* (1871), *The American Baron* (1872), *A Comedy of Errors* (1872), *An Open Question* (1873), *The Seven Hills* (1873), *The Living Link* (1874), *A Castle in Spain* (1878) and a historical novel *The Lily and The Cross: A Tale of Acadia* (1874). His *Elements of Rhetoric* on which he laboured for seven years appeared in 1878. *A Strange Manuscript* was published posthumously in 1888 and without the name of the author, while Archibald MacMechan edited his long poem *Behind the Veil* which he found in manuscript among de Mille's papers and published in 1893.

A unique work in the manner of Swift's *Gulliver's Travels* and Butler's *Erewhon, A Strange Manuscript Found in a Copper Cylinder* combines narrative, adventure and romance with a satiric comment on contemporary society. The manuscript is reputedly written by a seaman Adam More whose name suggests both the first man and Sir Thomas More, author of *Utopia*. The novel concerns More's encounter with the Kosekins, a race who speak a language similar to Hebrew and who live in the Antarctic within fifteen hundred miles of the south pole, and his attempt to reconcile their manners and customs with his own. The manuscript is discovered by four men becalmed between the Canary Islands and Madeira. The four, a rich Lord, a doctor, a Cambridge scholar and a cynical littérateur, entertain themselves by reading the tale, and their arguments underline de Mille's satire on his society. A sequel to the work was apparently planned but never completed.

TEXT:

A Strange Manuscript Found in a Copper Cylinder. New York: Harper's, 1888.

See also:

Archibald MacMechan in *Canadian Magazine,* September 1906, 404-16.

Introduction by R. E. Watters to *A Strange Manuscript Found in a Copper Cylinder.* Toronto: New Canadian Library, 1969.

From *A Strange Manuscript Found in a Copper Cylinder*

CHAPTER XV.

THE KOHEN IS INEXORABLE.

I determined to talk to the Kohen, and try for myself whether he might not be accessible to pity. This greatest of cannibals might, indeed, have his little peculiarities, I thought – and who has not? – yet at bottom he seemed full of tender and benevolent feeling; and as he evidently spent his whole time in the endeavor to make us happy, it seemed not unlikely that he might do something for our happiness in a case where our very existence was at stake.

The Kohen listened with deep attention as I stated my case. I did this fully and frankly. I talked of my love for Almah and of Almah's love for me; our hope that we might be united so as to live happily in reciprocal affection; and I was going on to speak of the dread that was in my heart when he interrupted me:

"You speak of being united," said he. "You talk strangely. Of course you mean that you wish to be separated."

"Separated!" I exclaimed. "What do you mean? Of course we wish to be united."

The Kohen stared at me as I said this with the look of one who was quite puzzled; and I then went on to speak of the fate that was before us, and to entreat his sympathy and his aid that we might be saved from so hideous a doom. To all these words the Kohen listened with an air of amazement, as though I were saying incomprehensible things.

"You have a gentle and an affectionate nature," I said – "a nature full of sympathy with others, and noble self-denial."

"Of course," said the Kohen, quickly, as though glad to get hold of something which he could understand, "of course we are all so, for we are so made. It is our nature. Who is there who is not self-denying? No one can help that."

This sounded strange indeed; but I did not care to criticise it. I came to my purpose direct and said,

"Save us from our fate."

"Your fate?"

"Yes, from death – that death of horror."

"Death – horror! What do you mean by horror?" said the Kohen, in an amazement that was sincere and unfeigned. I cannot comprehend your meaning. It seems as though you actually dislike death; but that is not conceivable. It cannot be possible that you fear death."

"Fear death!" I exclaimed, "I do – I do. Who is there that does not fear it?"

The Kohen stared.

"I do not understand you," he said.

"Do you not understand," said I, "that death is abhorrent to humanity."

"Abhorrent!" said the Kohen; "that is impossible. Is it not the highest blessing? Who is there that does not long for death? Death is the greatest blessing, the chief desire of man – the highest aim. And you – are you not to be envied in having your felicity so near? above all, in having such a death as that which is appointed for you – so noble, so sublime? You must be mad; your happiness has turned your head."

All this seemed like hideous mockery, and I stared at the Kohen with a gaze that probably strengthened his opinion of my madness.

"Do you love death?" I asked at length, in amazement.

"Love death? What a question! Of course I love death – all men do; who does not? Is it not human nature? Do we not instinctively fly to meet it whenever we can? Do we not rush into the jaws of sea-monsters, or throw ourselves within their grasp? Who does not feel within him this intense longing after death as the strongest passion of his heart?"

"I don't know – I don't know," said I. "You are of a different race; I do not understand what you say. But I belong to a race that fears death. I fear death and love life; and I entreat you, I implore you to help me now in my distress, and assist me so that I may save my life and that of Almah."

"I – I help you!" said the Kohen, in new amazement. "Why do you come to me – to me, of all men? Why, I am nothing here. And help you to live – to live! Who ever heard of such a thing?"

And the Kohen looked at me with the same astonishment which I should evince if a man should ask me to help him to die.

Still, I persisted in my entreaty for his help.

"Such a request," said he, "is revolting; you must be mad. Such a request outrages all the instincts of humanity. And even if I could do such violence to my own nature as to help you to such a thing, how do you think I could face my fellow-men, or how could I endure the terrible punsihment which would fall upon me?"

"Punishment!" said I. "What! would you be punished?"

"Punished!" said the Kohen. "That, of course, would be inevitable. I should be esteemed an unnatural monster and the chief of criminals. My lot in life now is painful enough; but in this case my punishment would involve me in evils without end. Riches would be poured upon me; I should be raised to the rank of Kohen Gadol; I should be removed farther away than ever from the pauper class – so far, indeed, that all hope in life would be over. I should be made the first and noblest and richest in all the land."

He spoke these words just as if he had said, "the lowest, meanest, poorest, and most infamous." It sounded like fresh mockery, and I could not believe but that he was amusing himself at my expense.

"This is cruel," said I. "You are mocking me."

"Cruel – cruel!" said he; "what is cruel? You mean that such a fate would be cruel for me."

"No, no," said I; "but alas! I see we cannot understand one another."

"No," said the Kohen, musingly, as he looked at me. "No, it seems not; but tell me, Atam-or, is it possible that you really fear death – that you really love life?"

"Fear death! love life!" I cried. "Who does not? Who can help it? Why do you ask me that?"

The Kohen clasped his hands in amazement.

"If you really fear death," said he, "what possible thing is there left to love or to hope for? What, then, do you think the highest blessing of man?"

"Long life," said I, "and riches and requited love."

At this the Kohen started back, and stared at me as though I were a raving madman.

"Oh, holy shades of night!" he exclaimed. "What is that you say? What do you mean?"

"We can never understand one another, I fear," said I. "The love of life must necessarily be the strongest passion of man. We are so made. We give up everything for life. A long life is everywhere considered as the highest blessing; and there is no one who is willing to die, no matter what his suffering may be. Riches also are desired by all, for poverty is the direst curse that can embitter life; and as to requited love, surely that is the sweetest, purest, and most divine joy that the human heart may know."

At this the Kohen burst forth in a strain of high excitement:

"Oh, sacred cavern gloom! Oh, divine darkness! Oh, impenetrable abysses of night! What, oh, what is this! Oh, Atam-or, are you mad? Alas! it must be so. Joy has turned your brain; you are quite demented. You call good evil, and evil good; our light is your darkness, and our darkness your light. Yet surely you cannot be altogether insane. Come, come, let us look further. How is it! Try now to recall your reason. A long life – a life, and a long one! Surely there can be no human being in a healthy state of nature who wishes to prolong his life; and as to riches, is it possible that any one exists who really and honestly desires riches? Impossible! And requited love! Oh, Atam-or, you are mad to-day! You are always strange, but now you have quite taken leave of your senses. I cannot but love you, and yet I can never understand you. Tell me, and tell me truly, what is it that you consider evils, if these things that you have just mentioned are not the very worst?"

He seemed deeply in earnest and much moved. I could not understand him, but could only answer his questions with simple conciseness.

"Poverty, sickness, and death," said I, "are evils; but the worst of all evils is unrequited love."

At these words the Kohen made a gesture of despair.

"It is impossible to understand this," said he. "You talk calmly; you have not the air of a madman. If your fellow-countrymen are all like you, then your race is an incomprehensible one. Why, death is the greatest blessing. We all long for it; it is the end of our being. As for riches, they are a curse, abhorred by all. Above all, as to love, we shrink from the thought of requital. Death is our chief blessing, poverty our greatest happiness, and unrequited love the sweetest lot of man."

All this sounded like the ravings of a lunatic, yet the Kohen was not mad. It seemed also like the mockery of some teasing demon; but the gentle and self-denying Kohen was no teasing demon, and mockery with him was impossible. I was therefore more bewildered than ever at this reiteration of sentiments that were so utterly incomprehensible. He, on the other hand, seemed as astonished at my sentiments and as bewildered, and we could find no common ground on which to meet.

"I remember now," said the Kohen, in a musing tone, "having heard of some strange folk at the Amir, who profess to feel as you say you feel, but no one believes that they are in earnest; for although they may even bring themselves to think that they are in earnest in their professions, yet after all every one thinks that they are self-deceived. For you see, in the first place, these feelings which you profess are utterly unnatural. We are so made that we cannot help loving death; it is a sort of instinct. We are also created in such a way that we cannot help longing after poverty. The pauper must always, among all men, be the most envied of mortals. Nature, too, has made us such that the passion of love, when it arises, is so vehement, so all-consuming, that it must always struggle to avoid requital. This is the reason why, when two people find that they love each other, they always separate and avoid one another for the rest of their lives. This is human nature. We cannot help it; and it is this that distinguishes us from the animals. Why, if men were to feel as you say you feel, they would be mere animals. Animals fear death; animals love to accumulate such things as they prize; animals, when they love, go in pairs, and remain with one another. But man, with his intellect, would not be man if he loved life and desired riches and sought for requited love."

I sank back in despair. "You cannot mean all this," I said.

He threw at me a piteous glance. "What else can you believe or feel?" said he.

"The very opposite. We are so made that we hate and fear death; to us he is the King of Terrors. Poverty is terrible also, since it is associated with want and woe; it is, therefore, natural to man to strive after riches. As to the passion of love, that is so vehement that the first and only thought is requital. Unrequited love is anguish beyond expression – anguish so severe that the heart will often break under it."

The Kohen clasped his hands in new bewilderment.

"I cannot understand," said he. "A madman might imagine that he loved life and desired riches; but as to love, why even a madman could not think of requital, for the very nature of the passion of love is the most utter self-surrender, and a shrinking from all requital; wherefore, the feeling that leads one to desire requital cannot be love. I do not know what it can be – indeed, I never heard of such a thing before, and the annals of the human race make no mention of such a feeling. For what is love? It is the ardent outflow of the whole being – the yearning of one human heart to lavish all its treasures upon another. Love is more than self-denial; it is self-surrender and utter self-abnegation. Love gives all away, and cannot possibly receive anything in return. A requital of love would mean selfishness, which would be self-contradiction. The more one loves, the more he must shrink from requital."

"What!" cried I, "among you do lovers never marry?"

"Lovers marry? Never!"

"Do married people never love one another?"

The Kohen shook his head.

"It unfortunately sometimes happens so," said he, "and then the result is, of course, distressing. For the children's sake the parents will often remain with one another, but in many cases they separate. No one can tell the misery that ensues where a husband and wife love one another."

The conversation grew insupportable. I could not follow the Kohen in what seemed the wildest and maddest flights of fancy that ever were known; so I began to talk of other things, and gradually the Kohen was drawn to speak of his own life. The account which he gave of himself was not one whit less strange than his previous remarks, and for this reason I add it here.

"I was born," said he, "in the most enviable of positions. My father and mother were among the poorest in the land. Both died when I was a child, and I never saw them. I grew up in the open fields and public caverns, along with the most esteemed paupers. But, unfortunately for me, there was something wanting in my natural disposition. I loved death, of course, and poverty, too, very strongly; but I did not have that eager and energetic passion which is so desirable, nor was I watchful enough over my blessed estate of poverty. Surrounded as I was by those who were only too ready to take advantage of my ignorance or want of vigilance, I soon fell into evil ways, and gradually, in spite of myself, I found wealth pouring in upon me. Designing men succeeded in winning my consent to receive their possessions; and so I gradually fell away from that lofty position in which I was born. I grew richer and richer. My friends warned me, but in vain. I was too weak to resist; in fact, I lacked moral fibre, and had never learned how to say 'No.' So I went on, descending lower and lower in the scale of being. I became a capitalist, an Athon, a general officer, and finally Kohen.

"At length, on one eventful day, I learned that one of my associates had by a long course of reckless folly become the richest man in all the country. He had become Athon, malek, and at last Kohen Gadol. It was a terrible shock, but I trust a salutary one. I at once resolved to reform. That resolution I have steadily kept, and have at least saved myself from descending any lower. It is true, I can hardly hope to become what I once was. It is only too easy to grow rich; and, you know, poverty once forfeited can never return except in rare instances. I have, however, succeeded in getting rid of most of my wealth, chiefly through the fortunate advent of Almah and afterwards of yourself. This, I confess, has been my salvation. Neither of you had any scruples about accepting what was bestowed, and so I did not feel as though I was doing you any wrong in giving you all I had in the world. Most of the people of this city have taken advantage of your extraordinary indifference to wealth, and have made themselves paupers at your expense. I had already become your slave, and had received the promise of being elevated to the rank of scullion in the cavern of the *Mista Kosek*. But now, since this event of your love for Almah, I hope to gain far more. I am almost certain of being made a pauper, and I think I can almost venture to hope some day for the honor of a public death."

To such a story I had nothing to say. It was sheer madness; yet it was terribly suggestive, and showed how utterly hopeless was my effort to secure the assistance of such a man towards my escape from death.

"A public death!" I said, grimly. "That will be very fortunate! And do you think that you will gain the dignity of being eaten up afterwards?"

The Kohen shook his head in all seriousness.

"Oh, no," said he; "that would be far beyond my deserts. That is an honor which is only bestowed upon the most distinguished."

Sara Jeannette Duncan (Mrs. Everard Cotes) (1862-1922)

Almost unrecognized in Canada as a novelist until the publication in 1961 of *The Imperialist* in McClelland and Stewart's New Canadian Library, Sara Jeannette Duncan is still little known today for her contribution to the literature of the small town in Ontario and, more important, for her Canadian treatment of James' international theme. Of her twenty-two novels, only one is set in Canada, but two others touch on Anglo-Canadian relations, *An American Girl in London* where the heroine is a guise for Duncan herself, and its sequel *Cousin Cinderella: A Canadian Girl in London,* while *A Social Departure* begins with an epic train journey across Canada taken two years after the opening of the Canadian Pacific Railway from sea to sea.

Sara Jeannette Duncan was born in Brantford on December 18, 1861, one of a number of writers to be born in the notable sixties. Eldest child of five, she was educated in Brantford, and at the Toronto Normal School. She taught public school for several years and then began a career in journalism, writing for the *Washington Post* (for whom she published an interview with the boots of William Dean Howells, standing outside his unanswered door) and then for the Toronto *Globe and Mail* under the pseudonym of Garth Grafton; she also published occasional pieces in *The Week* and the Memphis *Appeal.* In 1888 she became the special parliamentary correspondent of the Montreal *Star* and later in the same year she made a tour of the world, writing letters for the *Globe* which were reprinted in the Canadian and American Press, and published as a volume of essays "Saunterings." Her companion for this trip was Lily Lewis, later Mrs. Lilian Rood, and their experiences form the staple of her first novel *A Social Departure* or *How Orthodocia and I Went Round the World By Ourselves* (1890). In 1891 Miss Duncan married Everard Charles Cotes, a British journalist in India who was at the time curator of the Indian museum in Calcutta and later managing director of the Indian News Agency and the Indian Museum of Calcutta. The couple were in effect citizens of the British Empire for they were at home in both Calcutta and Simla, kept a flat in London and visited Brantford frequently. During the war, Mrs. Cotes took up residence permanently in England and their house became a centre of political and literary activity. She died in Ashstead, Surrey on July 22, 1922.

Miss Duncan wrote over twenty novels in her time. Of chief interest here are *A Social Departure or How Orthodocia and I Went Round the World by Ourselves* (1890), *An American Girl in London* (1891),

The Imperialist (1904), and *Cousin Cinderella, A Canadian Girl in London* (1908). Several others are set in India: *The Simple Adventures of a Mem Sahib* (1893), *The Story of Sonny Sahib* (1894), *His Honour and a Lady* (1896), *Set in Authority* (1906) and *The Burnt Offering* (1909). She also published: *A Daughter of To-Day* (1894), *Vernon's Aunt* (1894), *Hilda* (1898), *A Voyage of Consolation* (1898), *The Path of a Star* (1899), *On the Other Side of the Latch* (1901), *Those Delightful Americans* (1902), *The Pool in the Desert* (1903), *The Consort* (1912), *His Royal Happiness* (1914), *Title Clear* (1922), *The Gold Cure* (1924) and a book of drama *Julyann and Other Plays. His Royal Happiness* was produced as a play at the Royal Alexandra Theatre in Toronto.

The Imperialist is set in Brantford, the Elgin of the novel. It provides not only an analysis of a political situation, an element rare in Canadian fiction, but also an insight into the life of a small town, its values and traditions which anticipates Leacock's *Sunshine Sketches* by nearly a decade. *An American Girl in London* and its successor *Cousin Cinderella* are in a lighter vein. Duncan's versions of Twain's *Innocents Abroad*, they reveal a critical understanding of the differences between the Old and New Worlds, and of the problems, confusions and misunderstandings which these differences lead to. A sequel, *A Voyage of Consolation,* continues the adventures of Miss Mamie Wick in the same light vein.

TEXT:

An American Girl in London. London: Chatto & Windus, 1891.

See also:

Introduction by Claude Bissell to *The Imperialist*. Toronto: New Canadian Library, 1961.
F. Donaldson in *The Bookman*, London, 14 June 1898, 65-67.
M. MacMurchy in *The Bookman,* London, 48, May 1915, 39-40.

From *An American Girl in London*

CHAPTER VIII

'If I only had my own house in Portman Street,' Lady Torquilin remarked next day when we were having our tea in her flat, 'I could make you a great deal more comfy. Here we are just a bit cramped –

"crowded," as you say in America. But you can't eat your cake and have it too.'

'Which have you done, Lady Torquilin,' I inquired, 'with your cake?'

'Let it,' said my friend – 'twenty-five guineas a week, my dear, which is something to a poor woman. Last season it only brought twenty, and cost me a fortune to get it clean again after the pigs who lived in it. For the extra five I have to be thankful to the Duchess.'

'Did you really let it to a Duchess?' I asked, with deep interest. 'How lovely!'

'Indeed I did not! But the Duchess came to live round the corner, and rents went up in consequence. You don't know what it means to property-owners in London to have a duchess living round the corner, my child. It means *every*thing. Not that I'm freehold in Portman Street – I've only a lease,' and Lady Torquilin sighed. This led us naturally into matters of finance, and we had a nice, sensible, practical discussion about our joint expenses. It doesn't matter to anybody what our arrangement was, but I must say that I found great occasion for protest against its liberality towards me. 'Nonsense!' said Lady Torquilin, invariably; 'don't be a foolish kitten! It's probably less than you would pay at a good private hotel – that's the advantage to you. Every time we take a hansom it will be only sixpence each instead of a shilling – that's the advantage to me; and no small advantage it is, for cabs are my ruin. And you'll save me plenty of steps, I'm sure, my dear! So there, say no more about it, but go and get your boxes.'

So I drove back to the Métropole finally, and as I locked my last trunk I noticed a fresh card on the mantelpiece. It was another of Mr. Charles Mafferton's; and on the back was written in pencil: *I hope you are meeting with no difficulties. Should be glad to be of use in any way. Please let me know your permanent address as soon as possible, as the mother and sisters would like to call upon you. – C. M.'* This was nice and kind and friendly, and I tried in vain to reconcile it with what I had heard of English stiffness and exclusiveness and reserve. I would write to Mr. Mafferton, I thought, that very night. I supposed that by *the* mother he meant his own, but it struck me as a curious expression. In America we specify our parents, and a reference to 'the mother' there would probably be held to refer back to Eve. But in England you like all kinds of distinguishing articles, don't you?

Lady Torquilin's flat was a new one, of the regular American kind – not a second or third floor in an old-fashioned London house – and had a share, I am thankful to say, in a primitive elevator. The elevator was very small, but the man in the lower hall seemed to stand greatly in awe of it. 'To get them there boxes up in this 'ere lift, miss,' he said, when I and my trunks presented ourselves, 'she'll 'ave to make three trips at least' – and he looked at me rather reproachfully. ''Ware do you want 'em put out?' I said, 'Lady Torquilin's flat.' 'That's Number Four,' he commented, 'a good ways up. If you wouldn't mind a h'extra sixpence, miss, I could get a man off the street to 'elp me with 'em – they do be a size!' I said by all means, and presently my impedimenta were ascending with much deliberate circumstance, one piece at a time. The acoustic properties of Cadogan Mansions are remarkable. Standing at the foot of that elevator, encouraging its labours as it were, I could not possibly help overhearing Lady Torquilin's reception of my trunks, mingled with the more subdued voices of her housemaids. It was such a warm reception, expressed in such graphic terms, that I thought I ought to be present myself to acknowledge it; and the man put on two ordinary-sized valises next, to allow me to go up at the same time. 'We've got our orders, miss, to be pertickeler about wot she carries, miss,' he said, when I thought a trunk or two might accompany me. 'You see, if anything went wrong with 'er works, miss, there's no saying' ware we'd be!' – and we solemnly began to rise. 'Ladies in the Mansions don't generally use the lift such a very great deal,' he remarked further, 'especially goin' down. They complain of the sinkin'.'

'I shall always go up and down in it,' I said. 'I don't mind the sinking. I'm used to it.'

'Very well, miss. You 'ave only to press the button and she'll come up; an' a great convenience you'll find 'er, miss,' he returned, resignedly, unlocking the grated door on Lady Torquilin's flat, where my hostess stood with her hands folded, and two maids respectfully behind her, regarding the first instalment of my baggage. After she had welcomed me: 'It's curiosity in its way,' said Lady Torquilin; 'but what's to be done with it, the dear only knows – unless we sublet it.' It required some strength of mind to tell her that there were two more coming up. The next one she called an abnormity, and the third she called a barn – simply. And I must say my trunks did look imposing in Lady Torquilin's flat. Finally, however, by the exercise of ingenuity on our parts and muscle on the maids', we got the whole of my baggage 'settled up,' as Lady Torquilin expressed it, and I was ready for my first approved and endorsed experience in your metropolis.

It came that afternoon. 'I am going to take you,' said Lady Torquilin at lunch, 'to Mrs. Fry Hamilton's "at home." She likes Americans, and her parties – "functions," as society idiots call it – disgusting word – are generally rather "swagger," as they say. I daresay you'll enjoy it. Make yourself as tidy as possible, mind. Put on your pretty grey; tuck in that "fringe" of yours a bit too, my dear; and be ready by five sharp.'

'Don't you like my bangs, Lady Torquilin?'

'Say your fringe, child; people don't "bang" in England – except doors and the piano. No, I can't say I'm fond of it. What were you given a forehead for, if you were not intended to show it? I fancy I see Sir Hector, when he was alive, allowing me to wear a fringe!' And

Lady Torquilin pushed my hair up in that fond, cheerful, heavy-handed way people have, that makes you back away nervously and feel yourself a fright. I went to my room wondering whether my affection for Lady Torquilin would ever culminate in the sacrifice of my bangs. I could not say, seriously, that I felt equal to it then.

We went to Mrs. Fry Hamilton's in a hansom – not, as Lady Torquilin said, that she had the least objection to omnibuses, especially when they didn't drop one at the very door, but because there were no omnibuses very convenient to the part of Cromwell Road that Mrs. Fry Hamilton lived in. We inspected several before Lady Torquilin made a selection – rubber-tyred, yellow-wheeled, with a horse attached that would hardly stand still while we got in. I was acutely miserable, he went so fast; but Lady Torquilin liked it. 'He's perfectly fresh, poor darling!' she said. 'It breaks my heart to drive behind a wretched worn-out creature with its head down.' I said, Yes, I thought he was very fresh indeed, and asked Lady Torquilin if she noticed how he waggled his head. 'Dear beastie!' she replied, 'he's got a sore mouth. Suppose your mouth were perfectly raw, and you had a bit in it, and a man tugging at the reins – ' But I couldn't stand it any longer; I put my parasol up through the door in the top. 'Make him stop waggling!' I called to the driver. 'It's only a little 'abit of 'is, miss,' the driver said, and then, as the horse dropped his pace, he whipped him. Instantly Lady Torquilin's parasol admonished him. 'If you flog your horse,' she said emphatically, 'I get out.' I don't think I have ever driven in a hansom with Lady Torquilin since that our parasols have not both gone through the roof to point statements like these to the cabman, Lady Torquilin usually anguished on the dear horse's account, and I unhappy on my own. It enlivens the most monotonous drive, but it is a great strain on the nerves. I generally beg for a four-wheeler instead; but Lady Torquilin is contemptuous of four-wheelers, and declares she would just as soon drive in the British Museum. She says I will get used to it if I will only abstract my mind and talk about something else; and I am trying, but the process is a very painful one.

When we arrived at Mrs. Fry Hamilton's I rang the bell. 'Bless you, child!' said Lady Torquilin, 'that's not the way. They'll take you for a nursery governess, or a piano-tuner, or a bill! This is the proper thing for visitors.' And with that Lady Torquilin rapped sonorously and rang a peal – such a rap and peal as I had never heard in all my life before. In America we have only one kind of ring for everybody – from the mayor of the city to the man who sells plaster Cupids and will take old clothes on account. We approach each other's door-bells, as a nation, with much greater deference; and there is a certain humility in the way we introduce our personalities anywhere. I felt uncomfortable on Mrs. Fry Hamilton's doorstep, as if I were not, individually, worth all that noise. Since then I have been obliged to rap and ring myself, because Lady Torquilin likes me to be as proper as I can; but there is always an incompleteness about the rap and an ineffectualness about the ring. I simply haven't the education to do it. And when the footman opens the door I feel that my face expresses deprecatingly, 'It's only me!' 'Rap and ring!' says Lady Torquilin, deridingly, 'it's a tap and tinkle!' Lady Torquilin is fond of alliteration.

Inside quite a few people were ascending and descending a narrow staircase that climbed against the wall, taking up as little room as it could; and a great many were in the room on the ground-floor, where refreshments were being dispensed. They were all beautifully dressed – if I have learned anything in England, it is not to judge the English by the clothes they wear in America – and they moved about with great precision, making, as a general thing, that pleasant rustle which we know to mean a silk foundation. The rustle was the only form of conversation that appeared to be general, but I noticed speaking going on in several groups of two or three. And I never saw better going up and down stairs – it was beautifully done, even by ladies weighing, I should think, quite two hundred pounds apiece, which you must reduce to "stun" for yourself. Lady Torquilin led the way with great simplicity and directness into the dining-room, and got tea for us both from one of the three white-capped modestly-expressionless maids behind the table – I cannot tell you what a dream of peace your servants are in this country – and asked me whether I would have sponge-cake, or a cress sandwich, or what. 'But,' I said, 'where is Mrs. Fry Hamilton? – I haven't been introduced.' 'All in good time,' said Lady Torquilin. 'It's just as well to take our tea when we can get it – we won't be able to turn round in here in half an hour!' – and Lady Torquilin took another sandwich with composure. 'Try the plum-cake,' she advised me in an aside. 'Buszard – I can tell at a glance! *I* have to deny myself.'

And I tried the plum-cake, but with a sense of guilty apprehension lest Mrs. Fry Hamilton should appear in the doorway and be naturally surprised at the consumption of her refreshments by an utter stranger. I noticed that almost everybody else did the same thing, and that nobody seemed at all nervous; but I occupied as much of Lady Torquilin's shadow as I could, all the same, and on the way up implored her, saying, '*Have* I any crumbs?' I felt that it would require more hardihood than I possessed to face Mrs. Fry Hamilton with shreds of her substance, acquired before I knew her, clinging to my person. But concealment was useless, and seemed to be unnecessary.

'Have you had any tea?' said Mrs. Fry Hamilton to Lady Torquilin, her question embracing us both, as we passed before her; and Lady Torquilin said, 'Yes, thanks,' as nonchalantly as possible.

Lady Torquilin had just time to say that I was an American.

'Really!' remarked Mrs. Fry Hamilton, looking at me again. 'How nice. The only one I have to-day, I think.' And we had to make room for somebody else. But it was then that the curious sensation of being attached to a string and led about, which I have felt more or less in London ever since, occurred to me first – in the statement that I was the only one Mrs. Fry Hamilton had to-day.

Lady Torquilin declared, as she looked round the room, that she didn't see a soul she knew; so we made our way to a corner and sat down, and began to talk in those uninterested spasms that always attack people who come with each other. Presently – 'There is that nice little Mrs. Pastelle-Jones!' said Lady Torquilin, 'I *must* go and speak to her!' – and I was left alone, with the opportunity of admiring the china. I don't wonder at your fondness for it in London drawing-rooms. It seems to be the only thing that you can keep clean. So many people were filing in past Mrs. Fry Hamilton, however, that the china soon lost its interest for me. The people were chiefly ladies – an impressive number of old, stout, rosy, white-haired ladies in black, who gave me the idea of remarkable health at their age; more middle-aged ones, rather inclined to be pale and thin, with narrow cheek-bones, and high-arched noses, and sweet expressions, and a great deal of black lace and jet, much puffed on the shoulders; and young ones, who were, of course, the very first English young ladies I had ever seen in an English drawing-room. I suppose you are accustomed to them; you don't know what they were to me – you couldn't understand the intense interest and wonder and admiration they excited in me. I had never seen anything human so tall and strong and fine and fresh-coloured before, with such clear limpid eyes, such pretty red lips, and the outward showing of such excellent appetites. It seemed to me that everyone was an epitome of her early years of bread-and-butter and milk puddings and going to bed at half-past nine, and the epitomes had a charming similarity. The English young lady stood before me in Mrs. Fry Hamilton's drawing-room as an extraordinary product – in almost all cases five-eight, and in some quite six feet in height. Her little mamma was dwarfed beside her, and when she smiled down upon the occasional man who was introduced to her, in her tall, compassionate way, he looked quite insignificant, even if he carried the square, turned-back shoulders by which I have learned to tell military men in this country. We have nothing like it in America, on the same scale; although we have a great deal more air to breathe and vegetables to eat than you. I knew that I had always been considered 'a big girl,' but beside these firm-fleshed young women I felt myself rather a poor creature, without a muscular advantage to my name. They smiled a good deal, but I did not see them talk much – it seemed enough for them to be; and they had a considering air, as if things were new to them, and they had not quite made up their minds. And as they considered they blushed a good deal, in a way that was simply sweet. As I sat musing upon them I saw Lady Torquilin advancing toward me, with one of the tallest, pinkest, best-developed, and most tailor-made of all immediately behind her, following, with her chin outstretched a little, and her eyes downcast, and a pretty expression of doing what she was told.

'My dear,' said Lady Torquilin, 'this is Miss Gladys Fortescue. Gladys – Miss Wick, my young lady friend from Chicago. Miss Fortescue has a brother in America, so you will have something to chat about.'

'Howdj-do?' said Miss Fortescue. She said it very quickly, with a sweet smile, and an interesting little mechanical movement of the head, blushing at the same time; and we shook hands. That is, I think one of us did, though I can't say positively which one it was. As I remember the process, there were two shakes; but they were not shakes that ran into each other, and one of them – I think it was mine – failed to 'come off,' as you say in tennis. Mine was the shake that begins nowhere in particular, and ends without your knowing it – just the ordinary American shake arranged on the muscular system in common use with us. Miss Fortescue's was a rapid, convulsive movement, that sprang from her shoulder and culminated with a certain violence. There was a little push in it, too, and it exploded, as it were, high in air. At the same time I noticed the spectacles of a small man who stood near very much in peril from Miss Fortescue's elbow. Then I remembered and understood the sense of dislocation I had experienced after shaking hands with Mrs. Fry Hamilton, and which I had attributed, in the confusion of the moment, to being held up, so to speak, as an American.

'Do you know my brother?' said Miss Fortescue.

'I am afraid not,' I replied. 'Where does he live?'

'In the United States,' said Miss Fortescue. 'He went out there six months ago with a friend. Perhaps you know his friend – Mr. Colfax.'

I said I knew two or three Mr. Colfaxes, but none of them were English – had not been, at least, for some time back; and did Miss Fortescue know what particular part of the Union her brother and his friend had gone to? 'You know,' I said, 'we have an area of three million square miles.' I daresay I mentioned our area with a certain pardonable pride. It's a thing we generally make a point of in America.

I shouldn't have thought there was anyting particularly humorous in an area, but Miss Fortescue laughed prettily. 'I remember learning that from my governess,' she said. 'My brother is out in the West – either in the town of Minneapolis and the State of Minnesota, or the town of Minnesota and the State of Minneapolis. I never know, without looking out his address, which comes first. But I daresay there are a good many people in the United States – you might easily miss him.'

'We have sixty millions, Miss Fortescue,' I said; and Miss Fortescue returned that in that case she didn't see how we could be expected to know *any*body; and after that the conversation flagged for a few seconds, during which we both looked at the other people.

'I have never been to America,' Miss Fortescue said. 'I should like to go. Is it very cold?'

I did not mention the area again. 'In some places,' I said.

'I should not like that. But then, you have the toe-beganing – that must be nice.'

I assented, though I did not in the least know, until Miss Fortescue spoke of skating, what she meant. Miss Fortescue thought the skating must be nice, too, and then, she supposed, though it was cold, we always went out *prepared* for it. And the conversation flagged again. Fortunately, a gentleman at the other end of the room, where the piano was, began at that moment to sing something very pleading and lamentable and uncomfortable, with a burden of 'I love thee so,' which generally rhymed with 'woe' – an address to somebody he called 'Dear-r-r *Hear-r-r-t!*' as high as he could reach, turning up his eyes a good deal, as if he were in pain. And for the time it was not necessary to talk. When he had finished Miss Fortescue asked me if it was not delightful, and I said it was – did she know the gentleman's name? Miss Fortescue said she did not, but perhaps Lady Torquilin would. And then, just as Lady Torquilin came up, 'How do you like England?' asked Miss Fortescue.

* * *

'Well,' asked Lady Torquilin, as we drove home in another hansom, 'what did you and Gladys Fortescue find to say to each other?'

I said, quite truly, that I did not remember at the moment, but I admired Miss Fortescue – also with great sincerity – so enthusiastically, that I daresay Lady Torquilin thought we had got on splendidly together.

And what I wonder is, if Miss Fortescue had been asked about our conversation, what she would have said.

Gilbert Parker (1862-1932)

A prolific writer who published more than thirty-five works, Sir Gilbert Parker had an international reputation as a writer of short stories, novels, poetry, drama, travelogues and political commentary. He is the only Canadian writer to have his works published in a Scribner's Imperial edition uniform with collected works of Dickens, Meredith, Kipling and Henry James (23 volumes, 1912-23). Although Parker employs a wide variety of settings from Egypt to the South Seas, nearly half of his fiction is set in Canada.

Eldest son of a retired army officer turned village magistrate, Gilbert Parker was born in Camden East, Canada West on November 23, 1862. He attended Trinity College School in Port Hope and Ottawa Normal School. After teaching for a short time, he entered Trinity College, University of Toronto. In 1883 he was ordained in Kingston as a deacon of the Church of England and became a curate in Trenton. He did not however take up orders. He attended a course on elocution at Victoria University, Cobourg in 1884 and the following year he taught oratory at Queen's University. In 1885 he left Canada for Australia, giving lectures in a number of cities and journeying into the interior. He later took up a position on the Sydney *Morning Herald* with the proviso that he should spend three months of each year in travels to the South Seas.

Parker moved to England in 1889 where his extensive knowledge of Canada, South Africa and Australia stood him in good stead. Elected to the House of Commons as the unionist member for Gravesend in 1900, he represented the constituency for eighteen years. In 1903 he convened the first conference of universities of the Empire; for seven years he was chairman of the Imperial South African Association and during the war, was director of British publicity in America. During his later life he spent much time in America, particularly in California. He died in London in September, 1932.

Parker's literary career began in Australia where three of his plays, an adaptation of Faust, *No Defence* and *Heart of Gold* were produced profitably by the well-known actor George Rignold. He also wrote a sonnet sequence, "A Lover's Diary," published in Chicago in 1894, and a collection of lyrics, *Embers,* published by subscription in London in 1908. He brought out his first collection of short stories, *Pierre and his People,* in 1892, and from this time on, published thirty-two novels and short story collections in the next thirty-six years, with settings ranging from Canada to Egypt, the Channel Islands and the South Seas. Those set in Quebec are: *The Trail of the Sword* (1894), *When*

Valmond Came to Pontiac (1895), *The Pomp of the Lavilettes* (1896), *The Seats of the Mighty* (1896), *Born with a Golden Spoon* (1899), *The Lane that Had no Turning* (1900), *The Right of Way* (1901), *The Money Master* (1915), and *The Power and the Glory: a Romance of the Great Lasalle* (1925). *You Never Know Your Luck* (1914), *The World For Sale* (1916), and *Wild Youth and Another* (1919) are set in Saskatchewan, and the short stories in the collections *An Adventurer of the North* (1895) (published also as *A Romany of the Snows*) and *Northern Lights* (1909) take place mainly in the North-West. In addition, Parker wrote a book on travel *Round the Compass in Australia* (1892), and a book on the war, *The World in Crucible* (1915). He collaborated with Claude G. Bryan on *Old Quebec* and with Richard Dawson on *The Land, the People and the State* (1910, New York, 1913).

Parker's most interesting works are set in Canada. In *When Valmond Came to the Pontiac*, the hero poses as the son of Napoleon in a little Quebec village. *The Seats of the Mighty*, a novel of intrigue and adventure, is set like Kirby's *The Golden Dog* in the Quebec of the French regime before 1759; Parker took his information from Francis Parkman and from James Le Moine's *Maple Leaves* to create an authentic picture of the period. *Pierre and his People* is a collection of seventeen tales previously published in such magazines as the New York *Independent*. The settings range from Quebec to British Columbia but concentrate on the Canadian north-west before the transfer to the government in 1870 of the Hudson's Bay Company lands. Parker describes Pretty Pierre as combining the nonchalance and debonair qualities of the French with Indian coolness and nerve, and notes that he serves to link the tales together. Twenty-two more Pretty Pierre stories appear in a sequel, *An Adventurer in the North*.

TEXT:

Pierre and his People. Toronto: Copp Clark, 1894.

See also:
O. J. Stevenson. *A People's Best*. Toronto: Musson, 1927.
Desmond Pacey. *Creative Writing in Canada*. Toronto: Ryerson, 1958.

From *Pierre and His People*

THE STONE.

THE Stone hung on a jutting crag of Purple Hill. On one side of it, far beneath, lay the village, huddled together as if, through being close compacted, its handful of humanity should not be a mere dust in the balance beside Nature's portentousness. Yet if one stood beside The Stone, and looked down, the flimsy wooden huts looked like a barrier at the end of a great flume. For the hill hollowed and narrowed from The Stone to the village, as if giants had made this concave path by trundling boulders to that point like a funnel where the miners' houses now formed a *cul-de-sac*. On the other side of the crag was a valley also; but it was lonely and untenanted; and at one flank of The Stone were serried legions of trees.

The Stone was a mighty and wonderful thing. Looked at from the village direct, it had nothing but the sky for a background. At times, also, it appeared to rest on nothing; and many declared that they could see clean between it and the oval floor of the crag on which it rested. That was generally in the evening, when the sun was setting behind it. Then the light coiled round its base, between it and its pedestal, thus making it appear to hover above the hill-point, or, planet-like, to be just settling on it. At other times, when the light was perfectly clear and not too strong, and the village side of the crag was brighter than the other, more accurate relations of The Stone to its pedestal could be discovered. Then one would say that it balanced on a tiny base, a toe of granite. But if one looked long, especially in the summer, when the air throbbed, it evidently rocked upon that toe; if steadily, and very long, he grew tremulous, perhaps afraid. Once, a woman who was about to become a mother went mad, because she thought The Stone would hurtle down the hill at her great moment and destroy her and her child. Indians would not live either on the village side of The Stone or in the valley beyond. They had a legend that, some day, one, whom they called The Man Who Sleeps, would rise from his hidden couch in the mountains, and, being angry that any dared to cumber his playground, would hurl The Stone upon them that dwelt at Purple Hill. But white men pay little heed to Indian legends.

At one time or another every person who had come to the village visited The Stone. Colossal as it was, the real base on which its weight rested was actually very small: the view from the village had not been all deceitful. It is possible, indeed, that at one time it had really rocked, and that the rocking had worn for it a shallow cup, or socket, in which it poised. The first man who came to Purple Valley prospecting had often stopped his work and looked at The Stone in a half-fear that it would spring upon him unawares. And yet he had as often laughed at himself for doing so, since, as he said, it must have been there hundreds of thousands of years. Strangers, when they came to the village, went to sleep somewhat timidly the first night of their stay, and not infrequently left their beds to go and look at The Stone, as it hung there ominously in the light of the moon; or listened towards it if it was dark. When the moon rose late, and The Stone chanced to be directly in front of it, a black sphere seemed to be rolling into the light to blot it out.

But none who lived in the village looked upon The Stone in quite the same fashion as did that first man who had come to the valley. He had seen it through three changing seasons, with no human being near him, and only occasionally a shy, wandering elk, or a cloud of wild ducks whirring down the pass, to share his companionship with it. Once he had waked in the early morning, and, possessed of a strange feeling, had gone out to look at The Stone. There, perched upon it, was an eagle; and though he said to himself that an eagle's weight was to The Stone as a feather upon the world, he kept his face turned towards it all day; for all day the eagle stayed. He was a man of great stature and immense strength. The thews of his limbs stood out like soft unbreakable steel. Yet, as if to cast derision on his strength and great proportions, God or Fate turned his bread to ashes, gave failure into his hands where he hugely grasped at fortune, and hung him about with misery. He discovered gold, but others gathered it. It was his daughter that went mad, and gave birth to a dead child in fearsome thought of The Stone. Once, when he had gone over the hills to another mining field, and had been prevented from coming back by unexpected and heavy snows, his wife was taken ill, and died alone of starvation, because none in the village remembered of her and her needs. Again, one wild night, long after, his only son was taken from his bed and lynched for a crime that was none of his, as was discovered by his murderers next day. Then they killed horribly the real criminal, and offered the father such satisfaction as they could. They said that any one of them was ready there to be killed by him; and they threw a weapon at his feet. At this he stood looking upon them for a moment, his great breast heaving, and his eyes glowering; but presently he reached out his arms, and taking two of them by the throat, brought their heads together heavily, breaking their skulls; and, with a cry in his throat like a wounded animal, left them, and entered the village no more. But it became known that he had built a rude hut on Purple Hill, and that he had been seen standing beside The Stone or sitting among the boulders below it, with his face bent upon the village. Those who had come near to him said that he had greatly changed; that his hair and beard had grown long and strong, and, in effect, that he looked like some rugged fragment of an antique world.

The time came when they associated The Man with The Stone; they grew to speak of him simply as The Man. There was something natural and apt in the association. Then they avoided these two singular dwellers on the height. What had happened to The Man when he lived in the village became almost as great a legend as the Indian fable concerning The Stone. In the minds of the people one seemed as old as the other. Women who knew the awful disasters which had befallen The Man brooded at times most timidly, regarding him as they did at first – and even still – The Stone. Women who carried life unborn about with them had a strange dread of both The Stone and The Man. Time passed on, and the feeling grew that The Man's grief must be a terrible thing, since he lived alone with The Stone and God. But this did not prevent the men of the village from digging gold, drinking liquor, and doing many kinds of evil. One day, again, they did an unjust and cruel thing. They took Pierre, the gambler, whom they had at first sought to vanquish at his own art, and, possessed suddenly of the high duty of citizenship, carried him to the edge of a hill and dropped him over, thinking thereby to give him a quick death, while the vultures would provide him a tomb. But Pierre was not killed, though to his grave – unprepared as yet – he would bear an arm which should never be lifted higher than his shoulder. When he waked from the crashing gloom which succeeded the fall, he was in the presence of a being whose appearance was awesome and massive – an outlawed god: whose hair and beard were white, whose eye was piercing, absorbing, painful, in the long perspective of its woe. This being sat with his great hand clasped to the side of his head. The beginning of his look was the village, and – though the vision seemed infinite – the village was the end of it too. Pierre, looking through the doorway beside which he lay, drew in his breath sharply, for it seemed at first as if The Man was an unnatural fancy, and not a thing. Behind The Man was The Stone, which was not more motionless nor more full of age than this its comrade. Indeed, The Stone seemed more a thing of life as it poised above the hill: The Man was sculptured rock. His white hair was chiselled on his broad brow, his face was a solemn pathos petrified, his lips were curled with an iron contempt, an incalculable anger.

The sun went down, and darkness gathered about The Man. Pierre reached out his hand, and drank the water and ate the coarse bread that had been put near him. He guessed that trees or protruding ledges had broken his fall, and that he had been rescued and brought here. As he lay thinking, The Man entered the doorway, stooping much to do so. With flints he lighted a wick which hung from a wooden bowl of bear's oil; then kneeling, held it above his head, and looked at Pierre. And Pierre, who had never feared anyone, shrank from the look in The Man's eyes. But when the other saw that Pierre was awake, a distant kindness came upon his face, and he nodded gravely; but he did not speak. Presently a great tremor as of pain shook all his limbs, and he set the candle on the ground, and with his stalwart hands arranged afresh the bandages about Pierre's injured arm and leg. Pierre spoke at last.

"You are The Man?" he said.

The other bowed his head.

"You saved me from those devils in the valley?" A look of impregnable hardness came into The Man's face, but he pressed Pierre's hand for answer; and though the pressure was meant to be gentle, Pierre winced painfully. The candle spluttered, and the hut filled with a sickly smoke. The Man brought some bear skins and covered the sufferer, for, the season being autumn, the night was cold. Pierre, who had thus spent his first sane and conscious hour in many days, fell asleep. What time it was when he waked he was not sure, but it was to hear a metallic *click-click* come to him through the clear air of night. It was a pleasant noise as of steel and rock: the work of some lonely stone-cutter of the hills. The sound reached him with strange, increasing distinctness. Was this Titan that had saved him sculpturing some figure from the metal hill? *Click-click*! it vibrated as regularly as the keen pulse of a watch. He lay and wondered for a long time, but fell asleep again; and the steely iteration went on in his dreams.

In the morning The Man came to him, and cared for his hurts, and gave him food; but still would speak no word. He was gone nearly all day in the hills; yet when evening came he sought the place where Pierre had seen him the night before, and the same weird scene was re-enacted. And again in the night the clicking sound went on; and every night it was renewed. Pierre grew stronger, and could, with difficulty, stand upon his feet. One night he crept out, and made his way softly, slowly, towards the sound. He saw The Man kneeling beside The Stone, he saw a hammer rise and fall upon a chisel; and the chisel was at the base of The Stone. The hammer rose and fell with perfect but dreadful precision. Pierre turned and looked towards the village below, whose lights were burning like a bunch of fire-flies in the gloom. Again he looked at The Stone and The Man.

Then the thing came to him sharply. The Man was chiselling away the socket of The Stone, bringing it to that point of balance where the touch of a finger, the wing of a bird, or the whistle of a north-west wind, would send it down upon the offending and unsuspecting village.

The thought held him paralysed. The Man had nursed his revenge long past the thought of its probability by the people beneath. He had at first sat and watched the village, hated, and mused dreadfully upon the thing he had determined to do. Then he had worked a little, afterwards more, and now, lastly, since he had seen what they had done to Pierre, with the hot but firm eagerness of an avenging giant.

Pierre had done some sad deeds in his time, and had tasted some sweet revenges, but nothing like to this had ever entered his brain. In that village were men who – as they thought – had cast him to a death fit only for a coward or a cur. Well, here was the most exquisite retaliation. Though his hand should not be in the thing, he could still be the cynical and approving spectator.

But yet: had all those people hovering about those lights below done harm to him? He thought there were a few – and they were women – who would not have followed his tumbril to his death with cries of execration. The rest would have done so, – most of them did so, – not because he was a criminal, but because he was a victim, and because human nature as it is thirsts inordinately at times for blood and sacrifice – a living strain of the old barbaric instinct. He remembered that most of these people were concerned in having injured The Man. The few good women there had vile husbands; the few pardonable men had hateful wives: the village of Purple Hill was an ill affair.

He thought: now doubtfully, now savagely, now with irony.

The hammer and steel clicked on.

He looked at the lights of the village again.

Suddenly there came to his mind the words of a great man who sought to save a city manifold centuries ago. He was not sure that he wished to save this village, but there was a grim, almost grotesque fitness in the thing that he now intended. He spoke out clearly through the night:

"*Oh, let not the Lord be angry and I will speak yet but this once: Peradventure ten righteous shall be found there.*'"

The hammer stopped. There was a silence, in which the pines sighed lightly. Then, as if speaking was a labour, The Man replied in a deep, harsh voice:

"I will not spare it for ten's sake."

Again there was a silence, in which Pierre felt his maimed body bend beneath him; but presently the voice said, – "*Now!*"

At this the moon swung from behind a cloud. The Man stood behind The Stone. His arm was raised to it. There was a moment's pause – it seemed like years to Pierre; a wind came softly crying out of the west, the moon hurried into the dark, and then a monster sprang from its pedestal upon Purple Hill, and, with a sound of thunder and an awful speed, raced upon the village below. The boulders of the hillside crumbled after it.

And Pierre saw the lights go out.

The moon shone out again for an instant, and Pierre saw that The Man stood where The Stone had been; but when he reached the place The Man was gone. Forever!

E. W. Thomson (1849-1924)

A surveyor, civil engineer and journalist by profession, E. W. Thomson was also well known in his day for his poetry and for his short stories of voyageurs, habitants, Ontario Scots and veterans of the Civil War. *The Literary History of Canada* calls Thomson "one of the most skillful story-tellers of the Canadian writers of his day", and Desmond Pacey in his *Creative Writing* suggests that his most successful humorous stories are "worthy of Leacock at his best".

Edward Wills Thomson was born in Peel County, Upper Canada on February 12, 1849. His great grandfather Thomson was the first settler in Scarborough and his grandfather who had served under Brock at Queenston Heights, was a member of the Legislative Council and an opponent of William Lyon Mackenzie. Thomson was educated at the Brantford Grammar School and at Trinity College School, Weston. At the age of fourteen, he was sent to Philadelphia to live with an aunt and uncle, and here he became an "office junior" in a wholesale mercantile house. He enlisted in the Union Army during the American Civil War of 1864-5 and served in the Third Pennsylvanian Cavalry. After his discharge in 1865, he returned home to Chippewa and in the Fenian Raids of 1866 he served in the Queen's Own Rifles. In 1867 he entered the Profession of Civil Engineering and in 1872, he was registered as a land surveyor. It was during his work as surveyor in the lower Ottawa valley that he collected material for many of his short stories. In 1879, at the invitation of George Brown, he became chief editorial writer on the Toronto *Globe,* a position he held till 1883 and again from 1885 to 1891; the years between, those of the Manitoba land boom, he spent in Winnipeg as a land surveyor. In 1891, disagreeing with the Liberal policy of *The Globe,* he moved to Boston as revising editor for *The Youth's Companion.* He returned to Canada in 1902 and settled in Ottawa where he was foreign correspondent for the Boston *Transcript* and also an independent journalist. He died in Boston, March 5, 1924.

Thomson published three volumes of poetry: *Peter Ottawa* (1905), *When Lincoln Died and Other Poems* (1909) and *The Many-Mansioned House and Other Poems* (1909) as well as several books of stories: *Between Earth and Sky and Other Strange Stories of Deliverance* (1897), *Smoky Days* (1891), *Walter Gibbs, The Young Boss, and Other Stories for Boys* (1896), *Old Man Savarin and Other Stories* (1895) and *Old Man Savarin Stories: Tales of Canada and Canadians* (1917). He also published a verse translation in 1896 *This is of Aucassin and Nicolette.* He was made a Fellow of the Royal

Society of Literature in 1909 and a Fellow of the Royal Society of Canada in 1910.

The vogue of local colour fiction was at its height when Thomson began writing his short stories for Canadian and American magazines and many of his contemporaries including Gilbert Parker, Duncan Campbell Scott and Ralph Connor were taking advantage of the public taste for stories of French Canada, rural Ontario or the West. Thomson combined with his preference for rural settings, an appreciation for the realism of Howells and the naturalism of Zola and a strong sense of comedy. His best stories describe the real world of the Scots around Glengarry or the French Canadians along the Ottawa River in a simple and spare but vigorous style.

TEXT:

Old Man Savarin and Other Stories. Toronto: Briggs, 1895.

See also:

M. O. Hammond in *Queen's Quarterly* 38, January 1931, 123-39.

Old Man Savarin

OLD Ma'ame Paradis had caught seventeen small doré, four suckers, and eleven channel-catfish before she used up all the worms in her tomato-can. Therefore she was in a cheerful and loquacious humor when I came along and offered her some of my bait.

"Merci; non, M'sieu. Dat's 'nuff fishin' for me. I got too old now for fish too much. You like me make you present of six or seven doré? Yes? All right. Then you make me present of one quarter dollar."

When this transaction was completed, the old lady got out her short black clay pipe, and filled it with *tabac blanc.*

"Ver' good smell for scare mosquitoes," said she. "Sit down, M'sieu. For sure I like to be here, me, for see the river when she's like this."

Indeed the scene was more than picturesque. Her fishing-platform extended twenty feet from the rocky shore of the great Rataplan Rapid of the Ottawa, which, beginning to tumble a mile to the westward, poured a roaring torrent half a mile wide into the broader, calm brown reach below. Noble elms towered on the shores. Between their trunks we could see many whitewashed cabins, whose doors of blue or green or red scarcely disclosed their colors in that light.

The sinking sun, which already touched the river, seemed somehow the source of the vast stream that flowed radiantly from its blaze. Through the glamour of the evening mist and the maze of June flies we could see a dozen men scooping for fish from platforms like that of Ma'ame Paradis.

Each scooper lifted a great hoop-net set on a handle some fifteen feet long, threw it easily up stream, and swept it on edge with the current to the full length of his reach. Then it was drawn out and at once thrown upward again, if no capture had been made. In case he had taken fish, he came to the inshore edge of his platform, and upset the net's contents into a pool separated from the main rapid by an improvised wall of stones.

"I'm too old for scoop some now," said Ma'ame Paradis, with a sigh.

"You were never strong enough to scoop, surely," said I.

"No, eh? All right, M'sieu. Then you hain't nev' hear 'bout the time Old Man Savarin was catched up with. No, eh? Well, I'll tol' you 'bout that." And this was her story as she told it to me.

* * *

"Der was fun dose time. Nobody ain't nev' catch up with dat old rascal ony other time since I'll know him first. Me, I'll be only fifteen den. Dat's long time 'go, eh? Well, for sure, I ain't so old like what I'll look. But Old Man Savarin was old already. He's old, old, old, when he's only thirty; an' *mean – baptême!* If de old Nick ain' got de hottest place for dat old stingy – yes, for sure!

"You'll see up dere where Frawce Seguin is scoop? Dat's the Laroque platform by right. Me, I was a Laroque. My fader was use for scoop dere, an' my gran-fader – the Laroques scoop dere all de time since ever dere was some Rapid Rataplan. Den Old Man Savarin he's buyed the land up dere from Felix Ladoucier, an' he's told my fader, 'You can't scoop no more wisout you pay me rent.'

" 'Rent!' my fader say. ' *Saprie!* Dat's my fader's platform for scoop fish! You ask anybody.'

" 'Oh, I'll know all 'bout dat,' Old Man Savarin is say. 'Ladoucier let you scoop front of his land, for Ladoucier one big fool. De lan's mine now, an' de fishin' right is mine. You can't scoop dere wisout you pay me rent.'

" '*Baptême!* I'll show you 'bout dat,' my fader say.

"Next mawny he is go for scoop same like always. Den Old Man Savarin is fetch my fader up before de magistrate. De magistrate make my fader pay nine shillin'!

" 'Mebbe dat's learn you one lesson,' Old Man Savarin is say.

"My fader swear pretty good, but my moder say: 'Well, Narcisse, dere hain' no use for take it out in *malediction*. De nine shillin' is paid. You scoop more fish – dat's the way.'

"So my fader he is go out early, early nex' mawny. He's scoop, he's scoop. He's catch plenty fish before Old Man Savarin come.

" 'You ain't got 'nuff yet for fishin' on my land, eh? Come out of dat,' Old Man Savarin is say.

" '*Saprie!* Ain' I pay nine shillin' for fish here?' my fader say.

" '*Oui* – you pay nine shillin' for fish here *wisout* my leave. But you ain't pay nothin' for fish here *wis* my leave. You is goin' up before de magistrate some more.'

"So he is fetch my fader up anoder time. An' de magistrate make my fader pay twelve shillin' more!

" 'Well, I s'pose I can go fish on my fader's platform now,' my fader is say.

"Old Man Savarin was laugh. 'Your honor, dis man tink he don't have for pay me no rent, because you'll make him pay two fines for trespass on my land.'

"So de magistrate told my fader he hain't got no more right for go on his own platform than he was at the start. My fader is ver' angry. He's cry, he's tear his shirt; but Old Man Savarin only say, 'I guess I learn you one good lesson, Narcisse.'

"De whole village ain't told de old rascal how much dey was angry 'bout dat, for Old Man Savarin is got dem all in debt at his big store. He is grin, grin, and told everybody how he learn my fader two good lesson. An' he is told my fader: 'You see what I'll be goin' for do wis you if ever you go on my land again wisout you pay me rent.'

" 'How much you want?' my fader say.

" 'Half de fish you catch.'

" '*Monjee!* Never!'

" 'Five dollar a year, den.'

" '*Saprie*, no. Dat's too much.'

" 'All right. Keep off my lan', if you hain't want anoder lesson.'

" 'You's a tief,' my fader say.

" 'Hermidas, make up Narcisse Laroque bill,' de old rascal say to his clerk. 'If he hain't pay dat bill to-morrow, I sue him.'

"So my fader is scare mos' to death. Only my moder she's say, '*I'll* pay dat bill, me.'

"So she's take the money she's saved up long time for make my weddin' when it come. An' she's paid de bill. So den my fader hain't scare no more, an' he is shake his fist good under Old Man Savarin's ugly nose. But dat old rascal only laugh an' say, 'Narcisse, you like to be fined some more, eh?'

" '*Tort Dieu.* You rob me of my place for fish, but I'll take my platform anyhow,' my fader is say.

" 'Yes, eh? All right – if you can get him wisout go on my land. But you go on my land, and see if I don't learn you anoder lesson,' Old Savarin is say.

"So my fader is rob of his platform, too. Nex' ting we hear, Frawce Seguin has rent dat platform for five dollar a year.

"Den de big fun begin. My fader an Frawce is cousin. All de time before den dey was good friend. But my fader he is go to Frawce Seguin's place an' he is told him, 'Frawce, I'll goin' lick you so hard you can't nev' scoop on my platform.'

"Frawce only laugh. Den Old Man Savarin come up de hill.

" 'Fetch him up to de magistrate an' learn him anoder lesson,' he is say to Frawce.

" 'What for?' Frawce say.

" 'For try to scare you.'

" 'He hain't hurt me none.'

" 'But he's say he will lick you.'

" 'Dat's only because he's vex,' Frawce say.

" '*Baptême! Non!*' my fader say. 'I'll be goin' for lick you good, Frawce.'

" 'For sure?' Frawce say.

" '*Saprie!* Yes; for sure.'

" 'Well, dat's all right den, Narcisse. When you goin' for lick me?'

" 'First time I'll get drunk. I'll be goin' for get drunk dis same day.'

" 'All right, Narcisse. If you goin' get drunk for lick me, I'll be goin' get drunk for lick you' – *Canadien* hain't nev' fool 'nuff for fight, M'sieu, only if dey is got drunk.

"Well, my fader he's go on old Marceau's hotel, an' he's drink all day. Frawce Seguin he's go cross de road on Joe Maufraud's hotel, and *he's* drink all day. When de night come, dey's bose stand out in front of de two hotel for fight.

"Dey's bose yell an' yell for make de oder feller scare bad before dey begin. Hermidas Laronde an' Jawnny Leroi dey's hold my fader for fear he's go 'cross de road for keel Frawce Seguin dead. Pierre Seguin an' Magloire Sauve is hold Frawce for fear he's come 'cross de road for keel my fader dead. And dose men fight dat way 'cross de road, till dey hain't hardly able for stand up no more.

"My fader he's tear his shirt and he's yell, 'Let me at him!' Frawce he's tear his shirt and he's yell, 'Let me at him!' But de men hain't goin' for let dem loose, for fear one is strike de oder ver' hard. De whole village is shiver 'bout dat offle fight – yes, seh, shiver bad!

"Well, dey's fight like dat for more as four hours, till dey hain't able for yell no more, an' dey hain't got no money left for buy wheeskey for de crowd. Den Marceau and Joe Maufraud tol' dem bose it was a shame for two cousins to fight so bad. An' my fader he's say he's ver' sorry dat he lick Frawce so hard, and dey's bose sorry. So dey's kiss one anoder good – only all their close is tore to pieces.

"An' what you tink 'bout Old Man Savarin? Old Man Savarin is just stand in front of his store all de time, an' he's say: 'I'll tink I'll fetch him *bose* hup to de magistrate, an' I'll learn him *bose* a lesson.'

"Me, I'll be only fifteen, but I hain't scare 'bout dat fight same like my moder is scare. No more is Alphonsine Seguin scare. She's seventeen an' she wait for de fight to be all over. Den she take her fader home, same like I'll take my fader home for bed. Dat's after twelve o'clock of night.

"Nex' mawny early my fader he's groaned and he's groaned: 'Ah – ugh – I'm sick, sick, me. I'll be goin' for die dis time, for sure.'

" 'You get up an' scoop some fish,' my moder she's say, angry. Den you hain't be sick no more.'

" 'Ach – ugh – I'll hain't be able. Oh, I'll be so sick. An' I hain' got no place for scoop fish now no more. Frawce Seguin has rob my platform.'

" 'Take de nex' one lower down,' my moder she's say.

" 'Dat's Jawnny Leroi's.'

" 'All right for dat. Jawnny he's hire for run timber to-day.'

" 'Ugh – I'll not be able for get up. Send for M'sieu le Curé – I'll be goin' for die for sure.'

" '*Misère,* but dat's no *man!* Dat's a drunk pig,' my moder she's say, angry. 'Sick, eh? Lazy, lazy – dat's so. An' dere hain't no fish for de little chilluns, an' it's Friday mawny.' So my moder she's begin for cry.

"Well, M'sieu, I'll make de rest short; for de sun is all gone now. What you tink I do dat mawny? I take de big scoop-net an' I'll come up here for see if I'll be able for scoop some fish on Jawnny Leroi's platform. Only dere hain't nev' much fish dere.

"Pretty quick I'll look up and I'll see Alphonsine Seguin scoop, scoop on my fader's old platform. Alphonsine's fader is sick, sick same like my fader, an' all de Seguin boys is too little for scoop, same like my brudders is too little. So dere Alphonsine she's scoop, scoop for breakfas'.

"What you tink I'll see some more? I'll see Old Man Savarin. He's watchin' from de corner of de cedar bush, an' I'll know ver' good what he's watch for. He's watch for catch my fader go on his own platform. He's want for learn my fader anoder lesson. *Saprie!* dat's make me ver' angry, M'sieu!

"Alphonsine she's scoop, scoop plenty fish. I'll not be scoop none. Dat's make me more angry. I'll look up where Alphonsine is, an' I'll talk to myself: –

" 'Dat's my fader's platform,' I'll be say. 'Dat's my fader's fish what you catch, Alphonsine. You hain't nev' be my cousin no more. It is mean, mean for Frawce Seguin to rent my fader's platform for please dat old rascal Savarin.' Mebby I'll not be so angry at Alphonsine, M'sieu, if I was able for catch some fish; but I hain't able – I don't catch none.

"Well, M'sieu, dat's de way for long time – half-hour mebby. Den I'll hear Alphonsine yell good. I'll look up de river some more. She's try for lift her net. She's try hard, hard, but she haint's able. De net is down in de rapid, an' she's only able for hang on to de hannle. Den I'll know she's got one big sturgeon, an' he's so big she can't pull him up.

"*Monjee!* what I care 'bout dat! I'll laugh me. Den I'll laugh good some more, for I'll want Alphonsine for see how I'll laugh big. And I'll talk to myself: –

" 'Dat's good for dose Seguins,' I'll say. 'De big sturgeon will pull away de net. Den Alphonsine she will lose her fader's scoop wis de sturgeon. Dat's good 'nuff for dose Seguins! Take my fader platform, eh?'

"For sure, I'll want for go an' help Alphonsine all de same – she's my cousin, an' I'll want for see de sturgeon, me. But I'll only just laugh, laugh. *Non, M'sieu;* dere was not one man out on any of de oder platform dat mawny for to help Alphonsine., Dey was all sleep ver' late, for dey was all out ver' late for see de offle fight I told you 'bout.

"Well, pretty quick, what you tink! I'll see Old Man Savarin goin' to my fader's platform. He's take hold for help Alphonsine an' dey 's bose pull, and pretty quick de big sturgeon is up on de platform. I'll be more angry as before.

"Oh, *tort Dieu!* What you tink come den? Why, dat Old Man Savarin is want for take de sturgeon!

"First dey hain't speak so I can hear, for de Rapid is too loud. But pretty quick dey's bose angry, and I hear dem talk.

" 'Dat's my fish,' Old Man Savarin is say.

'Didn't I save him? Wasn't you goin' for lose him, for sure!?'

"Me – I'll laugh good. Dass *such* an old rascal.

" 'You get off dis platform, quick!' Alphonsine she's say.

" 'Give me my sturgeon,' he's say.

" 'Dat's a lie – it hain't your sturgeon. It's *my* sturgeon,' she's yell.

" 'I'll learn you one lesson 'bout dat,' he's say.

"Well, M'sieu, Alphonsine she's pull back de fish just when Old Man Savarin is make one grab. An' when she's pull back, she's step to one side, an' de old rascal he is grab at de fish, an' de heft of de sturgeon is make him fall on his face, so he's tumble in de Rapid when Alphonsine let go de sturgeon. So dere's Old Man Savarin floating in de river – and *me!* I'll don' care eef he's drown one bit!

One time he is on his back, one time he is on his face, one time he is all under de water. For sure he's goin' for be draw into de *culbute* an' get drown' dead, if I'll not be able for scoop him when he's go by my platform. I'll want for laugh, but I'll be too much scare.

"Well, M'sieu, I'll pick up my fader's scoop and I'll stand out on de edge of de platform. De water is run so fast, I'm mos' 'fraid de old man is boun' for pull me in when I'll scoop him. But I'll not mind for dat, I'll throw de scoop an' catch him; an' for sure, he's hold on good.

"So dere's de old rascal in de scoop, but when I'll get him safe, I hain't able for pull him in one bit. I'll only be able for hold on an' laugh, laugh – he's look *ver'* queer! All I can do is to hold him dere so he can't go down de *culbute*. I'll can't pull him up if I'll want to.

"De old man is scare ver' bad. But pretty quick he's got hold of de cross-bar of de hoop, an' he's got his ugly old head up good.

" 'Pull me in,' he say, ver' angry.

" 'I'll hain't be able,' I'll say.

"Jus' den Alphonsine she come 'long, an' she's laugh so she can't hardly hold on wis me to de hannle. I was laugh good some more. When de old villain see us have fun, he's yell: 'I'll learn you bose one lesson for this. Pull me ashore!'

" 'Oh! you's learn us bose one lesson, M'sieu Savarin, eh?' Alphonsine she's say. 'Well, den, us bose will learn M'sieu Savarin one lesson first. Pull him up a little,' she's say to me.

"So we pull him up, an' den Alphonsine she's say to me: 'Let out de hannle, quick' – and he's under de water some more. When we stop de net, he's got hees head up pretty quick.

" '*Monjee!* I'll be drown' if you don't pull me out,' he's mos' *cry*.

" 'Ver' well – if you's drown, your family be ver' glad,' Alphonsine she's say. 'Den they's got all your money for spend quick, quick,'

"M'sieu, dat scare him offle. He's begin for cry like one baby.

" 'Save me out,' he's say. 'I'll give you anything I've got.'

" 'How much!?' Alphonsine she's say.

"He's tink, and he's say, 'Quarter dollar.'

"Alphonsine an' me is laugh, laugh.

" 'Save me,' he's cry some more. 'I hain't fit for die dis mawny.'

" 'You hain' fit for live no mawny,' Alphonsine she's say. 'One quarter dollar, eh? Where's my sturgeon?'

" 'He's got away when I fall in,' he's say.

" 'How much you goin' give me for lose my big sturgeon?' she's ask.

" 'How much you'll want, Alphonsine?'

" 'Two dollare.'

" 'Dat's too much for one sturgeon,' he's say. For all he was not feel fit for die, he was more 'fraid for pay out his money.

" 'Let him down some more,' Alphonsine she's say.

" 'Oh, *misère, misère!* I'll pay de two dollare,' he's say when his head come up some more.

" 'Ver' well, den,' Alphonsine she's say; 'I'll be willin' for save you, *me*. But you hain't scooped by *me*. You's in Marie's net. I'll only come for help Marie. You's her sturgeon;' an' Alphonsine she's laugh an' laugh.

" 'I didn't lose no sturgeon for Marie,' he's say.

" 'No, eh?' I'll say myself. 'But you's steal my fader's platform. You's take his fishin' place. You's got him fined two times. You's make my moder pay his bill wis *my* weddin' money. What you goin' pay for all dat? You tink I'll be goin' for mos' kill myself pullin' you out for noting? When you ever do someting for anybody for noting, eh, M'sieu Savarin?'

" 'How much you want?' he's say.

" 'Ten dollare for de platform, dat's all.'

" 'Never – dat's robbery,' he's say, an' he's begin to cry like *ver'* li'll baby.

" 'Pull him hup, Marie, an' give him some more,' Alphonsine she's say.

"But de old rascal is so scare 'bout dat, dat he's say he's pay right off. So we's pull him up near to de platform, only we hain't big 'nuff fool for let him out of de net till he's take out his purse an' pay de twelve dollare.

"*Monjee,* M'sieu! If ever you see one angry old rascal! He not even stop for say: 'T'ank you for save me from be drown' dead in the *culbute!*' He's run for his house an' he's put on dry clo'es, an' he's go up to de magistrate first ting for learn me an' Alphonsine one big lesson.

"But de magistrate hain' ver' bad magistrate. He's only laugh an' he's say: –

" 'M'sieu Savarin, de whole river will be laugh at you for let two young girl take eet out of smart man like you like dat. Hain't you tink your life worth twelve dollare? Didn't dey save you from de *culbute? Monjee!* I'll tink de whole river not laugh so ver' bad if you pay dose young girl one hunder dollare for save you so kind.'

' 'One hunder dollare!' he's mos' cry. 'Hain't you goin' to learn dose girl one lesson for take advantage of me dat way?'

"'Didn't you pay dose girl yoursef? Didn't you took out your purse yoursef? Yes, eh? Well, den, I'll goin' for learn you one lesson yoursef, M'sieu Savarin,' de magistrate is say. 'Dose two young girl is ver' wicked, eh? Yes, dat's so. But for why? Hain't dey just do to you what you been doin' ever since you was in beesness? Don' I know? You hain' never yet got advantage of nobody wisout you rob him all you can, an' dose wicked young girl only act just like you give dem a lesson all your life.'

"An' de best fun was de whole river *did* laugh at M'sieu Savarin. An' my fader and Frawce Seguin is laugh most of all, till he's catch hup wis bose of dem anoder time. You come for see me some more, an' I'll tol' you 'bout dat.''

Index of Titles

Selected Bibliography

Canadian Literature. University of British Columbia. Quarterly 1959____.

Journal of Canadian Fiction. Fredericton. Quarterly, 1972____.

Atwood, Margaret. *Survival*. Toronto: Anansi, 1972.

Baker, Ray Palmer. *A History of English-Canadian Literature to Confederation*. Cambridge, Mass: Harvard University Press, 1920.

Bourinot, John G. *Our Intellectual Strength and Weakness* ed. Clara Thomas. Toronto: University of Toronto Press, (1893), 1973.

Brown, E. K. *On Canadian Poetry*. Toronto: Ryerson, 1944.

Eggleston, Wilfrid. *The Frontier and Canadian Letters*. Toronto: Ryerson, 1957.

Frye, Northrop. *The Bush Garden*. Toronto: Anansi, 1971.

Klinck, Carl F. and R. E. Watters. *Canadian Anthology*. Rev. Ed. Toronto: Gage, 1966.

Klinck, Carl F. *et al. The Literary History of Canada*. Toronto: University of Toronto Press, 1965.

Logal J. D. and Donald G. French. *Highways of Canadian Literature*. Toronto: McClelland, 1924.

Marquis, Thomas G. *English-Canadian Literature*. ed Clara Thomas. Toronto: University of Toronto Press, (1912) 1973.

Moss, John G. *Patterns of Isolation*. Toronto: McClelland and Stewart, 1974.

Pacey, Desmond. *Creative Writing in Canada*. Toronto: Ryerson, 1961.

_____. *Essays in Canadian Criticism*. Toronto: Ryerson, 1969.

_____. *Ten Canadian Poets*. Toronto: Ryerson, 1958.

Percival, Walter P. *Leading Canadian Poets*. Toronto: Ryerson, 1948.

Pierce, Lorne. *An Outline of Canadian Literature*. Toronto: Ryerson, 1927.

Rashley, R. E. *Poetry in Canada: The First Three Steps*. Toronto: Ryerson, 1958.

Stevenson, O. J. *A People's Best.* Toronto: Musson, 1927.

Storey, Norah, ed. *A Companion to Canadian Literature and History.*
Toronto: Oxford University Press, 1966.

Watters, R. E. and I. F. Bell. *On Canadian Literature 1806-1960* (Bibliography of Criticism). Toronto: University of Toronto Press, 1966.

Acknowledgements

Works by Charles G. D. Roberts reprinted by permission of Lady Joan Roberts.

Works by Bliss Carman reprinted by permission of McClelland and Stewart Limited, *The Canadian Publishers*, Toronto.

Works by Duncan Campbell Scott reprinted by permission of John G. Aylen, Ottawa, Canada.

Works by Robert Service reprinted from *Songs of a Sourdough* by Robert Service by permission of McGraw-Hill Ryerson Limited.

Work by Ernest Thompson Seton reprinted by permission of Charles Scribner's Sons from *Wild Animals I Have Known*, by Ernest Thompson Seton. Copyright 1898 Ernest Thompson Seton.

Work by Gilbert Parker reprinted by permission of Copp Clark Publishing Company, Toronto.